POWER I

STUDIES IN GOVERNMENT AND PUBLIC POLICY

POWER IN THE CITY

Clarence Stone and the
Politics of Inequality

Edited by

Marion Orr and Valerie C. Johnson

Foreword by Dianne M. Pinderhughes

University Press of Kansas

Published by the University Press of Kansas (Lawrence, Kansas 66045), which was organized by the Kansas Board of Regents and is operated and funded by Emporia State University, Fort Hays State University, Kansas State University, Pittsburg State University, the University of Kansas, and Wichita State University

Library of Congress Cataloging-in-Publication Data

Power in the city : Clarence Stone and the politics of inequality /
edited by Marion Orr and Valerie C. Johnson ; foreword by Dianne M.
Pinderhughes.

    p. cm. — (Studies in government and public policy)

  Includes index.

  ISBN 978-0-7006-1573-5 (pbk. : alk. paper)

  1. Municipal government—United States. 2. Metropolitan government—United States. 3. Urban policy—United States. 4. Stone, Clarence N. (Clarence Nathan), 1935–. I. Orr, Marion, 1962–. II. Johnson, Valerie C.

  JS331.P69   2008

  320.8092—dc22   2007043605

British Library Cataloguing-in-Publication Data is available.

Printed in the United States of America

10 9 8 7 6 5 4 3 2 1

To the professors in
the Department of Government and Politics at
the University of Maryland who taught us

To the memory of Linda Faye Williams,
a Maryland professor, mentor, and scholar extraordinaire

CONTENTS

FOREWORD

Clarence N. Stone is unquestionably among the most prolific and theoretically creative scholars of urban politics and American political science. The questions that he has and continues to pose to urban scholars form the bases for many important questions in the discipline as a whole. Although there has been considerable debate about the extent to which the study of urban politics is in decline, there are myriad opportunities for reflection and discussion about the vital connections between urban politics and other subfields comprising early twenty-first-century American political science.

When the editors of this volume, Marion Orr and Valerie Johnson, began discussing their plans to publish a Clarence Stone reader, I initially believed that it was intended as a sort of Festschrift, designed to honor a life and career well lived. Although a celebration of Clarence's work would surely be reason enough, I soon found that the book accomplishes much more than that. Although it pays tribute to Stone by republishing selected works spanning more than three decades, Stone has also contributed a new and significant piece on "Urban Politics Then and Now." Stone has not concluded his life's work, nor has he finished addressing the intellectual issues encompassing the urban subfield. As this volume demonstrates, Stone's contribution continues, and it is for this reason that I am pleased and honored to have been asked to write the foreword for *Power in the City: Clarence Stone and the Politics of Inequality.*

The editors' introduction to the volume, as well as the new contributions by Jennifer Hochschild and Stone, convey the task with which this book was conceived: to search for answers to several years' pressing questions: What is happening with the urban politics field in political science? Why does it seem to be in decline? What might be done about that?

The answer to the last question has obviously been shaped by the editors' decision to contribute to the field intellectually by exploring Stone's work over the decades from the "who governs" debates of post–World War II American urban politics, to the end of the twentieth century in its various approaches. The volume provokes a series of reactions and challenges. For one, many of the controversies that it revisits remain unresolved within urban politics. Second, as Hochschild suggests, the debates of urban politics have yet to be integrated into developments taking place in the rest of the discipline of political science. Finally, the volume challenges and encourages scholars in a variety of subfields of the discipline to take a new look at urban politics.

Questions related to the decline of urban politics can be answered by an examination of developments and growth taking place in comparative politics and various newly organized sections within the American Political Science Association (APSA). The political science of the early twenty-first century cannot be compared to the mid-twentieth-century version. The trajectory of political science has followed the world's transformation to a global society. Although it may be true that "all politics is local," it is surely no longer good enough to examine political behavior, institutions, and the nature of power in myopically local terms.

In addition to monumental changes taking place in how we define the world, the developments of new and emerging groups into the political arena have also had a significant impact on the political science discipline. When Stone began his academic career, the pressing questions were largely confined to the political behavior of the nation's white majority. Sorely lacking was an examination of the role and influence of African Americans, Latinos, gays and lesbians, and the ethnic groups of developing nations. There simply was no clear way of comprehending how even political history itself was defined within the narrow parameters of the dominant group. All of these developments form the tasks at hand for twenty-first-century political science.

As the world we once knew has shifted and changed, so too has political science. This fact is most vividly demonstrated in the generational shift underway as new scholars with new questions, ideas, experiences, and frames of reference enter the discipline—a shift that was particularly striking at the 1998 APSA meeting. For me and many others, it signaled the state of things to come.

At the time, I was the outgoing copresident of the Race, Ethnicity and Politics (REP) organized section and incoming president of the Urban Politics section. When I left the business meeting of REP and rushed to the business meeting of the Urban Politics section, I could not help but note—and subsequently discuss—the sharp difference in the two groups' constituencies. The REP meeting was largely made up of young scholars new to the profession, up-and-coming graduate students, and junior faculty, many of whom were Latino, Asian, African American, or mixed race. The urban politics meeting, on the other hand, comprised middle-aged and senior scholars, most white—or, in the new language of the newly complex urban communities of the West, Anglo.

What is interesting and most critical to this discussion, however, is that the work of political scientists who join REP and those who join urban politics is not mutually exclusive; much of the new racial and ethnic work is about groups centered in urban and metropolitan areas. If I were to offer one caveat to the processes that are taking place within the discipline, I would suggest that we not lose sight of the manner in which the approaches utilized and the questions that Clarence Stone has raised within urban politics remain relevant to American political science.

Several aspects of the urban politics subfield remain relevant to the study of American politics. One key aspect relates to its holistic nature. Unlike many other subfields, urban politics is concerned with all of the various aspects that comprise the discipline as a whole—political behavior, institutions, racial and ethnic politics, suburbanization, among many others.

Equally important is the manner in which urban politics has maintained a steady focus on power—not just as an abstraction, but as an important lens for examining issues of equity and social justice, including environmental racism, the distribution of public services, the position of business in a global economy, immigration, and, most recently, the Katrina debacle in New Orleans. The urban politics subfield provides an important frame of reference for understanding these critical dynamics and trends.

Last, the important and historical debates of American political science as a whole continue to be grounded in urban politics' focus on the reform tradition in major American cities and critiques of pluralism. From these studies we have, for example, witnessed APSA's concern with a responsible two-party system. These studies likewise form the concrete and practical basis of analyses of race, immigration, fiscal disparity, and class privilege, both domestically and internationally. Urban politics is not dead. Vital aspects of its tradition remain that continue to inform the discipline and provide vital links to seemingly disparate analyses. The key is to make these links more integrated into developments across the discipline.

One movement toward disciplinary integration might include a reconceptualization of American urban metropolitan areas as host to the complex array of racial and ethnic groups that have arrived in the decades since changes in American immigration policy in 1965. Those new arrivals, however, do not necessarily regard American cities as the end point of their search for economic prosperity, any more than did significant proportions of European ethnics early in the twentieth century. Today the surrounding areas of American cities—New York, Chicago, Los Angeles, Washington, South Bend, New Orleans, Atlanta, and many others—have significant immigrant populations. Those populations maintain close contact and interaction with their families, visiting them with some regularity, contacting them through cell phones and e-mail, and serving as a source of vital financial resources. Although Hochschild points to cities as sitting at the bottom of the American federal system, it is nonetheless true that these cities are also integrated in ways they were not, in the nineteenth and early twentieth centuries, integrated to the home countries of new residents.

We have seen these linkages in recent years in the increase in short courses in urban comparative politics at the APSA annual meetings. This very trend has affected the research focus of many political scientists, including my own. As I have begun to work on comparative racial and ethnic politics, looking in particular at the populations of African descent in Brazil and eventually other South American countries, I have by necessity had to consider a comparative urban politics research strategy.

Another possibility might include a series of cooperative research projects linking the overlapping concerns of scholars of APSA's Politics and History, Race, Ethnicity and Politics, and Public Opinion and Political Psychology groups with the urban politics field. Some of the unresolved questions that Stone revisits in his chapter and that are reviewed in his republished works will certainly be of interest to the membership of these organized sections. Developments in these sections may also shed new light on some of the questions long explored in urban politics. The cross-fertilization offered by cooperative research collaboration will no doubt strengthen all groups. The currency of Stone's work on regime theory, civic capacity, social capital, "power over," and "power to" will be familiar to many and will increasingly stimulate a broader exchange and focus as the discipline's transformation proceeds.

I expect that this new volume, which reframes a set of important questions in urban politics, will be of significant importance for some time to come.

Dianne M. Pinderhughes

PREFACE AND ACKNOWLEDGMENTS

There is no risk of overstatement to characterize Clarence N. Stone as a giant in the field of urban politics. For example, *all* of his major books have won awards. His first book, *Economic Growth and Neighborhood Discontent*, published in 1976, won the Southern Political Science Association's Chastain Award (now the V. O. Key Award) for the best book on Southern government and politics. *Regime Politics: Governing Atlanta, 1946–1988,* was awarded the American Political Science Association's (APSA) prestigious Ralph J. Bunche Award for the best scholarly work in political science that explores the phenomenon of ethnic and cultural pluralism. *Regime Politics* also won the APSA Urban Section's best book award. Stone's study of urban school reform (with Bryan Jones, Jeffrey Henig, and Carol Pierannunzia), *Building Civic Capacity,* won the APSA Urban Section's best book award. By publishing his writings in the major general political science journals, including *American Political Science Review, Journal of Politics,* and *American Journal of Political Science,* Stone successfully exported urban ideas to the broader discipline. Not many urban political scientists can make such a claim.

This book contains a selection of articles and essays on urban politics by Clarence Stone. For over four decades, Clarence has used the local lens to theorize and explore the nature of American democracy. Stone's writings, which have set trends in the field of political science, have encompassed, critiqued, debated, and recast large questions about democracy, power, and inequality. In 1962, Charles Press had the foresight to recognize the value of collecting some of Norton Long's most significant works and publishing them in a volume entitled *The Polity.* Norton Long (1910–1993) is considered to be one of the pioneers of modern U.S. urban political science. Inspired by Charles Press, it dawned on us that just as we benefit from *The Polity,* political science would greatly profit by having some of Clarence Stone's important articles and essays compiled and published in one collection. *Power in the City* is the result.

Stone has had a long career studying urban politics. Stone completed his B.A. degree in political science at the University of South Carolina (he is a South Carolina native), graduating at the top of his class and earning membership in Phi Beta Kappa. Stone completed the Ph.D. program in political science at Duke University in 1963, writing a dissertation that examined the city manager system as an avenue for municipal reform. In 1966–1967, as a fellow in the APSA's Congressional Fellowship Program, Stone used his year on Capitol Hill to learn firsthand how federal legislators and agencies considered and developed urban renewal programs. Stone was a founding member of the APSA's Urban Politics Organized Section and served as its president in 1988–1989. He taught at Emory University and spent the bulk of his career at the University of Maryland, becoming professor emeritus in 2001.

Few political scientists have had the distinction of having their ideas read, utilized, and criticized by so many scholars. Stone's ideas on urban regimes have generated considerable attention, and with this book, we hope to remind scholars how Stone's ideas on urban regimes were developed and have evolved. Hence, one goal of *Power in the City* is to redirect urbanists to important foundational aspects of the urban regime framework. For example, the essays in this volume remind us that Stone's work is steeped in Bachrach and Baratz's ideas about a "second face" of power, Schattschneider's notion of a "mobilization of bias," and "elite" theorists' views on social stratification. We hope to redirect the urban field's attention to the more dynamic attributes of Stone's work on regimes and a few of the elements of urban regime analysis that we think are understudied. Such a redirection, we believe, could lead to a more robust application of the regime concept and potentially to a reinvigoration of urban political science scholarship.

On the latter point, we purposely cast this volume to cover scholarly terrain that is much broader than the issues and controversies surrounding urban regime analysis. For example, some of the essays in this volume cover leadership, a significant factor in everyday political life, yet an understudied phenomenon in political science. Given what we know about power and the distribution of resources, what are the constraints on urban leadership? Given the structure of power in urban settings, what is the leadership task? The essays in this volume also flesh out the connection between electoral power and urban governance, as well as raise questions about the democratic nature of institutions of local government. Are there avenues for the lower social strata to shape policy that affect their families and communities? Why does it matter for local democracy? What role do race and racial politics play? How does all of this affect efforts toward social reform?

Within the discipline of political science, urban scholarship is considered to be at the periphery of the profession. Contemporary U.S. political scientists do not identify with cities the way early giants such as Frank J. Goodnow, Charles A. Beard, and William B. Munro did. Perhaps many contemporary political scientists believe that studying cities is provincial while studying national politics and comparative politics is chic and cosmopolitan. *Power in the City* is our attempt to remind those in the profession who are interested in discourse about democracy, representation, inequality, justice, and power of the advantages studying cities and other localities can bring to these important issues. Clarence Stone's scholarship superbly demonstrates how this can be accomplished.

Working on this book allowed us to revisit and reminisce about our days as graduate students at the University of Maryland. We acknowledge and thank all the

professors who taught us at Maryland. We especially thank Clarence for his support over the years and for agreeing to write an essay expressly for this volume. We
are also grateful that Jennifer Hochschild agreed to write an essay assessing and reflecting on Clarence's scholarship within the context of American political science.
Jennifer's primary research area is not urban politics. However, she keeps a close
eye on research in the urban politics subfield. As she notes in her chapter, Jennifer
is a member of the urban section of the APSA, and she is also a Stone watcher and
thoroughly familiar with Stone's works. We also thank Dianne Pinderhughes for
taking time out of her busy schedule to write the foreword. Dianne is the current
president of the APSA. She is the only contemporary APSA president to follow in
the tradition of Goodnow, Beard, and Munro (all past APSA presidents) whose
principal area of research is urban affairs.

We benefited from helpful feedback and comments from the anonymous re-
viewers who evaluated the book in manuscript. Their comments and suggestions
helped improve the volume tremendously. Major thanks go to Fred Woodward, the
director of the University Press of Kansas, for providing good advice throughout
this project. Susan Schott, Larisa Martin, and others at UPK did a superb job shep-
herding this book through publication.

Marion Orr and Valerie C. Johnson

1. Power and Local Democracy
Clarence N. Stone and American Political Science
Marion Orr and Valerie C. Johnson

> My own preference is for arrangements that foster an inverted form of Madisonian representativeness—one in which those who control much property are unable to dominate those who have little or none. Such representativeness seems to me to be essential (though not sufficient by itself) to achieving that form of public fairness which we call justice.
>
> —Clarence N. Stone (1987a, 294–95)

Political theorists have argued that the foundation for a democratic society must include the basics of economic and physical security for all citizens and a state that is responsive to the needs and preferences of all citizens. Democracy also entails the notion that everyone is entitled to have a voice in actions that affect them. Cities and other local communities have long been viewed as appropriate venues for exploring central concerns about democracy. Many of the modern political ideals about democracy, and related theories of inequality, justice, and liberty, began with the reflections of ancient political philosophers on the democratic institutions of Athens, Sparta, and other city-states. For over four decades, Clarence N. Stone has used the city to examine and explore the nature of American democracy. As several of the essays in this volume show, Clarence Stone disagrees with Robert Dahl, considered one of the nation's most preeminent modern democratic theorists, on many aspects of urban politics. Stone and Dahl, however, agree that studying local politics is essential to American democracy. Robert Dahl (1967) called the city the "optimal" site for analysis of democracy. Clarence Stone's scholarship effectively utilizes the city as a site to observe how American democracy works. For Clarence Stone, socioeconomic inequality constitutes a fundamental obstacle to the full realization of local democracy.

In this chapter, we consider Stone's scholarly contribution within the context of American political science and what his findings about inequality in the city tell us about our democracy. First, we contribute to ongoing debates about the direction of urban political science by considering the place of urban politics in the discipline. Below, we provide an historical perspective on the discussion about urban politics' "estrangement" from mainstream political science. We show that the study of cities and urban communities has long been on the periphery of political science. Although the discipline's interest in cities heightened in the 1960s and early 1970s, by the end of the 1970s, urban scholarship had returned to the periphery of the discipline. We discuss some reasons why. Next, we turn to Clarence Stone's scholarship, illustrating how his work on city politics addresses issues that are of concern to political scientists. We describe Stone's contribution to political science, paying close attention to the central themes and analytical concepts that form the focus of his work on power, leadership, and the nature of urban social reform. We highlight how well grounded Stone's work is in mainstream political science, something missing from the urban field otherwise.[1]

URBAN POLITICS AND POLITICAL SCIENCE

At the beginning of the 20th century, political scientists like William B. Munro, Charles Beard, and Frank Goodnow wrote about city governments. Many of these works were highly descriptive and legalistic tomes on city reform, administrative effectiveness, and structural differentiations.[2] Today, many urban scholars consider much of the work produced before World War II to be of little use today (see Peterson 1981, ix). As early as 1957, Lawrence Herson (1957), in a once-famous *American Political Science Review* (*APSR*) article, "The Lost World of Municipal Government," observed that much of this early work on local government had "very little . . . of substance sufficient to rise . . . into the general stream of political science." In that same *APSR* volume, Daland (1957, 506) quipped that if much of this research were destroyed, "political science would not be seriously touched."[3] Although critical of much of the pre–World War II work on cities, Daland (1957, 509) nonetheless viewed urban politics as "a vast untapped reservoir" and argued that the discipline would benefit from top-notch urban political analysis. Daland encouraged political scientists to pay more attention to urban government and politics.

After World War II, as cities underwent rapid and profound demographic transformation, urban political analysis began to shift away from formal institutions and administrative laws toward basic political, social, and economic forces that affected cities. It was during this era that urban political analysis added vitality to the study of local politics *and* generated theoretical propositions of interest across the discipline. Many theoretical issues got their start from local studies conducted during this period. James Q. Wilson's important work on organizational incentives and motivation started with his study of local Democratic clubs (Wilson 1962). Theoretical propositions concerning the usefulness of protest as a mechanism for powerless groups to obtain political influence were derived from local observation (Lipsky 1969; Piven and Cloward 1977). The community power debate of the 1960s was grounded in empirical observations generated by careful data gathering of urban political phenomenon. Foremost among these was the masterful study of Atlanta's leadership class by Floyd Hunter (1953), a sociologist. Dahl's *Who Governs?* (1961) provided urbanists with a comprehensive political analysis of local politics in New Haven. More significantly, it empirically tested a broad normative perspective (pluralism) about the extent to which interest groups segmented and dominated city decision making. Bachrach and Baratz (1962, 1970) used Baltimore politics to explore their thesis that some issues are deliberately left off the political agenda. Deciding not to decide is a decision. In effect, a second face of power exists that is not easily observable through examination and analysis of formal decision making processes. *Who Governs?* is one of the canonical works in political science. Bachrach and Baratz's "Two Faces of Power" article is also considered a classic—and not only among urbanists. According to a recent analysis of articles in *APSR*, as of 2005, it is the most widely cited article published since the journal's founding in 1906 (Sigelman 2006).

In the late 1950s and into the 1970s, urban politics was hot. During this period, a number of notable political scientists, including Edward Banfield, Robert Dahl, Heinz Eulau, Kent Jennings, Nelson W. Polsby, Raymond Wolfinger, Aaron Wildavsky, James Q. Wilson, and Theodore Lowi, used local politics to generate theories and to formulate and test hypotheses about power dynamics, voting behavior, ethnic politics, the relationship between voters and representatives, party politics, and other issues of central concern to political science. For a period, the city stood at the center of exciting research. There were clusters of political scientists writing about cities at several of the nation's major research universities, including Harvard, Yale, Columbia, Chicago, Northwestern, University of California–Berkeley, and MIT. Urban research units were established providing sponsorship and resources for urban politics research. For example, in 1958, with help from the Ford Foundation, the Joint Center for Urban Studies at Harvard and MIT was formed. In 1968, with urging from President Lyndon Johnson, the Urban Institute was founded. Research funds were available through the relatively new cabinet-level department devoted to local governments, the Department of Housing and Urban Development (HUD).

Many of the major philanthropic foundations were interested in and funded urban-related research. Sayre and Kaufman's (1960) encyclopedic study of New York City governance and David Greenstone and Paul Peterson's (1973) important study of community action programs were funded by the Russell Sage Foundation. In the late 1950s and early 1960s, the Ford Foundation supported a number of research projects on metropolitan reform and urban renewal (Marris and Rein 1973). Marilyn Gittell's (1967) important work on community control and school decentralization was also funded by the Ford Foundation. During the 1960s and early 1970s, Ford joined the American Political Science Association (APSA) in funding programs to advance the study of urban politics. For example, Ford and APSA supported intern programs "designed to increase interest in state and local government studies and to provide participant-observer opportunities to graduate students. Over a five year period the Association supported fifty-nine programs covering sixty-seven departments with financial aid to one hundred and eighty-six graduate students" (APSA 1973, iii). New Ph.D. graduates found exceptional opportunities in what was a stimulating research area. Beginning in the middle to late 1950s and into the 1970s, studying city politics was in vogue.

When viewed from the perspective of the 104-year history of the APSA, however, the 20-year period when urban politics generated wide interest in political science was an exception. Urban politics has historically been at the periphery of the discipline. Over a half century ago, Herson (1957, 330) described the study of American urban politics as "a stagnated area." And R. T. Daland (1957, 491) observed that "political scientists have been slow to study seriously the impact of urbanization on our governmental institutions and political life." Daland (1957, 491) added that "the professional journals of political science over the past fifty years have published but an insignificant number of studies concerned with urban governance."

When we systematically examined the articles in two of political science's oldest journals, *Political Science Quarterly* (founded in 1886) and *APSR* (founded in 1906), we discovered that only a tiny fraction of the articles in the selected journals are about urban issues (see Orr and Johnson 2007). Of all the articles published in the two journals between 1886 and 2002, we found that only 2% are on some aspect of the field. Our data confirm Daland's observation about political science journals and urban politics. When we isolated the urban articles across 116 years, we found only a handful of urban articles published in the late 1800s, an expansion of articles during the first decades of the 20th century, and then a drop in the number of articles in the middle of the 20th century. As expected, the number of urban-related articles rose during the 1960s and 1970s. However, they still represented a small percentage of the total number of articles. Jack Walker (1972) surveyed the subjects covered in five political science journals (*APSR, Journal of Politics, Midwest Journal of Political Science, Western Political Quarterly,* and *Polity*) during the 11 years from 1960 through 1970. His numbers are similar to ours. He found that during this period, only 2% of the articles focused on urban/metropolitan government. The number of urban-related articles in *APSR* and *Political Science Quarterly* declined by the end the 1970s. By the beginning of the 21st century, the number of urban articles tapered off, reaching the lowest number in over three decades. The urban politics subfield returned to its historical position at the margins of the study of American politics. The prominence of urban politics was short lived.

THE FLIGHT FROM THE CITY: POLITICAL SCIENCE AND URBAN POLITICS

In the early 1980s, in the preface to *City Limits,* Peterson (1981, ix–x) described urban politics as "removed once again to the periphery of the political science discipline. The field must struggle to gain representation on professional panels, course offerings in the area have peaked, and its attraction to graduate students has begun to wane." In the late 1980s, Bryan Jones (1989) struck a similar chord, arguing that urban scholars seldom "influence the direction of mainstream disciplinary work." The same theme was prevalent in the 1990s. Mark Schneider (1994, 24) declared that "the study of urban politics is in trouble. . . . Much of the work in the field diverges from the theoretical interests and terms of analysis found in other major subfields of the discipline." In 1996, Michael Danielson and Paul Lewis (1996, 203) concluded that the "work of political science's urbanists has not contributed as frequently to broad dialogues in the discipline." The pessimism continued into the new millennium. Dennis Judd (2005), who for nearly 20 years edited *Urban Affairs Review* and is the coauthor of an important urban politics textbook, recently observed that "urban politics has been at the periphery of the discipline for some time" and is now "estranged" from the political science profession. Finally, in 2007, Bryan Jones—who by this time had long ago made his famous exit from urban politics (see Judd 2005)—and his coauthors likened urban politics to a "black hole" (see Sapotichne, Jones, and Wolfe 2007). "Urban politics," they argued, had "drifted away from political science, both theoretically and methodologically."

There are competing theories about why urban politics continues to be marginalized in the discipline. In Chapter 13 of this volume, Jennifer Hochschild discusses some of these arguments. Judd (2005), like Hochschild, argued that ideological blinders and a reformist tradition colors urban political science scholarship, pushing it out of the mainstream. Danielson and Lewis (1996) maintain that urbanists remain wedded to the geographic boundaries of the central city while largely ignoring urban politics outside the city limits. According to Danielson and Lewis (1996, 206), "urban political science, by and large, has remained preoccupied with central cities despite their steadily declining relative importance." Peterson (1981) blames the marginalization on what he characterized as balkanization within the urban field. He notes, for example, that the number of urbanists working in specialized areas—transportation, health, housing, education, minority politics, and others— has exploded. Peterson also points to the influence of neo-Marxist determinism, a theoretical construct prevalent in urban political science research, especially in the 1970s. Sapotichne, Jones, and Wolfe (2007) maintain that the urban politics subfield constructed theoretical and methodological barriers that "insulate urban politics from the vigorous trends that have engulfed other parts of political science." Meanwhile, they point out, the interests and developments in the broader discipline prevent "the flow of ideas" from getting in and out of the urban subfield.

In-and-Out Urbanists

Few observers, however, have acknowledged that part of what happened to urban politics is that many of the scholars who helped elevate urban political analysis in the 1960s and 1970s moved on to other areas of political science. Many of these political scientists can best be described as in-and-out urbanists. Many of them came to the study of local politics with nonurban reputations, did a significant urban study, but then mainly worked elsewhere in the discipline. Robert Dahl fits the category of an in-and-out urbanist. He gained a reputation with the publication of *A Preface to Democratic Theory*, a critique of classic republican and populist conceptions of democracy published in 1956. *Who Governs?* appeared five years later. In his 1967 APSA presidential address, "The City and the Future of Democracy," Dahl highlighted the "advantage of the city as a unit for democratic government." Addressing his fellow political scientists just a short two months after deadly racial unrest in Detroit and Newark, Robert Dahl declared the city the "optimal" unit of government for examining democracy and "worthy of our best efforts" (1967, 964). After that fascinating lecture, Dahl did not return to urban political analysis.

Heinz Eulau is another example of an in-and-out urbanist. Considered one of the leaders of the "behavioral revolution" of the 1950s and 1960s, Eulau's research focus was on the theory and practice of political representation and electoral behavior. One of his important works examined the political behavior of state legislators (Wahlke et al. 1962). In the mid-1960s, Eulau launched a massive study exploring the linkage between voters and their elected city representatives, the City Council Research Project. The resulting book (several journal articles also resulted), *Labyrinths of Democracy*, does a number of things, including presenting a view of how local policy is formulated (Eulau and Prewitt 1973). The data were gathered by examining 82 city councils and interviewing 435 city councilors in San Francisco Bay area cities. It was a significant contribution to urban politics.

Eulau and his coauthor, however, make it clear in the preface of their volume that the book should not be considered a work of urban politics. As Eulau and Prewitt (1973,vii) put it, "How cities are governed and the policies stemming from governance are questions of great immediacy and importance. This comparative study of 82 city councils in the San Francisco Bay region is, however, something less than a study of urban governance, and it should not be so considered." Many years later, Eulau recalled that he "never had any overwhelming interest . . . in city councils" (Eulau 1991, 187). Eulau's subsequent work was decisively nonurban.

There is also a category of in-and-out urbanists who started their careers and built national reputations in the urban field (often producing several works in urban politics) but who then moved on to other areas of the discipline. Among this category are some of the titans of the modern political science profession, including Bryan Jones, Ira Katznelson, Paul Peterson, Nelson Polsby, Robert Salisbury, Jack Walker, James Q. Wilson, and Raymond Wolfinger. These in-and-out urbanists moved away from the urban subfield, shifting their research interest to national politics, presidential elections, Congressional studies, voting behavior, policy processes, bureaucracies, and interest groups. When such significant role models change their focus, however, it clearly influences the choices young graduate students make about dissertation topics.

Racial Politics and Urban Political Analysis

There are many reasons why political scientists decided to take the flight away from urban politics. Perhaps some may have been bothered by the race rebellions of the 1960s and concerned that their prior work failed to anticipate them. Dahl, Eulau, and several other in-and-out urbanists studied American cities during the height of the cold war. Within the context of the cold war milieu, American urban political scholarship seemed especially interested in exploring America's "openness" and extolling the virtues of democratic governments, including local municipalities. Even within the context of a diversity of peoples, communities, and interests, American local democracy seemed to work (Dahl 1961).

However, the racial polarization and civil disorders of the 1960s strongly suggested that local governments (and the national government for that matter) did not work as well for African Americans. With President Lyndon Johnson in the White House acknowledging the structural context of urban poverty and pursuing a war on poverty to combat it, it became ever more clear that one of the most challenging problems facing urban America centered around race. As central cities became managed by black mayors and other black public officials and disproportionately populated by poor African Americans, some political scientists considered academic research in urban politics to represent a kind of "social danger" that should be avoided (see Walton and McCormick 1997). Wilson (1987, 4–6) argues that after the angry reaction of many to the unflattering depictions of black family life in Daniel Patrick Moynihan's 1965 report, "The Negro Family: The Case for National Action," "serious research on minority problems in the inner city" was curtailed "as liberal scholars shied away from researching behavior construed as unflattering or stigmatizing to particular racial minorities." According to Wilson (1987, 5), liberal researchers avoided studying the urban "underclass" "either because of a fear of providing fuel for racist arguments or because of concern of being charged with 'racism' or with 'blaming the victim.'"

Beginning in the late 1960s and into the 1970s, just as big-city black mayors were first elected, a sizable proportion of the small number of African Americans who entered the profession during that period worked on various aspects of urban politics (Nelson and Meranto 1977; Rich 1984, 1989; Persons 1978; Pinderhughes 1987; Williams 1977).[4] These black political scientists established their professional reputations studying urban politics, going against the grain of mainstream political science (see Rich 2007; Orr and Johnson 2007). As the nation became predominantly suburban, American political science steered away from urban politics because urban became too closely associated with marginal populations. Mainstream political science, as Cathy Cohen (1999, xi) observed, is "accustomed to ignoring" "vulnerable" or "marginal" populations. Unlike studies of national elections or analyses of congressional markups and roll-call votes, a political scientist studying urban politics is likely to confront issues "directly tied to the daily survival of individuals and their communities" (Cohen 1999, ix; but see Thompson, forthcoming). The study of urban phenomenon often encompasses examination of poverty, socioeconomic and political inequality, and the "underclass." Cohen also notes that within mainstream social science, "research focused on the experiences of oppressed communities [is viewed] as non-scientific." As Walton and McCormick (1997, 231) argue, mainstream political scientists avoid researching and publishing on subject matters that are "seen by the larger culture as socially unacceptable and therefore socially dangerous."

Funding Political Science Research

Shifts in funding resources since the late 1970s encouraged the flight away from the urban politics subfield. Under Ronald Reagan, not only was federal assistance to local governments and low-income housing cut, but HUD funds for research were also sliced. Between 1980 and 1989, HUD's budget authority was cut from $74 billion to $19 billion in constant dollars.

Convinced that political science could benefit from greater appreciation for rigorous methods and scientific standards, several of the major foundations looked to fund research proposals that included cutting-edge quantitative methodological approaches. The Ford Foundation, for example, "embarked on a very aggressive program" to train Latin American political scientists how to conduct quantitative empirical research (Miller 1991, 235). Ford invested over a million dollars into the University of Michigan's Survey Research Center, whose researchers in turn exported their technology and methodology to Latin America.

Federal funding of the National Election Studies (NES) at the University of Michigan was also significant. The biennial national survey of voters in presidential and congressional elections had been conducted at Michigan's Survey Research Center since 1948 and supported by funds raised by faculty in the political science department during the 1950s and 1960s. By the early 1970s, the national surveys had become an exceptional resource for political scientists. In 1977, the National Science Foundation approved a proposal to fund the NES on a more permanent basis. With federal funding, the data from the NES would be collected and archived so that it could be shared by others. Scholars not involved in collecting data for the NES would have access to the information and could conduct secondary analyses of national elections going back many years. For several decades, graduate students have been trained to hone and develop sophisticated statistical skills, and they could use those skills to develop a quantitative model that is based on national survey data that have already been collected. No such nationally collected database exists for city politics.

Career Choices and Political Science

The flight from the study of city politics also reflected rational career choices. By the middle to late 1970s, the profession was feeling the full force of the "behavioral revolution" of the 1950s and 1960s. The behavioral approach focused on the individual, requiring the researcher to use such techniques and methods as probability statistics, survey research, correlation, and causal modeling. By the early 1970s, many of the major political science departments embraced sophisticated statistical and methodological techniques as important to graduate training. As early as 1967, for example, the chairman of Yale University's political science department proposed a "Program in the Mathematical Study of Politics" that would create a research center designed to forge collaboration between Yale's political science and mathematics departments (Merelman 2003, 84). Warren Miller, who played a key role in establishing the biennial surveys of voters in presidential and congressional elections, recalled that in the 1960s and 1970s graduate students at the University of Michigan understood that "if you wanted to be tabbed as something other than an area specialist, *if you wanted to be a political scientist,* you better have your credentials established by being a research assistant in the [survey research] institute, not a TA in the department" (Miller 1991, 234, emphasis added).

By the 1970s, expanding one's academic opportunities, professional standing, and capacity to obtain grants and awards meant utilizing and manipulating national-level data sets. This was especially the case in American politics. As Sigelman notes, "the American politics subfield was the leading edge of the discipline's embrace of statistics" (Sigelman 2006, 468). Sigelman's analysis of articles appearing in *APSR* shows that by the late 1970s, there was "widespread" and "nearly universal" adoption of quantitative research and survey research as data collection techniques in the American politics subfield; over 60% of the articles in *APSR* were survey-based analyses.

On the other hand, the number and percentage of small-sample-size case studies—the primary method used in urban politics—rarely appear in *APSR* or any of the other top political science journals (see Bennett, Barth, and Rutherford 2003). According to a recent survey of the major American political science journals, the proportion of articles presenting case studies in American politics fell: it was 12% in 1975, 7% in 1985, and 1% in 1999–2000 (Bennett, Barth, and Rutherford 2003). According to Yin (1994, xiii), the case study approach "has long been stereotyped as a weak sibling among social science methods." It is not considered legitimate or verifiable by many scholars in the American politics subfield.[5] Bennett, Barth, and Rutherford (2003, 377), however, concluded that "the dearth of case study" research in American politics "demands attention as to whether an important approach has been woefully neglected."

The rapid rise of quantitative research (especially in the 1970s, just as urban politics reached its zenith), backed up by the development of survey research methods, helped exacerbate the dismissive view of the discipline toward local politics. Political scientists trained and interested in utilizing and manipulating national-level data sets, especially survey-based research, were seen as attractive to faculty recruitment committees. As the major political science departments successfully recruited them, scholars who used quantitative methodological techniques came to dominate the faculty. The clusters of political scientists camped out in major political science departments, and conducting urban political analysis soon disappeared. Today, most major political science departments appear to have at most one faculty member who specializes in urban politics. Many more departments lack even that.

CLARENCE STONE AND LOCAL DEMOCRACY

Unlike the in-and-out colleagues of his generation, Stone has been in the field for the long haul. His dissertation was a study of the city manager system as an avenue for municipal reform (Stone 1963a). As an APSA Congressional Fellow in the late 1960s, Stone worked on federal urban renewal policy. As a young scholar, he published work on party and constituency as an aspect of legislative politics (see Stone 1963b, 1965, 1966). However, while several in his cohort took the flight away from studying the city, Stone built and sustained his reputation studying urban and local politics.

Stone also distinguished himself by not fully embracing the new methodological paradigms in behavioral sciences that were gaining traction just as his academic career commenced. For Stone, contemporary American political science adheres too closely to Occam's razor. "There is a drive toward parsimony, toward identifying key variables and formulating general propositions," Stone observed. This approach, he adds, has "limited capacity to expand understanding." "Most outcomes have multiple causes that are never easy to sort out," he notes. "Contexts and the salience of various causal forces change, confounding our efforts to amass a body of scientific knowledge that can be replicated through repeated observations" (Stone 1987a, 18). For Stone (1989, 257), the empirical challenge is "analyzing the *conjunction* of factors, not isolating single variables." As Jennifer Hochschild notes later in this volume, Stone's approach to political science aligns closely with Lanyi's balloon.

Stone sees great value in the historical approach, and he puts it to good use in his case studies of Atlanta. Identifying "general tendencies" within a flow of historical events and sorting out "what conjoins to enable" some actions (i.e., policy decisions) to prevail over others are the keys to the research enterprise, according to Stone. "By following events sequentially, we gain some understanding of what remains constant, what changes, and what is associated with each. Given a significant degree of social inertia, a historical sequential process is a rough counterpart to laboratory control. . . . By observing the flow of events over time, we can see what combination of factors have recurring weight and what changing factors alter the course of events" (Stone 1989, 257–58). In the right hands, such a study would delineate the complexity of urban political phenomenon and generate testable propositions. Stone's detailed research on Atlanta is illustrative of how case studies, infused with a deep emphasis on historical analysis and contexts, can advance the discipline's understanding of big questions like the status of local democracy and the distribution and use of political power.

Social Stratification and Systemic Power

Clarence Stone has consistently held up for attention what urban politics tells us about American politics and how American democracy works. His findings show how social and economic inequality perpetuates a political system that is biased in favor of the well-off. Stone's scholarship also shows how tensions inherent in a system of social and political inequality tend to be reconciled in terms that favor the upper strata. Stone confronts an age-old issue of the consequences of social inequality for democracy. If one theme unites Stone's scholarship, it is that urban politics is embedded in a system of social stratification that tilts the political balance, perpetuates inequality, and weakens local democracy.

Stone embraces a Tocquevillian view of democracy, seeing politics as centered in and "reflecting the associational life of a community" (Stone 1989, 238). A close reading of Stone's scholarship also reveals the influence of the political theorist Hannah

Arendt (1961). Arendt described politics as people acting together to make things happen that would otherwise not occur. Stone (1989, 238) reminds us that "how people are grouped" and on what terms are crucial aspects of local politics. Stone's views of politics emphasize building relationships, as well as how those relationships are arranged, modified, and sustained, and on whose terms. This conceptualization moves the weight of local politics away from electoral power and the aggregation of individual policy preferences toward one that emphasizes the formation and reformation of governing arrangements. Stone observed that "An integral part of politics, no less in democracies than in other forms of government, is the coordination of institutional capacities in the task of governance" (Stone 1989, 234–35). Groups vary in their capacity to contribute to the shaping of the governing arrangement and to determining the route to achieve its goals. "For that reason," according to Stone, "inequalities in economic situation, social status, and organizational position carry great weight in building relationships for governing" (Stone 2005a, 325). Throughout his scholarship, Stone emphasizes how business control of substantial resources gives business leaders significant power in a city's governing arrangement.

In several major publications in the 1970s and 1980s, Stone developed a conceptualization of power centered on "the capacity to affect the context within which decisions are made" (Stone 1976, 20). Building on Bachrach and Baratz's (1962) "two faces of power" argument, Stone's work highlights three interrelated dimensions of political power. In his first book, *Economic Growth and Neighborhood Discontent*, Stone writes about the business community having "positional advantage," a dimension of power linked to the ability "to gain cumulative policy benefits at the expense of competing groups" (Stone 1976, 205). Later, in an important *APSR* article (Chapter 2 of this volume), Stone (1980) advanced what he called "systemic power" in which a group's wealth and economic power predisposes public officials to favor that group's interests. Finally, in an article that appeared in the *American Journal of Political Science*, Stone (1988) formulated the concept "preemptive power" in which a group has a strategic advantage because it is able to set the policy direction of a community's governing coalition, allowing it to protect its privileged position. Garnering any of these dimensions of power, however, does not come easily. "Only those groups with substantial, multiple, and expendable political resources are likely to be able to devote their resources to gaining and maintaining" these dimensions of power (Stone 1976). While acknowledging that such power exists among upper-strata groups (upper- and middle-class communities, for example), Stone notes that the business community possesses the high levels of resources to gain systemic power, ensuring it a significant role in the local governing arrangement.

The theoretical contributions of Stone's "position advantage," "systemic power," and "preemptive power" concepts moved the community power debate beyond the

on-again–off-again elite versus pluralist discussion, what Stone called "an intellectual dead end" (Stone 1976, 17).

> We need to get away from the question of whether power is exercised by one group or
> many. It is, of course, exercised by many groups. But to say that power is not monopo-
> lized by a single elite is not the same as saying that lines of influence are fluid or that
> communities are controlled by "shifting coalitions of participants drawn from all areas
> of community life." It is this very fluidity and changeability of power relations that needs
> to be reconsidered. . . . Policy is made and power is exercised within *a structured set of*
> *relationships*. These relationships are neither neutral nor easily changed. They confer
> advantages and disadvantages on various groups in the local community in the form of
> preferences and predispositions of leading local officials (Stone 1976, 17, emphasis added).

In the late 1980s, first in *The Politics of Urban Development* and later in *Regime Pol-*
itics, Stone developed the concept "urban regime" as a further elaboration of systemic and preemptive powers and as an analytical tool to explore the politics and
policy implications of local governing arrangements. Urban regimes are manifested
in a set of relationships shaped by a principal feature of American liberal democracy: a division of labor between state and society (see also Elkin 1987). Public matters are concentrated in the hands of the state, while ownership and authority of
productive assets are typically controlled by the private sector. To be effective (to
carry out major decisions), local leaders in both the public and private sectors must
accommodate the division between state and society, and this accommodation
often involves a significant role for civil society and how the civic sector is organized. This accommodation is what Stone calls an urban regime. For Stone, the real
work of local governance takes place through urban regimes, those "informal
arrangements by which public bodies and private interests function together in
order to be able to make and carry out governing decisions" (Stone 1989, 6).

While recognizing that local regimes include a broad array of private interests,
including labor union officials, political party leaders, officers in nonprofit groups
or foundations, leaders of neighborhood organizations, and church leaders, Stone
emphasizes the central role of business leaders. In local politics, economic elites,
especially those from the business community, carry great weight in shaping and
sustaining a viable governing arrangement. As Stone (1989, 7) declares, "the economic role of businesses *and the resources they control* are too important for these
enterprises to be left out completely." The significant imbalances in the distribution of resources present in the system of stratification, especially evident in central cities, favors the business elites and others of high social and economic status.
Across a city's community sectors, the business community is typically the most
influential, with the resources reaching the threshold required to be a part of the

governing arrangement and to influence the terms that shape local policy. This is the nature of "positional advantage" and "systemic" and "preemptive powers."

The Atlanta Regime: Politics Still Matters

When we entered the graduate program in political science at the University of Maryland in the late 1980s, urban political scientists were especially interested in shedding light on central questions surrounding urban economic redevelopment policy. Who was involved in shaping local redevelopment policy? Who were the winners and losers in the area of urban economic development? In his influential book, *City Limits* (1981), Paul Peterson argued that economic conditions and goals determine most of the city's political agenda and structured urban politics. Because most capital is mobile, Peterson explained, cities find that they must compete with other jurisdictions in order to attract and retain businesses, investment capital, and nonpoor residents. According to Peterson, downtown economic development dominated the local policy agenda because of a community consensus that economic development policy is good for the general welfare of the city. The economic imperative drives urban economic development policy and structures urban politics. For Peterson, that redevelopment projects are typically carried out through a "highly centralized decision-making processes involving prestigious businessmen and professionals" is less an indication of weakened local democracy and more of a reflection of a community consensus in favor of economic growth (1981, 132). This thesis put Peterson at odds with Stone's view of urban politics (see, e.g., Stone 1984; Stone and Sanders 1987).

Stone's analysis of urban politics is based on his years of closely observing and writing about politics in Atlanta. Stone's first book, *Economic Growth and Neighborhood Discontent,* is a close examination of Atlanta's urban renewal program over a 20-year period (1950–1970). It shows how social stratification and political inequality shaped the context through which urban renewal policy was formulated in Atlanta. The context favored the city's business community, and policy was shaped in its interests. Urban renewal proposals supported by Atlanta's business community were much more successful at gaining support and being implemented than proposals from other community sectors. The city constructed new office buildings, a new civic center, and a new downtown stadium. Neighborhoods were bulldozed to make room for commercial and other forms of nonresidential development. Thousands of poor black residents were displaced by government action in the process. Stone observed that "the quiet and subtle influence of the business community was a major determinant of policy" and concluded that Atlanta's urban renewal program was shaped in the interest of the business community (Stone 1976, 131).

In his classic *Regime Politics,* an examination of Atlanta's famous biracial governing coalition over a period of more than 40 years, Stone shows how redeveloping Atlanta's downtown came to occupy and maintain top billing on the city's policy agenda. Downtown redevelopment was the central policy strategy for transforming Atlanta into an international city, a key goal of the city's business-leaning biracial coalition. A new $400 million airport was constructed, and MARTA, a complex and expensive rapid transit system, was completed. New highways were built and existing ones rerouted. By the late 1980s, glitzy office towers, high-end hotels, luxury apartments, and state-of-the-art sport facilities dominated the city's downtown, enhancing the city's appeal as a tourist and convention attraction and as a home for residents interested in an active and culturally rich nightlife. Issues such as neighborhood preservation, public education, and affordable housing, however, were neglected or short lived. Working- and lower-class populations were displaced and bore the brunt of economic redevelopment policies. According to Stone, Atlanta's public policy agenda during much of the second half of the 20th century was "regressive" (1989, 166). As Stone notes, "It favors the interests of upper-strata groups and disregards or harms the interests of lower strata groups" (166). Stone uncovered a pattern in which major public policies supported by the few but opposed by the many were nevertheless implemented. The policy followed was the one favored by the business community.

Business is neither a reluctant nor a passive partner in governance. Atlanta's postwar political experience is a story of active efforts by the business elite to make the most of their economic and organizational resources in setting the terms on which civic cooperation occurs. Thus, downtown business has not been content to sit back and be courted as a source of investment capital. Instead, the business elite have engaged actively in formulating a policy agenda and in structuring a set of arrangements to advance that agenda (Stone 1989, 233).

A key manifestation of Atlanta's business community's systemic power is its attractiveness as an ally for those advancing a policy agenda, especially public officials (Stone 1980). The business community is an important ally if one is trying to promote and carry out a policy agenda. "If one is seeking credit, donations, technical expertise, prestigious endorsements, organizational support, business contacts, media backing, or in-depth analyses of problems, then very likely one is thrown into contact with the civic network that emanates from the activities of the downtown business elite" (Stone 1989, 192). Stone, for example, noted that Atlanta's business community was "indispensable" to the city's goal of becoming an international city. Public officials who embrace an activist agenda quickly recognize that not much can be accomplished without the cooperation of the business community. "While public officials enjoy significant autonomy in decision making, their autonomy is constrained by the fact that they operate in the broad context of a highly stratified socioeconomic system. This system predisposes officials to favor upper- over lower-strata interests" (Stone 1980, 989). In Atlanta, city hall's "favored interests" were business leaders. Mayors and other public officials managed conflict, timed proposals, and shaped issues in a way that was to the advantage of the city's business community. According to Stone, if one is to fully understand the scope and nature of the urban democracy, one must come to grips with the propensity of elected officials to be drawn into a governing arrangement with members of the upper strata, especially the business community. Stone illustrates that this is the nature of systemic power.

Stone is nevertheless mindful of the importance of civil society and the nature of the relationships within the civic sector (see, e.g., Stone 2005b; Stone, Orr, and Worgs 2006). For instance, Stone (1989) shows that the African American church, the Butler Street YMCA, the headquarters of the city's black leadership during the period, the Urban League, neighborhood associations, historic preservationists, civil rights organizations, and other community-based organizations were part of Atlanta's "civic fauna" and contributed in a variety of ways to governance (see Rae 2003). Atlanta's civic sector was not inconsequential.

However, Atlanta's business community's systemic power raised the opportunity costs for those desiring a different course and also served as a "gravitational force" that enabled the economic elite and others with substantial resources to entice groups poised to oppose the status quo into their orbit (Stone 1989, 194). As Stone (1989, 132) notes, "The business elite operated with a high level of cohesion and continuity and with a daunting array of resources. Its power added up to more than the sum of its parts. Even potential rivals found it easier to move with than against the business elite." In Atlanta, the neighborhood movement eventually faltered in the 1980s not only because of low budgets and internal fragmentation, but also because of the "potency" of the business-led rival coalition (Stone 1989, 132). The business community used its slack resources to achieve the cooperation of the city's black middle class and to mold it into an important partner in the governing coalition. As a group, Atlanta's black middle class benefited from new housing areas and later from employment and business opportunities. It is the classic "go along to get along" phenomenon that Stone clarifies by incorporating intervening political-psychological variables such as "small opportunities" and "limited cognition" and emphasizing the important role that "selective incentives" play in encouraging cooperation.

An underlying question throughout Stone's Atlanta studies has been why one governing arrangement—with its dominant and regressive policy of downtown economic redevelopment—has prevailed over others. From Stone's perspective, the answer is that the policy orientation of the community "grows out of governing arrangements" (Stone 1987b, 273). "It behooves us," Stone continues, "to give attention to the arrangements by which policy is made and conflict is managed. If these arrangements are flawed in some fundamental way, we cannot expect to have good

policy over the long run. Development policy will reflect the weaknesses of political arrangements" (282). In Atlanta during much of the postwar period, business
leaders played a substantial role in shaping the governing arrangement and setting
the terms of cooperation. They also controlled "resources in a quantity and of a
kind that can lead groups to ally with one set of arrangement instead of another"
(Stone 1989, 238–39). Atlanta's business leaders were uniquely cohesive and exceptionally involved. However, the urban regime concept holds out the possibility for
a different arrangement (see Stone 1987b; Stone, Orr, and Imbroscio 1991). Given
that power is "interwoven with institutional arrangements" (Stone 1989, 238), efforts
to elevate policies other than economic development onto the local agenda will fall
short unless local leaders have the power to restructure relationships and broaden
representation in the city's governing arrangement (see Imbroscio 1997).

Urban Political Leadership

An often overlooked aspect of Clarence Stone's scholarship has been his contribution in the area of political leadership. Political leadership is difficult to quantify,
yet both empirical research and historical studies reveal the crucial importance of
political leaders (see Burns 1978). Operating within an urban context of unequal
distribution of resources, complex relationships, and limited governmental authority, urban leadership raises the issue of structure and agency (Sewell 1992). Structuralists believe that urban actors are heavily constrained and limited by economic
and systemic forces. They believe, for example, that the economic logic of capital
mobility forces mayors and other city leaders to promote and pursue urban redevelopment policies. From this perspective, urban leadership is constrained and
less determinative (see Savitch and Kantor 2002). Agency, however, suggests that
city leaders are capable of exerting some degree of control. Agency implies room
for political leadership.

Stone acknowledges, recognizes, and takes seriously structure but is foursquare
on the side of agency (Stone 1989, 9–10). "Structural constraints are real," he
observes (Stone 2005a, 322). However, Stone argues that structures are real but not
fixed, opening the door for creative leadership. "Structures," Stone writes, "are reinforced, challenged, and modified by agents that operate from considerations that
are more immediate and complex than submission to broad structural pressures"
(2005a, 323). As Stone, Whelan, and Murin (1986, 203) observe:

> Power is based on the resources of groups, and those resource distributions don't change
> much on a year-to-year basis. Yet resource distributions are not self-enabling phenom-
> ena. Individual leaders are instrumental in bringing groups together and in devising the
> means by which coalitions function as systems of cooperation. Power is thus manifest

in the actions of individuals, and individuals do matter. Still, the actions of individual leaders should be seen as efforts to mobilize and sustain the use of resources. For that reason, political leaders do not operate independent of the social structure or of the nature of the economy. At the same time, social structures and economies don't devise and install political arrangement. That is the role of political leaders. Political leaders must work with the resources they can mobilize (and anticipate what competing leaders might be able to mobilize). At the same time, they are not confined to a single pattern of arrangements. Leadership is in part a creative exercise.

According to Stone, Atlanta's Mayor William Hartsfield was such a leader. Mayor Hartsfield, who came to office in 1937 with strong ties to the city's corporate leadership, had an ambitious vision of making Atlanta an international city. To make it happen, Hartsfield needed a reliable electoral base. As Stone explains it, Hartsfield's reform-style politics did not appeal to working-class whites (who, business leaders feared, if given a strong electoral voice would lead Atlanta to duplicate the explosive and economically damaging racial tensions found in other cities in the Deep South), and good government middle-class whites were increasingly moving to the suburbs. In response, Hartsfield used his leadership position to help forge a governing coalition consisting of city government, the white business community, and middle-class African Americans. Hartsfield is credited with coining the organizing slogan "Atlanta—the city too busy to hate." Black voters supplied the electoral support needed to keep unreconstructed whites from controlling city government and potentially ruining the city's image and economic future. Atlanta's biracial governing coalition was shaped by and responded to a potentially disabling scenario of racial chaos.

In *Regime Politics,* Stone also introduces the reader to several African American leaders who used their skills, relationships, institutional resources, and creativity to help incorporate the black middle class into Atlanta's governing arrangement. Grace Hamilton, A. T. Walden, and John Wesley Dobbs, for example, were formidable leaders in Atlanta's African American community during the 1940s and into the 1970s. They also played key roles in the city's governing regime. Stone, for example, observed that as the executive director of the Atlanta Urban League, Hamilton "was a central connector in the city's governing coalition" (1989, 34). Hamilton also had numerous personal, professional, and institutional relationships that ran deep into Atlanta's black community, especially the city's black middle class. Walden, an attorney, was a leader in the city's Republican Party until he switched to the Democrats in the 1940s. Walden was then active in the Democratic Party and cofounded with Dobbs an important citizen organization devoted to black voter registration (see Stone 1989, 33). He also assumed leadership roles in a number of community organizations. He served as chair of the executive boards of Butler Street YMCA and the Atlanta Urban League, and he was president of the

Atlanta Branch of the NAACP. With these visible political positions, Walden was able to exercise great political influence on behalf of black Atlantans. In the context of the Deep South in the 1940s, significant progress was made in the black community, such as street and sewer improvements and the hiring of black policemen in African American neighborhoods. Black leaders were not only interested in material benefits. They also managed gradually to bring around the city's white leaders to see race relations in a different light.

Although Mayor Hartsfield and other local leaders operated in a setting deeply structured by race, they framed racial peace as a purposeful way of bridging that structural divide. In his younger days, Hartsfield had been a staunch defender of Jim Crow and a vocal critic of the NAACP. However, faced with the damage that racial conflict could bring about, Hartsfield, and the city's white leaders, accepted with growing appreciation the aim of racial goodwill. In this way, Atlanta became the first Deep South city to embrace peaceful school desegregation. Under Hartsfield's successor, Ivan Allen, the structural remnants of Jim Crow were further weakened by a biracial dinner honoring Martin Luther King Jr.'s Nobel Peace Prize. Not everyone viewed the dismantling of Jim Crow with equal favor, but as Stone shows, a broad purpose can provide a means through which transformed relationships could be achieved and solidified.

Stone first highlighted purpose in an analysis of James MacGregor Burns's (1978) treatment of "transactional and transforming" leadership (Stone 1990). His scholarship also added the significance of purpose to the discussion of leadership. "People are motivated to pursue purposes," writes Stone (2005a, 316). Drawing on Burns (1978), Stone believes that part of the leadership challenge is motivating and mobilizing people to act on a shared broad purpose. As Stone (1990, 13) puts it, "Leaders appeal to followers by invoking worthy causes, and that in some circumstances followers respond, not as free riders expecting others to make the needed effort, but as moral agents willing to make personal sacrifices on behalf of the causes they are committed to." Because people or groups are confronted with competing worthy purposes, they are likely to coalesce around those purposes that are viewed as feasible. Feasibility often means reaching the threshold of resources necessary to achieve a purpose (see also Stone, Orr, and Worgs 2006). It is the leaders' role to assemble the resources and convince followers that resources are available, their participation necessary, and their purposive goals obtainable. "The genius of leadership," writes Stone (1990, 13), "lies partly in vision—in seeing what cause can serve to mobilize followers and their resources. But it also lies partly in how the cause is presented—how followers are motivated."

Stone's work on political leadership is also consistent with his emphasis on coalition formation and reformation as central to urban politics. Coalitions are collections of groups. As representatives of the group, leaders control the group's resources. Stone emphasizes that groups differ in the types, amounts, range, and durability of resources under their command. The political activities of groups are orchestrated by group leaders. "Groups don't simply exist and await discovery. They are brought into political being and oriented by the actions of political leaders" (Stone, Whelan, and Murin 1986, 199). From Stone's perspective, a central part of the leadership task is having the capacity to transform political arrangements that can effectively operate in a socially, economically, and politically complex urban setting. "Each set of political arrangements," Stone reminds us, "is built by the action of political entrepreneurs" (Stone, Whelan, and Murin 1986, 200–201). Stone's scholarship reminds us that effective leadership is a prerequisite for any consideration of reshaping political arrangements and working toward a more just policy agenda.

The Politics of Urban Regeneration: School Reform

Throughout his many articles, books, and essays on urban development policy and politics, Clarence Stone consistently raised implicit and explicit questions about systemic bias and socioeconomic inequality. *Regime Politics* includes a chapter entitled "Equity and Effectiveness" in which Stone questioned the "justness" of Atlanta's urban redevelopment policies (Stone 1989, 201). For example, despite Atlanta's 40-plus years of downtown redevelopment, poverty remained high, the public school system was failing, the homeless population expanded, and crime and violence were serious problems. Stone (1989, 209) concluded that Atlanta's redevelopment regime "produced no palpable policy inroads in employment, education, and affordable housing." He believes that if Atlanta and other cities pursued a broader economic redevelopment strategy of education and training, safe and affordable housing, and other policies, it "would make for a socially healthier community" (Stone 1989, 205).

Because of the linkage of labor force preparedness and broader economic redevelopment strategies, any comprehensive effort at social reform and inner-city regeneration would include public school reform as a high priority. The bulk of Stone's work in the area of social reform has been devoted to the politics of reforming urban schools (Stone 1998a; Stone et al. 2001). Many of the efforts to improve urban education tend to be partial, narrow, and ephemeral. Most central cities fall short when it comes to carrying out systemic school reform. Clarence Stone's work helps us understand why cities have fallen short and how they might chart a different course. Here Stone moves from the purely descriptive-analytical to policy prescription.

Much of this work is informed by what Stone calls "civic capacity" (Stone 1998b, 2001). Consistent with urban regime analysis, civic capacity is about relationships and how those relationships can be realigned to focus and tackle a community-wide concern like systemic school reform. Civic capacity refers to the mobilization of an array of local stakeholders in support of a community-wide goal. It is about community members participating and contributing in a supportive way to pursuing a policy priority. It is also about the efficacy of cooperation in the face of pending disaster. Civic capacity calls for coalition building across community sectors and collective problem solving. "Civic capacity comes into play when people see an issue as a community problem, one that therefore calls for a collective (that is to say, civic) response" (Stone 1998b, 15).

Like his earlier work on urban economic development policy, Stone views politics as central to urban school reform. If relationships and coalition formation are the crux of politics, the issue for advocates of school reform is how to rearrange and modify the political arrangements that currently shape the scope and nature of urban education. For education reform to take hold requires a political arrangement where leaders across community sectors are supportive and have the civic capacity to bring together the necessary resources to demonstrate that school reform appears feasible and to make it happen.

Drawing on data gathered from an 11-city comparative study of education reform, Stone argues that cities vary in their ability to shape such arrangements around school reform. One of the major challenges in generating the civic capacity to carry out school reform is overcoming the tendency for community leaders to disagree about the nature of the problem (Stone et al. 2001). Although nearly everyone agrees that urban school reform should be a high priority, Stone observes, community leaders bring divergent perspectives concerning the challenges facing children and education. For example, many see the problem as mainly financial (more resources for schools); others maintain that the health and social problems confronting children and their families are the central reasons for poor education performance. There is "a lack of consensus on the basic issues facing urban education" (Stone et al. 2001, 113). Where there is little agreement about the nature of the problem and divergent views about policy priorities, civic mobilization around urban school reform is likely to be low or nonexistent. "Only where communities share a common perspective on the problem facing them is major reform likely to be put into place and kept in place" (Stone et al. 2001, 102). Divergent problem definition leads to a breakdown in political mobilization, thus limiting civic capacity.

Even when there is general agreement about the need for school reform, different groups bring different concerns and interest to the education issue. In many communities, corporate leaders bring concerns about taxes and efficiency. As Stone observed, "parents and educators . . . share the goals of good schooling for children, but educators also have a strong interest in professional prerogatives that make them wary of an active parental role" (Stone 1998c, 262). Education has also long held historical symbolic importance to African Americans (see Anderson 1988). Urban school systems provided the avenue for black political influence and a source of black middle-class opportunities (Henig et al. 1999; Orr 1999).

Race is another challenge that hampers the building of civic capacity around school reform, especially in large urban school districts. In Atlanta, Baltimore, Detroit, and Washington, D.C., for example, educational policies embraced by black educators and their black school activist allies were typically opposed by white corporate elites, noncity education professionals, and white politicians (Orr 1999; Henig et al. 1999). Browning, Marshall, and Tabb (1984) have argued that building coalitions across racial and ethnic groups was a significant avenue for changing local public policy. However, in some multiethnic cities, Asian and Hispanic residents have had difficulty breaking through the school desegregation policy legacies established in the 1960s and 1970s (Clarke et al. 2006).

In the final analysis, Stone believes that urban school reform (and perhaps social reform more generally) requires various segments of the community to "act on a problem in a way that is out of the ordinary" (Stone 2001, 614). Stone often cites El Paso, Texas, as a good example of a city in which various sectors of the community worked on systemic school reform "in a way that is out of the ordinary." He notes, for example, that in El Paso, "grassroots and elite-level consultation and deliberation are ongoing activities" (Stone 2001, 606). Ordinarily, in many school reform efforts, elite-level actors develop reform initiatives and then try to arrange grassroots support. In El Paso, "not only is there a major community-based organization involved, but the development of parent and community leadership and the promotion of grassroots engagement are also part of the ongoing activity" (Stone 2001, 606). These kinds of collaborations, combined with highly planned forms of cross-sector consultation and the institutionalization of community-wide deliberation (supported via the El Paso Collaborative for Academic Excellence), has led El Paso's leaders to embrace a shared purpose of transforming the political arrangements that promote and support systemic school reform (Staudt and Stone 2007; see also Orr 2007).

In his empirical work on urban school reform, Stone demonstrated that for most urban school districts, "genuine reform will not come easily" (Stone et al. 2001, 142). The primary obstacles to systemic school reform are not a lack of clever ideas, an indifference to education, or a lack of willingness to try new things. The primary obstacles are political in nature; they are rooted in the fact that various groups have distinct interests that often lead them to work against one another in ways that dissipate energies and blunt reform efforts (140). In the end, Stone's work on urban social reform and regeneration returns to the observation that "politics matter."

———

We would emphasize that local *politics* matter. There are particular advantages that the study of urban political analysis brings to political science and other areas of the discipline could learn from a closer connection to urban politics. For example, urban politics is somewhat unique in taking a holistic approach to the study of politics. The local arena is a polity in miniature, allowing for a manageable and in-depth examination of how varied components fit together into a complex form of governance. It is possible to look at the whole system, including voting behavior, the executive, the legislature, interest groups, and formal structures of government. Urban politics provides a multiplicity of accessible points of observation that can serve the discipline well and enhance our opportunity to approach large questions from many particular angles.

The manageable scale also permits for comparative analysis. Browning, Marshall, and Tabb's (1984) important study of 10 California cities presented a path-breaking analysis that showed variation in how government responded to the political demands of racial and ethnic minorities. Although Eulau and Prewitt (1973) attempted to distance *Labyrinths of Democracy* from the urban politics subfield, their study of 82 city councils nevertheless illustrated the comparative advantage of city politics, demonstrating that "cities are best thought of as real-world laboratories where one can observe the workings out of some, by no means all, of the governing processes relevant to democracy" (vii). Indeed, some important state studies show many of the advantages of looking comparatively across a number of smaller polities below the national level. For example. V. O. Key's (1949) *Southern Politics in State and Nation* and Daniel Elazar's (1966) *American Federalism: A View from the States* remain American political science classics. More recently, Rodney Hero's (1998) *Faces of Inequality* is considered a monumental theoretical contribution. Although these studies are not what is narrowly construed as local, they nevertheless show the advantages that can be derived by examining several sub-national polities.

Another advantage of urban politics is that scholars working in the area have maintained a steadier focus on power, especially when compared with other scholars who study American politics and government (but see Hochschild, this volume). "Power reconsidered" was the central theme of the 2006 annual meeting of the APSA. It was the hope of organizers that the meeting would encourage political scientists to "devote more time and energy" to the study and analysis of power (Valelly 2006). According to Valelly, who cochaired the 2006 conference, American political science had exhibited a "silence about power," and he wished to revive "a somewhat dormant discussion" of the concept. If there were a closer connection with urban politics, it is possible that the discipline would not have lost sight of a concept that is, as Valelly put it, "truly indigenous to political science" (Valelly 2006). For most urbanists, power is not treated as an abstraction but as an important lens for seeing issues of equity and social justice. Because urban politics often brings the researcher to a closer examination of "the experiences and life quality of marginal individuals and groups in this society" (Cohen 1999, ix.), urbanists are much more likely to develop a political analysis that sheds light on the distribution of power and how it is skewed in a manner that renders the poor and marginalized into a subordinate and powerless status. The suffering among New Orleans' black poor in the aftermath of Hurricane Katrina in 2005 may have been an eye-opener for many political scientists, but for urbanists, it was, sad to say, no surprise.

Stone and Whelan (2007) point out that work by a new generation of urban historians illustrates ways in which local experiences have restructured the foundations of national politics. As Stone points out in Chapter 12 of this volume, the urban context continues to evolve, and as it does so, the potential for further restructuring national politics is likely at work. Therefore, even if their concern is a better understanding of national politics, we believe that urban politics should matter to more political scientists.

Urban politics' "estrangement" from mainstream political science is unfortunate because political science could richly benefit from the theories and questions addressed in urban political analysis. Although it might be fair to place some of the blame for the subfield's marginalization on urbanists, it is also clear that the larger discipline's emphasis on national-level politics may be neglecting some important contributions within urban politics. Although we would not make the claim that all politics is local, we think a strong case can be made that urban politics provides a useful lens through which to explore many issues of concern to political scientists. The urban setting can be put to good use and can advance more generally our understanding of political science and American democracy. The scholarship of Clarence Stone shows how this can be most astutely accomplished.

OVERVIEW OF THE BOOK

In compiling this volume, we selected some of Stone's most illuminating published articles, essays, and book chapters. We have grouped the selections under four sections. Part 1 includes some of Stone's significant theoretical work on urban political power. Chapter 2 describes "systemic power" and explains the predisposition of local public officials to be drawn into an alliance with the city's upper strata. Chapter 3 looks closely at what some critics of classic pluralism called "nondecision making" and builds an argument for the usefulness of studying the nondecision process. Chapter 4 explains urban regime analysis, emphasizing that for a regime to be viable, it must be able to mobilize the resources commensurate with its main policy agenda. The chapter develops a typology of regimes, comparing the nature and difficulty of various regime types.

Part 2 examines political leadership in community politics. Although there is no well-developed theory of political leadership, Stone has attempted to define the scope and nature of political leadership in an urban context. Given their visibility and access to significant resources, the position of mayor is no doubt a leadership position. Chapter 5 examines the nature of democratic political leadership in U.S. cities. The leadership performance of four big-city mayors—James Michael Curley of Boston, Fiorello La Guardia of New York, and Richard J. Daley and Harold Washington of Chicago—is discussed. Urban regime analysis, however, reminds us that mayoral leadership takes place within a set of political arrangements. In Chapter 6, Stone explains the environmental influences that mayors operate in.

Part 3 examines race, class, and political power in Atlanta. Situated in a context of Southern segregation and racial division, Atlanta's biracial coalition provided much of the empirical data Stone used to develop his theoretical insights on urban regimes and coalition formation. Chapter 7 argues that black electoral incorporation is no match for the economic power of white economic elites. Continuing the theme that African American electoral power is severely limited by white economic power, Chapter 8 develops the thesis that a "coalitional bias" constrains electoral power and that Atlanta's biracial coalition was centered around an accommodation between the city's African American middle-class and white civic elites. Chapter 8 emphasizes the role of race *and* class in the structure and function of the Atlanta regime.

Part 4 is about the politics of social reform and urban regeneration. In this section, Stone considers how cities develop the "civic capacity" to carry out an agenda devoted to urban school reform. Throughout the essays, we see connecting themes from Stone's earlier work on downtown redevelopment policy: education improvement can come about only through governmental *and* nongovernmental action. Chapter 9 compares four school districts' efforts to carry out school reform. Chapter 10 explains the findings of the Civic Capacity and Urban Education Project, an 11-city study of urban school reform. The essay describes conflicts around urban school reform and argues for concerted and sustained engagement among institutional elites and a grassroots base through which ordinary citizens are engaged. Chapter 11 discusses two conceptions of power: "power over" and "power to." The essays explain the nature of political relationships that shape preferences for school reform and other social reform activities.

Part 5 includes two new essays. In Chapter 12, Stone engages in clarification and introspection. He also paints a vision for an important new urban agenda. Few authors have had the distinction of having their ideas read and used by so many scholars. This is testimony to the saliency of Stone's ideas and the timeliness of his analyses. We are pleased that Stone agreed to comment on his own work. The volume concludes with an essay by Jennifer Hochschild. In Chapter 13, Hochschild carefully locates Stone's scholarship within political science, pointing out many of its strengths. Like us, she laments the marginalization of urban politics. She also believes that much can be learned by cross-fertilization of the subfields. Hochschild also provides some sharp points about omissions in Stone's work.

ACKNOWLEDGMENTS

We thank Peter F. Burns, Ramona L. Burton, Bryan D. Jones, Wilbur C. Rich, Heywood T. Sanders, Josh Sapotichne, and Clarence N. Stone for helpful comments and suggestions on earlier drafts of this chapter.

NOTES

1. Stone is among the most cited political scientists in the discipline. See the recent citation rankings by Masuoka, Grofman, and Feld (2007).

2. There have long been political scientists working in the field of public administration who did urban-related research. See, e.g., Holden (1964) and Lockard (1962).

3. Of the works on local politics published before World War II, perhaps the pioneering research and findings of Charles Merriam and his student, Harold Gosnell, stand out as classics and remain worthy of consultation.

4. A 1995 study of major political science departments, for example, found that many of the African American professors concentrated "in fields of study traditionally reserved for blacks, such as urban affairs, southern politics, civil rights, and African politics" (*Journal of Blacks in Higher Education* 1995/1996, 11).

5. This critique has come from some within the urban subfield. Robert C. Wood (1963, 120) notes that the case study's "capacity to advance positive knowledge and to build new generalizations on the present opportunistic basis by which cases are selected remains sharply limited."

REFERENCES

American Political Science Association (APSA). 1973. *Political science and state and local government*. Washington, D.C.: American Political Science Association.

Anderson, J. D. 1988. *The education of blacks in the South, 1860–1935*. Chapel Hill: Univ. of North Carolina Press.

Arendt, H. 1961. *Between past and future*. New York: Viking Press.

Bachrach, P., and M. S. Baratz. 1962. The two faces of power. *American Political Science Review* 56:947–52.

———. 1970. *Power and poverty: Theory and practice*. New York: Oxford Univ. Press.

Bennett, A., A. Barth, and K. R. Rutherford. 2003. Do we preach what we practice? A survey of methods in political science journals and curricula. *PS: Political Science and Politics* 36:373–78.

Browning, R., D. Marshall, and D. Tabb. 1984. *Protest is not enough*. Berkeley: Univ. of California Press.

Burns, J. M. 1978. *Leadership.* New York: Harper & Row.

Clarke, S. E., et al. 2006. *Multiethnic moments: The politics of urban education reform.* Philadelphia: Temple Univ. Press.

Cohen, C. J. 1999. *The boundaries of blackness: AIDS and the breakdown of black politics.* Chicago: Univ. of Chicago Press.

Dahl, R. A. 1961. *Who governs?* New Haven, Conn.: Yale Univ. Press.

———. 1967. The city in the future of democracy. *American Political Science Review* 61:953–70.

Daland, R. T. 1957. Political science and the study of urbanism. *American Political Science Review* 51:491–509.

Danielson, M. N., and P. G. Lewis. 1996. City bound: Political science and the American metropolis. *Political Research Quarterly* 49:203–20.

Elazar, D. J. 1966. *American federalism: A view from the states.* New York: Crowell.

Elkin, S. 1987. *Regimes and the American republic.* Chicago: Univ. of Chicago Press.

Eulau, H. 1991. Interview with Heinz Eulau. In *Political Science in America: Oral Histories of a Discipline,* ed. M. Baer, M. Jewell, and L. Sigelman, 179–94. Lexington: Univ. of Kentucky Press.

Eulau, H., and K. Prewitt. 1973. *Labyrinths of democracy: Adaptations, linkages, representation, and policies in urban politics.* Indianapolis, Ind.: Bobbs-Merrill.

Gittell, M. 1967. *Participants and participation: A study of school policy in New York City.* New York: Praeger Press.

Greenstone, D., and P. Peterson. 1973. *Race and authority in urban politics: Community participation and the war on poverty.* Chicago: Univ. of Chicago Press.

Henig, J., R. C. Hula, M. Orr, and D. S. Pedescleaux. 1999. *The color of school reform.* Princeton, N.J.: Princeton Univ. Press.

Hero, R. E. 1998. *Faces of inequality: Social diversity in American politics.* New York: Oxford Univ. Press.

Herson, L. 1957. The lost world of municipal government. *American Political Science Review* 51:330–45.

Holden, M., Jr. 1964. The governance of the metropolis as a problem in diplomacy. *Journal of Politics* 26:627–47.

Hunter, F. 1953. *Community power structure.* Chapel Hill: Univ. of North Carolina Press.

Imbroscio, D. L. 1997. *Reconstructing city politics: Alternative economic development and urban regimes.* London: Sage.

Jones, B. D. 1989. Why weakness is a strength: Some thoughts on the current state of urban analysis. *Urban Affairs Quarterly* 25:30–40.

Journal of Blacks in Higher Education. 1995/1996. Blacks in political science departments at the nation's highest-ranked universities. *Journal of Blacks in Higher Education* 10:10–12.

Judd, D. R. 2005. Everything is always going to hell: Urban scholars as end-times prophets. *Urban Affairs Quarterly* 41:119–31.

Key, V. O. 1949. *Southern politics in state and nation.* New York: Alfred A. Knopf.

Lipsky, M. 1969. *Protest in city politics.* Chicago: Rand McNally.

Lockard, D. 1962. The city manager: Administrative theory and political power. *Political Science Quarterly* 77:224–36.

Marris, P., and M. Rein. 1973. *Dilemmas of social reform: Poverty and community action in the United States.* 2nd ed. Chicago: Aldine.

Masuoka, N., B. Grofman, and S. L. Feld. 2007. The political science 400: A 20-year update. *PS: Political Science and Politics* 40:133–45.

Merelman, R. 2003. *Pluralism at Yale.* Madison: Univ. of Wisconsin Press.

Miller, W. E. . 1991. Interview with Warren E. Miller. In *Political science in America: Oral histories of a discipline*, ed. M. Baer, M. Jewell, and L. Sigelman, 231–47. Lexington: Univ. of Kentucky Press.

Moynihan, D. P. 1965. *The negro family: The case for national action.*Washington, D.C.:Office of Policy Planning and Research, U.S. Department of Labor.

Nelson, W. E., and P. Meranto. 1977. *Electing black mayors: Political action in the black community.* Columbus: Ohio State Univ. Press.

Orr, M. 1999. *Black social capital: The politics of school reform in Baltimore.* Lawrence: Univ. Press of Kansas.

———, ed. 2007. *Transforming the city: Community organizing and the challenge of political change.* Lawrence: Univ. Press of Kansas.

Orr, M., and V. C. Johnson. 2007. Race and the city: The view from two political science journals. In *The state of the political science discipline: An African-American perspective*, ed. W. C. Rich, 308–24. Philadelphia: Temple Univ. Press.

Persons, G. A. 1978. Atlanta: Black mayoral leadership and the dynamics of political change. Ph.D. diss., Massachusetts Institute of Technology.

Peterson, P. 1981. *City limits.* Chicago: Univ. of Chicago Press.

Pinderhughes, D. M. 1987. *Race and ethnicity in Chicago politics: A reexamination of pluralist theory.* Urbana: Univ. of Illinois Press.

Piven, F. F., and R. Cloward. 1977. *Poor people's movements: Why they succeed, how they fail.* New York: Vintage Books.

Rae, D. 2003. *City: The end of urbanism.* New Haven, Conn.: Yale Univ. Press.

Rich, W. C. 1984. *The politics of urban personnel policy: Reformers, politicians, and bureaucrats.* Port Washington, N.Y.: Kennikat Press.

———. 1989. *Coleman Young and Detroit politics.* Detroit: Wayne State Univ. Press.

———, ed. 2007. *African-American perspectives on political science.* Philadelphia: Temple Univ. Press.

Sapotichne, J., B. D. Jones, and M. Wolfe. 2007. Is urban politics a "black hole"? Analyzing the boundary between political science and urban politics. *Urban Affairs Review* 43:76–106.

Savitch, H. V., and P. Kantor. 2002. *Cities in the international marketplace.* Princeton: Princeton Univ. Press.

Sayre, W., and H. Kaufman. 1960. *Governing New York City: Politics in the metropolis.* New York: Russell Sage.

Sewell, W. H. 1992. *A theory of structure: Duality, agency, and transformation.* Chicago: Univ. of Chicago Press.

Schneider, M. 1994. Review of *Renewing cities. American Political Science Review* 88:224–25.

Sigelman, L. 2006. The coevolution of American political science and the American political science review. *American Political Science Review* 100:463–78.

Staudt, K., and C. N. Stone. 2007. Division and fragmentation: The El Paso experience in global-local perspective. In *Transforming the city: Community organizing and the challenge of political change,* ed. M. Orr, 84–108. Lawrence: Univ. Press of Kansas.

Stone, C. N. 1963a. The city manager and community power: Leadership and policy making in a council-manager city. Ph.D. diss., Duke Univ.

———. 1963b. Inter-party constituency differences and congressional voting behavior: A partial dissent. *American Political Science Review* 57:665–66.

———. 1965. Issue cleavage between Democrats and Republicans in the U.S. House of Representatives. *Journal of Public Law* 14:343–58.

————. 1966. Congressional party differences in civil liberties and criminal procedure issues. *Social Science Quarterly* 47:161–71.

————. 1976. *Economic growth and neighborhood discontent: System bias in the urban renewal program of Atlanta.* Chapel Hill: Univ. of North Carolina Press.

————. 1980. Systemic power in community decision making: A restatement of stratification theory. *American Political Science Review* 74:978–90.

————. 1984. City politics and economic development: Political economy perspectives. *Journal of Politics* 46:286–99.

————. 1987a. The study of the politics of urban development. In *The politics of urban development,* ed. C. N. Stone and H. Sanders, 3–22. Lawrence: Univ. Press of Kansas.

————. 1987b. Summing up: Urban regimes, development policy, and political arrangements. In *The politics of urban development,* ed. C. N. Stone and H. Sanders, 269–90. Lawrence: Univ. Press of Kansas.

————. 1988. Preemptive power: Floyd Hunter's "community power structure" reconsidered. *American Journal of Political Science* 32:82–104.

————. 1989. *Regime politics: Governing Atlanta, 1946–1988.* Lawrence: Univ. Press of Kansas.

————. 1990. Transactional and transforming leadership: A re-examination. Paper presented at the Annual Meeting of the American Political Science Association, San Francisco, Calif.

————, ed. 1998a. *Changing urban education.* Lawrence: Univ. Press of Kansas.

————. 1998b. Introduction: Urban education in political context. In *Changing Urban Education,* ed. C. N. Stone, 1–22. Lawrence: Univ. Press of Kansas.

————. 1998c. Civic capacity and urban school reform. In *Changing Urban Education,* ed. C. N. Stone, 250–76. Lawrence: Univ. Press of Kansas.

————. 2001. Civic capacity and urban education. *Urban Affairs Review* 36:595–619.

————. 2005a. Looking back to look forward: Reflections on urban regime analysis. *Urban Affairs Review* 40:309–41.

————. 2005b. Institutions count but resources decide: American mayors and the limits of formal structure. In *Transforming local political leadership,* ed. R. Berg and N. Rao, 180–94. New York: Palgrave Macmillan.

Stone, C. N., J. R. Henig, B. D. Jones, and C. Pierannunzi. 2001. *Building civic capacity: The politics of reforming urban schools.* Lawrence: Univ. Press of Kansas.

Stone, C. N., M. Orr, and D. Imbroscio. 1991. The reshaping of urban leadership in U.S. cities. In *Urban Life in Transition,* ed. M. Gottdiener and C. Pickvance, 222–39. Urban Affairs Annual Reviews 39. Thousand Oaks, Calif.: Sage Publications.

Stone, C. N., M. Orr, and D. Worgs. 2006. The flight of the bumblebee: Why reform is difficult but not impossible. *Perspectives of Politics* 4:529–46.

Stone, C. N., and H. T. Sanders. 1987. Reexamining a classic case of development politics. In *The Politics of Urban Development,* ed. C. N. Stone and H. T. Sanders, 159–81. Lawrence: Univ. Press of Kansas.

Stone, C. N., and R. K. Whelan. 2007. The short and exaggerated life of public regardingness: The continuing evolution of urban political study. Paper presented at the Urban Affairs Association Annual Meeting, Seattle, Wash.

Stone, C. N., R. K. Whelan, and W. J. Murin. 1986. *Urban policy politics in a bureaucratic age.* Englewood Cliffs, N.J.: Prentice-Hall.

Thompson, J. P. Forthcoming. Race and urban political theory. In *Theories of Urban Politics,* 2nd ed. London: Sage.

Valelly, R. M. 2006. Political scientists' renewed interest in the workings of power. *Chronicle Review* 52:B6.

Wahlke, J. C., H. Eulau, W. Buchanan, and L. C. Ferguson. 1962. *The legislative system.* New York: John Wiley.

Walker, J. 1972. Brother can you paradigm. *PS: Political Science and Politics* 5:419–22.

Walton, H., Jr., and J. P. McCormick. 1997. The study of African-American politics as social danger. *National Political Science Review* 6:229–44.

Williams, L. F. 1977. Race, class, and politics: The impact of American political economy on black Detroit. Ph.D. diss., Univ. of Chicago.

Wilson, J. Q. 1962. *The amateur Democrat: Club politics in three cities.* Chicago: Univ. of Chicago Press.

Wilson, W. J. 1987. *The truly disadvantaged.* Chicago: Univ. of Chicago Press.

Wood, R. C. 1963. The contributions of political science to urban form. In *Urban Life and Form,* ed. W. Z. Hirsch, 99–127. New York: Holt, Rinehart and Winston.

Yin, R. A. 1994. *Case study research: Design and methods.* Thousand Oaks, Calif.: Sage Publications.

Part One

Power, Social Stratification, and Local Democracy

Clarence Stone's conceptualization of community power, especially the urban regime framework, is one of his greatest contributions to the study of urban politics. Key to understanding Stone's contribution is his thoughtful reflection on how inequalities in the socioeconomic political system limit the promises of local democracy. In Chapter 2, the question that Stone poses is why, when all of their actions are taken into account, do public officials seem to favor upper-strata interests over lower-strata interests? Why do they sometimes act in apparent disregard to the contours of electoral power, which are predicated on majority rule? The answer is the result of what Stone terms "systemic bias."

Systemic bias takes into account that public officials operate in an environment that is class stratified. Power is not only a matter of intention; it is also a matter of context. It is situational. The nature of the socioeconomic system places groups in a position where their power is regarded despite the fact that they are not intentionally attempting to have their power advanced; it is just a reality of a class-stratified system. Therefore, systemic power is that type of power furthest removed from open competition, and purposeful or intentional activity.

In Chapter 3, Stone takes the systemic bias argument one step further by challenging the pluralist critique of nondecision making. In the process, he explains how seemingly insignificant political activity (activity that is broad and diffused) manifests power just as much as overt activity (decisions). Although pluralists place emphasis on decision making, Stone argues that policy efforts are shaped by activities that are beyond the boundaries of decisional politics. Policy is shaped by actions and arrangements that appear peripheral to the process of making big decisions, and represents a less visible or "second" face of power that is distinctive from decisional power. Stone addresses the major criticism lodged against the concept nondecision making by illustrating how it can be studied empirically. He also shows how pluralists fail to appreciate how broad and diffused activities are conditioned by structural factors, systemic constraints, and mobilization of bias, and how public-private arrangements have policy consequences.

In Chapter 4, Stone sets forth the guiding assumptions of urban regime analysis. According to Stone, the extent to which the politics of urban regimes have positive economic and political consequences depends on the character of the governing coalition. Regimes vary from city to city. Although some are devoted to downtown development, and thus can be termed *entrepreneurial* or *corporate regimes*, others are devoted to broader citizen and neighborhood interests and thus can be termed *progressive regimes*. Regime analysis suggests that public policies or governing decisions that do evolve are shaped by three factors: the composition of the coalition that governs under these arrangements; the nature of the relationships among members of the governing coalitions; and the resources that the members bring to the governing coalition. The unequal distribution of resources has a substantial impact on the character of the governing coalition—again, what is important is not who controls, but who can assemble the resources to bear on decisions that need to be made. The difference between development regimes and middle-class progressive regimes is the greater ability of the former to amass resources and side payments for projects. The necessary ingredient essential for progressive regimes to work becomes an attentive electorate and the organization and active involvement of the lower strata. Progressive mandates often rest on a base of active popular support. The difficult part is maintaining commitment by setting goals that are feasible but also socially significant. The pursuit of progressive mandates, as Stone asserts, is a more difficult governing task than development, but nonetheless is in fact possible.

2. Systemic Power in Community Decision Making

A Restatement of Stratification Theory

Clarence N. Stone

Students of power have long probed beneath the surface fiction of political equality for the imbalances of influence that are invariably present in the governance of communities. But this search is complicated by the fact that power is often present without being visibly exercised. In trying to understand the less visible influences surrounding public decision making, scholars have variously developed such concepts as nondecisions, anticipated reactions, and indirect influence. Useful as they are, these concepts don't take us far enough. It seems that there is a dimension of power beyond what the accepted concepts suggest—a dimension best termed "systemic."

Consider these circumstances. Contrary to reasonable expectations, electoral strength, whether potential or manifest, appears to be an unreliable indicator of political power. Major business enterprises and other upper-strata interests seem to have an influence on local decisions not warranted by their numbers or their overt participation in political and governmental affairs. For example, while business influence in particular controversies is not very impressive (business interests are often divided or defeated), business influence seems to be important in a way not measured by victories and losses. Conversely, lower-strata groups seem to face fewer handicaps in politics than in other areas of community life (cf. Dahl 1961, 293–96), but they make little use of political activity to further their position and, when they do, they are often disappointed by the transitory nature of their influence.

Peter Bachrach and Morton Baratz (1970) confronted this problem of a less visible face of power, setting forth the notion of nondecision making. By this term, they meant the capacity of elite groups to restrict the scope of community decision making. G. William Domhoff (1978) has added the assertion that there is a national upper class based on corporate wealth which is able to control the agenda of public debate and maintain ideological dominance. However, nondecision making has proved difficult to research; critics charge that it is not possible to study nonevents and that what in fact is studied is a special kind of decision making.

Whether the critics have fairly characterized nondecision making is debatable (see Crenson 1971), but there does seem to be more to the "hidden face" of power than agenda control. Despite efforts to contain them, a variety of issues do surface; during the 1960s, for example, redistributive issues were prominent. The missing element in the community power puzzle seems to be in the predispositions of public officials. Why, when all of their actions are taken into account, do officials over the long haul seem to favor upper-strata interests, disfavor lower-strata interests, and some times act in apparent disregard of the contours of electoral power? Can this systemic pattern be treated in power terms?

In the discussion below, I will argue "yes" to this last question. The core of my argument is that we must take into account contextual forces—the facet of community decision making I label "systemic power." In brief, this argument runs as follows: public officials form their alliances, make their decisions and plan their futures in a context in which strategically important resources are hierarchically arranged—that is, officials operate in a stratified society. The system of stratification is a motivating factor in all that they do; it predisposes them to favor upper- over lower-strata interests. Systemic power therefore has to do with *the impact of the larger socioeconomic system on the predispositions of public officials.*

The class character of community decision making does not result from a conscious calculation. As Norton Long has argued, rationality is "a function of the parts rather than the whole" (1958, 251). What I shall elaborate below is the argument that because officials operate within a stratified system, they find themselves rewarded for cooperating with upper-strata interests and unrewarded or even penalized for cooperating with lower-strata interests. In selective ways described later, public officials experience strategic dependencies predisposing them to favor upper- over lower-strata interests. Thus some groups are in a position to receive official cooperation, while others encounter substantial resistance. Put another way, different strata operate from different footings and therefore face different opportunity costs (cf. Harsanyi 1962). The particular interactions and relationships (the parts) yield an overall pattern of decision making that is unplanned and unforeseen. It does, however, bear a class imprint not predicted by pluralist theories of community power and it comes about in ways requiring no ruling elite.

The overall argument is developed in three steps: (1) a definition and explanation of the concept of systemic power, (2) a highlighting of systemic features underlying specified power imbalances, and (3) an examination of empirical findings bearing on the notion of systemic power used here.

SYSTEMIC POWER: TOWARD AN EXPLANATION AND DEFINITION

Everyone recognizes that system features in some way affect the distribution of power. But how does one relate those system features to the power relationships among determinate actors?

Power is most readily seen in overt and purposive activity among individuals. But students of politics (such as Anton 1963) have long recognized that power relationships are more complex than what can be observed in that form:

1. Power is not only *interpersonal;* it is also *intergroup* (including relationships between classes and strata). Few would quarrel with this position.

2. Power is not only a matter of intention; it is also a matter of context, of the nature of or "logic" of the *situation*. Here there is a need for some clarification.

Most students of power agree that there is a phenomenon called "anticipated reactions." *A* may influence the behavior of *B* because *B* is fearful of the reactions of *A* to a given course of conduct; or *B* may be accommodating to *A* because *B* wants to stay in the good graces of *A* for future advantage. To illustrate, Robert Dahl observes that "elected leaders keep the real or imagined preferences of constituents constantly in mind in deciding what policies to adopt or reject" (1961, 164). In this latter instance especially, it is not necessary that the passive "actor" intend that its preferences be taken into account or even be conscious that a power relationship exists. Indeed, Dahl makes much of the indifference and unconcern of the electorate. All that is required for this to be a power relationship is that elected officials take into account preferences of the electorate because the electorate is in a position to give or withhold something of value—in this case, votes. Any actor may, just by possessing a politically useful resource, enjoy a power advantage.

Furthermore, it is not necessary that the superordinate member in a power relationship has gained that position by some intended activity. Inherited wealth is not politically valueless because it was inherited, nor is advantage gained through a fortuitous change in circumstances any less an advantage because the change was fortuitous. Power can therefore be situational in a twofold sense: (1) a participant need not make a conscious effort to get into a power position for that position to be power relevant, and (2) the participant need not be aware of the particular consequences of the power position (cf. Oppenheim 1978). This means therefore that, if the *situation* is such that *B* feels a need to be accommodating to *A*, then *A* has power over *B*, whether *A* sought that position or is even aware of it or not. Moreover, the strength of the relationship is not governed by motivation. In an anticipated reaction, the strength of the relationship is determined by the vulnerability of *B* to *A* (cf. Emerson 1962). Vulnerability hinges on the *structure of the situation,* and that is separate from the motivation or effort that went into creating or even exploiting the situation. This is not to say that motivation, sharply defined intention, or conscious effort to gain an advantage are never important, only that they are not essential to a power relationship.

3. Power relationships are not only *direct;* they may also be *indirect.* Again, there is need for clarification, and there is also a need for keeping in mind the difference between the situational element of power and the indirect element of power.

Power is most often viewed as a conflict relationship. When there is direct conflict, the exercise of power is not in doubt. This is the standard "*A* gets *B* to do what *B* would not otherwise have done." This is a clear case of the "power over" relationship. But suppose there is no overt threat, not even an implicit threat to use sanctions. Rather, participants have an unequal opportunity to further their interests. *A* has a greater capacity to achieve goals than *C* has (excluding *B* from consideration for the time being). We say that *A* is more powerful than *C*—that, for example, Mayor Lee is more powerful than the corner grocer. But is this a power relationship since there is no *direct* conflict between *A* and *C*? This relationship has been treated as a "power to" rather than a "power over" relationship, and therefore not as a conflict relationship. However, the "power to" relationship is a conflict relationship if *A* and *C* are in *indirect* competition to achieve their goals. If *A*, by getting *B* to do *x* makes it unlikely that *C* can get *B* to do *y*, then there is a conflict relationship—but it is indirect because *A* and *C* are not competing directly with one another. This is implied in the nondecision-making argument. *A* excludes *C*'s items from the agenda of decision making, not only because *C*'s items may be threatening in some direct way, but *because the agenda is limited and there is competition for the space available.* An unequal capacity to achieve goals is therefore a conflict relationship to the extent that the actors are in competition for a limited opportunity to further their interests. If *A* uses superior resources to structure a pattern of agenda setting and *C* finds that s/he cannot change the agenda, *A* has exerted power over *C* even in the absence of direct conflict between *A* and *C*.

DEFINING SYSTEMIC POWER

For purposes of the present discussion, let us assume that we need be concerned only with durable, not transient, power conditions. Let us also assume that we are concerned only with intergroup power relationships. What we are looking for is a way to treat the durable features of the larger socioeconomic system as an element of the power relationships among groups.

By putting together the different elements of power in their various combinations (and concentrating on durable conditions), one may derive the following classification scheme. Systemic power appears as that type of power *furthest* removed from open competition (*direct* power relationships) and purposive activity (involving a conscious *intention*) among individuals (*interpersonal*). Yet it is made up of elements that are acknowledged to be aspects of power.

Systemic power can be defined as that dimension of power in which durable features of the socioeconomic system (the *situational* element) confer advantages

Table 2.1. Types of Power Relationships

Elements in Relationship	Type of Relationship
Intergroup, intentional and direct	Decisional
Intergroup, situational and direct	Anticipated reaction
Intergroup, intentional and indirect	Nondecision making
Intergroup, situational and indirect	Systemic

and disadvantages on groups (the *intergroup* element) in ways predisposing public officials to favor some interests at the expense of others (the *indirect* element).

At the intergroup level, when situational and indirect elements of power are put together in the political context, the combination brings to light the situational dependency of official decision makers on one set of participants that prevents other participants from having an equal chance to further their interests through the political process. Beneficiaries of that situational dependency need not have made a conscious effort to create that dependency for political purposes. All that is necessary for that dependency relationship to qualify as part of a power relationship is that some visible gain be allocated to the beneficiary group and that the gain be, at least indirectly, at the expense of some competing group.

To be sure that the various dimensions of power are differentiated, let us trace the recession from direct and open conflict based on active intention. If a business organization contributes money and mounts a successful campaign to defeat a candidate, it is exercising decisional power. This represents an intentional use of resources under conditions of direct conflict to gain a specific objective.

Anticipated reactions differ from decisional power only in that while conflict is direct, it is not overt, but tacit. It arises from the structure of the situation rather than from an open and intentional mobilization of resources. Consider a hypothetical example. Because only the local chamber of commerce is capable of putting together an effective challenge, an incumbent administration interested in running for reelection courts the good favor of the chamber by being attentive to its interests. The mere presence of mobilizable resources produces results because the responding actor (the mayor) wants to avoid sanctions from the superordinate party (the chamber). Consequently, the chamber exercises power without any active effort.

In contrast to the above examples, nondecision making falls into the category of power relationships involving no direct conflict. The point made so forcefully by Peter Bachrach and Morton Baratz (1970) is that contending groups exercise power not only to influence the outcomes of specific issues but also to shape the context of decision making and thereby influence how, and even whether, an issue develops. It is important to remember that the superordinate party in nondecision making is not totally passive. We could, for example, observe a chamber of commerce promoting city manager government, or school administrators reinforcing the view that education is nonpolitical. Bear in mind, however, that what is being observed is not a superordinate party exercising power over a subordinate party (hence the power relationship is not one of direct conflict) but rather the superordinate party using resources to influence the context (institutions, procedures, and norms) of community decision making. Nondecision-making power differs from decisional power in that it is not a matter of winning particular decisional struggles but of determining how conflict will be shaped or opposition prevented (Frey 1971). It is most telling when it so diffuses the conflict relationship that a direct and even tacit confrontation is avoided.

Systemic power differs from nondecision making on the important dimension of intention and situation. That is, like nondecision making, systemic power does not entail a relationship of direct conflict, but, unlike nondecision making, systemic power is *purely situational.* By this I mean both that members of the power relationship may be unaware of the particular consequences of their power position and that they need have made no active effort to build up or defend their power advantage. Systemic power, as such, involves no overt attempt to influence the context of decision making. It lies in the imperatives of the situation and requires no elite group engaged in changing or maintaining institutions, procedures, or norms. Because its operation is completely impersonal and deeply embedded in the social structure, this form of power can appropriately be termed "systemic."

How, then, can systemic power be studied? The answer is that its consequences can be observed. Like other elements of community power, systemic features impinge on the behavior of official decision makers, and that impingement can be translated into power terms by means of the concept "opportunity costs." As John Harsanyi (1962) has pointed out, if some actors encounter less resistance than others, they must expend fewer resources to achieve their goals—in short, their opportunity costs are lower. Hence their power position is stronger than the position of those actors who have higher opportunity costs. Now we can link that idea directly to systemic power. Because system features predispose officials to favor some interests and to oppose others, those system features lower the opportunity costs for some groups while raising them for others—thereby having an important impact on the community's overall set of power relationships.

The concept of opportunity costs makes it clear why influence is not proportional to the effort expended on political activities. If, for example, one candidate for public office has to make a great effort to be elected and another sails through with an easy campaign, we don't conclude that the first candidate was more powerful because s/he overcame more resistance. It is often the case that the weak must struggle while the strong have only to ask. And if those with few resources encounter official resistance, they may find that they quickly face political bankruptcy. Edward Banfield recounts how Mayor Richard Daley, on assuming office, wrote to three or four of Chicago's major business leaders, "asking them to list the things they thought most needed doing" (1961, 251). The poor of Woodlawn, by contrast, had to engage in protests, voter-registration drives, and other highly visible forms of political action to call attention to their concerns. The truly powerful are often able to achieve their aims with little effort whereas those who are less powerful must make a much greater effort to achieve the same results.

A method of analysis that looks only at conflict or even at amount of energy expended politically is therefore likely to concentrate mainly on the struggles of the less powerful to have some influence on decision makers. It would miss systemic power and overlook the advantages that some groups enjoy in the form of favorable predispositions of public officials. Hence we need a conception of power that encompasses more than direct conflict between two actors. Some power relationships are triadic, and that makes indirect conflict possible. The triad we are considering here has public officials at the focal point. Their tendency to cooperate with some interests and resist others is itself an aspect of community power through its effects on the opportunity costs involved in influencing decisions. Bear in mind that the *indirect* power relationship referred to is not between public officials and favored groups, but between favored and unfavored groups. Note also that if this indirect relationship leads to overt conflict, it is not the favored groups but rather public officials (the intervening presence in the triad) who are likely to be the target of discontent.

Community power relationships thus manifest themselves through the behavior of public officials. That is why recruitment patterns are so important. But systemic power refers to something more fundamental even than recruitment. It refers to the circumstance that officeholders (regardless of personal background, nature of electoral support, network of associations, etc.) are, by virtue of their position, more situationally dependent on some interests than others. Because this dependency is inherent in the situation, officials are inescapably predisposed to favor some interests over others.

The tendency for officials to favor some interests at the expense of others can be the result of many factors—overt pressure, anticipated reactions, or a nondecision process, for example. But the central point here is that one source of that tendency is a set of situational dependencies that grow out of the larger socioeconomic system. Because the impact of these dependencies is indirect and because they are not the product of overt and purposive political activity, they are often overlooked. However, systemic features do affect the power positions of competing groups with a stake in community decision making. By employing the notion of opportunity costs, we can see that systemic power does not mean that power is exercised by the system, but rather that *the system affects power relationships in ways that are situational and indirect.*

SOCIAL STRATIFICATION AND SYSTEMIC POWER

Up to this point, systemic power has been treated abstractly. Now it is time to turn to the palpable inequalities that are part of the larger socioeconomic system, particularly as they relate to the process of community decision making. To make this matter more manageable, we can look to a well-developed body of writing concerned with social stratification. Most studies of stratification treat hierarchical differentiation as having several dimensions (economic, associational, and social) and many layers (one or more middle strata as well as upper and lower strata). The separability of dimensions makes analysis possible on something other than a straight ruling-class/subordinate-class basis. However, because the separate dimensions of differentiation are highly intercorrelated, inequalities are likely to be *cumulative* rather than dispersed.

At the same time, stratification bears on the pluralist argument that numbers can counterbalance wealth. Modern systems of stratification tend to be diamond shaped: a small top stratum, large (and multiple) middle strata, and a relatively small bottom stratum (Matras 1975, 130–33). The advantage of numbers thus does not accrue to those at the bottom, but rather to the middle strata. The nature and composition of the middle strata are of special importance. They are often the source of change and conflict, variously challenging the dominance of those higher up and resisting upward movement by those at the bottom of the social hierarchy.

Our concern, however, is with a static tendency of social structure, that is, with the relatively stable impact of inequalities in opportunities and resources. Drawing on the literature on stratification, we can differentiate among three major kinds of inequality, each of which fits the diamond-shaped distribution of opportunities and resources and each of which has special relevance to community decision making. While the three facets of socioeconomic inequality discussed here do not exhaust the elements of stratification impinging on community decision making, they serve to highlight systemic power.

1. *Economic position.* The top stratum possesses great wealth and command of major economic enterprises; the middle strata have job skills, job entitlements, moderate amounts of personal wealth, and property; the bottom stratum is characterized mainly by economic dependency. This distribution has special significance for public decision makers because, as one moves toward the top of the diamond, economic strata are perceived as more strongly revenue producing, while as one

moves toward the bottom of the diamond, economic strata are perceived as more strongly service demanding. Officials naturally lean in the direction of favoring revenue producers because they are essential to institutional maintenance.[1]

2. *Associational position.* The top stratum possesses hierarchical power, that is, command of the resources of major organizations. Moreover, because these organizations are either essentially self-directing hierarchies or small membership-based associations, they have no collective action problem (Olson 1965). While the middle strata possess power, they are organized for collective action through employment-related and other voluntary associations. These organizations are relatively stable and, as in the case of unions, sometimes enjoy a legally recognized position. They may have sufficient and continuing funding to have a permanent staff, and in this regard may approximate hierarchical power. However, because they are serving a mass base, they face the "law of oligarchy" problem (a disjunction of goals between officials and rank-and-file members). And because they must sometimes mobilize the membership base to be effective, they cannot escape the collective action problem. The bottom stratum, though a less numerous segment of the population, also has mass power. However, it is either organized into unstable and ad hoc voluntary associations or simply not organized at all. When organized, its associations are without permanent staff; and in all cases the problem of collective action is acute.

Associational position requires some explanation. Insofar as organization represents a capacity to mobilize support for or against a decision, it is an element in anticipated reactions (or, if activated, an element in decisional power). In this sense there is substance to the pluralist argument that a numerous mass can counterbalance an elite group. But even in this realm of anticipated reactions, it is important to keep in mind the diamond-shaped distribution. Mass as a counterbalance to elite resources applies, *as an anticipated reaction,* to middle versus upper strata. It does not readily apply to lower versus upper strata. And, in those not infrequent cases of conflict between middle and lower strata, the lower strata seldom enjoy the advantage of numbers (see Shefter 1977).

Our main concern here, however, is not with anticipated reactions, but with systemic power. There is a parallel with economic position. In the case of economic position, we focused on revenue production, not on the use of wealth in campaign contributions and the like. Campaign contributions can be limited, and the masses can raise large sums through small donations. In this way, the *immediate advantage* of the wealthy few can be overcome. But their *systemic advantage* as major revenue producers would be unaffected. The masses cannot counterbalance this advantage because, as a mass, they are more visible as service demanders than as producers of revenue.

Associational position has a similar facet which constitutes one element of systemic power. Mass power (that is, numbers without organization) isn't useful for aggregating resources in furthering a policy objective. Suppose, for example, that the objective is to upgrade a neighborhood and improve or eliminate substandard housing. Suppose further that the alternative ways of achieving that goal are (1) through the expansion of a medical complex—a use of hierarchical power, or (2) a rehabilitation effort by a large number of small property owners—a use of mass power thus requiring some kind of collective action. Clearly, the first alternative is easier, and public officials would be more inclined to consult and work with a few key organizational officials than with a mass of property owners. Even aside from the ability-to-pay factor (which could be overcome by a subsidy program), an effort that requires mass action is more difficult (and the greater the mass, the greater the difficulty) than one that requires an organization to act. Having differentiated systemic advantage from nonsystemic power, we can now draw a general conclusion. The significance of differences in associational position *as a dimension of systemic power* is that, as one moves toward the top of the diamond, associational strata are perceived as possessing a greater capacity to mobilize and sustain resources for goal attainment, while as one moves toward the bottom of the diamond, associational strata are perceived as being more dependent on unsteady forms of collective action.

3. *Social position and lifestyle.* The top stratum (probably most readily identified by level of education and type of skills required in work role) enjoys high esteem and status. Members of this group are self-assured and widely believed to be cosmopolitan, to be concerned with the future, and to have a high sense of civic responsibility and competence. They are also generally perceived to be achievement oriented. Members of the middle strata are thought to have these characteristics to a limited degree, and they are only moderately esteemed. Those of the bottom strata are not esteemed and are perceived to possess cultural handicaps. They are not self-assured, their goals are seen as immediate and limited, and they are regarded as likely to engage in psychologically protective or escapist behavior (behavior believed to limit their ability to achieve their full potential as productive members of society). The distribution of social status that accompanies these general beliefs and perceptions has special significance for public decision makers because, as one moves toward the top of the diamond, social strata are regarded as not only more admirable but also more interesting and fruitful to work with (upper-status children, for example, are deemed to be more desirable students to teach), while, as one moves toward the bottom of the diamond, social strata are regarded as less admirable and more frustrating and unrewarding to work with. The point is not that public officials are uncompassionate toward the poor. Often they regard the poor as victims of circumstances, but, even so, officials see members of the lower strata as unlikely to succeed individually and unlikely to contribute collectively to the well-being of the whole community.

The three dimensions of socioeconomic differentiation discussed here enable us to view systemic power in a clearer light. Given the likelihood that public officials, elected and appointed, will want to enhance their own careers and assure the well-being of the organizational units they are affiliated with (cf. Downs 1967; Frohlich and Oppenheimer 1978), their behavior will be patterned by the system of stratification. Specifically, systemic power grows out of the fact that as officeholders make decisions, they take into account: (1) economic considerations—especially the government's revenue needs; (2) associational considerations of various groups to engage in and sustain policy and other goal-oriented actions; and (3) social status and lifestyle considerations as they bear on professional and career accomplishments.

The overall argument here is that upper-strata interests do "exert" extraordinary influence, but that this influence is not usually overt. It flows more from the position they occupy than from the covert action they take. Upper-strata influence *and lower-strata weakness* are traceable to the predispositions that inevitably accompany public office holding in a society characterized by hierarchical differentiations of wealth, organization position, and esteem. These predispositions facilitate the exercise of influence by upper-strata interests (lower their opportunity costs) and thereby enhance upper-strata power.

These predispositions are not identical with the general cultural biases of the society, nor are they direct products of the general process of opinion formation. Instead, they grow out of the pressures particular to office holding. Because the predispositions that make up systemic power are different from the prevailing consensus on the economic, political, and social order, their impact is most noticeable as one examines the least visible aspects of decision making. In other words, systemic power has greater impact as decisions are further removed from the external pressures of public sentiment and are therefore more exclusively a matter of the internal pressures of office holding.

Underlying systemic power are these two points: (1) public officeholders want not only to hold office but also to achieve objectives so that the institutions they direct will thrive and their own individual careers will blossom; and (2) as they are engaged in achieving objectives—that is, governing—officeholders are especially mindful of the resources, both cultural and material, possessed by various segments of society.

Systemic power—based, as the name suggests, in the system of social stratification—can be contrasted with other, more visible forms of power. Formal political equality, for example, has mainly to do with the election process—a highly public activity. That activity nudges officeholders in the direction of greater responsiveness to all segments of society, but especially to those of the numerous middle strata. By contrast, as we have seen, systemic power has mainly to do with governing and it tilts the political balance toward the upper strata. Thus, while the total community power configuration is influenced by election outcome, the systemic element of that configuration is not.

EXAMINING THE IMPACT OF SYSTEMIC POWER

If systemic power is indeed systemic and not a matter of an elite group exercising power in some observable form, how can it be studied? The question can be answered in two parts. First, the heart of the above argument is that systemic power manifests itself in the behavior of public officials; therefore we need to look at decisional activity (broadly defined). To the extent that systemic power is present, it should result in (1) decisional outcomes that are consistent with the various strategic dependencies of public officials, and (2) patterns of interaction in which those of the upper and lower strata encounter different degrees of resistance from officials. Second, the argument can be used to derive testable propositions. While at this stage there are no studies of decision making keyed specifically to systemic power, it is possible to illustrate how the argument can account for concrete patterns of behavior. The argument does refer to observable regularities in decision making about which there are relevant findings. Let us then turn to the overall argument as a basis for pertinent generalizations.

We started the discussion with the point that public officials might be expected to base their actions on popular acceptability, thus appealing to the most numerous and most interested segments of their constituencies. We also noted that official behavior doesn't always conform to this seemingly reasonable expectation, and the subsequent discussion indicated why public officials are subject to forces other than those emanating directly from the electoral system. Though they are the least numerous segment of the population, members of the upper strata possess resources strategically important to public officials. Public officials thus operate under *dual pressures*—one set based in electoral accountability and the other based in the hierarchical distribution of economic, organizational, and cultural resources.

From this review of the argument, we can see that systemic power enjoys no monopoly; hence its impact will be selective. Two general propositions seem warranted: (1) upper-strata influence is neither comprehensive nor undifferentiated—it is particular to the way in which public officials derive career and institutional benefit; and (2) upper-strata advantage is greatest where popular constraints are weakest.

Let us turn now from these general propositions to a discussion of how systemic power might be concretely manifested. The application of the general proposition about upper-strata influence being neither comprehensive nor undifferentiated requires first a reminder that the system of stratification involves an economic, an associational, and a social (lifestyle) dimension. The argument here thus differs from the elitist notion that there is a ruling class exercising general dominance. Instead, the systemic power argument holds that the nature of upper-strata advantage and lower-strata disadvantage varies with the dimension of stratification under consideration. The argument here thus offers a possible explanation for some otherwise puzzling findings in the literature on urban politics. Let us consider each of the three dimensions briefly.

Business Influence and the Economic Dimension

Writers such as Domhoff who argue that there is a ruling class run into difficulty when they find that business influence is more pronounced in some areas than others. Domhoff, for example, is unable to explain why business, though manifestly interested in both areas, has so much less influence in governmental reform than in redevelopment (1978, 168–69).

Business influence is embedded in the imperatives of the situation in which local government operates. And business interests prevail not because a ruling-class network promotes pro-business proposals, but because governments are drawn by the nature of underlying economic and revenue-producing conditions to serve those interests (cf. Lindblom 1977). It is this set of circumstances that constitutes one facet of systemic power. Business influence is therefore greater in a policy area like urban renewal that is related to revenue production than in an area like governmental reform that is unrelated to revenue production. The notion of systemic power developed here therefore accounts for variations in business influence that Domhoff's ideological-dominance thesis cannot explain.

The Power of the Few and the Associational Dimension

As a dimension of systemic power, associational position helps explain what otherwise is a political paradox. One of the recurring conflicts in urban politics is over expansion of institutions such as hospitals and universities into surrounding residential neighborhoods. The behavior of these institutions is easy to explain, but why do local officials cooperate with and promote their expansionist aims? While hospitals and universities provide employment and sometimes upgrade surrounding property, they also take land off the tax rolls—a problem of considerable consequence for many central cities. If the surrounding neighborhood is a slum, city hall support for institutional expansion might be credited to economic considerations—to the removal of a service-demanding and therefore costly population. But how do we explain city hall support for expansion of an institution when the surrounding neighborhood is composed of the tax-paying and vote-casting middle class? The answer surely must lie with the associational aspect of systemic power. Officials want to see change and activity that they can claim a role in. They want to see the institutions in their jurisdictions grow and prosper, and large institutions have the wherewithal and the organization to assure that major projects are executed and that change occurs. Official decision makers have a natural inclination to work with those best able to accomplish visible successes.

In describing an issue involving strong neighborhood opposition to the construction of a new library by New York University, Douglas Yates assesses Mayor Lindsay's decision to support library construction this way:

> In terms of political costs and benefits the Mayor gained support in the nonprofit sector (but few votes) and lost support in a neighborhood whose votes were thought to be very important for any liberal, reform politician running in the city (1977, 123).

If elected officials are guided by a desire for popular support, how does a mayor come to choose an alternative that is not only favored by the least numerous side but also opposed by the group that is at the heart of his own electoral coalition? The problem was not one of miscalculation or lack of information; the opposition was too vocal and too intense for its preference to be misunderstood. Pluralism cannot account for this issue outcome. Systemic power, on the other hand, affords a reasonable explanation for why public officials choose courses of action sought by the few but opposed by the many. The few are better positioned to bring off complex projects and achieve tangible goals.

Agency Autonomy Reinterpreted in Light of the Social Dimension

Most studies of urban administration conclude that public service bureaucracies enjoy a high level of autonomy. In the provision of routine services, bureaucratic decision rules seem to be based mainly on internal considerations—administrative convenience, economizing scarce resources, and professional considerations (Mladenka and Antunes 1976). Many agency operations appear well insulated from external pressures. Even in areas such as public education where citizens are active, community groups don't seem to have much impact. Civil rights groups and their allies, for example, have a long history of achieving apparent concessions only to be frustrated by failures in implementation (Rogers 1968). Such experiences have engendered a neopluralist interpretation of urban politics, namely, that administrative fragmentation and unmanaged social conflict have given us an "ungovernable city" (Yates 1977).

Throughout, but especially in the provision of routine services, researchers find little evidence of a class bias in the allocational decision of administrative agencies. Instead they find "unpatterned inequalities" (Lineberry 1977). Yet while it is clear that class is by no means the only factor at work in service delivery, there is substantial evidence that the client's social position does indeed have an impact. The systemic-power argument directs us to the phase of service delivery where class is a factor.

A puzzling feature of findings about "unpatterned inequalities" and administrative fragmentation is how to account for the higher level of dissatisfaction with service delivery among lower-income and minority groups. Why does level of satisfaction with and trust in government vary with social status? One possible answer is that lower-status groups have a greater need for government services. But there is a more direct way of explaining lower-status attitudes, and this is that lower-status clients are treated differently interpersonally (Clark 1965).

Much of the unpatterned inequality in service delivery concerns agency decisions about the location of physical facilities, the allocation of dollars, or the frequency of response to service demands. It does not concern the actual behavior of individual service deliverers interacting with clients. It is at this interpersonal level of decision making that a class bias becomes evident, and differences in social position and life style have an impact. One close student of bureaucratic decision rules concludes:

> Street level bureaucrats develop stereotypes which suggest that lower class citizens are less deserving of a service or that attempts to deliver services to them will be unsuccessful. Consequently, the foot soldiers give low priority to delivering services to lower class clients. The result is that although agency decision rules produce "unpatterned inequalities," individual decision rules create "patterned inequalities" (Greene 1979, 11–12).

Most students of bureaucracy find that professional norms are an important basis for decision rules. But they don't examine closely the political nature of these norms. However, professional norms apply a value framework to clients, and one aspect of that framework is a definition of who is worthy of being served (Greene 1979, 9). Another aspect is a judgment about how professionals should expend their efforts. Career advancement and professional recognition go to those professionals whose clients show visible improvement from treatment or who are "interesting" in some way (Schon 1970). Professional norms and mores are biased toward those clients with the greatest "potential," and potential is often perceived to be class related and intergenerationally transmissible. Upper-class clients—whether public school students, mental health patients, juvenile offenders, or library patrons—generally receive the best service and the most highly trained personnel. And, perhaps most important of all, they are the ones treated with the most positive attitudes (Hollingshead and Redlich 1958; Rosenthal and Jacobson 1968).

Thus, the aspect of systemic power involving social position and lifestyle does account for a significant inequality in service delivery and may well account for some of the dissatisfaction of poor and minority groups with local government. Even though service-providing professionals are largely autonomous, social inequality can enter service delivery through the norms and mores of various occupational groups. Variations in client treatment thus may not be random occurrences nor determined purely by internal agency considerations. Instead, the treatment of clients may be conditioned by the degree of social esteem they enjoy. If so, further research should support the tentative conclusion drawn here—that class bias is more characteristic of the interpersonal and labor-intensive aspects of service delivery than of other areas.

In light of the numerous defenses available to service bureaucracies, their patterns of client interaction are highly resistant to change, and disadvantaged groups find such matters as teacher attitude very hard to alter. Further, as we shall see in the following section, top-level officials have no incentive to reverse class bias in service delivery.

Class Bias in Program Implementation: The "Ungovernable City" Reconsidered

Turning to the matter of fragmentation and government immobility, we need to remember that while the social dimension is separable from the economic and associational dimensions, the three aspects of systemic power are in fact highly correlated. Those well-off in one regard tend to be well-off in other regards also. What this means is that community decision makers are operating within a common system of stratification. Even though the mayor, the rezoning board, the redevelopment agency, the school system, the transit authority, the planning commission, and the finance department may all have a certain amount of autonomy and room for independent action, they nevertheless share basic predispositions that—if not identical—are at least highly compatible. Thus they may act in concert on many matters, but balk on others—especially those that hold the risk of altering the city's social composition (cf. Peterson, 1976, 173–78).

Local governments are not uniformly immobilized in all areas of policy. They continue to provide a wide range of services, regulate many activities and do so effectively, build huge public works projects, redevelop vast areas, and institute new transportation systems. Immobility is selective. It is most likely to occur when some group presses a demand that runs counter to ingrained system biases described above. Major efforts to upgrade housing for low-income families, to integrate schools, to institute a comprehensive public health program, and to expand economic opportunities for the poor are likely to encounter serious resistance and be abandoned, subverted, or diverted to some other purpose. But efforts to revitalize business districts, expand prestige institutions, and provide amenities to the affluent middle class do not have a poor record of implementation. Of course, no major project is going to proceed without some resistance, but, if the project involves an accommodation of upper-strata interests, it is likely to garner the kind of priority concern by, and continuing attention from, public officials that leads to breaking impasses and circumventing roadblocks. On the other hand, if the project is suspect as being a "magnet for the poor," official support is likely to be lukewarm or short-lived, and resistance may go unchecked (Stone 1976). Though the many actors in policy making may be autonomous, they share a tendency to favor upper over lower strata. While policy is usually made by the accretion of many small and apparently autonomous decisions, the cumulative impact often has a class bias. Decision making need not be unpatterned just because it is incremental.

Systemic power provides the key to how this may occur. Even where community groups are active, the opportunity costs of overcoming ingrained system resistance are enormous. In his study of more than 10 years of contention over school desegregation, David Rogers concluded: "Civil rights leaders were so demoralized by this time and so tired after their long series of defeats that many of them temporarily retired from the desegregation struggle" (1968, 29).

The disadvantage to those who must overcome official resistance compared to the advantage of those who have only to reinforce official inclinations goes far toward explaining how groups otherwise evenly matched in political resources can fare so differently. The systemic power argument offers a plausible explanation for variations of citizen dissatisfaction, distrust, and alienation along class lines; and that explanation seems to fit the facts better than arguments about administrative fragmentation and unpatterned bias. The neopluralist argument fails to account for significant variations in implementation success. While class bias is not omnipresent, the systemic power argument enables us to see where and how it might be at work and what effect it might have in the governance of cities.

The Overt Behavior of Political Actors

Thus far the evidence of systemic power has consisted of broad-stroke patterns. It has been argued that systemic power accounts for decision outcomes unaccounted for by either neo-Marxists/neo-Millsians like Domhoff or latter-day pluralists like Yates. The main thrust of my presentation is that systemic power affects policy outcomes in select ways, depending on the particular nature of the systemic advantage enjoyed by the upper strata. We can now turn from decision outcomes to patterns of overt behavior.

To focus more finely on the behavior of decision makers, let us recall the second general proposition: upper-strata advantage is greatest where popular constraints are weakest. Because systemic forces are different from electoral pressures, public officials can be expected to manifest their inner predispositions to favor upper-strata interests when they are least accountable to the general public. Since not all stages of decision making are equally salient to the public, systemic power should be most evident under conditions of low visibility and least evident under conditions of high visibility.

While most studies of decision making don't focus specifically on visibility, the available evidence does correspond with expectations. A study of redevelopment policy in Atlanta traced urban renewal proposals through three stages and found that pro-business demands enjoyed no advantage over pro-neighborhood demands at the highly visible stage of "official disposition." However, at the preliminary stage of screening demands for further consideration—a low-visibility stage of decision making—business enjoyed a wide advantage, and also enjoyed some advantage at the implementation stage—a relatively low-visibility stage of demand processing (Stone 1976, 190–92). Similarly, business advantage was most evident when controversy was absent, while neighborhood interests fared better under conditions of conflict (Stone 1976, 193–94; see also Morlock 1974, 324). Patterns of conflict themselves indicated that officials were predisposed to favor business interests; pro-business demands were most likely to encounter opposition after they were under active consideration by officials, but conflict surrounding pro-neighborhood demands was most likely to take the form of community groups trying to overcome official resistance to giving a proposal sympathetic consideration (Stone 1976, 194–95). Overall, this study uncovered a pattern of behavior in which public officials clearly preferred to advance pro-business demands and did so except when community opposition was intense. Pro-neighborhood proposals received quite different treatment, being advanced mainly only when external pressures on officials were present. In short, opportunity costs varied greatly from one group to the other.

A related pattern of behavior concerns coalition formation. In a complex urban community, political coalitions can be put together in multiple ways, and different kinds of coalitions are formed for different purposes. Electoral coalitions appear to be quite pluralistic. However, once the highly visible election campaign is over, officials display a marked preference for involving upper-strata interests in planning and formulating policy proposals. For instance, a reanalysis of 32 case studies found that business contacts began earlier and took a more intimate (low-visibility) form than did the contacts of other groups with these same public officials (Davis and Weinbaum 1969, 70–76). Coalition formation in governing, especially the early and low-visibility phase of consultation and support building, thus tends to have a class character not evident in other phases of politics. In a similar vein, there are indications that mayors *elected* with strong lower-strata support nevertheless feel constrained to form policy alliances with business interests (Stokes 1973). While the evidence at this stage is impressionistic, officials regardless of electoral base appear to be drawn by the unequal distribution of material, organizational, and cultural resources to favor working closely and intimately with the upper strata.

The Observable Impact of Systemic Power: Summary

Systemic power is elusive but not unobservable. By drawing attention to predispositions and related behavior patterns of public officials, the systemic power argument lends itself to the formulation of propositions and helps account for some important aspects of community decision making. While this review of evidence has necessarily been fragmentary, a number of generalizations have been adduced that can be tested further—if not quantitatively, then at least by means of observed regularities in behavior. First, the systemic power argument enables us to account for reported variations in business influence. Because business influence is tied in closely with the revenue-production needs of local government, business influence declines as policy concerns become more remotely related to revenue production. Second, it enables us to account for paradoxical situations in which elected officials side with the few (e.g., hierarchically directed institutions) against the many (e.g., activated groups of citizens). Third, it enables us to account for class bias in service delivery and to pinpoint that bias is most likely to occur in those places where personal interaction is especially important and where subjectively defined client attributes are most pertinent. In addition, it puts fragmented policy making in a new light, suggesting that implementation success varies according to the class character of program benefits. Finally, systemic power, resting as it does on a foundation that has to do with governing rather than winning elections, leads to the conclusion that public officials favor upper-strata interests more strongly in the least visible phases of decision making and that, regardless of patterns of electoral cleavage, officials come to consult closely and informally with upper-strata interests.

CONCLUSION

The systemic power argument is at heart an argument about the behavior of public officials. They are the most active element in a triadic relationship in which high-strata interests enjoy a power advantage over lower-strata interests. As officials pursue their own interests, being especially mindful of the particular institutions and processes they are part of, they are guided by a set of strategic dependencies that grow out of a stratified socioeconomic system. This contextual force is what throws off the pluralist prediction that electoral competition and administrative fragmentation will yield shifting coalitions and unpatterned biases. The argument here suggests that, in governing, public officials are strongly drawn to the upper strata and their decisions reflect this attraction. Yet the systemic power argument differs from the ruling-class thesis. Systemic power is not a general form of upper-strata dominance through agenda control. Because the upper strata are strategically advantaged, their extraordinary influence is not so much exercised as it is selectively manifested in the predispositions and behavior of public officials. The argument here can be summarized briefly:

1. While public officials enjoy significant autonomy in decision making, their autonomy is constrained by the fact that they operate in the broad context of a highly stratified socioeconomic system.
2. This system predisposes officials to favor upper- over lower-strata interests.
3. *These predispositions grow out of public office holding itself;* public officeholders are motivated by a desire for career success. For the institutions they are affiliated with to flourish and for their individual careers to advance, officeholders pursue various policy objectives.
4. As officeholders pursue their objectives, the logic of their situation confers advantages on some groups, disadvantages on others. That is, officeholders are predisposed to accommodate some interests while resisting others. In this way, system features lower the opportunity costs for some groups and raise them for others—thereby having an impact on the overall distribution of power.
5. The system attributes that influence the predispositions of officeholders are of at least three kinds: economic, associational, and social; and the impact of systemic power varies accordingly with the nature of the policy problem.
6. Systemic power is not absolutely controlling or always overriding; it is most evident in the least visible phases of policy making.
7. While systemic advantage is only a facet of the total community power picture, it has wide-ranging importance. It affects who has intimate access to decision making, which proposals are considered, and how they are promoted.

Public officeholders are predisposed to interact with and to favor those who can reciprocate benefits (cf. Blau 1964). Thus they respond to dual pressures. Formal democracy conditions the highly visible actions and campaign strategies of public officials so that they are especially responsive to those of the numerous middle strata of society. Actual governing, however, heightens responsiveness to upper-strata interests, especially when policy activities are technically complex or so diffuse in time and place as to involve no single focused dramatic event—that is, where public oversight is least effective.

It should be acknowledged that there are important limitations of the systemic power argument. It is not intended to explain how the present system of stratification came into being. Rather, it focuses on the results of the system—how system features affect power relationships and the pattern of community decision making. The argument does help explain how the system of stratification is maintained. Advantage perpetuates itself. Public officeholders seldom find it feasible to challenge those who hold strategically important resources. As officeholders, their performance is tied closely to a need to cooperate with those who possess material, organizational, and cultural advantages. It is almost always easier to come to terms with the advantaged than to overthrow them. In their innermost selves, public officials may doubt that the system is just or even the best possible, but in their roles as public officials they nevertheless feel impelled to be "realistic" and accommodate to the existing distribution of strategically important resources.

The fragments of empirical evidence examined here suggest that socioeconomic inequalities do affect the behavior of public officials, and, in this way, leave a class imprint on policy decisions. The system of stratification thus seems to undercut the formal equalities of citizenship and put various groups on different political footings. In that way, socioeconomic inequalities become part of the total community power picture.

NOTES

"Systemic Power in Community Decision Making: A Statement of Stratification Theory," by Clarence N. Stone, *American Political Science Review*, Vol. 74 (December 1980), pp. 978–90. Reprinted with the permission of Cambridge University Press.

1. It should be noted that local governments are especially dependent on property taxes and they show a particularly strong concern with revenue production because of their place in the federal system. The strategic dependence of local officials on business is thus partly a matter of a market economy and partly a matter of the federal system. On the former, see Lindblom (1977) and Miliband (1969); on the latter, see Peterson (1978).

REFERENCES

Anton, T. J. 1963. Power, pluralism, and local politics. *Administrative Science Quarterly* 7:425–57.
Bachrach, P., and M. S. Baratz. 1970. *Power and poverty*. New York: Oxford Univ. Press.
Banfield, E. C. 1961. *Political influence*. New York: Free Press.
Blau, P. 1964. *Exchange and power in social life*. New York: John Wiley.
Clark, K. B. 1965. *Dark ghetto*. New York: Harper and Row.
Crenson, M. A. 1971. *The un-politics of air pollution*. Baltimore: Johns Hopkins Univ. Press.
Dahl, R. A. 1961. *Who governs?* New Haven, Conn.: Yale Univ. Press.
Davis, M., and M. G. Weinbaum. 1969. *Metropolitan decision processes*. Chicago: Rand McNally.
Domhoff, G. W. 1977. *Who really rules? New Haven and community power reexamined*. New Brunswick, N.J.: Transaction Books.
Downs, A. 1967. *Inside bureaucracy*. Chicago: Little, Brown.
Emerson, R. M. 1962. Power-dependence relations. *American Sociological Review* 27:31.
Frey, F. W. 1962. Comment: On issues and non-issues in the study of power. *American Political Science Review* 65:1081–101.
Frohlich, N., and J. A. Oppenheimer. 1978. *Modern political economy*. Englewood Cliffs, N.J.: Prentice-Hall.

Greene, K. R. 1979. The impact of agency and individual decision rules on the delivery of urban services. Paper presented at the annual meeting of the Midwest Political Science Association, Chicago.

Harsanyi, J. C. 1962. The measurement of social power, opportunity costs, and the theory of two person bargaining games. *Behavioral Science* 7:67–75.

Hollingshead, A. B., and F. C. Redlich. 1958. *Social class and mental illness.* New York: John Wiley.

Lindblom, C. A. 1977. *Politics and markets.* New York: Basic Books.

Lineberry, R. L. 1977. *Equality and urban policy.* Beverly Hills, Calif.: Sage Publications.

Long, N. 1958. The local community as an ecology of games. *American Journal of Sociology* 64:251–61.

Matras, J. 1975. *Social inequality, stratification, and mobility.* Englewood Cliffs, N.J.: Prentice-Hall.

Miliband, R. 1969. *The state in capitalist society.* New York: Basic Books.

Morlock, L. L. 1974. Business interests, countervailing groups and the balance of influence in 91 cities. In *The search for community power,* ed. W. D. Hawley and F. M. Wirt, 309–28. Englewood Cliffs, N.J.: Prentice-Hall.

Olson, M. 1965. *The logic of collective action.* Cambridge, Mass.: Harvard Univ. Press.

Oppenheim, F. E. 1978. "Power" revisited. *Journal of Politics* 40:598–608.

Peterson, P. E. 1976. *School politics Chicago style.* Chicago: Univ. of Chicago Press.

———. 1978. The politics of taxation and expenditure—A unitary approach. Presented at the annual meeting of the American Political Science Association, New York.

Rogers, D. 1968. *110 Livingston Street.* New York: Random House.

Rosenthal, R., and L. Jacobson. 1968. *Pygmalion in the classroom.* New York: Holt, Rinehart and Winston.

Schon, D. A. 1970. The blindness system. *Public Interest* 18:25–38.

Shefter, M. 1977. New York City's fiscal crisis: The politics of inflation and retrenchment. *Public Interest* 48:98–127.

Stokes, C. B. 1973. *Promises of power.* New York: Simon and Schuster.

Stone, C. N. 1976. *Economic growth and neighborhood discontent.* Chapel Hill: Univ. of North Carolina Press.

Yates, D. 1977. *The ungovernable city.* Cambridge, Mass.: MIT Press.

3. Social Stratification, Nondecision-Making, and the Study of Community Power

Clarence N. Stone

As any reader of *The Prince* knows, politics is less about monolithic control than about maneuvering for and capitalizing on strategic advantages. There is no such thing as absolute power, and in democracies especially, elites rule more by persuasion, inducement, and habit than by command and coercion. If we start with this elementary political understanding, we can discard much that has been said in the community power debate. Just as pluralists do not argue that citizens enjoy perfect equality, their critics do not maintain that elites exercise total domination.

In a world of imperfect and incomplete systems of control, politics has to do with how various groups go about obtaining, maintaining, and changing strategic advantages and seeking to avoid strategic disadvantages. What, then, is the best way to study these advantages and disadvantages? Is it, as pluralists have maintained, by examining the "big decisions," or is it, as nonpluralists contend, by searching for a second and less visible face of power—the process of nondecision making?

The question is a crucial one. Concepts and evidence interplay in a way that makes the study of social phenomena very difficult. Concepts guide us toward some kinds of evidence, but they may also deflect consideration from other kinds. The study of community power illustrates both. It shows how assumptions have much to do with what we look for and how we go about examining what we see.

In the new edition of *Community Power and Political Theory*, Nelson Polsby contends that there is no convincing case that pluralists have looked at the wrong data, and states that when attempts are made to study the concept of nondecision-making "the second face of power in practice merges with the first and they become identical" (1980, 212). I intend to argue the contrary position—a position based on a version of stratification theory. This view is that there is a less visible face of power that differs in important ways from decisional power. Just as the economy involves more than buying and selling consumer goods, so the polity involves more than pressures and counterpressures on discrete policy choices. Decisional politics is, in a manner of speaking, the politics of the consumer market, not the politics of investment and production. And, to continue the analogy, expending time and resources on particular substantive decisions is often a low-return form of political activity. The return is higher if one can invest in crediting or maintaining arguments and beliefs through which a strategic advantage is secured.

The point is *not* that nondecision making involves the absence of observable phenomena; it does not. Rather, the point is to be attentive to what nondecision making does involve: activities not directly or immediately related to the resolution of major policy issues. These activities are part of a nondecision process to the extent that they influence which proposals take shape, why they assume one shape rather than another, and on what terms various actors participate in policy making.

Is there a theoretical reason for believing that influences surrounding nondecision making (some might prefer "predecision making") are different from those surrounding decision making? I will argue that indeed there is and, further, that the nondecision process can be studied empirically.

The first step is not to muddle the two kinds of influences by treating activities as if everything can indiscriminately be labeled "decision making." As the new edition of Polsby's book illustrates, pluralists fail to distinguish between what they have examined carefully and what their critics feel they have given insufficient attention to. Though they sometimes imply that "decision making" includes all observable activities in a community's political life, pluralists continue to focus on actors and activities most proximate to official decisions on major policy proposals (see, e.g., Polsby 1980, 185–86). Other activities with seemingly small and remote public consequences are neglected or downplayed. Yet it is often arrangements and beliefs rooted in what is thought of as the "private sector" that profoundly shape community relationships. While activities related to these beliefs and arrangements are frequently only indirectly related to public decision making, they provide strategic advantages and disadvantages in determining how public affairs will be conducted. Thus, when Polsby (1980) assures us that pluralists use eclectic research methods, he tells us only part of the story—pluralists apply their eclectic approach to a restricted band of activities. There is much they do not look into.

Yet while the inadequacies of pluralism have been debated for 20 years (major criticisms include Anton 1963; Bachrach and Baratz 1970; Clark 1968; Crenson 1971; and Lukes 1974), there is not a widely accepted alternative in the study of power. Confusion continues to becloud what nondecision making is and what its theoretical foundations are. As a result, Polsby (1980), Wolfinger (1971), and other critics have not given nondecision making and the stratification theory on which it is based a fair test.

The notion of nondecision making, all admit, is difficult to work with. While the basic idea that there is a process through which some potential issues are kept off or removed from the agenda of decision making is clear enough, operationalization of the idea for research purposes is not easy. Methods of studying power should, however, be guided by theory, not ease of research. Little is to be gained by rigorous analysis of too narrow a body of evidence. For this reason, we should not give up the concept of nondecision making. In the following discussion I shall argue the side of the nonpluralists, and in doing so shall attempt to make several points. First, I argue that pluralists misunderstand their adversaries' position and thereby fail to look in the right places or in an appropriate way for nondecision making. Second, they fail to appreciate that "decisions" come in a variety of sizes and shapes and that, because pluralists consider only a restricted kind of decisional activity, the term "nondecision-making" can be fruitfully applied to various types of activity that might otherwise be overlooked. Third, I present a schema of power that provides specifically for nondecision making and for the system of stratification as a contextual influence on both decision making and nondecision making. Fourth, I suggest how the schema might help us to understand better the problem of political quiescence and political mobilization as a dimension of community power. Finally, I return to the matter of evidence. While my main concern here is to synthesize and lay out a nonpluralist view of community power as a way of providing theoretical grounding for the concept of nondecision making, I attempt to show how, in existing studies, there is evidence of a nondecision process. In some ways the problem of understanding power is not a problem of seeking new kinds of data, but of being properly attentive to the evidence researchers have been uncovering for many years. Overall, my aim is not so ambitious as to "prove" a complex theory of community power, but I shall try to set forth the rationale for a broadened examination of evidence.

REEXAMINING PLURALIST ASSUMPTIONS

Stratificationists are concerned with the broad matter of who has the capacity to further their interests, how, and why (to rephrase Lasswell). To stratificationists, focusing on decisional activity is a little like examining power relations between native Americans and white settlers by examining specific battles and particular negotiated settlements. The Battle of Little Bighorn is fascinating history, but not a very revealing phase of the overall power struggle. Stratificationists would have us look not at various skirmishes on the border of a larger struggle, but at the larger struggle itself—at the distribution of social rewards and how it is maintained. Their point is not that power is the same as "who benefits" any more than pluralists argue that power is the same as decisional outcome. Rather, the stratificationist's view is that "who benefits" is the outcome we should attempt to explain, and that we should allow for the possibility that power is a *part* of the explanation. Stratificationists concerned with power do not deny that unequal rewards are inevitable or in some sense desirable. But they do believe, as Dennis Wrong (1976, 120) puts it, that "conflicts between unequally rewarded groups and a sense of injustice on the part of the less privileged may be just as endemic in society as the necessity for unequal rewards itself." They also believe that there are degrees of unequal reward, and that the character of political and social arrangements affects the size of the disparity in reward and privilege.

For students of social stratification, the pluralist concentration on decisional activity is a matter of being unable to see the forest for the trees. Let us consider how this occurs.

Pluralists make two crucial assumptions about how power is manifested, and through these assumptions they narrow the range of power activities considered. Polsby, for example, assumes first that the public and private sectors of life are largely separate and autonomous, and second that most people most of the time are unconcerned about public affairs. Because of these two assumptions, he believes that the best test of power is the test of who prevails in particular decisional struggles. In the pluralist world, people are free to calculate whether their interests are better pursued publicly or privately, and generally they choose private and, as pluralists see it, nonpolitical activities. Further, those who are well off privately are believed to have no extraordinary advantage in the public sector and also no particular incentive to pursue political influence (Dahl 1961, 71). As Polsby (1980, 117) says, if a person's occupation is banking, "the pluralist presumes he spends his time at the bank, and not in manipulating community decisions." This view does not acknowledge that the normal activities of financial institutions lead to extensive involvement in a wide range of community matters and that many of these activities influence public affairs at least indirectly. By neglecting these considerations, pluralists equate political involvement with direct efforts to influence electoral processes and the outcome of public policy decisions.

This narrow conception of political involvement is intertwined with one of the basic pluralist assumptions—that of inertia. According to the pluralist view, most people have the resources to exert some power, and most groups know their interests and are able to act freely on behalf of these interests when motivated to do so. However, they are motivated only to influence a few occasional matters of immediate concern. Hence, the pattern of power is dispersed and specialized. The unstated premise in this pluralist view of the world is that the exercise of power consists of overcoming inertia (acting and motivating others to act in the public arena) and that only a few—mostly public officials guided by ambition and an accompanying need for popular support—have the drive and skill to be influential over a large number of matters. Given the inertia assumption, pluralist researchers are drawn automatically to decisional activity, and they see as powerful only those who prevail in the give and take of that activity.

There are two problems with the pluralist approach. The first and most fundamental of these is that it does not take into account functional interdependence, and pluralists therefore fail to see how strongly public officials are impelled to accommodate the interests of upper-strata groups. There is a natural tendency for public officials to form a governing alliance with business and other upper-strata interests; these interests therefore enjoy easy access and a ready reception for requests for action and cooperation (see Stone 1980). Consequently, in a stratified society, politically relevant activity is less costly for some than it is for others, and behavior is influenced accordingly. The tendency to be inert is not uniformly distributed throughout all sectors of society. Some groups are able to expend resources for strategic purposes, thus protecting their interests against a sustained attack or even prolonged neglect.

The second problem with the pluralist approach is that it takes too narrow a view of activity and thereby fails to examine many of the ways in which the strategic level of power plays upon the decisional level. Strategic power is used to influence the structure and procedures of public *and* private institutions, the formation of alliances and associational networks (some of which may not be overtly political), the climate of community opinion, and cultural norms and beliefs that often are only indirectly political in content. Thus, there is a realm of activity beyond the give and take over specific policy decisions, a realm where numerous calculations are made about what is feasible and what is infeasible, about what is desirable and what is to be avoided, about what is worth following through and what may well be left alone. It is at this level that upper-strata groups are able to use and maintain strategic advantages in the protection and promotion of their interests. These are activities only indirectly, but still importantly, related to public decision making. And because these activities are neglected by the pluralists' approach to decision making, we can speak about a nondecision-making process. It is to a closer look at that process that we should now turn.

TOWARD A CLARIFICATION OF NONDECISION MAKING

Both defenders and critics are unclear about the notion of nondecision making. They seem, at least some of the time, to be talking about different phenomena. Confusion is compounded because the term "nondecision-making" is not totally apt for what the critics of pluralism have in mind. Bachrach and Baratz (1970, 44), for example, leave themselves open to criticism by describing a nondecision as a special kind of *decision*—one that "results in suppression or thwarting of a latent or manifest challenge to the values or interests of the decision maker." Thus, what they are describing is a form of activity they believe previous community studies have neglected. Their point is that pluralists have examined only certain kinds of decisions, especially decisions that have reached a certain stage of public visibility. It seems to me that Bachrach and Baratz were on the right track and that there is something to be gained by differentiating between those activities directly involved in making concrete and particular policy decisions and those activities that lie behind this process and may bear only indirectly on such decisions.

There is another distinction that should be kept in mind. In arguing that pluralists do not look at the wrong data, Polsby (1980, 217–18) notes that pluralists "are under an injunction to look at actual 'decisions'—even decisions not to expand the community agenda." In doing so, Polsby assumes that the agenda is controlled by fairly explicit and concrete decisions to consider or not consider various policy alternatives. As he sees it, an issue is admitted or not; it is on or off. However, the alternatives are not necessarily so sharply defined. Many issues make a brief and superficial appearance, but they are not sustained policy efforts. The durability of an issue and therefore its genuine significance are not likely to be evident until time passes and a number of actions, some seemingly small and inconsequential, have been taken. Thus, nondecision making need not be about nonevents; it may be about a pattern of events, and "events" may be made up of many low-visibility actions, spread out over time. A major reason for talking about nondecision making is to emphasize how important choices may be made in some form other than the clear-cut selection between highly visible and concrete alternatives.

There is, then, an ample range of activities not covered by the pluralist approach. It is these activities that are encompassed by the term "nondecision-making," at least as it is used here. Hence, the nondecision-making process, as contrasted with the decision-making process studied by the pluralists, includes activities with the following characteristics.

1. Actions that are strategic in nature and are only indirectly related to particular policy decisions. Put another way, these are actions that need not be focused on particular outcome but do include diffuse efforts to influence the context in which (a) specific opinions are formed, (b) particular expectations develop, and (c) tacit calculation are made about what is desirable and feasible (which is why reputation for power and "potential" power are not insignificant parts of the overall picture).
2. Actions that encompass private arrangement and public-private arrangement. It is often these arrangements that facilitate or constrain actions by various groups and determine lines of allegiance and conflict.
3. Low-visibility, small-scale actions (public and private), such as obligation-building and cue-giving through such means as charitable donations, favor granting, and informal socialization into norms of community behavior. It is often these actions that solidify, modify, or alter private and public-private arrangements.

In comparison to decision-making, nondecision-making has a wider scope and a less sharply defined outcome. It takes in such subprocesses as agenda setting, conflict management, and support building; and its study requires a longer time perspective than does the examination of particular decisional outcomes. While the two processes are not unrelated, the impact of nondecision making on decision making becomes evident, in part, by looking at decisional outcomes (big and little) over time. If we are concerned about a group's durable capacity to further its interests, we should not treat decisions as discrete and unrelated events. Each decisional outcome takes its meaning from where it fits into the ongoing succession of decisions. Some proposals are vetoed, some are not, and some of those vetoed are replaced by slightly revised later editions. Some proposals survive but lead a lonely existence as token efforts in one direction or another, while other proposals become part of an aggregation that represents a substantial policy effort. It is therefore important not to regard decisions as isolated events but to see them as part of a flow of actions from a more general and perhaps even loose set of influences. Because the boundaries of policy making are continually tested, there is no authoritative test of group influence. Power in the sense of the capacity to promote or protect interests is therefore not just the ability to influence the outcome of a particular decision but rather the capacity to shape and take advantage of a set of arrangements that will produce an ongoing flow of favorable actions (see Elkin 1980). Nondecision-making, then, has to do with the shape of the larger political landscape, and that is a different order of questions from the influencing of a particular decision. It involves the capacity to exploit the larger social context and deploy resources on matters that provide indirect and long-term payoffs rather than just immediate and concrete benefits.

"Nondecisions" (the products of nondecision-making) thus are not necessarily issues that have been kept off the agenda. They also include issues that make it onto the agenda but lose steam and prove to be of little lasting significance. What makes such issues nondecisions is that their lack of staying power is related to the kinds of activities included in the nondecision-making process. The proponents of some issues are strategically disadvantaged and may therefore be unable to sustain an issue even if they are able to raise one.

Finally, it is important also to realize that a set of strategic advantages and disadvantages—we can use Schattschneider's term, "mobilization of bias"—is not solely the result of consciously strategic maneuvering. Power is the product of something more than the intentional activity to create it.

SOCIAL STRATIFICATION AND THE THREE-TIERED SCHEMA OF POWER

We can now turn to a restatement of the stratificationist position and see how community power can be visualized as a three-tiered process of influence. The restatement of the stratificationist view of community power includes the following points:

1. The formal equalities of citizenship are countermanded by inequalities in (a) wealth, (b) organizational position, and (c) social status/lifestyle.
2. Inequalities in wealth, organizational position, and social status come about because those who play functionally important roles and have socially valued skills and attributes control resources and enjoy privileges; others do not have the same reservoir of resources to draw on.
3. The unequal distribution of politically relevant resources helps shape the pattern of political activity and explain the pattern of overt, observable conflict.
4. Activities vary in the extent to which they bear directly on concrete and specific decisional outcomes. There are three levels of activity on which power can be exercised, ranging from focused pressures on particular and concrete policy decisions to diffuse efforts to shape and take advantage of general features of the social system.
5. The scope and extent of effort that various strata make *and* sustain are influenced by the resources they possess, the resistance they encounter (that is, the opportunity costs they pay), the likelihood of success, and the immediacy of costs and benefits.
6. The upper strata are better positioned to exercise power that is wide in scope and diffuse in impact (nondecision-making power). The lower strata are positioned to do little more than try to influence narrow decisions of immediate impact.

To move from these general points about political inequality, and the reciprocal relationship between the system of social stratification and the power behavior of strata, we need to look closely at the three levels of power and what they suggest about the structure of community influence. The three levels of power can be represented in schematic form. The power schema presented in Table 3.1 gives us a way of seeing the interplay of direct and contextual factors. Decisions are the immediate result of both decisional activity and mobilization of bias. The schema thus treats official decision makers not as actors who are neutral arbiters of group conflict, but as actors with predilections to favor some groups and disfavor others. Thus they form their alliances, manage conflict, formulate proposals, and implement programs in accord with the direct and indirect influences on them and on positions they occupy.

Mobilization of bias is itself partly a product of overt and focused activity, but is also a product of more diffuse activity directed at prevailing norms, informal practices, and the climate of opinion. A mobilization of bias thus cannot be substantially altered just by legislating institutional changes and enacting new procedures, though these changes might have some impact. There are also systemic conditions that are an influential contextual force impinging on mobilization of bias. Systemic constraints themselves are influenced by the diffuse but observable efforts of political actors, but they too are in good measure the product of contextual forces that are essentially beyond the realm of what is political except in the most indirect way. Even the overt and observable exercises of power are not necessarily explicitly political. For example, efforts to maintain or oppose a market system of production or to

Table 3.1. Three Levels of Power

Overt and therefore directly observable exercises of power (horizontal arrows)	System bias path: contextual and therefore indirectly observable influences (vertical arrows)
	structural conditions, consists of such matters as underlying value orientation and nature of technology; and therefore involve no necessary role for agents who have conscious political intentions
	systemic constraints, results are logics of success & failure for individuals and institutions.
	mobilization of bias, as manifested in processes through which agendas are set and tended, conflict managed, and support is built and maintained; these processes shape the predispositions of community actors as they formulate, develop, and act upon policy matters.
	decisions, results are particular and concrete allocations of benefits through official and unofficial governmental actions.
third level of power: general and diffuse strategic activities consisting of such things as the promotion of ideas & interaction patterns that ascribe vital attributes to various groups & processes; content need not be directly political & activity doesn't necessarily involve a conscious exercise of political power.	
second level of power: contains both diffuse and focused strategic activities, consisting of such things as efforts to influence the climate of opinion, to create alliances & patterns of consultation, to shape notions about what is proper, desirable, or feasible, and to change or maintain institutions & procedures both formal and informal.	
first level of power: express support for or opposition to specific policy proposals.	
latent but perceived support for or opposition to specific policy proposals—manifested as anticipated reactions.	

realm of nondecision

realm of decision making

maintain or oppose meritocratic measures of social worth can be made without actors being aware of their political power consequences. Intended consequences are not a prerequisite for the exercise of power (Oppenheim 1978). Therefore, actions can be politically relevant without the actors intending that their efforts affect something as abstract but important as systemic constraints.

With the basic framework in mind, let us turn to the specific features of the second and third nondecision levels of power. Mobilization of bias is by now a familiar idea. The way in which politics is organized—the institutions and processes through which officials are selected and decisions made—is not neutral. A given form of organization makes it easier for some kinds of support to be mobilized (and sustained), but other kinds of support have difficulty. Thus, it is easy for some issues to be addressed, while others tend to be neglected. This bias in the organization of politics manifests itself in the predispositions of public officials as they play leading roles in formulating proposals, aggregating support behind these proposals, overseeing their implementation, and managing the conflict they engender.

Seen without reference to contextual influences, the mobilization of bias appears to be little more than the result of a freewheeling game in which some political actors get ahead because they are more ambitious, farsighted, smarter, luckier, or perhaps more energetic than others. In this light, mobilization of bias is not necessarily of great, long-lasting consequence. Those who are consistently disadvantaged in concrete and particular decisions might eventually come to understand the circumstances that bring about that condition and seek to change the mobilization of bias. To be sure, producing change is always harder than maintaining the status quo. But enough accumulated grievances could generate a new political alignment and lead to a challenge of the established order.

The contextual influences (systemic constraints) on mobilization of bias show us, however, that there is more than the inertia of the status quo to be considered. Just as the mobilization of bias assures that not all issues will have an equal chance of developing, systemic constraints assure that not all political alignments will have an equal chance of forming and lasting. (Political alignments are not to be equated with voting alignments; rather they are the alignments for bringing together the support—public and private, physical and mental—to act on a program.) The structural conditions of society in interaction with the third level of power give rise to systemic constraints—logics of success and failure for individuals and institutions.

Briefly, there are in the United States four major systemic constraints that have special relevance to the political order (Stone 1980). These are:

1. Legal or formal-political, which concerns citizenship rights such as suffrage and legal standing. This is the area that most nearly approaches equality and dictates that electoral success requires mass support.

2. Economic, which concerns the means of production. The market system of private ownership makes government, especially local government, dependent on business activity as a source of revenue and other social benefits.
3. Associational, which concerns the organization of people and material. Bureaucratic structures are the dominant way of organizing for specified, task-oriented programs.
4. Social, which concerns lifestyle and the possession of various cultural advantages. Formal education, professional and managerial skills, and a cosmopolitan orientation are the favored attributes.

Significantly, only one of the four systemic constraints is egalitarian. The others provide the ingredients in a multilayered, multidimensional system of social stratification that is essentially diamond shaped (Matras 1975). The logics of success and failure follow the lines of social stratification. A political alignment that has a prominent place for business interests, the directors of staffs of major institutions (nonprofit as well as profit), and the upper status has promise of much success. One that consists mainly of the dependent poor, those without organizational leverage and staying power, and the lower status offers little hope of success and a high probability of failure. Thus the system of stratification is far from neutral in its effects on political alignments, and the mobilization of bias is greatly influenced by the constraints that reflect the system of social stratification.

As we consider the influences of the second and third levels of power, we can see that they mix with and compound the inequalities that emerge from the structural conditions of society to constitute a system bias path. In this way, structural conditions give rise to systemic constraints much as tangible resources like wealth and numbers give rise to anticipated reactions. Neither structural conditions nor anticipated reactions involves an overt *exercise* of power, but both have important power consequences. In the case of anticipated reactions, the impact on decisions is direct and particular. In the case of structural conditions, their impact is more indirect and their influence on decisions more remote, but the central point, as we shall see later, is that they nevertheless affect the opportunity costs in exercising power; they thus bear importantly on the strength and weakness of various groups as actors in the community power arena.

In addition to showing the various paths of influence on decisions (decisions involving concrete and particular allocations of benefits through governmental action), the schema shows that overt and directly observable exercises of power vary in scope. Some are narrowly and concretely focused on specific decisions; at the other extreme are diffuse efforts to influence the broad social and political context in which decisions are made. While some efforts are aimed at institutions and procedures, others are aimed even more broadly at reinforcing or changing sentiments about the social worth of various groups and the processes of which they are a part. Thus, politically relevant activity spreads over a range of targets, from the narrow and focused to the broad and diffuse, from those that are consciously and directly political to those in which political intent is indirect and perhaps not even explicit in form. Our next steps are to amplify the theoretical argument by clarifying how system bias is a dimension of power and then by examining how the distribution of resources conditions the power behavior of various strata.

TOWARD AN UNDERSTANDING OF SYSTEM BIAS AS A DIMENSION OF POWER

Let me be explicit about the meaning of the term "power" as it is used here. The aspect of community power under examination concerns the capacity of social collectivities to influence the course of government action. However, to talk about "power over" government states the problem wrongly. The ultimate concern is *the differential capacity of various groups and strata to influence the actions and inactions of government,* including but not restricted to particular and concrete decisions about allocations of benefits. I am making an important assumption that should not be overlooked. This differential capacity to exert influence is a competitive matter. It is, in a sense, a zero-sum game. One competitor's gain is another's loss; one's advantage is another's disadvantage.

I am therefore imputing to political actors an interest in avoiding any disadvantage in influencing the decision of government. If they cannot enjoy an advantage, they certainly want neutrality. Indifference about bestowing political privileges on others is precisely what is contradicted by support for such ideas as universal suffrage and "equal protection of the laws." It is not unreasonable, then, to believe that there is widespread and genuine interest in an open and neutral process of governing. At the very least we can assume that few people want to labor under a political disadvantage.

In concrete terms, the absence of neutrality means differing rates of resistance for various groups and social strata. To understand how bias constitutes a dimension of power, we need to take into account the idea of opportunity costs. These costs are the link between system features and the overt behavior of political actors. As John C. Harsanyi has argued so persuasively, the measurement of power should take into consideration the resistance encountered. If some actors meet greater resistance than others, they must expend more resources to achieve their goals—that is, their opportunity costs are greater. Those actors with greater opportunity costs are weaker. Hence, "the influence of actors can and should be compared in terms of what they can achieve at comparable costs" (Harsanyi 1962, 69). The absence of neutrality on the part of official decision makers *and* the absence of neutrality in the institutions, norms, and practices that encase them constitute a systemic basis on which social collectivities vary in their capacity to influence policy. Some groups encounter relatively less resistance and are advantaged by that condition. Others encounter relatively great resistance and are disadvantaged by that reason. Once the idea of opportunity costs is introduced, the conclusion is inescapable that, other things being equal, the advantaged are more powerful than the disadvantaged. Given a disinclination by any actor to be politically disadvantaged, we cannot regard acquiescence in this state of affairs to be a matter of consent.

POWER-RELATED BEHAVIOR AND THE DISTRIBUTION OF RESOURCES

If system bias is an important dimension of power, we should consider not only how it comes into existence but also why it goes largely unchallenged. We need to understand how the system of social stratification might condition the exercise of power and in this way serves to protect the very inequality it creates.

The argument being made here is that overt and therefore directly observable exercises of power are determined by three factors: (1) the immediacy of the costs or benefits at stake, (2) the amount of resistance encountered (the opportunity costs), and (3) the supply of resources available. The first step in the argument is as follows. Those with few resources must use them cautiously and reserve them mainly for those matters of immediate concern. They have little to expend, are likely to encounter resistance, and can expect uncertain results at best. Those with abundant resources can use them more freely and invest them in ways that promise a long-term return. They have much to expend, are likely to encounter receptiveness, and can be reasonably optimistic about results. Consequently the scope of power activity by various strata is conditioned by the supply of power resources available and the extent to which they are available for delayed payoffs. The system of stratification thus has a dual effect: a direct effect on the distribution of resources itself and an indirect effect on how resources are used. It is therefore likely that overt exercises of power at the nondecisional level reinforce rather than counterbalance the system bias that originates in structural conditions.

The overall argument implicit in the schema can now be stated. Structural conditions give rise to a system bias that follows a path running through systemic constraints on to mobilization of bias and ultimately has an impact on particular and concrete decisions. Structural conditions also bestow unequal material and cultural resources on various elements of society (giving rise to social strata) but allow for formal, legal equality. Formal, legal equality is not enough, however, to prevent great imbalances in political resources. Those with few resources confine their political efforts to concrete and focused actions with immediate consequences. Those with more resources extend their political efforts over a wider scope. Those with abundant resources are able to afford a long-term view and invest some effort into such broad and diffuse activities as maintaining or altering biases and indirect constraints on policy making. Those with abundant resources also face lower opportunity costs and therefore can easily afford the efforts to reinforce or modify the system bias that originates in structural conditions. System bias thus has a certain amount of built-in inertia. It would take a large expenditure of resources to overcome system bias, but those with large resources are generally oriented toward reinforcing rather than changing system bias.

While those who are disadvantaged might in an abstract sense be motivated to work for system change, their concrete circumstances suggest otherwise. Those with few resources have every reason to avoid exercises of power with remote and unspecified payoffs. They can ill afford to contend with high opportunity costs at all, but the effort is especially unpromising when the benefits are not only unlikely but unspecified as well. There is a sense in which the disadvantaged do not even have a strong incentive to vote; even though voting is a relatively costless form of political activity, it is also what Verba and Nie (1972) call a "blunt" instrument of participation and therefore by itself does not convey very precisely targeted pressure. Standing alone, it offers few benefits.

Because people have no taste for waging costly battles they are sure to lose, much goes uncontested. The disadvantaged are likely to use their resources on the issues of most immediate impact—decisions involving concrete and particular allocations of benefits and costs—and these are the issues where overt and direct conflict is most frequent. While the mobilization of bias is occasionally, as in the 1960s, an object of open conflict, such occurrences are infrequent, and the contestants rarely divide strictly along class lines.

We come back then to our original query about the acquiescence of the lower strata in a system that disadvantages them. I conclude that, while the disadvantaged are generally passive, their acquiescence does not necessarily signal consent or even indifference. Nor is it necessary to argue that the disadvantaged do not know their true interests. Rather, it may be the case that their position in society does not lend itself to the expression of those interests in a strategic or even highly programmatic form. The absence of such expression does not mean that they are unmindful of their own interests; it may signify only that they are not well positioned to pursue far-reaching change. Certainly, studies of participation indicate that the lower strata not only engage in political activity at a low rate, but also that they tend toward modes of participation that are not addressed to structural or institutional causes, at least not in an instrumental way (see, e.g., Verba and Nie 1972; Booth et al. 1968; Brill 1971; Banfield and Wilson 1971; Gans 1967; Carlin 1970).

The point is not that the lower strata are intrinsically incapable of collective action on long-range problems or that they are uniquely disinterested in such action (see, for example, the discussion of the problems of and experience with collective action in poor neighborhoods by O'Brien 1975). Rather, the point is that the logic of their situation heightens their concern for tangible and short-term outcomes. As Greenstone and Peterson (1973, 257) observed in their study of the Community Action Program, lower-strata groups often appeared erratic in their political loyalties because they were drawn toward "whatever group happened to best articulate their most pressing grievances at a particular election" (see also Agger et al. 1964, 158–67, on an earlier period).

The passivity of the lower strata with regard to strategic biases, their low level of participation generally, and their tendency to opt for immediate remedies are themselves indications that the influences surrounding the nondecision process may be class biased in a way that influences surrounding the decision process are not. The theoretical justification for this view, I have argued, has to do with how it is possible for power advantages or disadvantages to be cumulative. An imbalance of resources is not only a power factor itself, but it can influence how various strata behave politically and why some groups may be able and inclined to pursue and make use of strategic advantages while others tend to accept what comes along or confine their activities to first-level (that is, decisional) efforts to influence the outcomes of particular issues.

THE NONDECISION PROCESS IN OPERATION

If the above line of argument is sound, it should call into question the pluralist idea that communities are governed by "shifting coalitions of participants drawn from all areas of community life" (Merelman 1968, 451). The nonpluralist argument developed here holds that there are class differences in how groups participate in the political life of communities, and these differences affect the strength and durability of political support behind various policy alternatives. Looked at in another way, the nondecision process serves to make some alignments more vulnerable and unstable than others. Assuming that the argument is plausible, one may still ask if there is evidence that supports it. In addressing that question, this section is *not* intended to show that there are at present authoritative findings. Instead its purpose is simply to suggest that there is some empirical as well as conceptual merit to the nonpluralist position. There are a few studies broad enough in their coverage to allow some preliminary examination of the question of whether the nondecision process has a prevailing class bias. Specifically, there are book-length studies of urban redevelopment policy in Atlanta (Stone 1976), of the civil rights movement in Greensboro, North

Carolina (Chafe 1980), and of the poor in Clear Fork Valley, an Appalachian mining community (Gaventa 1980). Each affords an opportunity to see how policy efforts are shaped by activities outside the level of decisional politics.

The major difference between these three studies and the pluralist approach is that each of the three treats as the power arena the diffuse and historically elongated process in which the mobilization and countermobilization of support and opposition to a broad policy effort occur. This contrasts with the pluralist concentration on the disposition of concrete and highly specific proposals for public action—the "big" decisions Polsby (1980, 96) specifies as appropriate for study. According to Polsby, it is important not to be concerned with "trivial" issues (1980, 54) or attach great significance to preliminary "plans, proposals, committees, wishes and ambitions" (1980, 185). In the nonpluralist approach, small and preliminary actions are appropriate objects of study but not so much in the form of discrete and separately important events as in the form of "markers" in the ongoing flow of policy events, and as indicators that private and public-private arrangements have policy consequences, albeit sometimes delayed or indirect.

Very briefly, then, what do the three studies indicate about the nondecision process? First, the flow of policy actions took the following shape.

Atlanta's redevelopment policy provided land and facilities for central business district revitalization, but efforts to promote a sustained program of neighborhood and housing improvement faltered.

Greensboro's desegregation policy eliminated the legally and quasi–officially sanctioned Jim Crow system, but efforts to maintain black solidarity around a program of promoting black consciousness and redistributing economic benefits (raising wages, improving housing, and expanding opportunities for the lower class) proved to be short lived.

Clear Fork Valley and pertinent governmental jurisdictions provided low taxation and general support for an absentee-owned corporation, the American Association, that controlled much of the land in the area and engaged in capital-intensive strip mining, thus leaving many local people unemployed and impoverished; local efforts at community development and antipoverty action were highly constrained and largely unsuccessful.

Each of these three sets of cumulative actions can be linked to a pattern of actions through which support was aggregated and maintained behind one policy alternative, while support behind the other dissipated and was not maintained. Put another way, "coalitions" involving a central place for upper-strata interests were durable and resilient, while those centering more on lower-strata interests proved to be highly fragile and unstable.

Why did this pattern emerge? What is it that enabled upper-strata groups to occupy superior strategic ground? The following four categories of factors seemed to provide the context in which support built up or diminished around various proposals and policy concerns:

1. *Broad strategic actions* of at least two kinds: (a) disseminating ideas and beliefs, such as that business leaders are especially enlightened and community minded (Atlanta), that civility and moderation should be adhered to in regulating social conflict (Greensboro), and that community harmony should be preserved (Clear Fork Valley); and (b) creating a network of obligations and dependencies through such actions as providing voluntary contributions (Atlanta and Greensboro) and allowing the families of formerly employed workers to use company housing and land (Clear Fork Valley). Just as one example of how these strategic factors served to channel conflict away from an upper-strata group, consider this event in Atlanta's political history: black leaders with close ties to the mayor and the business establishment defused intense black opposition to housing and urban renewal policy and kept such opposition out of the election of 1961 by arguing that it was important not to alienate responsible white leaders.

2. *Focused strategic actions and arrangements,* especially those that provide private interests with representation on public bodies or that give them special access to public officials. One more or less self-explanatory example was mine-owner domination of the Board of Reclamation Review of the State Surface Mining Department in its refusal to overturn a strip-mining permit for a subarea of Clear Fork Valley. The importance of informal access is illustrated by the contrast in the handling of racial crises in Greensboro. Faced with a need to respond to the issue of racially restricted public accommodations, the mayor convened a meeting of 23 civic leaders. Every prominent banker and corporate executive was invited; but when faced with campus and community militance and a felt need to take steps to have the National Guard sent into a black college campus in the city, the mayor consulted no black leaders.

3. *Differences in the capacities and stability of organizations,* which show up in several ways: (a) in the resources available; for example, neighborhood-based protest organizations in all three communities lacked staff and could do little analysis or tracking of trends; (b) in having means for handling leadership succession and perpetuating themselves; for example, upper-strata interests often work through incorporated and bureaucratized organizations such as the Georgia Baptist Hospital in Atlanta and the mining company, the American Association, in Clear Fork Valley; and (c) the use of specialized units or front organizations, such as the Uptown Association in Atlanta, which was ostensibly a neighborhood organization but was established by business interests to prevent blacks from moving into the northern section of the city. Differences in resources and capacities need no elaboration, but the problem of leadership succession may not be fully appreciated. To illustrate the point, let us consider a single example from Atlanta. For a

short time, one of the city's most effective protest organizations was U-Rescue. At the core of this group's official leadership were two key figures: (a) a black minister, who received a promotion in his church hierarchy that involved a completely new set of responsibilities and a move out of the neighborhood, and (b) a white merchant, who was killed in an automobile accident. Neither was replaced by someone of equal skill and determination; the organization lapsed into passivity before the issue of neighborhood redevelopment was settled in final form.

4. *Asymmetrical vulnerabilities to co-optation and sanction,* which take many forms, from a willingness to accept personal favors and recognition of an inclination to take care of the maintenance needs of religious and neighborhood organizations. All three communities provide numerous examples of the disadvantaged being co-opted by the acceptance of immediate and particularistic benefits— including jobs (all three), land for housing developments (Atlanta), church donations (Clear Fork Valley), generous prices for churches in the clearance areas of urban renewal projects (Atlanta), opportunities to be sponsors for nonprofit housing (Atlanta), appointments to public office (Greensboro), and the chance to become members of prestigious civic organizations (Atlanta and Greensboro). Those who are resource poor had little to offer as inducements to the powerful, but they did attempt to use embarrassing publicity as a threat. However, as Gaventa (1980) documents in some detail in the case of Clear Fork Valley, business corporations have multiple devices for obscuring responsibility for unsavory actions and are not highly vulnerable to this form of sanction.

Identifying these four categories of nondecision forces is only part of the picture. The sum of nondecision making is greater than its parts. The parts contribute to the view that successful community actions require at least the absence of opposition from the powerful and resource rich, and in most cases, their active cooperation. The powerful and resource rich act within this understanding to give cues about what is acceptable through the projects they support or do not support. In Greensboro, the chamber of commerce supported a campaign to promote a better "human relations" understanding to accompany public school desegregation, but they later encouraged the resignation of the progressive staff member who was aggressive in extending the chamber into a number of areas of community concern, thus signaling an end to their social activism. In Atlanta, business leaders refused to form a "blue ribbon" committee to work out interracial agreements about housing patterns. The mining company of Clear Fork Valley refused land for such purposes as a health clinic, a housing project, and a child development program, thus dampening community development efforts by the poor. In these and similar actions, the powerful and resource rich signaled what would have high opportunity costs and what would not.

Let us be clear about what is being claimed here. The claim is *not* that this very brief description of just a few instances in which groups enjoyed and made use of strategic advantages constitutes an empirical test of any set of propositions. All that is being claimed is that (1) nondecision making can be examined empirically, and (2) the evidence from three separate, single-community studies (all three Southern, it might be noted) provides examples of what can be found, and these examples support the view that the nondecision process has a class bias. The specific examples are cited not to try to prove class bias, but to show how such a bias could grow out of events that are only indirectly related to major policy decisions—events many of which might seem on an individual basis to be inconsequential. There is not room here to show how the four categories of factors outlined above serve to shape agenda setting, conflict management, and support building, nor to indicate how these activities constitute continuing processes that impinge on community policy making. But the three studies from which the illustrations are drawn are sufficiently detailed to allow readers to see why it is valuable to follow the flow of decisions and other actions over a long period of time. In this way, it becomes apparent that policy is shaped greatly by actions and arrangements that seem peripheral to the making of "big" decisions. Over time, upper-strata influence in these three studies appears pervasive and enduring to an extent not evident in the resolution of discrete and highly visible policy issues.

CONCLUSION

The conception of power presented here draws together various strands of non-pluralist argument and combines them with a version of stratification theory. In brief, this argument is that, because some elements of society play roles that are functionally important and possess socially valued skills and attributes, they are able to garner substantial social rewards and privileges. The socioeconomic inequalities that result are perpetuated politically. These inequalities provide an imbalance of resources and encourage a set of arrangements in which that imbalance is protected and maintained. Far from motivating have-nots to challenge established arrangements, the imbalance encourages them to be passive and reserve what little influence they have for issues of pressing concern. These issues may center on benefits of a particularistic and even personal kind or on a defense against some imminent and specific cost or threat.

A conception of power as operating on multiple levels enables us to see the strategic dimension of politics—how expenditures of resources may be invested in securing and maintaining arrangements that are one or even two steps removed from the making of immediate decisions about matters of substantive policy. By taking into account the strategic dimension of politics, we are impelled to make a broad and inclusive search for factors and processes that are at some remove from the resolution of major decisional issues. This search does not deny that public officials play a significant role in rallying support behind proposals and in choosing between policy alternatives, but it does require that we question the adequacy of pluralism's inertia assumption as a guide to the study of nondecision making. By making alternative assumptions we can see how private activities and arrangements may be very much a part of the community power picture. While their *direct* role in public decision making on the "big" issues is often minor, they shape the successive actions through which agendas are set and tended, conflict managed, and support aggregated and maintained. In this way private activities and arrangements influence what the "big" decisions are, how they are considered, and what predispositions public officials and other community actors bring to their resolution. Activities and arrangements that on the face of things appear to be apolitical and inconsequential, may, on further examination, prove to be important links in the community power chain.

The argument developed here provides a rationale for this broader search for evidence. Such a search should refine our knowledge about how various strata fit into the political life of urban communities. And, if the argument about the nondecision is sound, then we need to discard some bits of pluralist wisdom about "shifting conditions," "slack" in the system, and the role of immediacy and intensity of interest in creating power out of powerlessness.

NOTE

"Social Stratification, Nondecision-Making and the Study of Community Power," by Clarence N. Stone, *American Politics Quarterly*, Vol. 10 (July 1982), pp. 275–302. Reprinted with the permission of Sage Publications.

REFERENCES

Agger, R. E., et al. 1964. *The rulers and the ruled.* New York: John Wiley.
Anton, T. J. 1963. Power pluralism and local politics. *Administrative Science Quarterly* 7:425–57.
Bachrach, P., and M. S. Baratz. 1970. *Power and poverty.* New York: Oxford Univ. Press.
Banfield, E. C., and J. Q. Wilson. 1971. Political ethos revisited. *American Political Science Review* 65:1048–62.
Booth, A., et al. 1968. Social stratification and membership in voluntary associations. *Social Quarterly* 9:427–39.
Brill, H. 1971. *Why organizers fail.* Berkeley: Univ. of California Press.
Carlin, J. F. 1970. Store front lawyers in San Francisco. *Transaction* 7 (Apr.): 64–74.

Chafe, W. H. 1980. *Civilities and civil rights.* New York: Oxford Univ. Press.

Clark, T. N. 1968. *Community structure and decision making.* San Francisco: Chandler Press.

Crenson, M. A. 1971. *The un-politics of air pollution.* Baltimore: Johns Hopkins Univ. Press.

Dahl, R. A. 1961. *Who governs?* New Haven, Conn.: Yale Univ. Press.

Elkin, S. L. 1980. Cities without power: The transformation of American urban regimes. In *National Resources and Urban Policy,* ed. H. E. Ashford. New York: Methuen.

Gans, H. J. 1967. *The Levittowners.* New York: Pantheon.

Gaventa, J. 1980. *Power and powerlessness.* Urbana: Univ. of Illinois Press.

Greenstone, D., and P. E. Peterson. 1973. *Race and authority in urban politics.* New York: Russell Sage.

Harsanyi, J. C. 1962. The measurement of social power, opportunity costs and the theory of two person bargaining games. *Behavioral Science* 7:67.

Hunter, F. 1953. *Community power structure.* Chapel Hill: Univ. of North Carolina Press.

Lukes, S. 1974. *Power: A radical view.* London: Macmillan.

Matras, J. 1975. *Social inequality, stratification, and mobility.* Englewood Cliff, N.J.: Prentice-Hall.

Merelman, R. M. 1968. On the neo-elitist critique of community power. *American Political Science Review* 62:451–60.

O'Brien, D. 1975. *Neighborhood organization and interest-group processes.* Princeton, N.J.: Princeton Univ. Press.

Oppenheim, F. E. 1978. "Power" revisited. *Journal of Politics* 40:598–608.

Polsby, N. W. 1980. *Community power and political theory.* 2nd ed. New Haven, Conn.: Yale Univ. Press.

Schattschneider, E. E. 1960. *The semi-sovereign people.* New York: Holt, Rinehart & Winston.

Stone, C. N. 1976. *Economic growth and neighborhood discontent.* Chapel Hill: Univ. of North Carolina Press.

———. 1980. Systemic power in community decision making: A restatement of stratification theory. *American Political Science Review* 74:978–90.

Verba, S., and N. H. Nie. 1972. *Participation in America.* New York: Harper & Row.

Wolfinger, R. E. 1971. Nondecisions and the study of local politics. *American Political Science Review* 65:1063–80.

Wrong, D. H. 1976. *Skeptical sociology.* New York: Columbia Univ. Press.

4. Urban Regimes and the Capacity to Govern

A Political Economy Approach

Clarence N. Stone

To a casual observer, regime analysis might appear to be a return to classical urban pluralism, the reigning wisdom of 30 years ago and earlier. After all, the executive-centered coalition described in *Who Governs?* (Dahl 1961) bears all the earmarks of a regime. Both pluralism and regime analysis emphasize coalition building as an integral part of the governing process and both bodies of thought subscribe to the view that politics matters. There, I intend to show, the similarity ends. Fundamental differences separate the two approaches to urban politics.

Centrally concerned with such matters as the assimilation of immigrant groups and the political consequences of increasing social differentiation, the urban strain of classic pluralism drew heavily on a political culture approach (Banfield 1961; Banfield and Wilson 1963; Dahl 1961), whereas the analysis of urban regimes stems from a political economy perspective (Elkin 1987; Fainstein et al. 1986; Logan and Molotch 1987; Shefter 1985; Stone 1989a; Swanstrom 1985). Other differences abound. In particular, pluralism assumes that governmental authority is adequate to make and carry out policies promoted by top officials so long as those officials do not lose popular favor. Regime analysis posits a different and more complex process of governance. Specifically, it recognizes the enormous political importance of privately controlled investment, but does so without going so far as to embrace a position of economic determinism. In assuming that political economy is about the relationship between politics and economics, not the subordination of politics to economics, regime analysts explore the middle ground between, on the one side, pluralists with their assumption that the economy is just one of several discrete spheres of activity and, on the other side, structuralists, who see the mode of production as pervading and dominating all other spheres of activity, including politics.

In regime analysis, the relationship between the economy and politics is two way. At any given time, economic forces both shape and are shaped by political arrangements. Historically, the market economy of capitalism was established by a political process and remains subject to political modification (Polanyi 1957). At the same time, the economy shapes politics and is a major source of issues (Fainstein 1990).

Theorizing always involves taking some conditions as given in order to examine the relationship between others. Urban regime theory takes as given a liberal political economy, one that combines two conditions. One is a set of government institutions controlled to an important degree by popularly elected officials chosen in open and competitive contests and operating within a larger context of the free expression of competing ideas and claims. Second, the economy of a liberal order is guided mainly, but not exclusively, by privately controlled investment decisions. A regime, whether national or local, is a set of arrangements by which this division of labor is bridged (Elkin 1987).

The version of regime theory propounded here holds that public policies are shaped by three factors: (1) the composition of a community's governing coalition, (2) the nature of the relationships among members of the governing coalition, and (3) the resources that the members bring to the governing coalition. Of course, this does not mean that the governing coalition operates in a social and economic vacuum; the socioeconomic environment is a source of problems and challenges to which regimes respond.

In writing about the international sphere, Krasner (1983, 1) says that regimes are "intervening variables between basic causal factors on the one hand and outcomes and behavior on the other." This formulation is akin to psychology's longstanding treatment of stimulus and response. Psychology came to understand early that, instead of simply stimulus and response, the response is mediated through the organism. Hence $S > R$, becomes $S > o > R$. In regime theory, the mediating "organism" is the regime. The full reality is, of course, more complicated than this, but the point is that in the role of intervening factor, urban regimes are potentially an autonomous force. As Krasner (1983, 5) says of their international counterparts, "they are not merely epiphenomenal." Politics matters.

Of course, politics can matter in different ways. Dahl's understanding of New Haven's executive-centered coalition is one version. Regime analysis, I shall argue, puts that same coalition in a different light, but one that is nonetheless still political. In setting forth differences between the two schools of thought, I will first present some key assumptions of urban pluralism and then offer contrasting assumptions from regime theory. In the process I will show how New Haven's executive-centered coalition can he reinterpreted and offer my own version of what urban regimes are about. The point I will emphasize is that a governing capacity has to be created and maintained. It is not just "there" for the taking, by electoral or other means.

URBAN PLURALISM: AN OVERVIEW

Pluralism is not to be equated with complexity; it is not just the absence of mono-lithic control. Classic urban pluralism is a particular explanation of how demo-cratic politics works in a liberal order. Its principal tenets include the following:

1. In the U.S. and its localities, the citizenry provides consensual support for the basic features of the system: a democratic governmental form, an economy of mainly private ownership, and a nonaristocratic social order. This consensus is a genuine expression of popular sentiment, not an engineered consciousness.
2. Consistent with the requirements of democracy, state authority is subject to popular control by means of open and free elections.
3. Operating within a framework of popular consent, the state enjoys a high degree of self-sufficiency, enough to be capable of allocating substantial benefits and imposing significant costs, and doing so on its own. Local government is the state writ small.
4. Consensus extends only to broad features. On more specific issues, the fragmented and unstable character of popular majorities makes public officials responsive to even small groups or those who are socioeconomically disadvantaged.
5. Politics involves aggregating the relatively stable and autonomously formed preferences of individual citizens. While amenable to persuasion about larger community interests, citizens are especially protective of their roles in the social order and of what affects them directly and immediately.
6. Power consists of a capacity to overcome resistance and gain compliance. Because control has the dimensions of domain, scope, and intensity, the cost of compliance assures that no one group can exercise comprehensive social control.
7. Political change is guided by a process of modernization.

Before showing how regime theory modifies or contradicts these elements of urban pluralism, I want to provide some elaboration of the pluralist position.

STATE CAPACITY, ELECTIONS, AND POLITICAL INFLUENCE

Pluralist analysis rests first and foremost on the assumption of an autonomous state, capable of allocating substantial benefits and imposing significant costs. Per-haps because the state is conventionally defined in terms of a monopoly of legiti-mate violence, the legal authority of government is seen as sufficient for governing. Dahl (1961, 96) talks about government as "the single most effective institution for coercion" and assumes the adequacy of legal authority.

Add to this understanding of the state the condition of democratic control and voting strength becomes the key factor in political power. To be sure, pluralism acknowledges that resources other than the franchise come into play, but the vote remains central. For example, Dahl's study of New Haven stresses the place of elections in countering any concentration of power, treating even the problem of inequality as election centered. Dahl makes the following observation: "Running counter to [the] legal equality of citizens in the voting booth, however, is an unequal distribution of the resources that *can be used for influencing the choices of voters,* and between elections, of officials" (Dahl 1961, 4, emphasis added). The problem of inequality is thus described as one of how the uneven distribution of wealth and other resources modifies the formal equality of the franchise.

Popular majorities are typically the controlling force, but they are composed of temporary and unstable coalitions. Though there is consensus on fundamentals, a complex and highly differentiated social order with increasing occupational and role specialization provides fertile ground for conflict over particular and limited issues. Class cleavage is secondary, at most, to the specific, often short-term conflicts associated with interest group policies (Polsby 1980, 117–18).

In this system of fragmented and unstable political attachments, small size is not a disqualifying condition for political influence. Given that alignments are fluid and that on any particular issue many people will be inattentive or indifferent, a group with small membership may enjoy the strategic advantage of controlling the balance of power in a political contest. Politicians are thus constantly mindful of the need to seek the support of even small groups and avoid encouraging their opposition. While the power to govern rests on popular support, this support is always tenuous. Ordinarily "control over any given issue-area gravitates to a small group which happens to have the greatest interest in it" (Dahl 1961, 191). Influence is specialized and impasse is an ever-present possibility.

Fragmentation can lead to stalemate (Sayre and Kaufman 1965, 716–19), but does not have to. After all, the New Haven of Mayor Richard Lee was a place of enormous and politically significant physical restructuring. In Dahl's (1961, 201) words, "rapid comprehensive change in the physical pattern of a city is a minor revolution," and Richard Lee's New Haven underwent such a revolution.

Dahl explains Lee's success in redevelopment as a matter of skill in activating latent support and skill in negotiating through a tangle of particular costs and benefits. Consider a significant detail in how Dahl works this out. Parallel with this discussion of redevelopment, Dahl argues that African Americans in New Haven made exceptional use of voter influence. He observes, "Some citizens . . . have fewer alternatives to political action than others. Probably the most significant group in New Haven whose opportunities are sharply restricted by social and economic barriers are Negroes" (Dahl 1961, 293). Dahl (1961, 294–95) then cites higher voter participation by blacks in New Haven as evidence that they make use of formal political equality to pursue their goals. By contrast, he argues, those who are better off socioeconomically prefer to pursue their goals in the private sector (Dahl 1961, 294).

In this view, government authority, as an allocator of opportunities, assures a form of societal mutual accommodation in which everyone is able to gain at least something. The public and private sectors are treated as distinct and government is seen as an autonomous power, checked primarily by the reciprocal relationship between public officials and their constituents. Thus, by treating the public and private sectors as politically distinct and downplaying the complex interrelationships between government and the economy, Dahl can show how specialization of influence is consistent with change. Redevelopment, he admits, was of special benefit to downtown property interests, but only as part of a policy of "shared benefits to citizens in general" (Dahl 1961, 61). Overall, then, Dahl sees New Haven, not as a place locked into the status quo, but one in which socioeconomically disadvantaged groups can use their leverage as strategic voting blocs to open up opportunities and move ahead.

PREFERENCE FORMATION, POWER, AND POLITICAL CHANGE

Radical critics have made the pluralist understanding of consensus a special target. If class cleavage arises to the surface only infrequently, radical analysts charge, it is because the dominant class exercises ideological hegemony. It has inculcated the subordinate class with a politically disabling outlook (Abercrombie, Hill, and Turner 1980). In response, pluralists argue that the media of communication and the process of socialization themselves are pluralistic. Competing ideas can be heard and information is sufficiently available for the public to find out about any issue that concerns it. Because most issues involve complex trade-offs, Polsby (1980, 116) maintains no one should second-guess citizen preferences. He says, "the imputation of 'false class consciousness' suggests that the values of analysts are being imposed arbitrarily on groups in the community" (Polsby 1980, 116). If there is consensus, it is presumed genuine.

Preferences on particular issues stem from the individual's position in a complex society. In Graham Allison's (1971, 176) terms, "where you stand depends on where you sit." Consistent with the expectations of James Madison in *Federalist* No. 10, pluralists believe that social heterogeneity prevents any single group from gaining dominance. In their view, politics is essentially a matter of aggregating preferences. This means that coalitions are inherently unstable (Polsby 1980); hence competition is easily preserved.

The rejection of false consciousness takes on added importance in the light of the pluralist conception of power. Pluralism adheres to what I call a social control model of power in which the crucial factor is the cost of compliance (Stone 1989a,

1989b). This is the Weberian formulation about *A* getting *B* to do what *B* would not otherwise have done. Evan Dahl's (1982, 33) later works subscribe to this concept and continue to describe power as inevitably dispersed. The cost of compliance makes that pattern inevitable, given that power involves scope (range of activities) and intensity (depth of what is asked of actors) as well as the extent or domain (number of actors subject to the exercise of power). On the other hand, radical critics argue, if preference formation is not autonomous, resistance is undercut; the cost of compliance ceases to restrict those who would exercise social control (Lindblom 1973, 201–13).

As one peels back the assumptions underlying the pluralist concept of power, an inconsistency emerges. Power consists of comprehensive social control; hence in almost any complex society, it is certain to be extremely limited. The cost of compliance restricts the reach of power and makes most power relationships reciprocal. So, while government is the principal institution for achieving and maintaining social control, it cannot do much without voluntary compliance. To anticipate the regime argument, how significant is electoral control of government? What does it mean for weak public officials to be responsive to small or socioeconomically disadvantaged groups?

To treat elections as centrally important is to assume that the governments they control and guide are significant instruments of power. However, the social control model of power, emphasizing as it does the cost of compliance, suggests that government is mainly an aggregator of preferences; hence it operates largely by incrementalism and mutual adjustment.

In the pluralist view, because no one has much power, social change is largely apolitical. It is a process of modernization, involving both the transition from a traditional to a modern outlook and heightened social differentiation. Machine versus reform politics is a culture clash, reflecting the faster process of modernization for the educated middle class. In *Who Governs?*, the transition from "the patricians" through "the ex-plebes" to "the new men" is shorthand for modernization and highlights a process of increasing role differentiation (Stone 1989b). In Dahl's (1961, 59) view, because "political heterogeneity follows socioeconomic heterogeneity," social differentiation increasingly disperses power. Thus power and conflict are shaped by, but do not contribute to, social change.

The economy is largely absent from pluralist accounts of political cleavage. Race is seen as a stubborn problem, but ethnic ties as a source of conflict are described as yielding to a process of modernization and assimilation. Political leaders vary in role, from caretakers who do little, through brokers who mediate conflicts, to entrepreneurs who play active parts in putting together large and complex projects. Social differentiation makes concerted action a problem. Banfield (1961, 252) observes of Daley's Chicago that it "is too big a place, and the interest in it too diverse, for agreement to occur very often." Political leadership consists mostly of aggregating preferences that emerge from the processes of social change and power is exercised within those bounds (Dahl 1961, 204). Governance rests on popular consent in an increasingly diverse constituency.

SUPPLANTING URBAN PLURALISM

Regime theory modifies or contradicts the above principles of urban pluralism. Let us turn to the specifics.

Sufficiency of the State

Urban regime theory assumes that the effectiveness of local government depends greatly on the cooperation of nongovernmental actors and on the combination of state capacity with nongovernmental resources. Economic well-being is contingent on private investment (Peterson 1981). The point, however, is a broader one: To be effective, governments must blend their capacities with those of various nongovernmental actors (Crenson 1983).

The distinction between the public sector and the private sector can be made conceptually, but can also be a highly misleading guide to empirical reality (Mitchell 1991). That reality is one in which government and business activities are heavily intertwined, as are government and nonprofit activities. This is not to say that government is an inconsequential institution or that public officials are unable to rally support and mobilize efforts on behalf of broad social purposes. Rather, it is to emphasize that, in a liberal order, many activities and resources important for the well-being of society are nongovernmental and that fact has political consequences.

According to regime theory, holding a public position in and of itself enables officeholders to do relatively little, especially by way of introducing new practices and relationships. This is not to deny that the writ of national authority is generally greater than the writ of local authority, and the writ of authority in European countries appears to be significantly greater than in the U.S. The main point is that even at the national level in a so-called "strong state" country, the character of a liberal society is that many essential activities are nongovernmental, and in rearranging these activities, government authority needs the cooperation of private actors. Coercive uses of authority can contribute to a rearrangement, but that can be most readily achieved where there is an active and cooperating constituency supporting the coercion and monitoring compliance.

The act of governance requires the cooperation of private actors and the mobilization of private resources. Talk about state autonomy should not obscure that fact.

Electoral Power Reassessed

If holding public office were sufficient warrant to govern, then elections would be centrally important. The important questions would be about how voters are influenced and elections won. In regime theory, these are not trivial questions, but they also are not the central questions. Often the winning electoral coalition is not the governing coalition (Ferman 1985). The reason is that government authority is inadequate for governing; hence the cooperation and participation of nongovernmental actors becomes essential.

Why belabor the obvious point that in a liberal order many important activities are nongovernmental? Consider a definition of politics offered by Bernard Crick:

> Politics . . . can be simply defined as the activity by which different interests within a given unit of rule are conciliated by giving them a share of power in *proportion to their importance to the welfare of the whole community* (Crick 1982, 21, emphasis added).

Crick never elaborates on the stipulation "in proportion to their importance to the welfare and survival of the whole community" but it is surely in need of some comment. For one thing, the question of who contributes what to the general well-being is itself subject to debate and conflict. Even so, it directs attention to a fundamentally different proposition from one person–one vote.

The definition emphasizes that politics is a great deal more than voting for and holding public office. If governance is furthering the welfare and assuring the survival of a body of citizens, then actors and activities labeled private are de facto an integral part of the governmental process and elections are of limited importance. Furthermore, once the sufficiency of formal authority for governance is in doubt and elections come to be regarded as inadequate forms of popular control, the conditions that make government responsive to socioeconomically disadvantaged groups are no longer met.

Power: From Social Control to Social Production

In the eyes of some, the dual weakness of government authority and of electoral control of government constitute conditions under which a private elite can exercise control. That, however, is not the regime argument. Instead, regime analysis concedes to pluralism the unlikelihood that any group can exercise comprehensive social control but also holds that the absence of monolithic control is so universal as to be uninteresting. Because the pluralist conception of power is in many ways uninstructive, regime theory offers as an alternative a social production model of power (Stone 1989a). This is a facilitative concept, "power to" rather than "power over" (Arendt 1961; Pitkin 1972; Parsons 1969; Clegg 1989).

A social production model of power makes the usefulness of Crick's definition of politics more apparent. Instead of the power to govern being something that can be captured by an electoral victory, it is something created by bringing cooperating actors together, not as equal claimants, but often as unequal contributors to a shared set of purposes.

There is an admitted kinship between pluralism and the social production model of power. In regime theory, the capacity to govern is always partial and it is subject to the centrifugal forces to which pluralists are sensitive. Yet a basic difference remains; governance is not the issue-by-issue process that pluralism suggests. There are several reasons why. One is that nongovernment resources are highly skewed and reflect a stratified society. Once the equalizing effect of one person–one vote is heavily discounted, the classic pluralist argument about dispersed inequalities cannot be sustained. As Rokkan (1966, 105) said, "Votes count but resources decide."

There is an undeniably high level of specialization of interest and role differentiation does characterize modern society, but the question of political involvement is more complicated than that. Those actors rich in resources by that fact have much to protect. Downtown banks, for example, have extensive investments, loans, and trust holdings. These concerns lead them directly into redevelopment, transportation, and tax policy. Social peace, race relations, and police practices are also salient, as are education and the quality of the workforce. With such wide policy concerns, not to mention the possibilities of serving as holder of government deposits and lender of money to municipal authorities, downtown banks have a very strong incentive to care about the character of city government, the community's political climate, and the allies on whom they can count. Extensive involvement in city affairs is thus to be expected.

Public choice literature tells us that coalitions tend to cycle, that is, to be unstable (Oppenheimer 1975). That would surely be the case if politics were simply a matter of aggregating preferences about the distribution of a given body of benefits. Occurrences of coalition stability point to a different concept of politics, one in which politics is about the production rather than distribution of benefits. Moreover, we need not treat preferences as fixed; they evolve through experience and therefore are informed by available opportunities (Cohen and March 1986, 220–21).

On the surface, the argument offered here appears counterintuitive: that fixed preferences give rise to unstable coalitions and fluid preferences to relatively stable ones. However, the key assumption is in the accompanying assumption about the nature of politics. If we start from the premise that the amount and kind of benefits and opportunities depend upon the creation and maintenance of cooperative arrangements, then we can see how attachments form and are reinforced.

A concept borrowed from economics amplifies the point: Transaction costs mean that established relationships have great value in facilitating future cooperation. Hence, once formed, a relationship of cooperation becomes something of value to be protected by all of the participants. Furthermore, because a governing coalition produces benefits it can share or withhold, being part of an established coalition confers preemptive advantages (Stone 1988). Hence, there is an additional reason to preserve rather than casually discard coalition membership.

For those on the outside, gaining membership in a governing coalition possesses considerable appeal. Of course, several considerations may be at work and the concessions required to gain membership may be too great to be met by an outside group. Even so, there is a cost, a set of foregone opportunities, that attaches to being an outsider. Indeed, this point exposes a fundamental difference between the social control and social production models of power. The social control model focuses on control and resistance, with the cost of compliance serving to limit the power of the superordinate actor in accordance with the subordinate actor's will to resist. This is what March (1966) calls a power-depleting model. The social production model makes being on the outside (the counterpart to resistance) costly to the subordinate actor. The social production conception is what March calls a power-generating model. The power-generating aspects of governance help explain how a prevailing coalition, such as the biracial coalition that governs Atlanta, can have such durability.

The social production model of power offered by regime theory thus differs in important respects from pluralism. While accepting the obvious point that society is too complex to be controlled by a single force, regime theory suggests that universal suffrage and social differentiation have limited explanatory power for urban politics. Such democratic concepts as one person–one vote and equality before the law are significant, but the unequal distribution of economic, organizational, and cultural resources has a substantial bearing on the character of actual governing coalitions, working against the kind of fluid coalition and power dispersion predicted by pluralist theory. As we turn next to the topic of preference formation, we will see that the "power to" of the social production model translates into a form of "power over." The translation is, however, far from simple and direct.

PREFERENCE FORMATION AND CONSENT

Because people respond mainly to what is immediate and concrete, the pluralist notion of consensus possesses little explanatory power. There is little reason to believe that broad and vague ideas control particular and concrete actions and at least some reason to think that action often precedes belief (Cohen and March 1986; Fantasia 1988; Pitkin 1972, 324). Furthermore, as Tilly (1984) has argued, society is more appropriately thought of as a loosely coupled network of interactions than as a cohesive unit bound together by common beliefs.

Let us turn, then, to the question of preferences on particular issues and let us assume narrow cognition: that ordinarily, people respond to what is familiar, immediate, and concrete. This view underlies the long-standing concept of satisficing (March and Simon 1965) and has long been used in psychology (Milgram 1974, 38). Narrow cognition is consistent with the pluralist view that individual preferences, at least on particular issues, derive mainly from one's place in a highly differentiated society. However, we radically alter our understanding of politics if we think about preferences as being formed not in the context of a static social structure, but rather in a context of dynamic social interactions that sometimes reveal new possibilities and offer changing opportunities (Darnton 1989). Combined with narrow cognition, this step suggests that policy preferences are relatively fluid.

What, then, are preferences based on? Are human beings rational egoists or are they shaped by some more complex process at work (Grafstein 1992)? Are preferences formed atomistically or is there a social dimension? Classic pluralism did not face this question because a static position in the social structure allows for a comfortable convergence between rational egoism and highly specialized socialization into a role.

Though my own thoughts are preliminary, it might be fruitful to posit some elementary principles of motivation. There is an economizing side to the self that drives us to get what we can with minimum effort and expenditure. However, the principle of polarity tells us not to expect behavior to consist of a single tendency (Muir 1977). A single tendency leaves nothing to explain; it just is. By contrast, polarity or opposing tendencies present the possibility of explanation in the form of specifying the conditions under which one or the other tendency prevails.

As a preliminary step toward identifying an appropriate polarity, let us assume that behavior is guided by mixed motives. Specifically, let us assume that, varying with the circumstances, the economizing tendency is counterpoised by a social purpose tendency. How, it might be asked, can a social purpose tendency be reconciled with limited cognition? Part of the answer has to do with the purposive side of the self and desire to be associated with something larger than the life of an asocial individual (Muir 1977; Margolis 1990; Chong 1991). Another part of the answer is that narrow cognition is not a stationary condition. Vision can be expanded by discussion and interaction, leadership, exposure to a social movement, participation in a set of activities that point beyond the immediate, and much more.

Social relationships and experiences make a difference. Of course, if these relationships and experiences are characterized by treachery and distrust, then one learns to be guarded and withdraw into the economizing self. Ordinarily, narrow cognition does not result in the extreme of personal withdrawal. Instead, for most of us most of the time the purposes we pursue involve small, familiar groups and the responsibilities attached to those groups and to our careers (Barnard 1968, 267–68). Centrifugal forces are real, but stop well short of solipsism.

As individuals move up in an organization or take up new activities, the social purposes they are cognizant of may expand or at least change. Large purposes may become more attractive than small ones. Why would a Martin Luther King forego personal wealth, comfort, and safety for a life of danger and modest material reward? It was hardly stereotypical economizing behavior. Presumably the magnitude and nobility of the cause had an appeal (Stone 1990).

Still, not all grand and noble causes enlist active supporters. For that matter, over time, many a would-be social reformer becomes cynical and opportunistic. What, then, explains the differential appeal of causes? People may, of course, disagree about whether a cause is socially useful or harmful. Among those considered good and socially useful an important consideration is perceived feasibility. Lost causes or hopeless causes command few supporters. After all, the current cliche is about wanting "to make a difference," not about searching for a chance to make a futile gesture.

There is circularity in the relationship between commitment to a cause and its feasibility. The more people support a cause, the greater its feasibility. The point tells us something about the nature of leadership. The role of leaders is not simply to depict causes as socially worthy; they also try to convince followers that the cause is achievable and that the time is right to act (Stone 1990; Chong 1991). Of course, this also means that the leader-follower interaction is very complicated and that the follower-to-follower relationship plays a vital role, in some cases even blurring the distinction between leader and follower (Burns 1978).

FLUID PREFERENCES AND GOVERNANCE

Now we can see why it is important to reject the idea that politics is merely preference aggregation. If preferences are fluid, then their aggregation cannot be compartmentalized from the prior question of their creation. The interactions people engage in and the relationships they form (negotiations and coalition building, for example) shape preferences, including understanding about what is feasible and what is not. In this process, those with more resources (especially resources that can build additional support or advance a policy purpose) have a superior opportunity to rally support to the cause they favor. To be sure, the cause is likely to undergo modification and elaboration as support is built and conflict managed, but those with the most to contribute have a larger voice. Those with fewer resources to contribute have a lesser voice and may well be confined to what I have called elsewhere "small opportunities," particular projects and individual benefits that are essentially by-products of the main policy thrust (Stone 1989a).

Fluid preferences thus refer to the potential for change, and the phrase is not meant to suggest that they are highly volatile and change on a day-to-day basis. An established pattern of interaction and structure of resources has substantial staying power (Baumgartner and Jones 1991).

Resources need not be material. As pluralists have long argued, they can consist of skill, ability to inspire, organizational capacity, technical expertise, or other intangible factors. However, material resources are especially useful. They are serviceable for almost any project and they can be shifted from one purpose to another. They are also especially useful in initiating an interaction around some shared objective. Material transactions frequently provide immediate results, requiring no stretching of narrow cognition. They also do not require a high level of trust; hence they are quite workable in an impersonal and socially heterogenous setting, characterized by uncertainty and shallow relationships. Moreover, through repeated face-to-face exchange, material transactions can lead to less shallow and more complex relationships.

The relationship between preference formation and material resources is more complicated than the simple fact that some actors have more dollars than others. Some purposes are more readily coordinated and promoted by material means, and once a climate or ecology of material transactions is established, other such transactions are readily made (Crenson 1971, 170–76). For that reason some purposes may be more tractable than others. In short, the ready availability of means rather than the will of dominant actors may explain what is pursued and why. Hence, hegemony in a capitalist order may be more a matter of ease of cooperation around profit-oriented activities than the unchallenged ascendancy of core ideas.

If people are purposive, but purposive in the sense of wanting to be involved in achievable goals, and if some goals are more readily achieved than others, then people will tend toward those goals that are achievable. This may be the case even when hard-to-achieve goals are deemed desirable. It matters, then, how much effort it takes to organize people to do something. Russell Hardin (1982, 221) argues, "social states of affairs are often much more to be explained by what can be tacitly coordinated than by what anyone's preferences or reasoned outcomes might be." This is not to discount reflection and deliberations as elements in the human condition. They play a creative role, but they are likely to have a lasting impact only to the extent that they are embodied in concrete activities and vital social relationships.

With these general points in mind, let us reconsider the case of urban redevelopment in New Haven. Was Mayor Lee acting on preferences already held? Yes, in the sense that there was widespread sentiment in favor of revitalizing the city. However, because redevelopment also involved considerable displacement (20% of the city's population), social disruption that accompanied large-scale change in land use, delays and uneven success in rebuilding, numerous opportunity costs, and many unanticipated consequences, vague sentiment about city revitalization is hardly the whole issue. The real question is how the program could be sustained in the face of substantial opposition.

Raymond Wolfinger's (1974, 343) comment about one of the major components of redevelopment is instructive: "The [Church Street] project's inception, development, and survival depended on four important advantages possessed by the Lee Administration: technical skill, public relations talent, Lee's control of his government and party, and his alliance with businessmen and Yale." Encouraged by the availability of federal money, urban redevelopment in New Haven could claim high priority, not because of popular demand or even because popular resistance was lacking, but because a few resource-rich and executive-controlled sectors of the city supported the program and could provide the means necessary for its execution. It was what could be done; it was what could be coordinated.

Maintaining routine services can, of course, be coordinated even more easily than carrying out a controversial program, but urban redevelopment in New Haven met the needs of the regime members described by Wolfinger. It provided Mayor Lee with a highly visible program and a chance to make a name as a person of action. It offered cosmopolitan professionals the opportunity to make their mark. It was consistent with the patronage needs of the party organization, and it enabled downtown business and Yale to make an effort to improve their environment. Redevelopment was also a generator of jobs, contracts, and such socially worthy small opportunities as new school buildings and housing for the elderly. It could therefore generate supplementary support and help manage conflict. In short, it was the social production model of power in operation.

The lesson of New Haven is not that an urban regime must be activist. Rather, it is that political leaders and professional administrators of an activist inclination need coalition partners who can provide resources useful in launching major projects and managing the resulting conflict. This is not to suggest that activist efforts are necessarily successful. Program activism sometimes loses. In Kalamazoo, for example, tax-conscious small property holders used the referendum process to veto that city's program of redevelopment (Sanders 1987).

The real lesson of New Haven is that we should treat power with special care. It is not enough to see the city's story as one in which a set of strategically positioned and resource-rich actors imposed their will on others. Nor is it enough to debate whether the prevailing group represented majority sentiment or just a form of acquiescence. That scenario misses the point about fluid preferences.

If preference is influenced by perceived feasibility, then the will of the governing coalition was shaped by what was seen as achievable. The availability of federal money and the structure of the urban renewal program were strong inducements for the formation of a business-government partnership. Although the partners were far from unwilling to join together, it is perhaps significant that there were no similar inducements for other coalitions. Federal money and the structure of the urban renewal program were only one set of factors. Redevelopment is amenable to execution in a way that many other policy initiatives are not. Redevelopment requires mainly the coordination of effort among a small number of elite actors. They can command the essential resources, and if they reach agreement, the program can move ahead even in the face of significant opposition. Moreover, redevelopment carries with it an abundance of selective incentives that a policy issue such as educational reform lacks. The logic of the situation in New Haven made a coalition with business attractive and redevelopment appealing to city hall. The achievability of redevelopment shaped preferences, especially those of key public officials.

In urban pluralism, preferences form in a manner exogenous to the power relationship. Power is a contest of wills, that is, a contest over whose preference will prevail. In this contest, resources may be unequal, but everyone has limited resources and therefore a limited capacity to impose his will on someone else. By contrast, the social production model treats preference formation as endogenous to the power relationship. Preferences are influenced by practicability: Achievable goals are attractive; difficult-to-achieve goals are unattractive. Of course, feasibility is not the only factor that influences preference; other considerations also enter the picture. We should remember as well that practicability need not be an all-or-nothing matter. Even with these caveats, one can still say that the logic of the situation in New Haven favored urban redevelopment in the Richard Lee era.

Once we think about the logic of the situation, given fluidity of preferences, power ceases to be simply a question of whether dominant actors can freely impose their will. Intention is partially shaped by the situation. Just as some actors possess more resources than others, some actions are more compelling than others. Ease of coordination enters the picture.

Let us add one final dimension to the matter of preference formation. Preferences do not emerge from atomistic relationships. Social bonds matter enormously, not only because they inform us, but because we want to maintain them. What the isolated individual might prefer is modified by a desire or need to take into account the consequences of that want on someone else. This is what Crick's definition of politics is about: a situation in which differing interests take one another into account by sharing in governance. This ideal is seldom met on a universally inclusive basis, but a significant degree of mutual "account taking" is surely an integral part of building and maintaining a coalition.

Hannah Arendt (1961, 164) captures the point nicely when she observes, "All political business is, and always has been, transmitted within an elaborate framework of ties and bonds for the future." For Arendt, the process of governing is one of acting within a set of relationships and acting with an eye on the future state of these relationships. Coalition partners thus educate one another in two ways. One is a simple exchange of information. The other is educating one another about the nature of their interdependence. Mere information about another can be disregarded. The understanding of an interdependent relationship is a more insistent matter. Indeed, at its most profound level, such an understanding may redefine identity. That is a major reason why the composition of a governing coalition and the nature of the relationship between its members have a profound effect on policy.

As coalitions form and change, new considerations and new understandings come into play and preferences modify. Tensions may abound within a coalition, but those who can bring the necessary resources together and coordinate their efforts have an opportunity to constitute a governing coalition. The chance to pursue significant policy aims can have the effect of subduing differences and reshaping outlooks. The very act of cooperating with other people enlarges what is thinkable, and it may give rise to new or expanded preferences.

Preferences change because understanding changes. In this process we alter the boundaries of social intelligence, not by force of intellectual effort, but by the experience of interacting purposefully with others. The nature and composition of a governing coalition is thus vitally important, not only for who is included, but also for who is not. A narrow governing coalition means that policy is guided by a narrow social understanding and a struggle to alter participation in the coalition may ensue. It is appropriate, then, to turn to the issue of political conflict and policy change.

POLITICAL ECONOMY AND THE SOURCES OF POLITICAL CONFLICT

In classic urban pluralism, the economy is considered principally for its social consequences. Increasing levels of education, the expansion of the middle class, and ethnic assimilation diminish class and ethnic cleavage, foreordain "good government" opposition to machine politics, and promise the eventual triumph of a reform morality.

Mainly, the pluralist world is divided into discrete spheres of activity. People go about their specialized activities largely unconcerned about or unbothered by those outside their own narrow sphere. As Nelson Polsby (1980, 117) says, "If a man's major life work is banking, the pluralist presumes he will spend his time at the bank and not in manipulating community decisions." The economy and political affairs are thus seen as separate arenas. Aside from issues of political morality, conflict is largely internal to discrete spheres of activity and the prevailing pattern is one of mutual adjustment. Moreover, pluralists believe that blockage in one area (minorities in private employment in Dahl's example) leads to increased effort elsewhere. Given pluralist assumptions about dispersed power, one would indeed expect social practice overall to offer something to everyone. Dispersed power also leads to expectations about equilibrium and incremental change.

Social, economic, and technological changes might temporarily disrupt various points of equilibrium, but mutual accommodation would work to restore them. In a system of dispersed power, slack political resources, Dahl argues, can be used to correct felt wrongs and open needed opportunities. Any political action that imposes one-sided costs is likely to be opposed by mobilization to redress the balance.

Regime theory generates no such expectation. Power as social production capacity ("power to") is not assumed to be dispersed and spheres of activity are not assumed to be discrete. Regime theorist Susan Fainstein's (1990, 123) political economy perspective makes a sharp contrast with pluralism. In her view, "political forces are ultimately rooted in the relations of production." To be sure, she argues, political forces enjoy a degree of autonomy and they are affected by noneconomic as well as economic factors, but the agenda of political struggle is closely tied in with the economy. Still, the politics-economy relationship follows neither fixed pattern nor set trajectory. In a sense, history is a series of momentous struggles over the terms of that relationship, with no predetermined outcome.

In a political economy perspective, redevelopment is a response to a far-reaching process of economic restructuring, a response:

> to the transformation of the economic bases of cities in the advanced capital world from manufacturing to services; the rapid growth of the producer services sector within cities at the top of the global hierarchy; the simultaneous concentration of economic control within multinational firms and financial institutions, and decentralization of their manufacturing and routine office functions (Fainstein 1990, 120).

Economic change raises questions of equity: Who will benefit and who will bear the cost? It also forces decision makers to ask how various economic and noneconomic considerations are to be weighed against one another (Logan and Molotch 1987). The pace as well as the exact form of restructuring is an issue. As Karl Polanyi (1957, 36–37) has argued, "The rate of change is often of no less importance than the direction of the change itself."

Classic pluralism suggests that the costs and benefits of restructuring should be widely spread and that the capacity of adversely affected groups to mitigate harmful actions should make for slow and orderly change. By contrast, regime theory predicts that restructuring will reflect the concerns of the governing coalition and its capacity to understand and appreciate the consequences of its actions. The small opportunities attached to redevelopment work against a countermobilization, as does the limited importance of electoral power.

Restructuring does not itself dictate that a city like New Haven must concentrate on the physical reconstruction of its central business district and displace one-fifth of its population without adequate attention to relocation facilities. Nor does it dictate that a city like Baltimore must concentrate for years on converting its harbor area to convention and tourism uses while neglecting its school system (Orr 1991). Regime theory focuses on the nature and composition of the governing coalition, and instead of assuming a widespread capacity to redress imbalances, asks how and why some concerns gain attention and others do not.

By embracing a political economy perspective, regime theory rejects the notion that modern life consists of discrete spheres of activity, largely insulated from one another. The physical redevelopment of the city can be seen as part of a fundamental process of restructuring. Through the modification of land use, redevelopment spills over into all areas of community activity.

With community life unsegmented in a political economy perspective, conflict and policy change come into a different light. In the process of economic restructuring, physical redevelopment competes with education for priority. If the conditions of employability and the pathway to economic productivity are changing, why has human investment policy not enjoyed a higher priority? Restructuring in and of itself cannot answer that question; nor can pluralism with its assumptions about dispersed power. By contrast, regime theory can provide an answer and can suggest as well what would help to alter urban policy priorities. Before turning to the specifics, I want to address briefly the larger issue of the character of political change and the context within which regime-building efforts occur.

POLITICAL CHOICE AND POLITICAL CHANGE

Regime theorist Martin Shefter (1976, 19) rejects the view "that political institutions mechanistically reflect, and are uniquely determined by, an underlying configuration of social forces." He argues instead that governing arrangements are artifacts, formed in an intentional manner. Tracing the evolution of the Tammany machine in New York, Shefter follows the coalition-building efforts and strategic maneuvers of contending elites, and shows "that alternative political structures can exist in a given social environment." He thus joins Barrington Moore in treating history as an opportunity to explore "suppressed possibilities" (Moore 1978, 376; Smith 1983); that is, Shefter views political change as a process in which choice and struggle play a part as some arrangements gain sway over others.

To talk of choice and struggle is not to suggest that elites have a clear and comprehensive vision of the alternatives they shape and advance. Narrow cognition precludes that scenario. Nor is it to suggest that elites have free rein to pursue whatever their political imaginations can bring forth. Elites cannot easily ignore powerful trends such as economic restructuring, and they find themselves constrained by such forces as the mobility of capital.

Political explanation is not simply the realm of choice left over when constraints are taken into account. It is, in part, a matter of how constraints are modified or maneuvered around. Jones and Bachelor (1986, 212) use the term "creative bounded choice." Hannah Arendt (1961, 117) writes about, not subordination to, but "the domination of necessity." Political freedom, she says, is about people deliberating and acting together to modify what would otherwise be an expected course of events (Arendt 1961, 168–71).

Modifying an expected course of events calls for more than deliberation and expression of intent. It requires a set of arrangements that brings together needed resources and motivates participants to play their essential parts. Action is central. Mobilization, organization, and the generation of new capabilities within the nongovernment sector, is as important as, or more so than, making a legislative claim. Hence, we come back to the question of the adequacy or inadequacy of government authority. In a liberal order, important resources lie outside the government sector and behavior is not closely guided by exertions of authority. A substantial rearrangement of established and therefore "expected" social and economic practice (that is, a major policy innovation) typically requires some form of effort that joins government and nongovernment resources. It is to the nature of that effort I now turn.

REGIME AND GOVERNING CAPACITY

By emphasizing the inadequacy of legal authority for bringing about policy change, regime theory can perhaps clarify what is at issue with the rediscovery of the state. When studied historically, the state emerges as a political entity with a limited and variable capacity to govern (Skowronek 1982; Badie and Birnbaum 1983). Further, as Skocpol (1985, 17) says, there is an "unevenness [in capacity] across policy areas" as well. In regime theory, because "stateness" guarantees no given level of effectiveness, those who would govern find themselves drawn toward interdependence with various societal interests (Skocpol 1985, 19). The special weakness of the American local state reinforces the point.

Some discussions of state capacity focus on technical competence, on the training of officials, and the expertise they possess. While technical capacity is not inconsequential, I want to emphasize a different aspect of capacity: the capacity to stimulate the cooperation of private actors. Responding effectively to a challenge like economic restructuring means bringing about substantial change in established social and economic practice, and that means drawing on nongovernment resources and enlisting nongovernment actors. The character of that undertaking depends on the policy aim pursued.

The inadequacy of government authority standing by itself accounts for the frequent discrepancy between the winning electoral coalition in a locality and the coalition that actually governs the locality. The inadequacy of government authority is also a reason why, in order to explain the policy action of a regime, it is necessary to go beyond the composition of the governing coalition. Because members of the coalition are not simply dividing the spoils of office, the nature of the relationship among the coalition members matters. It is particularly significant that this relationship includes the resources members bring to bear on the task of governance.

In order for a governing coalition to be viable, it must be able to mobilize resources commensurate with its main policy agenda. Participation in governance, especially for those who are not public officials, is based heavily on the goals they want to achieve. Participation may modify these goals, but participation is still purposeful. It follows that, if a coalition cannot deliver on the agenda that holds it together, then the members will disengage, leaving the coalition open to reconstitution. In the same manner, doable actions help secure commitments and perhaps attract others with similar or consistent aims.

A TYPOLOGY

Let us now move from general proposition to concrete cases. In doing so, I offer four types of regimes, regimes that vary in the difficulty of the governing tasks their policy agendas call for. Three of the four represent regimes that correspond to types well documented in research on American cities. The fourth is at least partly hypothetical and represents an extension, not a recounting, of the experience in a few American communities. I have not crafted the typology to the cross-national experience because differences in central government structure, national policy, and party system can mean that locality-to-locality comparisons across nations are extremely complicated (Keating 1991). Even within the U.S., the types represent simplifications.

The purpose of the typology is not to illuminate the complexity of concrete cases, but rather to show how, if policy change is to be brought about, the resources must match the requirements of the proposed agenda. The typology makes concrete the argument that governance requires more than the capture of elected office. The logic of the typology is that those who would exercise political choice and alter current policy can do so only by making use of or generating an appropriate body of nongovernmental resources.

1. *Maintenance regimes* represent no effort to introduce significant change. They provide us with a benchmark against which to compare other types of regimes. Because maintenance regimes involve no effort to change established social and economic practice, no extensive mobilization of private resources is necessary and no substantial change in behavior is called for. Such regimes center on the provision of routine services and require only periodic approval at the ballot box.

Motivational demands are minimal. Skepticism or indifference is not a problem. A desire to keep tax levels down is often at work, but support for that position calls only for occasional participation in elections. Few demands are placed on elites.

Since maintenance regimes require little of public officials and low taxes are usually popular, why are maintenance regimes not more prevalent (as they once were)? The answer is that, while demands are few, rewards are small. For nongovernment actors, maintenance calls for contentment with things as they are and "as they are" may include a state of decline. For public officials, maintenance means foregoing opportunities to make a mark on the world and names for themselves. Maintenance is appealing mostly to provincials who are content to operate in a small arena populated by friends and neighbors.

2. *Development regimes* (such as Lee's coalition in New Haven) are concerned primarily with changing land use in order to promote growth or counter decline. Therefore they represent efforts to modify established social and economic patterns, and they involve the linking of private investment to public action. For private investors to commit their resources, they must believe that positive change is feasible, and they may well see a series of public actions as necessary steps to assure that feasibility. These steps may consist of acquiring and clearing land, building public facilities, or providing other subsidies.

Because they involve change and disruption, development projects are often controversial. They provoke opposition and contain risks for public officials who back them. Hence, development activities are often insulated from popular control (Friedland 1983). They impose no motivational demands on the mass public and are advanced easiest when the public is passive. What they do require is coordination between institutional elites. Coordination may involve some inducements, but little coercion. A set of actors must move in concert, but the number is small. It is not inherently difficult for them to frame a shared vision, and inducements do not have to be spread widely.

Given that there are risks of popular disapproval, elected officials could be expected to be wary about identifying themselves with large development projects. However, in America's post–World War II cities, mayors have consistently associated their administrations closely with development activity. Such activity is a response to economic restructuring, and it meets a need for quick and visible action. The immediate negative consequences are usually localized, and mayors have tended to identify themselves more closely with the announcement of plans than with the details of implementation (Sanders and Stone 1987). Still, some, such as Boston's Kevin White, have paid the price of electoral unpopularity.

Development activity not only gives rise to controversy, it also generates an abundance of selective incentives and small opportunities: jobs, contracts, fees, new schools, parks, theater facilities, and many more. These can help enormously in managing conflict and softening or dividing the opposition. In terms of degree of difficulty in the governing task, development does not rank very high. It calls mainly for elite coordination and, to help manage conflict, insider transactions. Insofar as the mass public is concerned, all that is required is that they not inflict electoral defeats. The resources needed are those of legal authority (principally the power of eminent domain), private investment monies, development expertise, transaction links within the business sector, and public funds for various forms of subsidy. Over the years, federal and state governments have provided substantial public money to localities for development purposes.

3. *Middle class progressive regimes* focus on such measures as environmental protection, historic preservation, affordable housing, the quality of design, affirmative action, and linkage funds for various social purposes (Clavel 1986; Conroy 1990; Kann 1986; Shearer 1989). Because exactions are part of the picture, if they are to amount to anything, development must be encouraged or at least not prevented. Progressive mandates thus involve monitoring the actions of institutional elites and calibrating inducements and sanctions to gain a suitable mix of activity and restriction. The governing task consists of a complex form of regulation.

Unlike the development regime, the government-business relationship in a progressive regime is not a largely voluntary relationship. Coercion plays a larger part than in development regimes. On the other hand, the relationship is not purely coercive. Business has the option of disinvesting. Some might argue that the difference between development regimes and progressive regimes is that progressive cities simply are more attractive as investment sites. That, however, misses part of the picture. Even cities faced with economic decline often have areas within them that are quite attractive to investors; hence some form of negotiated arrangement is possible. At the same time, many cities that are highly attractive to private investment nevertheless impose few restrictions.

Furthermore, investment partnerships can be worked out between government and nonbusiness interests; for example, New York City's long-running progressive housing policy rested partly on the use of financial resources from labor unions (Fainstein and Fainstein 1989). Nonbusiness investors may be inexperienced and, for that reason, more difficult to work with than their business counterparts. None of this is to deny that cities differ in attractiveness to private investors and differences in attractiveness affect the potential for progressive measures, but there is clearly more to it than that.

A progressive regime requires an attentive electorate. Progressive mandates often rest on a base of active popular support. If the referendum process is a keystone in regulation, as in San Francisco (DeLeon 1990), then dependence on mass support is direct and central. Regulation does not require extensive participation by masses of people, but because progressive mandates may involve significant trade-offs, citizen participation is useful in informing citizens about the complexities of policy while keeping them committed to progressive goals. The difficult part is maintaining that commitment by setting goals that are feasible but also socially significant. Citizen involvement in community affairs and in oversight boards and commissions may help preserve that commitment. Progressive regimes show that elections are not an insignificant part of the government process, but they also illustrate the need for something more than periodic approval.

The pursuit of progressive mandates is a more difficult governing task than development. The coordination of institutional elites is as much a part of the progressive task as the development task, and it may be more difficult because action is less voluntary. The involvement of citizen groups and the need for active and informed public support heighten the difficulty of the task. The resources required include those needed for development plus the organizational capacity to inform, mobilize, and involve the citizenry.

Perhaps it is appropriate at this point to add a comparative or cross-national dimension to the discussion. The U.S. context is one of weak and, especially at the local level, nonprogrammatic parties. Moreover, the U.S. to an unusual degree leaves responsibility for planning in local hands. Consequently, in the area of land use regulation, U.S. local governments have more to do with weaker political organizations than almost any other advanced industrial society. It is not surprising, then, that most progressive communities in the U.S. have large middle-class populations. The weakness of party organization gives special importance to nonpolitical civic organizations and to organizational and technical skills that the middle class can provide on a volunteer basis. At the same time, even in such a different national setting as Paris, France, the middle class plays a crucial role in progressive government (Body-Gendrot 1987).

4. *Regimes devoted to lower-class opportunity expansion* would involve enriched education and job training, improved transportation access, and enlarged opportunities for business and home ownership. In the U.S., such regimes are largely hypothetical, but there are hints of such regimes in community organizations, such as Baltimore's BUILD, which has gained a place in that city's governing coalition (Orr

1991). A few cities, Chicago under Harold Washington, for example, have moved in that direction from time to time.

I use the term *opportunity expansion* rather than *redistribution* to suggest that the programs need not be zero sum, as the word *redistribution* suggests. The lower class can be treated as something more than claimants for greater service; efforts can be directed toward expanding opportunities through human investment policies and widened access to employment and ownership. As the quality of the workforce rises and ownership becomes more widespread, there are potential gains, both economic and noneconomic, for the community at large. The challenge, of course, is how to organize a community so that such admirable aims can actually be pursued.

A regime of lower-class opportunity expansion involves the same difficulties as progressive regimes plus some of its own. To be done on a significant scale, enlarged opportunities for employment and for business and home ownership require altering practices in the private sector, but without driving away investment. Achieving these goals calls for coordination among institutional elites, but not on a purely voluntary basis. It requires regulation, and regulation is most sustainable when backed by a popular constituency. Because a lower-class constituency lacks some of the skills and organizational resources that a middle-class constituency would start with, the effort to equip it for that watchdog constituency role is more substantial than the effort needed to mobilize a middle-class constituency, and that is only part of the story.

A major challenge is the motivational one. A lower-class population is conditioned to restricted opportunity and is skilled in coping with disappointment and frustration. This is the circumstance that leads some to talk about a culture of poverty, but that term is too antiseptic to describe the concrete reality on which limited expectations are based. It carries with it an element of "blame the victim." Its only usefulness is to highlight the difficulty of changing expectations based on long conditioning. But then, why talk about culture? Why not talk about the conditioning, which, for the most part, is ongoing?

Altering opportunities on a class basis calls for more than loose references to self-help or pep talks to individuals about working hard to get ahead. In the first place, the process requires that opportunities be real, that those who meet education or training requirements be offered decent jobs, not dead-end jobs with no future (Bernick 1987). School compacts that guarantee jobs to high school graduates or that assure financial support for a college education are the kinds of practices that make opportunities real. A few individual opportunities or scattered chances to compete for a restricted set of positions are not enough.

The availability of the opportunities is only the first step. Lower-class children also need to believe that the opportunities are real and that they are actually attainable. Given a background that encourages low expectations and cynicism about life chances, members of the lower class are likely to pursue opportunities only if they are encouraged and supported not only individually but also through their families and their peers. Put another way, changing conditions on paper is not enough. Previously conditioned expectations have to be altered. To do that, it is necessary to create a complex set of incentives that are extensive enough to affect classwide views and that are intensive enough to sustain ongoing personal commitments to make use of expanded opportunities.

For opportunity expansion regimes, the coordination task is immense. Given that the participation of elites may be less than fully voluntary, coordination among them is itself no simple matter. Given the needs they must meet, they may find that coordinating resource allocation among themselves is not enough; they may also feel compelled to make concerted efforts to garner assistance from the state government or other extralocal sources. Mobilizing a lower-class constituency itself is another immense task, requiring the combined efforts of government and non-government actors (Henig 1982).

The most difficult feature in the entire process is achieving congruence between the provision of opportunity by established institutions and the use of those opportunities by the lower class. If the opportunities are not available to a high degree, then lower-class expectations will not modify. However, if opportunities are made available and are poorly used, then the institutions providing those opportunities will withdraw or divert their efforts to a different task.

The kind of large-scale campaign needed to expand opportunities on a class basis would be long and hard. It would offer few quick returns to individual officeholders (and American politics, especially at the local level, is very much an instrument of personal political organizations). Overcoming a cycle of disappointment and cynicism is a governing task far more difficult than even the pursuit of the mandates of middle-class progressives. It would require all of the resources needed for a progressive regime plus the creation of a capacity for mass involvement in supporting and making use of programs of opportunity expansion. Though it need not be done all at once, it has to be done on large enough scale and at fast enough pace to encourage and sustain a changed outlook within the lower class. In addition, it would probably require funding or other program supports beyond what can be raised within urban localities.

A SCHEMATIC REPRESENTATION

If we return to the earlier proposition about policy agendas and resources, we can now present it schematically (see Fig. 4.1). The horizontal axis represents increas-

Figure 4.1. Regime viability.

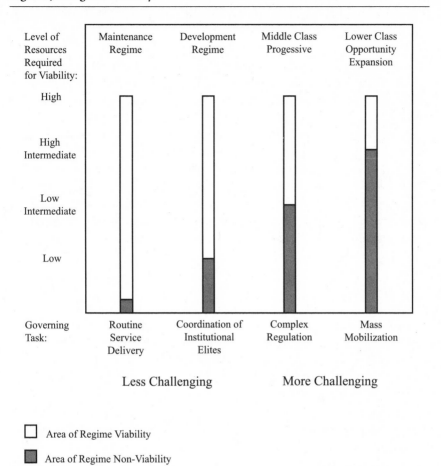

ing degrees of difficulty in the governing task. The vertical axis represents increasing levels of resources needed as the difficulty of the task increases. Where resources are commensurate with the tasks that characterize various regimes, we have an area of regime viability. Where resources and task are not commensurate, regimes lack viability.

With this figure in mind, we can then return to the earlier issue about political choice and policy action. Promoting development, pursuing progressive mandates, and seeking opportunity expansion for the lower class are not choices available through a simple process of enactment. To pursue these policy alternatives means to marshal the resources required for their achievement. Policy choice, then, is a

matter of regime building, of bringing together the essential partners on a basis
that enables them to meld together the resources commensurate with the governing responsibility undertaken. There is a role for reflection and deliberation, but
the role is not simply one of choosing desirable goals. Instead, it is one of devising
a means whereby the government and nongovernment sectors can cooperate fruitfully. To fail to treat the question of means adequately is to invite disillusionment
and the abandonment of socially worthy goals. Cynicism and opportunism are sure
to follow.

A first step in understanding the issue of means is to grasp the fact that governmental authority, standing alone, is inadequate. I have attempted to use regime
theory to show why. Another step is to abandon the analytically convenient but
politically inappropriate notion that governance is about aggregating relatively stable policy preferences. These preferences are fluid, and the ones deemed worthy
will thrive only if provided a supportive environment. Regime theory provides a
way of thinking about what constitutes a supportive environment.

CONCLUSION

In facing the challenge of regime building in American cities, two features of the
national political economy must be reckoned with. One is a large and varied nongovernment sector that not only controls most investment activity but also contains most of society associational life. The other is that government authority relies
more on inducing actions than it does on simply issuing commands. It is not
enough, then, to put good people into office. There is little they can do on their
own. Even their use of coercion depends on an actively supportive constituency.

If the restructuring of the economy is to be dealt with constructively, if urban
poverty and racial division are to be ameliorated, appropriate regimes are required,
that is, arrangements that combine government and nongovernment efforts. Building and maintaining appropriate urban regimes entails overcoming two related
barriers. One is the inherent difficulty of promoting policy change: The other is the
tendency for coalition formation to be guided by the availability of selective material incentives.

Machiavelli (1985, 23–24) captured the difficulty of innovation in *The Prince*,
observing:

> nothing is more difficult to handle, more doubtful of success, nor more dangerous to
> manage, than to put oneself at the head of introducing new orders. For the introducer
> has all those who benefit from the old order as enemies, and he has lukewarm defenders
> in all those who might benefit from the new orders. This lukewarmness arises partly

from fear of adversaries who have the laws on their side and partly from the incredulity of men, who do not truly believe in new things unless they come to have a firm experience of them.

If Machiavelli is right, the motivation to support change comes more easily after the fact, but political reality calls for active support as a precondition of basic policy change. The challenge for political leadership is how to make a new order believable before it is experienced, how to generate and maintain active support for "new things" before the public has had an opportunity "to have a firm experience of them." This is unlikely to be purely a matter of rhetoric; basic policy change is perhaps more likely through concrete efforts that demonstrate how small steps can cumulate into larger moves.

If few resources are readily available, the easiest regime to build is one devoted to the maintenance of routine services, but that would mean not responding to economic restructuring and its attendant social problems. Given a determination to act, the easiest response is a development regime. Of course, it may arouse neighborhood opposition and see proposals blocked, but it has the capacity to model proposals or present alternatives. The resilience of development policy lies partly in the selective incentives it generates. Development is not an all-or-nothing matter. It consists of an aggregate of discrete projects, each of which offers tangible and immediate benefits to the operational actors: They stand to receive contracts and fees as well as a chance to play a part in visible accomplishments. For operational actors especially, reinforcement is immediate. The general and long-term benefits may be in doubt, but the project is, nevertheless, visible and can be touted as an improvement. Tangible and immediate benefits to private actors (profits) can be tapped directly or indirectly to provide tangible and immediate benefits to public actors (e.g., campaign funds). Because the benefits are easily divisible, they can be used to bridge racial or other social divides and to bypass ideological differences.

Political leadership, that is, the creative exercise of political choice, is not about following the path of least resistance. In the case of urban regimes, it consists neither in doing nothing nor simply making use of the incentive already in place. It is about developing a larger view of what might be and then crafting the arrangements that advance that vision. After all, associational life is not built entirely on selective incentives and pursuit of material reward.

It should be possible to bring groups together around broader issues. Suburban communities, for example, often give public education top priority. How is this possible? Ideology seems to have little to do with it. Suburbs are communities in which civic participation is often oriented to family concerns such as education for their children. The suburban resident who is also a manager in a business corporation, as a suburban resident, has different priorities from those she or he might have as corporate official. Suburban civic participation is often organized around support for education through PTAs and related organizations. Participants come together in their role as proponents of a good school system. Their individual concerns are merged into a shared concern. Their tendency to be purposeful is given social expression. Furthermore, in middle-class suburbs, an educational thrust is a highly viable policy purpose, reinforced by the ready availability of both public revenue and a community environment that nurtures belief in the availability of opportunity and the social capital to take advantage of it.

In the city, if family concerns and concerns about the quality of community life are not given public expression, business profitability will fill the vacuum. Business interests control resources that can be devoted to civic activity, and business executives are based in an organizational setting that emphasizes obligations to stockholders and other business executives (Stinchcombe 1968, 181–86). In this setting, purpose is defined in terms of material gain and people cooperate in order to further material gain. If city policy is to pursue a wider agenda than development, then nonbusiness actors have to be brought into the regime. Participants, business and nonbusiness alike, must occupy roles that focus on social concerns and on ways of addressing those concerns, but social concerns cannot be sustained in a vacuum. Fiscal resources and concerted efforts to provide a supportive environment are also needed. In the affluent suburb, priority for education is easy; it can be built on strong supports in the private lives of residents and the tax base they provide. In the city, the coordination of public and private efforts requires effort and leadership skill. The political challenge is greater.

The development experience can be misleading. Because material incentives play a large part, it may appear that they play the only part. Similarly, because participation in an achievable small purpose is more attractive than participation in an unachievable large purpose, it may appear that only small purposes are attractive. In expanding policy choice, the role of political leadership is to weave material and nonmaterial incentives together and to combine achievable small purposes in a way that contributes to a large purpose.

In his analysis of organizational leadership, Chester Barnard (1968, 284) said, "the morality that underlies enduring cooperation is multidimensional." Contrary to the assumptions of some analysts, cooperation is not an unnatural act that people have to be coerced or bribed to perform. To be sure, the centrifugal force of individual interest and immediately achievable purpose have to be reckoned with, but there is also the possibility of tapping the human yearning for a larger social purpose. Indeed, Barnard (1968, 282) argues, without a larger purpose, an organization is likely to be short lived.

If freedom consists of being able to exercise choice, political freedom for American cities requires a capacity to build regimes with broad agendas. For that to happen, urban political leaders have to envision the city as more than a location for physical development, and they must be able to devise arrangements that involve nonbusiness elements of the community in governance. The weakness of formal authority leaves a vacuum that business interests have the ready resources to fill. The existence of progressive regimes, instances of community-based organizations, such as Baltimore's BUILD, and the capacity of suburbs to support alternative forms of civic cooperation all indicate that regimes capable of pursuing more inclusive agendas are possible. The creation of such regimes depends as much on what happens in the nongovernment sector as in the government sector. Ultimately, however, it depends on how and in what ways the two sectors are joined.

ACKNOWLEDGMENTS

For comments on an earlier draft, I am indebted to Susan Fainstein, John Mollenkopf, John Portz, Sanford, Mary Stone, Hal Wolman, and Austin Works. I also wish to thank Dean Sue M. Smock and the College of Urban, Labor, and Metropolitan Affairs of Wayne State University for a research appointment that enabled me to do the groundwork for this paper.

NOTE

"Urban Regimes and the Capacity to Govern: A Political Economy Approach," by Clarence N. Stone, *Journal of Urban Affairs*, Vol. 15, p. 1028. Reprinted with the permission of Blackwell Publishing.

REFERENCES

Abercrombie, N., S. Hill, and B. S. Turner. 1980. *The dominant ideology thesis.* London: Allen and Unwin.
Allison, G. T. 1971. *Essence of decision.* Boston: Little, Brown.
Arendt, H. 1961. *Between past and future.* Cleveland: Meridian Books.
Badie B., and P. Birnhauni. 1983. *The sociology of the state.* Chicago: Univ. of Chicago Press.
Banfield, E. C. 1961. *Political influence.* New York: Free Press.
Banfield, E. C., and J. Q. Wilson. 1963. *City politics.* Cambridge, Mass.: Harvard Univ. Press.
Barnard, C. I. 1968. *The functions of the executive.* Cambridge, Mass.: Harvard Univ. Press.
Baumgartner, F. R., and B. D. Jones. 1991. Agenda dynamics and policy subsystems. *Journal of Politics* 53:1044–74.
Bernick, M. 1987. *Urban illusions.* New York: Praeger Press.
Body-Gendrot, S. N. 1987. Grass-roots mobilization in the Thirteenth Arrondisement of Paris. In *The politics of urban development,* ed. C. N. Stone and H. T. Sanders. Lawrence: Univ. Press of Kansas.
Burns, J. M. 1978. *Leadership.* New York: Harper and Row.
Chong, D. 1991. *Collective action and the civil rights movement.* Chicago: Univ. of Chicago Press.
Clavel, P. 1986. *The progressive city.* New Brunswick, N.J.: Rutgers Univ. Press.

Clegg, S. R. 1989. *Frameworks of power.* Newbury Park, Calif.: Sage Publications.

Cohen, M. I., and J. G. March. 1986. *Leadership and ambiguity.* 2nd ed. Boston: Harvard Business School Press.

Conrov, W. J. 1990. *Challenging the boundaries of reform: Socialism in Burlington.* Philadelphia: Temple Univ. Press.

Crenson, M. A. 1971. *The un-politics of air pollution.* Baltimore: Johns Hopkins Univ. Press.

———. 1983. *Neighborhood politics.* Cambridge, Mass.: Harvard Univ. Press.

Crick, B. 1982. *In defense of politics.* New York: Penguin Books.

Dahl, R. 1961. *Who governs?* New Haven, Conn.: Yale Univ. Press.

———. 1982. *Dilemmas of pluralist democracy.* New Haven, Conn.: Yale Univ. Press.

Darnton, R. 1989. What was revolutionary about the French Revolution? *New York Review of Books* (Jan. 19): 3ff.

DeLeon, R. E. 1990. The triumph of urban populism in San Francisco? Paper presented at the Annual Meeting of the American Political Science Association, San Francisco.

Elkin, S. L. 1987. *City and regime in the American republic.* Chicago: Univ. of Chicago Press.

Fainstein, S. S. 1990. Economies, polities, and development policy. In *Beyond the city limits,* ed. J. R. Logan and T. Swanstrom. Philadelphia: Temple Univ. Press.

Fainstein, S. S., and N. Fainstein. 1989. New York City: The Manhattan business district, 1945–1988. In *Unequal partnerships,* ed. G. Squires. New Brunswick, N.J.: Rutgers Univ. Press.

Fainstein, S. S., et al. 1986. *Restructuring the city: The political economy of urban development.* New York: Longman.

Fantasia, R. 1988. *Cultures of solidarity.* Berkeley: Univ. of California Press.

Ferman, B. 1985. *Governing the ungovernable.* Philadelphia: Temple Univ. Press.

Friedland, R. 1983. *Power and crisis in the city.* New York: Schoken Books.

Grafstein, R. 1992. Rational choice inside and out. *Journal of Politics* 54:259–68.

Hardin, R. 1982. *Collective action.* Baltimore: Johns Hopkins Univ. Press.

Henig, J. R. 1982. *Neighborhood mobilization.* New Brunswick, N.J.: Rutgers Univ. Press.

Jones, B. D., and L. W. Bachelor. 1986. *The sustaining hand.* Lawrence: Univ. Press of Kansas.

Kahn, M. E. 1986. *Middle class radicalism in Santa Monica.* Philadelphia: Temple Univ. Press.

Keating, M. 1991. *Comparative urban politics.* Hants, England: Edward Elgar Publishing.

Krasner, S. D. 1983. *International regimes.* Ithaca, N.Y.: Cornell Univ. Press.

Lindblom, C. E. 1977. *Politics and markets.* New York: Basic Books.

Logan, J. R., and H. L. Molotch. 1987. *Urban fortunes.* Berkeley: Univ. of California Press.

Machiavelli, N. 1985. *The prince.* Trans. H. C. Mansfield. Chicago: Univ. of Chicago Press.

March, J. G. 1966. The power of power. In *Varieties of political theory,* ed. D. Easton. Englewood Cliffs, N.J.: Prentice-Hall.

March, J. G., and H. A. Simon. 1965. *Organizations.* New York: John Wiley and Sons.

Margolis, H. 1990. Dual utilities and rational choice. In *Beyond self-interest,* ed. J. Mansbridge. Chicago: Univ. of Chicago Press.

Milgram, S. 1974. *Obedience to authority.* New York: Harper.

Mitchell, T. 1991. The limits of the state: Beyond statist approaches and their critics. *American Political Science Review* 85:77–96.

Moore, B. 1978. *Injustice: The social bases of obedience and revolt.* White Plains, N.Y.: M. E. Sharpe.

Muir, W. K. 1977. *Police: Streetcorner politicians.* Chicago: Univ. of Chicago Press.

Oppenheimer, J. 1975. Some political implications of vote trading and the voting paradox: A proof of logical equivalence. *American Political Science Review* 6:963–66.

Orr, M. E. 1991. Mayor Schmoke and the Baltimore regime. Paper presented at the Annual Meeting of the Urban Affairs Association, Vancouver, British Columbia.

Parsons, T. 1969. *Polities and social structure.* New York: Free Press.

Peterson, P. E. 1981. *City limits.* Chicago: Univ. of Chicago Press.

Pitkin, H. F. 1972. *Wittgenstein and justice.* Berkeley: Univ. of California Press.

Polanyi, K. 1957. *The great transformation: The political and economic origins of our times.* Boston: Beacon Press.

Polsby, N. W. 1980. *Community power and political theory: A further look at problems of evidence and inference.* New Haven, Conn.: Yale Univ. Press.

Rokkan, S. 1966. *Norway: Numerical democracy and corporate pluralism.* In *Political oppositions in western democracies,* ed. R. A. Dahl, 70–115. New Haven, Conn.: Yale Univ. Press.

Sanders, H. T. 1987. The politics of development in middle-sized cities. In *The politics of urban development,* ed. C. N. Stone and H. T. Sanders. Lawrence: Univ. Press of Kansas.

Sayre, W. S., and H. Kaufman. 1965. *Governing New York City.* New York: W. W. Norton.

Shearer, D. 1989. In search of equal partnerships. In *Unequal partnerships,* ed. G. D. Squires. New Brunswick, N.J.: Rutgers Univ. Press.

Shefter, M. 1976. The emergence of the political machine: An alternative view. In *Theoretical perspectives on urban politics,* ed. W. D. Hawley, et al. Englewood Cliffs, N.J.: Prentice-Hall.

———. 1985. *Political crisis/fiscal crisis: The collapse and revival of New York City.* New York: Basic Books.

Skocpol, T. 1985. *Bringing the state back in.* In *Bringing the state back in,* ed. P. B. Evans, D. Rueschemeyer, and T. Skocpol. New York: Cambridge Univ. Press.

Skowronek, S. 1982. *Building a new American state.* New York: Cambridge Univ. Press.

Smith, D. 1983. *Barrington A. Moore, Jr.: A critical appraisal.* Armonk, N.Y.: M. E. Sharpe.

Stinchcombe, A. L. 1968. *Constructing social theories.* Chicago: Univ. of Chicago Press.

Stone, C. N. 1988. Preemptive power: Floyd Hunter's "community power structure" reconsidered. *American Journal of Political Science* 32:82–104.

———. 1989a. *Regime politics: Governing Atlanta, 1946–1988.* Lawrence: Univ. Press of Kansas.

———. 1989b. Paradigms, power, and urban leadership. In *Leadership and politics,* ed. B. D. Jones. Lawrence: Univ. Press of Kansas.

———. 1990. Transactional and transforming leadership: A re-examination. Paper presented at the Annual Meeting of the American Political Science Association, San Francisco.

Stone, C. N., and H. T. Sanders. 1987. Reexamining a classic case of development politics: New Haven, Connecticut. In *The politics of urban development,* ed. C. N. Stone and H. T. Sanders. Lawrence: Univ. Press of Kansas.

Swanstrom, T. 1985. *The crisis of growth politics.* Philadelphia: Temple Univ. Press.

Tilly, C. 1984. *Big structures, large processes, huge comparisons.* New York: Russell Sage.

Wolfinger, R. E. 1974. *The politics of progress.* Englewood Cliffs, N.J.: Prentice-Hall.

Part Two
Urban Political Leadership

Much writing in urban politics takes the constraints, limitations, and complexities facing urban governments as its points of departure. From this vantage point, several conclusions are drawn that suggest that politics does not matter, and by implication, that leadership does not matter. The city, it has been concluded, has undergone transition and is limited and ungovernable. The extent of government action must be confined to the narrow purview of brokering, economic development, or that which is shaped by bureaucrats and technical experts. Clarence Stone takes a decisively different position. "Leadership," Stone and his coauthors write, "is not a process of presiding over what is inevitable. It is about making something happen that, given the ordinary course of events, would not occur" (Stone, Orr, and Imbroscio 1991, 236).

As noted in Part 1, a significant criticism that Clarence Stone has of the pluralist and economistic models are their limited appreciation for the role of politics. Politics surely matters and need not be subject to economic imperatives or the complexities of contemporary society. There are, to be sure, several options available, and uncontrollable forces do not confine these options, although they must be taken into consideration. Just as politics matters for Stone, leadership also matters and is a basic determinant of coalition building as well as the options that are likely to be pursued.

Stone is keenly aware of the manner in which models of urban politics have served as blinders in our understanding of leadership and urban governance. Assumptions about constraints, limitations, and complexities extract politics and leadership from local governance. In this regard, Stone's writing forges an alternative theoretical path and leads us to a broader understanding about the role of leaders, the leadership task, and the options that are available. Rather than ask what can't be done, Stone asks what can be done. How do urban actors (leaders) go about responding to the world as they experience it?

For Stone, governing coalitions are not static, and by extension, neither are leaders and policy responses. All are subject to modification based on challenges emanating from the world, either local or extralocal. In Stone's conception of urban governance, there is a significant place or role for market-based activities, government-based activities, civic- or voluntary-based activities, and community-based activities (be they racial, ethnic, or class based in character) as they arise. Neither is by necessity held hostage to the other. Each sphere of influence carries out activities in pursuit of its particular interests. But what happens when the interests of seemingly autonomous spheres collide and tension arises (the point at which autonomy is clearly seen as a faulty assumption)? For Stone, the answer rests not in some command-and-control structure, but rather in cooperation (a key element of governance)—a factor often promoted, or in some instances, hampered and/or attenuated by leadership.

In Chapter 5, Stone argues that our understanding of power and leadership in the local community is shaped by the paradigms we apply to the study of urban politics. These in turn affect the questions we ask. He examines the modernization paradigm (a new lens for an examination of the pluralist model) and the economistic paradigm to illustrate how they serve as blinders to a broader perspective of urban leadership. As is typical of his work, Stone once again departs from routine questions of mayoral skills and abilities inherent in the modernization and economistic paradigms, and he forges a path for a clearer understanding of the leadership task.

In Chapter 6, Stone clarifies our common definition of leadership and sets forth a number of characteristics from which we may better assess leadership performance. His conception of leadership is fluid, not static; intentional, not determinant; and interactive, not commanding. For Stone, leadership goes to the heart of politics, and because politics matters, leadership matters, affecting the capacity of people to work together on shared concerns.

REFERENCE

Stone, C. N., M. Orr, and D. Imbroscio. 1991. The reshaping of urban leadership in U.S. cities. In *Urban Life in Transition,* ed. M. Gottdiener and C. Pickvance, 222–39. Urban Affairs Annual Reviews 39. Thousand Oaks, Calif.: Sage Publications.

5. Paradigms, Power, and Urban Leadership

Clarence N. Stone

Leadership in the urban community has long been a subject of study. Classic examinations of community power, in particular Robert Dahl's *Who Governs?* (1961) and Edward C. Banfield's *Political Influence* (1961), are centrally concerned with leadership by elected executives. More recent studies, such as the *Ungovernable City* (1977) by Douglas Yates and *Governing the Ungovernable City* (1985) by Barbara Ferman, are similarly focused on mayoral leadership. Even writers who are concerned mainly with the impact of an impersonal market on city policy and politics, notably Paul Peterson in his influential *City Limits* (1981), contrast more effective and less effective forms of executive leadership. While there is a common tendency to treat leadership in highly personal terms, the lasting studies, such as those mentioned above, never stop at that. They show a high level of awareness of the context in which leadership is exercised, and they embody some underlying conception of what the leadership task is.

In this chapter, I want to follow in that tradition and to extend it. Specifically, I want to focus attention on the question of leadership's task, conceptions of power that are intertwined with that question, and the contextual dimension of power and leadership. I do not propose to talk in detail about these issues here. Instead, I want to consider how we come to think about these questions. In the following pages, I will argue that our understanding of power and leadership in the local community is shaped by the paradigms we apply to the study of urban politics. From an initial paradigm of modernization, we have moved to an economistic paradigm, and we now stand on the threshold of a regime paradigm. Each of these paradigms shapes how we look at power and what we think the nature of the leadership task is.

By focusing on paradigms, I aim to show not only why it is important to see urban leadership in broader terms than the skills and abilities of individuals who occupy the office of mayor, but also why it is important that we be fully aware of the conception of the leadership task that is embodied in our analyses. None of this is intended to deny that at the community level mayors are our most visible leaders. And I do not mean to characterize the personal qualities of mayors as inconsequential. They are significant. But I think the proper beginning point is the nature of the leadership task. To understand that, we must begin by looking at different

111

conceptions of the community and what its governance entails. As will be evident, my preference is for the regime paradigm. At the same time, I hope to show that there are connecting threads that tie the regime paradigm to its predecessors.

THE MODERNIZATION PARADIGM

As I indicated above, two of the most important books in urban political science are Robert Dahl's study of New Haven, *Who Governs?*, and Edward Banfield's study of Chicago, *Political Influence*. Both did much to focus attention on mayoral leadership, and both rightly are considered pillars of pluralism. My labeling of them here as pillars also of the modernization paradigm may strike some readers as odd or even perverse. Why talk about a modernization paradigm when pluralism is already a widely used and much discussed term?

One reason for talking about a modernization paradigm is that it is indeed a new label—one that I hope will enable readers to see some classics in a new light. A second reason for using the term "modernization" is to emphasize that both Dahl and Banfield saw urban politics in a context of social change. Neither saw city politics as static. Dahl, in particular, made extensive use of a historical perspective. For Banfield, too, although the point is made more emphatically in the book he coauthored with James Q. Wilson (1963), city politics is to be understood as an activity shaped by the transition from a traditional ethos of private regardingness to a modern ethos of public regardingness. For example, in Banfield's eyes, Mayor Richard Daley was not merely a skillful broker of particular conflicts; he was also the master broker between Chicago's tradition-minded inner wards and its modern-minded outer wards (1961, 246–47). Dahl made a related argument. He described New Haven's move away from politics based on ethnic conflict, arguing that assimilation had blurred the class character of the original cleavage between Yankee Protestant and Catholic immigrants. Dahl's counterpart to public regardingness is the set of policies that New Haven's Mayor Richard Lee engineered, policies that emphasized "shared benefits to citizens in general rather than specific categories" (Dahl 1961, 61). As further evidence of the change away from the old ethnic-based politics of patronage, Dahl suggested that the significant new actors so visible under Mayor Lee were professionally qualified program specialists. Dahl (1961, 62) concluded that the new power actors "in local politics may very well prove to be bureaucrats and experts—and politicians who know how to use them." These new figures in New Haven politics received follow-up study in books by Raymond Wolfinger (1974) and Russell Murphy (1971).

Banfield gave less attention to bureaucrats and experts, but he nevertheless described the Chicago political landscape in "modernized" terms. He did not ignore the machine, of course, but he did not make it the center of his explanation of city policy. Instead he observed that civic controversies, from which policy in Chicago grew, arose "out of the maintenance and enhancement needs of large formal organizations" (Banfield 1961, 263). He, like Dahl, saw these issues as being resolved in a context of popular control and against a background of consensus on fundamentals.

For reasons that I will explore below, both Banfield and Dahl treated urban politics as a matter of many small, nonclass conflicts. If the two differed much, it is that Dahl placed more emphasis on the autonomy of political leaders and their capacity to activate latent support for an ambitious policy agenda. New Haven's entrepreneurial mayor, Richard Lee, stands in contrast to Chicago's political broker, Mayor Richard Daley. Whereas Dahl (1961, 6) talked about the "potential of the cunning, resourceful, and masterful leader," Banfield (1961, 270–71) offered a classic rendition of pluralist brokerage:

> According to the Chicago view, a policy ought to be framed by the interests affected, not by the political head or his [this was before Jane Byrne's mayoralty] agents. In this view, the affected interests should work out for themselves the "best" solution of the matter (usually a compromise). The political head should see that all principally affected interests are represented, that residual interests (i.e., "the general public") are not entirely disregarded, and that no interest suffers unduly in the outcome.

Of course, it was easier to talk in such terms as the 1950s came to a close—the time in which Banfield and Dahl wrote their classics. At that time, the mayors of New Haven and Chicago seemed to represent the spectrum of effective city leadership. The urban scene, after all, appeared basically tranquil, with issues confined largely to narrow-gauge conflicts between the parties immediately affected by particular policies. Yet it would be highly unfair to Banfield and Dahl to suggest that they were merely reporting what was visible at the time. Their analyses were much too penetrating for that. To be sure, their conceptual "blinders" prevented them from foreseeing the turmoil ahead, but they were still able to probe an underlying character of political arrangements. For this reason, we need to consider further the label "modernization" as an adjective for the paradigm they employed.

Modernization

Modernization can be defined in various ways. Banfield, in particular in his work with James Q. Wilson, talked about urban conflict primarily in terms of a cleavage between a provincial and tradition-minded ethos linked to machine politics and a cosmopolitan and modern-minded ethos linked to good government reform.[1] This cleavage, rather than class or racial conflict, was the focus of Banfield and Wilson's (1963) understanding of city politics. Dahl differed mainly in placing more emphasis on consensus than on conflict. Yet while both Banfield and Dahl were much influenced by the concern with political culture and political socialization so prevalent at the time they were writing, both also had a more profound understanding of what modernization is about.

For both, modernization meant social differentiation and a high level of role specialization. That understanding of modernization informed their understanding of conflict: for them, conflict occurred along lines of highly refined social differentiation, not along the broad break of class associated with early industrialization. Perhaps the key sentence in Dahl's *Who Governs?* is this: "political heterogeneity follows socioeconomic heterogeneity" (1961, 59).

From the early differentiation between social notables and business elites to Mayor Lee's introduction of program experts and policy professionals into an increasingly middle-class community, Dahl's New Haven story is about how socioeconomic heterogeneity fosters political heterogeneity and forms the foundation for a pluralist distribution of power. In *Political Influence*, Banfield (1961, 252) was much less historical; nevertheless, he reached the related conclusion that "Chicago is too big a place, and the interests in it too diverse, for agreement to occur very often."

According to both Dahl and Banfield, social differentiation causes fragmentation, and the political task is to cope with that fragmentation. According to Banfield (1961, 258), Daley accomplished this by being the master broker. He brokered a necessary amount of cooperation in a community with "limitless opportunities for obstruction." For Dahl, Mayor Lee was an extraordinary public leader because he created an executive-centered coalition capable of promoting a broad program of action. According to Dahl (1961, 204) this program generated substantial popular support, and it represented a major achievement because it was brought about in a situation in which "the centrifugal forces in the system were . . . persistent and powerful." Lee's political skill was evident in his ability to prevent the elements in his coalition "from flying off in all directions" (Dahl 1961, 204) despite a natural tendency to do so.

Power as a Cost-of-Compliance Problem

Both Banfield and Dahl base their view of power on this view of modernization as a fragmenter of social life. For both of them, power represents a cost-of-compliance problem. They draw on the Weberian formulation that power is the capacity of A to get B to do what B would not otherwise do. Seen in this way, power in a complex system is inevitably distributed in a pluralist pattern. As Dahl (1982, 33) has argued, "control is almost always to some extent costly to the ruler." To obtain B's compliance A has to expend resources. Banfield (1961, 241) observed: "In a system in which the political head must continually 'pay' to overcome formal decentralization and to acquire the authority he needs, the stock of influence in his possession cannot all be 'spent' as he might wish." Given that compliance never comes free of charge, one can argue that control, particularly in a formally democratic system, can be exercised only over a small domain and a limited range of activities, especially if more than a thin level of compliance is being sought (Dahl 1982, 32–36; see also Wrong 1980).

The linking of this line of argument to Weber's definition of power is notable. In a premodern world, control might be expanded by sacred myth, but Weber argues that the modern world has been "disenchanted." Furthermore, in such a world, a world of instrumental rationality, specialists acquire autonomy as their expertise removes them from effective control by their superiors.[2] When functional specialists are brought together bureaucratically, Dahl (1982, 33) reminds us that formal organizations develop an impulse toward independence. Compliance is costly because, in Chester Barnard's terminology, the zone of indifference for most people most of the time is quite narrow. Achieving compliance requires some kind of reciprocal benefit, in the absence of a pervasive system of coercion, which itself would be costly to maintain. According to Banfield (1961, 313), "the terms upon which control may be acquired (assuming that it may be acquired at all) are established through a process of bargaining." Dahl (1961, 89) adds that "the relationship between leaders and citizens in a pluralist democracy is frequently reciprocal."

Banfield's view of the virtual impossibility of achieving broad-scale control and coordination eventually became a foundation of neoconservative skepticism about liberal social reform. From Jeffrey L. Pressman and Aaron Wildavsky's (1984) complexity of joint action to Charles Morris's (1980) critique of Mayor John Lindsay's "arrogant overreachings," the message is that overambitious executives who are not mindful of the intractable character of social problems invite disappointment and defeat, if not outright disaster. In *The Ungovernable City*, Douglas Yates (1977, 146–65) tamed the rhetoric considerably and the argument a little, but his street-fighting pluralism is in the same vein. Mayors with limited resources should not undertake social crusades.

Dahl's *Who Governs?* is connected to a somewhat different line of thought. It is, I contend, a contributor to an economistic paradigm, as exemplified in Paul Peterson's *City Limits*. Before turning to that discussion, let me summarize what I have said about the modernization paradigm and the view of power and leadership it encourages.

Summary

According to Thomas Kuhn (1970), a paradigm provides a set of assumptions and a way of seeing the world. Because the assumptions themselves play a part in what we see, or perhaps more importantly, what we do not see, observation is never pure observation. It is colored by predisposition. That is the case with the modernization paradigm no less so than with others.

The modernization paradigm holds that the contemporary world is characterized by a high level of social differentiation and that the differentiated actors in this world (whether they be individuals, informal groups, formal organizations, or some larger social entity) enjoy considerable autonomy. The prevailing force is centrifugal: it is a natural tendency for complex arrangements to come apart. Imposing order and coordination on this world is difficult; achieving compliance is costly. No matter how skillful leaders are, they must have substantial resources, and even then, they lead mainly by bargaining and consent. Because control is costly, coalitions tend to be unstable. Typically they form and dissolve, issue by issue. In this pluralist scenario, a comprehensive plan of control is virtually impossible. Because subjects of power exercises are autonomous, they can resist and drive up the cost of obtaining their compliance. No elite group can monopolize sufficient resources and command enough know-how to establish a large and effective domain of control. Leadership consists of the capacity to mediate conflicts, to bargain in order to overcome differences by using mutually beneficial cooperation, and to anticipate what will garner popular approval. It follows, some might argue, that an overly ambitious agenda of public action will result in frustration. Neoconservatives were quick to use that characterization for liberal social reformers such as Mayor John Lindsay in New York. Furthermore, it could be argued that public officials, appointed as well as elected, have a self-serving interest in expanding public activity and that if that propensity is not curbed, society will suffer from political overload (see, e.g., Bruce-Briggs 1979).

THE ECONOMISTIC PARADIGM

Whereas the modernization paradigm offers a complex world in which centrifugal movement is prevalent, the economistic paradigm pictures the world as a market. Here also there is no command center and, in some respects, leadership does not much matter. The mobility of investment capital is the dominant feature, and the laws of the market shape the world. The primary exposition of this view is Paul Peterson. It should be noted that his *City Limits* acknowledges a debt not only to public-choice economists but also to structural Marxism (Peterson 1981, xii).

Structural Marxism, as the name implies, plays down the role of leadership in favor of attention to the laws of economic development. Structuralism is not the only Marxist position now current, but to try to unravel the various strands of Marxism and the process by which a new appreciation of autonomous state action has evolved would take us too far afield.[3] Suffice it for now to say that Marxism holds that cities are among the entities that are compelled to some degree to promote investment and thus to facilitate capital accumulation. This need to attract investment encourages the exploitation of have-nots and, in general, elevates the exchange value of property over its use value (Harvey 1973). While those who are exploited by this process can counter it to some extent by engaging in a struggle to challenge the social legitimacy of the established order, the most telling imperative is that of capital accumulation (Fainstein and Fainstein 1982).

Peterson's *City Limits* is a purer rendition of the economistic paradigm for urban politics. In Peterson's account, the federal system produces an intergovernmental division of labor in which cities are particularly subject to the forces of economic competition. Cities are impelled to be highly responsive to investment interests, and for this reason, they avoid progressive measures of redistribution. The national government is therefore the body most responsive to social-welfare needs (Peterson, Rabe, and Wong 1986).

Peterson's formulation of the city's position in the larger political economy is particularly significant for its bearing on his treatment of power and leadership. First, insofar as developmental policy and social welfare are concerned, he gives little emphasis to the particular conflicts that are such a pervasive part of the pluralist world depicted in the modernization paradigm. Peterson confines conflict to the arena of allocational policies (service distribution and employment rules). For the remainder, as "shareholders" in the city, citizens have a unitary interest in developmental policy and in avoiding welfare responsibilities as well. From this it follows, in Peterson's words:

> In the development arena, power is not best understood as a "zero sum" game, where one person or group wins at the expense of another. Instead, power is better understood in systemic terms; it is the capacity of the community as a whole to realize its objectives. What is needed is not so much the capacity to enforce one's will over others as the leadership ability that can persuade others to contribute to a common cause (Peterson 1981, 148).

As an example of such leadership, Peterson turns to New Haven's Mayor Richard Lee. Because Dahl had described Lee, particularly in promoting redevelopment, as someone who activated latent support, Lee's leadership appears to be that of a facilitator rather than an overrider of opposition. Peterson's view of the social context, unlike the Marxist view, defines away conflict. Playing on Dahl's view of Mayor Lee as someone who activated latent support, Peterson transforms power from a cost-of-compliance problem to an efficiency problem. The transformation requires only that conflict not be present to a significant degree.

How does the community best act to further its shared interest in economic advancement? The external threat of economic competition presumably makes business executives and other relevant actors amenable to mayoral persuasion. Besides, Peterson adds, support for development enables business executives to enhance their reputations as civic leaders: "The politics of development is particularly enticing to otherwise apolitical businessmen, because successful effort on behalf of a project that benefits the community as a whole has a halo effect" (Peterson 1981, 142).

Peterson's formulation bypasses the cost-of-compliance issue by defining the situation as consensual. This transforms the problem from one of overcoming opposition to one of surmounting the free-rider problem—how to get individuals to exert themselves on behalf of a collective good. This is the efficiency problem. Working deductively, Peterson solves the problem by positing an individual interest on the part of business executives in enhancing their reputations as civic leaders and in achieving a halo effect. Significantly, Peterson's argument is silent on the individual and group gains that may accrue from developmental projects. Civic reputations and halo effects fit nicely with a non-zero-sum scenario of power, and similarly, persuasion appears to be appropriate for the leadership role. By contrast, consideration of particular gains and benefits invites questions about who bears the costs and how economic losers in development fit into the picture. Focusing on these issues poses a different kind of leadership challenge, one that the economistic paradigm does not highlight. As Kuhn maintained, paradigms have a propensity to direct attention to some questions and facts and away from others. The economistic paradigm is no exception.

Taking Stock

Paradigm-guided research—which all research is according to Kuhn—is a mixture of assumptions and observations. Kuhn also suggests that each paradigm enables us to answer some questions but not others. A paradigm is ascendant as long as it directs attention to interesting questions and holds some promise of yielding answers. But as new questions emerge, perhaps from anomalous findings that become increasingly hard to dismiss, the ground is prepared for a paradigm shift. It should be remembered that a paradigm shift does not mean that findings from a previous paradigm have been invalidated; it only means that a new way of looking at the world is being attempted with the hope of generating new findings that bear on more pressing questions. This is not the occasion to try to trace the intellectual origins of the various paradigms, but it is in order to give some brief indication of how the modernization and economistic paradigms fit into the historical context. The modernization paradigm, with its pluralist scenario, could explain a world in which urban conflict was relatively low key and in which the most visible cleavage was between city machines and good-government reformers. With the eruption of more intense conflict during the 1960s and the emergence of sharp cleavages along racial lines, the conventional modernization paradigm no longer seemed adequate. The political-overload/street-fighting pluralism modification had some appeal for a time, but a subsequent lessening of overt conflict and a lowering of political temperatures left that revised version of the modernization paradigm with little to offer as a research agenda.

Marxism could explain conflict and even fluctuations in the intensity of conflict, but it faced several difficulties, not the least of which was its dubious legitimacy in the larger political arena. Marxism's appeal historically was tied to its joining of theory and practice. Structural Marxism does that poorly, all the more so when the political tide is running against radical change and events offer no promise of a crisis capable of supporting system transformation. At least in its vulgar interpretation, structural Marxism provides weak ground for political involvement and plays down the role of leadership.[4] It is not surprising, then, that some Marxist scholars have moved toward an increasingly flexible notion of the autonomy of politics and, I would argue, toward a renewed respect for the work of Max Weber.[5] This line of intellectual development has merged with historical sociology and is one of the sources that feeds the emerging paradigm of regime theory (Abrams 1982; Skocpol 1984; Tilly 1981).

Paul Peterson's *City Limits* represents a different line of development. As the most influential work in the economistic paradigm, *City Limits* has an affinity with public choice as a school of thought. But that is not its primary appeal. Indeed, as indicated above, *City Limits*, by focusing on the city as a corporate unit and what is rational for that unit, fails to probe very much into the incentives that motivate individuals. It does not answer the question of why, given that behavior generally is to be understood as a matter of expedient self-interest, individuals would act on behalf of some larger good.[6]

Still, *City Limits* has a twofold appeal. It provides a plausible account of federalism from the New Deal up to recent years. Specifically, it suggests why city governments in particular are unreceptive to assuming responsibilities for welfare. It also offers an explanation of the tendency for city officials and business executives to form a close working alliance, including those circumstances in which a mobilized black electorate succeeds in putting a black mayor in city hall. Peterson's achievement is a significant one, strengthened by the fact that he has put together a parsimonious and logically consistent argument.

There are chinks in Peterson's armor, however. It is a deductive argument, and close observation of the facts turns up anomalies. Peterson's argument about cities in the federal system is ahistorical; it fails to account for a pre–New Deal period in which urban machines were more responsive to welfare concerns than the national government was (Erie 1988). Moreover, the present era of Republican presidential ascendancy, in which New Deal priorities have been overturned and megadeficits have put a squeeze on social spending, also fits poorly Peterson's view of federalism.

At the city level itself, Peterson's argument characterizes developmental policy as consensual, based on the city's unitary interest in economic advancement. Again, the facts fit imperfectly. Conflict often surrounds development, and much of the dispute involves the issue of which policy is best for the city (see Stone and Sanders 1987). Perhaps the most telling anomaly is the fact that urban-development policies have not diminished urban poverty and cities are characterized by segmented economies in which a large proportion of the population appears to be blocked away from the benefits of economic growth and change.[7] A final specific inadequacy is that Peterson describes urban leadership as being engaged primarily in persuasion. Especially when viewed historically, that appears to be an anemic way of picturing the role of leadership.

This description and assessment of the modernization and economistic paradigms have focused on particular features and specific anomalies. The two paradigms also share a general feature, which I regard as more serious than anomalous findings. Neither points to the question of abuse of power, and that strikes me as a serious inadequacy. To be sure, structural Marxism focuses on class exploitation as the inevitable consequence of capitalism. But that is much too sweeping and too general to serve very well as a basis for evaluating specific urban regimes and their performance. It condemns a system, not the actions of specific agents within that system. To be sure, the Marxist response to this observation is to say, "That is the point." I beg off debating the issue on this occasion by asserting simply that we have choices less grand than acceptance or rejection of capitalism. To talk about urban regimes, as I propose to do, is to consider how local political arrangements are put together and altered. These arrangements can be more representative or less so. Put another way, they can be more faction dominated or less so. In the Madisonian tradition, we have a responsibility to try to make them less so. The first step is to consider how factionalism and representativeness are at issue. This is the question that regime theory addresses, and the modernization and economistic paradigms do not.

In the case of the modernization paradigm, the conception of power as a matter of command and compliance treats abuse of authority as an unlikely event. Leaders can be unskillful and ineffective, but in the pluralist scenario overreaching the proper bounds of power in the service of factional advancement is seen as untenable over the long run. The dispersion of power assures that. Resistance can always drive up the cost of control and undercut the position of those who abuse their power.

The economistic paradigm treats power in a similar manner. In the developmental arena (redistributive policy is the opposite side of the same coin), Peterson explicitly refuses to treat power as the ability to enforce one's will over others. Instead, power is defined as a system capacity to act—it is "power to" rather than "power over." The challenge facing leaders is how to aggregate efforts for a common purpose. Viewed in this way, leadership can fail. It can, as in the pluralist scenario, be unskillful and ineffective, but there is no strong reason to worry about abuses of authority, because power is not defined as the capability of one element of the community to dominate and exploit another.

To treat power and leadership as a matter of efficiency undercuts the critical role of analysis. To be sure, the economistic perspective can serve to question how effective a city is in the developmental efforts it makes. But economics is an efficiency-driven discipline; it never speaks with confidence about matters of equity. It has little to say about conflict, and it tends to see politics as irrational (see, e.g., Schultze 1977). Consequently, economics often treats equity as subordinate to efficiency. The favored rhetoric, whether in popular or technical terms, is that which talks about policies that result in virtually no one's being worse off and at least some being better off—hence, Peterson defines power in the developmental arena as non–zero sum.

That the modernization and economistic paradigms fail to direct attention to the possibility of the abuse of power does not mean that these paradigms have taught us nothing. By focusing on power as a cost-of-compliance problem, the modernization paradigm shows us that an elite group is unlikely to control a community by means of coercion and deception. By focusing on the need to aggregate efforts in support of a common purpose, the economistic paradigm indicates that authority can serve a worthy purpose and, indeed, that weak or ineffective authority can be detrimental to a community's well-being. What is needed, then, is a paradigm that (1) shows how power can be concentrated, although not in the form of a centralized command-and-control structure and (2) appreciates the good that authority can do while making us mindful of the ways in which it can be abused. A regime paradigm, coupled with the concept of preemptive power, can, I believe, meet these two needs (see Stone 1988).

Urban Regimes

Regime theory has many antecedents. Martin Shefter's (1976; see also Shefter 1985) reinterpretation of machine politics; Harvey Molotch's (1976) work on "the growth machine"; John Mollenkopf's (1983) analysis of coalition building at the national level; the study of political incorporation by Rufus Browning, Dale Rogers Marshall, and David Tabb (1984); a general body of literature on historical sociology with its roots in Marx and Weber; "the two faces of power" argument by Peter

Bachrach and Morton Baratz (1970), the discussion of sectarchy by Bryan Jones and Lynn Bachelor (1986); and the work of Stephen D. Krasner (1983) and others in international politics—all are among the contributors to this emerging paradigm. Important as these various works are, the two sources I have found most compelling are Floyd Hunter's (1953) *Community Power Structure*, as an antecedent of preemptive power, and Stephen L. Elkin's (1980; 1985) formulation of urban regimes as arising in a political-economy context. Hunter's work I will return to later. Elkin's contribution is at the heart of the concept of regime itself.

According to Elkin, the task facing those who would govern is one of putting together arrangements that cope with the division of labor between state and economy. This means satisfying the principle of popular control of public authority while fostering a climate suitable for investment by privately controlled capital. Elkin thus takes into account the economic imperative that is so central in Peterson's analysis, but he does not treat it as a single, overriding determinant. Regime character is formed by an accommodation between the need for private investment and a community's political arrangements. Furthermore, this accommodation is not merely coexistence. Business interests attempt to shape politics, and they possess important political resources in their efforts. In the other part of this accommodation, along with seeking popular support, political actors pursue strategies that affect investment; governmental decisions do much to shape investment opportunities.

While accommodation is essential, the relationship between these two centers of activity is fraught with tension. Under regime theory, political conflict ceases to appear as an irrational distraction from the pursuit of a community's well-being. Instead, because community well-being involves an accommodation between two principles, one largely economic and the other political, struggle can be seen as the natural result of efforts by various groups to shape that accommodation on terms that are favorable to their interests. Conflict is thus part of the struggle to determine how the two principles, though in tension with one another, will be reconciled. While the structural boundaries of this struggle are set by the political-economy context, any particular settlement is subject to alteration. A change in either the economic situation or the political landscape can result in new or modified arrangements. The regime paradigm is therefore particularly well suited to consider questions of political change and continuity—change originating either in the economic or in the political sphere and continuity based in the persistence of a structural relationship.

Implicit in this view of the urban community is an understanding of leadership as an activity that involves the creation, maintenance, and modification of a governing regime—the prevailing arrangements through which economic and political imperatives are accommodated. As in the previous two paradigms, the leadership task is intertwined with a conception of power, and I now turn to that discussion.

Preemptive Power

Elsewhere I have spelled out the connection between the concept of preemptive power and Floyd Hunter's community power structure; I won't repeat that discussion here (Stone 1988). I will, however, remind the reader that the basic argument of Hunter's original study is quite compatible with the current emphasis on political economy. In looking at Atlanta, Hunter observed a formal division of authority between the public arena of government and the private arena of business ownership and investment. This formal division, Hunter argued, was bridged by an informal structure, for which he coined the phrase "community power structure." In an argument parallel to Robert K. Merton's (1957) analysis of the latent functions of the machine, Hunter argued that this informal structure persisted because it met a community need for leadership, for some group capable of responding to social change and of easing various forms of friction in the community. Leadership consists of devising adaptive responses and mobilizing community resources so as to put those responses into effect. Note that Hunter does not argue that this group runs the community in command-and-control fashion. He is arguing only that some group keeps an eye on the need to modify community practices and puts together efforts to adopt what it regards as essential new policies (cf. Selznick 1957). This is the leadership function, which Hunter found in Atlanta to be filled by an informal structure that he regarded as highly unrepresentative.

The conception of power surrounding this leadership role is what I call preemptive power, and it involves two aspects. One is the power advantage that comes from occupying that role and being able to take the initiative and to frame proposed actions as *community* responses—to say, in effect, if the community acts, then its action will take *this* form. Alternative proposals can be and are made, but they are often piecemeal, or they may be attempts to veto proposed actions. Rarely are they part of a broad effort to exercise governing responsibilities. More importantly, even if they are broadly conceived, proponents may command too few resources to make them viable. That brings us to the second aspect of preemptive power, the capacity to hold together enough resources and positions of institutional strength to foreclose any rival group or coalition from exercising the power of governance. This is the least understood and least explored aspect of preemptive power. Yet it is precisely this capacity to bring together *and hold together* a coalition capable of exercising governing responsibilities that is at the heart of the concept of preemptive power. Interestingly enough, Hunter views this situation as contingent. His argument is not that an elite group inevitably dominates. Instead, he maintains that the insider coalition controls the leadership function not only because it is well endowed with resources but also because it works at making the most politically (in a broad sense) of these resources. Those on the outside are too fragmented, uninformed, and apathetic to counter the insider monopoly of the capacity to govern.

There are three sets of institutions that are key to the capacity to govern. Government itself is only one. Corporate business is a second, and Hunter regards it as inevitable that business interests will be part of any effective governing coalition. The third arena is the network of civic organizations which conducts much of the public debate on policy issues and harnesses and directs much of the volunteer activity in the community. *Community Power Structure* describes how business control extended to that arena in the Atlanta of the period immediately after World War II. It is in that arena, Hunter believed, that business presence could be, but was not, countered by a broader set of community interests.

In harmony with Bachrach and Baratz, one can argue within the regime paradigm that leadership has two faces. One is a policy face, leadership engaged in deciding particular policy questions. The other is a regime face, leadership engaged in creating, maintaining, and modifying the de facto governing arrangements of the community.

Regime leadership is important because formal public authority is weak. The operating assumption of the regime paradigm is that the authority of a community's official government is too weak to govern autonomously. As we have come to appreciate, a winning electoral coalition is not the same as a coalition capable of governing.[8] Consequently, a governing coalition can be created only by putting together an informal structure that joins public and private resources and institutions.

The question that this conclusion raises, then, is one of how the membership in the governing coalition is determined. That is what preemptive power is about, and a political-economy perspective on this question becomes important in providing an explanation for why significant business involvement is essential. Business control of credit and investment activity is simply too important to be bypassed.

The matter doesn't end there, however, because the question of popular control and the involvement of civic and community organizations of various kinds has much to do with exactly how the governing regime is shaped and how it conducts itself. Political and economic actors need to achieve cooperation. On the one side, business investment is intertwined with a variety of publicly provided services and facilities. On the other side, economic growth is a popular campaign theme. However, cooperation is not automatic. What everyone agrees on in the abstract quickly becomes a source of friction when it is made concrete. Group conflict and personal aspirations stand as formidable obstacles to any collective effort. Under these conditions, it is no easy task to see that policy goals are articulated and resources mobilized behind them. For a community to be governed, group conflict must be managed and personal ambition harnessed. Although governance does not entail comprehensive control, it does require that cooperation and exchange occur and that critical decisions be made (cf. Selznick 1957). That is what urban regimes are about, and it is through civic organizations and informal networks that much of the essential cooperation, exchange, and consequent mobilization of resources occurs.

The capacity to exercise leadership—whether preemptively or not—thus depends heavily on a community's associational life. The creation and shaping of networks of cooperation and exchange are important aspects of regime leadership, and such activities are not necessarily tied to the mayor's office.

Within the regime paradigm, leadership is a complex activity, occurring at various stages. The regime paradigm assumes that a stable structure of cooperation and exchange is widely useful to urban communities. That being the case, any coalition capable of providing that structure is powerful because of that fact. Community dependence on such a structure undergirds that power.[9] However, the members of the governing coalition are preemptively powerful only to the extent that they are able to monopolize enough resources and positions of institutional strength to prevent themselves from being displaced by a rival structure of cooperation and exchange. The difficulty of changing such a structure is what gives the incumbent coalition its distinctive power. If that structure can be changed easily, it holds no preemptive advantage.

It is important, then, to see that a preemptive advantage is contingent. This advantage can be modified. Moved one way, the situation heightens factional domination of the structure of cooperation and exchange. Moved another way, that role becomes more representative. Thus the regime paradigm puts business's role in community governance in a light quite different from the one shed by the economistic paradigm. Whereas Peterson sees the alliance between business leaders and city officials as an effort to promote the city's economic interest efficiently, the regime paradigm sees the potential for factional exploitation in such an arrangement, unless it is expanded to include a broad representation of community interests.

The question of representation assumes special importance in the regime paradigm because it is assumed that the policy face of leadership is governed by the regime face. Policy is shaped by the composition of the governing coalition *and* by the terms on which its members are related to one another. Put another way, because membership in the governing coalition is so coveted, members have a strong incentive to maintain the coalition, and its maintenance needs thus help to shape policy.

The reader should bear in mind that the preemptive-power argument does not hold that the governing coalition is free to control the tides of social change and to impose any policy solution of its own choosing. The claim is the much more modest one that the governing coalition shapes policy responses to social change. Its control is only that of adaptive *responses*; it does not control the *sources* of social and economic change.

The preemptive-power argument further holds that adaptive responses are always partial and incomplete. Policy is made by an unending succession of attempts to cope satisfactorily with an ongoing process of change. The process is very much one of trial and error, with the governing coalition determining not only which trials will be made, but also deciding what constitutes an error. If the governing coalition is inadequately representative, then its capacity to detect error is also inadequate. As Pressman and Wildavsky (1984, 135) observed in their study of implementation: "Learning fails because events are caused and consequences are felt by different organizations." If the governing coalition is a mediating agent between such external forces as economic competition among localities, or various forms of social change, on the one side, and, on the other side, the impact of these changes on the mass public, then representation becomes enormously important. This is the reason regime composition and preemptive advantage are worth studying. The argument I am making, it should be noted, assumes that the response to external pressures, such as economic competition and various social changes, are political; they do not possess a technically defined character. The regime argument assumes there is no one best way, dictated by known facts. Priorities are too much at issue and policy solutions are too uncertain for technical solutions to hold sway.

The regime paradigm thus has us look at leadership in a way different from both the economistic and the modernization paradigms. Efficiency or effectiveness in countering centrifugal forces is not enough. It is by no means rendered irrelevant—a governing coalition still faces the challenge of being effective. But regime leadership is also subject to the critical test of how representative are the arrangements that it creates and maintains.

Regime leadership is also much broader than mayoral leadership. When elected executives assume office, they confront an established set of civic relationships—formal and informal organizations within the business community and within the broader community as well. Business and other community-based leaders constitute part of the force that shapes these civic relationships, and these relationships, I have suggested, are a major element in the picture of preemptive power.

Faced with a limited base of resources and a need for showing quick results, a newly elected mayor is to a great extent bound by existing civic relationships. Unusual skill and timely circumstances may afford a mayor some opportunity to reshape those relationships. Richard Daley, Fiorello La Guardia, Richard Lee, and John Lindsay are among the mayors who appear to have been able to achieve some reshaping. But the preemptive-power argument tells us not to restrict our atten-

tion to the holders of governmental office. Other community actors are also important. Race relations in Atlanta, for example, have been powerfully shaped by business leadership (Stone 1986). In Flint, Michigan, the Charles S. Mott Foundation
plays a central part in community affairs (Jones and Bachelor 1986, 183–84). In Minnesota's Twin Cities, foundations and such business-backed organizations as the
Citizens League play a major role in setting the civic agenda (Brandl and Brooks
1982). The examples could be multiplied.

THE REGIME PARADIGM AND REGIME LEADERSHIP

Regime leadership never operates with a completely free hand. Societal trends, the
particular traditions of a community and established institutions, as well as national
policies and political alignments provide a context within which urban regimes are
formed, reformed, and modified. Richard Daley did not create his centralized political structure out of whole cloth. Fiorello La Guardia reshaped New York City's politics by capitalizing on the New Deal.

Each individual case is somewhat unique, reflecting the differing skills and
visions of various urban leaders as well as the particulars of time and place. Yet the
building and reshaping of urban regimes are also constrained by societywide forces.
Thus, while regime character cannot be predicted from a set formula, it is possible
to focus on some matters of general importance. These fall into two categories, one
involving societal trends over time and the other cross-city comparisons.

As indicated earlier, those who employ the modernization paradigm see an
overriding trend toward social differentiation and a consequent fragmentation of
power. However, the concept of preemptive power calls into question the connection between social differentiation and dispersed power. Complexity does more
than run up the costs of compliance and coordination. It also gives rise to new
forms of exchange and organization; it leads to change in how people act together
for shared ends (North 1984; and see, e.g., Tilly, Tilly, and Tilly 1975). With the rise
and maturation of industrial society, personal and small-scale social action based
on communal groups gives way to more impersonal and large-scale social action
based on formal organizations. This increase in scale almost certainly contributes to
a shift in political form, from legislative centered and ward based to executive centered and functionally oriented (Stone, Whelan, and Murin 1986, 214–18).

In making a case for sectarchy rather than pluralism, Jones and Bachelor (1986,
203–10) challenge Dahl's view that industrial society disperses resources. They see a
trend in which advanced industrialism confers an advantage on large size and in
which politics often consists of bargaining between powerful peak organizations in
the various sectors of community life. In a society of large-scale actors, the ability

to act in a forceful and sustained manner is beyond the capacity of most small community-based groups. Hence the policy agenda is controlled by those who work through peak associations and other big entities.

Although the modernization paradigm colored Dahl and Banfield's interpretation of what they observed, both authors were aware of the change in the scale of urban political life. Banfield acknowledged this directly in arguing that civic controversies in Chicago grow out of the maintenance and enhancement needs of large-scale formal organizations. The picture is a complicated one, however. Relatively homogeneous suburbs and small cities are still able to represent the interests of modest property holders and neighborhood-oriented citizens, but such groups can easily find themselves left out of the decision processes of the large metropolis (Danielson and Doig 1982, 77–78; Miller 1981; Stone and Sanders 1987; Jones and Bachelor 1986; Stone 1976).

By examining the secular trend of industrial society toward big entities and concentrations of resources, we can see how urban regimes can be constituted so as to leave a significant set of community interests unrepresented. In order to get a fuller picture, it is important, however, to consider cross-city differences as well as trends over time. The economistic paradigm focuses attention on differences in the economic position of cities. Cities with declining economies are impelled to court business assiduously; those with a strong investment position can pursue more varied development strategies. It follows also that cities that are heavily dependent on a single firm or industry are more constrained than are those that have diversified economies (Jones and Bachelor 1986, 214).

The regime paradigm shifts the cross-city focus considerably by directing attention to community civic life. In this paradigm, investment strategies in the economic sector and electoral strategies in the political sector are not isolated activities. In some sense, they must be reconciled with one another. In an era of ward-based party politics, the urban machines provided the mediating mechanism. With the erosion and replacement of those old forms, the "nonpartisan" civic life of the community has become the arena in which issues are debated, cooperation is elicited, and forms of exchange are articulated (cf. North 1984). It is in the shaping of a community's civic institutions, that regime leadership is exercised. If only a city's commercial elite are active in this endeavor, then business priorities and concerns are likely to dominate the civic as well the economic sector. As large-scale enterprises, businesses individually and in their peak associations have the money, the professional staff, and the organizational capacity to play a dominant civic role. Of course, in a given community, it matters whether the commercial elite operates within a tradition of civic involvement and public unity or whether business enterprises with particular stakes in governmental policy go their individual ways (Elkin 1987,

61–82). But perhaps even more important is the question of whether nonbusiness interests are sufficiently organized and command enough resources to be a durable countervailing force in a community's civic life. Labor unions, churches, and ethnic associations are among the possible sources of a more diverse civic life; but it is not their mere presence that matters. The question is whether or not they are constituted in such a way as to take an active and independent part in civic affairs (Bellush and Bellush 1984; Jones and Bachelor 1986, 214–15; Shefter 1985). There is the further question of the presence and involvement of the educated middle class on a basis other than employment in large economic enterprises. The knowledge and professional skills of such a population can enhance the place of nonbusiness groups in a community's civic life (see Clavel 1986). Of course, the character of a regime is not just a matter of the composition of the groups that make up the governing coalition. Regimes also differ in the norms that guide their governing elites (cf. Krasner 1983). These elites may be disposed to be a closed group, or they may be disposed to operate more openly and inclusively.

In shaping urban regimes, leaders are constrained by the givens of the situation. But leadership is also capable of reshaping, within limits, these givens. The task of urban leadership is therefore not merely to build regimes that can govern effectively; they also have a responsibility to shape regimes that will govern equitably. This means giving attention to the community's associational life. Particularly as older neighborhood-based channels of representation are abandoned, efforts are needed to develop institutions through which diverse concerns and experiences can gain expression. Without these efforts, large business enterprises are likely to dominate a community's public life. Businesses not only control investment activity; they also are organizationally capable of establishing and running a system of civic cooperation and exchange that is narrowly attentive to business interests.

CONCLUSION

At this point it should be clear that paradigms influence how we view leadership as well as what questions we ask. Thus it is important to be aware of paradigmatic assumptions. They color our interpretation of what we observe, and they make some issues prominent while leaving others in the background.

The modernization paradigm highlights social differentiation and the centrifugal effect it has. Operating from a cost-of-compliance conception of power, this paradigm emphasizes the fragmenting effect that social differentiation has on the power of command. Leadership, it suggests, is a matter of overcoming a centrifugal tendency through skillful bargaining and persuasion, aimed at potential areas of agreement that cut across various lines of social differentiation.

Peterson's version of the economistic paradigm provides a logical extension of this classic pluralist view of leadership. Peterson simply argues that the competitive economic situation in which local governments are located gives various community interests a common stake in securing the economic well-being of their city as a territorial entity. This unitary interest in the city's economic standing, according to Peterson, transcends the pluralistic interests that social differentiation otherwise generates. In the treatment of the leadership task, the difference between the modernization and the economistic paradigms is mainly a matter of emphasis. Looking at the large and complex city of Chicago, Banfield accentuated Mayor Daley's brokerage role as a mediator among the community's competing interests. In looking at the developmental arena, Peterson gave cardinal attention to executive leadership in mobilizing community efforts. He cited New Haven's Mayor Lee as a prime example.

Neither the modernization paradigm nor Peterson's version of the economistic paradigm invites attention to the possibility of exploitation by a dominant group. In the modernization paradigm, dissatisfied groups can simply resist and drive up the cost of control, so that domination becomes impossible.[10] In Peterson's model, the external threat of economic competition promotes to the top priority a shared concern with the corporate body's financial well-being. Because this concern is shared by everyone, there is no room for exploitation.

Concern with exploitation is evident in structural Marxism, but it is largely an abstract, system-level concern—essentially beyond the actions and inactions of community-level leaders, except perhaps at the point of *system* crisis. Concern with exploitation is, however, incorporated into the regime paradigm. In this paradigm, because the governing coalition and the arrangements it rests on help to shape policy, it matters who makes up the governing coalition and how the members are related to one another and to the larger community. Leadership is not solely a matter of policy making; it is also a matter of building, maintaining, and modifying a governing regime. This is the leadership task shared by both elected officials and other community actors.

The notion of preemptive power that is embodied in the regime paradigm exposes the possibility of exploitation in the form of factional domination. However, it is important to understand just what form this possibility may take. The concept of preemptive power does *not* remove power as a cost-of-compliance problem from the scene. It does *not* deny that the capacity to command is highly fragmented. It does direct our attention to a different level of power or, in the words of Bachrach and Baratz, a different face of power.

While highlighting the possibility of factional domination, the preemptive-power argument does not treat such domination as inevitable. Indeed, it treats it as contingent. That is why leadership is so important in the regime paradigm. Preemptive power is a concept that draws both on the usefulness of power in serving community needs (in that sense, it has kinship with Peterson's view of power) and on the potential for abusing power. The assumption is that it is useful for the members of a community to be guided by some set of arrangements through which adaptive responses can be made to social change and through which potential conflict will be contained (Hunter 1953, 69; Simon 1980). That such a structure is useful is, however, no guarantee that it will exist or that it will be used fairly.

The practical political question raised by the concept of preemptive power is one of how such power can be perpetuated if, in the eyes of various segments of the community, it is being wielded unfairly. The answer is complex, and it has been detailed elsewhere (Stone 1988). Suffice it to say here that the usefulness of governing arrangements means that segmented acts of resistance are easily overridden. To be effective, opposition has to be organized and coordinated. If it is to replace an established coalition, it has to be able to bring together and hold together a coalition of its own capable of assuming the responsibilities of governance. In short, it has to create an alternative regime that will be able to maintain itself over time. Passive resistance alone will not do. To effect significant change, the alternative regime has to be at least capable of withholding something vital from the existing coalition as a condition of being incorporated into a modified set of governing arrangements.

Most discussions of authority get entangled in a consideration of legitimacy and the assumption that authority entails a morally binding quality. I view authority in a somewhat different light. My argument is that the formal authority of local government is inadequate for effective governance. For that reason, an informal set of arrangements may fill that vacuum. To those who know little about these arrangements, their status may be cloudy. To those who do know about such an informal structure, it will be regarded as legitimate to the extent that it is perceived to be the best *available* arrangement for filling the community's needs (Schepple and Soltan 1987). If this structure entails cooperation with Daley's machine in Chicago, then the attitude may be one of "so be it." If it means an alliance with white business elites in Atlanta in order to hold racial demagogues in check, then again the attitude may be one of "so be it." This means not that the authority of such an informal structure has a sacred quality, but that it appears to be the most practical way of meeting an important need for a workable form of governance. Much as inmates generally go along with a system of control in a prison because they prefer an orderly and predictable form of constraint to random violence and harassment, so elements of a community may cooperate with or acquiesce to an informal structure because they regard it as preferable to no structure at all.

Authority in the preemptive-power argument thus does not necessarily entail moral obligations. Such obligations may or may not be present. I frame the issue this way in order to make the point that a given structure is not necessarily weakened by pointing out its moral shortcomings. So long as it is regarded as the best available structure, those who are subject to its form of authority are likely to acquiesce. The structure can be challenged only by convincing enough people with enough institutional positions of strength that an alternative structure can be created and made to work, or by convincing substantial segments of the community that no authority is better than the existing structure. This puts an enormous burden on those who would oppose, a far greater burden than can be imagined from thinking about power in terms of the cost of compliance. Indeed, the urban-regimes paradigm reverses the impact of the cost factor on power relations. It emphasizes the cost of opposing and replacing a system of governance. This does not mean that the cost of achieving compliance is inconsequential for an established regime. It does mean, however, that an established regime is not easily replaced, and a challenge to it may be expensive.

At the same time, the preemptive-power argument does not treat any given system of authority as inevitable. Authority is contingent. Any system of governance can be weakened by showing that an alternative set of arrangements is possible, but change can be made only by showing that the alternative is better in some sense, whether moral or self-interested, *and* by showing that the alternative is workable. Preemption thus involves more than occupying a position of governing authority; it also entails securing a governing role in such a way that one cannot be easily displaced—driving up the cost to any challenge group. Preemptive power can be exercised only by those who control enough resources of the kind that are especially useful in governance and that cannot be readily duplicated. Leadership is the activity of bringing resources together in such a way that a set of governing arrangements is created and maintained. Responsible leadership entails the creation and maintenance of such arrangements in a way that does not serve the factional interest of some segment of the community at the expense of others. That is a particularly difficult task because there is always tension between representativeness and the capacity to govern. The first step, however, is to gain a clear understanding of what the task is and of the tensions it must deal with. That understanding, I believe, can be furthered by research conducted within an urban-regimes paradigm.

NOTES

"Paradigms, Power, and Urban Leadership," by Clarence N. Stone, in *Leadership from Political Science Perspectives*, ed. Bryan D. Jones. Lawrence: Univ. Press of Kansas, 1989, pp. 135–59. Reprinted by permission of the University Press of Kansas.

1. This is the organizing theme for *City Politics;* see also Banfield (1958) and Ladd (1969).

2. See Gerth and Mills (1958, 232–35). On the problem of achieving compliance in an organizational setting, see also Crozier (1964).

3. But see Carnoy (1984).

4. Note the shift away from economic determinism by Castells (1983).

5. On trends in Marxist thought, see Carnoy (1984).

6. Contrast the analysis of behavior within business firms presented in Cyert and March (1963).

7. Interestingly, one of the best discussions of this problem is in a book edited by Paul Peterson; see Kasarda (1985).

8. See Ferman (1985); and more generally Rokkan (1966).

9. On power and dependence, see Blau (1964); and Emerson (1962).

10. See the discussion of "slack resources" in Dahl (1961, 308–10).

REFERENCES

Abrams, C. 1982. *Historical sociology.* Ithaca, N.Y.: Cornell Univ. Press.

Bachrach, P., and M. Baratz. 1970. *Power and poverty.* New York: Oxford Univ. Press.

Banfield, E. 1958. *The moral basis of a backward society.* New York: Free Press.

———. 1961. *Political influence.* New York: Free Press.

Banfield, E., and J. Q. Wilson. 1963. *City politics.* Cambridge, Mass.: MIT Press.

Barnard, C. 1938. *The functions of the executive.* Cambridge, Mass.: Harvard Univ. Press.

Bellush, J., and B. Bellush. 1984. *Union power and New York.* New York: Praeger.

Blau, P. 1964. *Exchange and power in social life.* New York: John Wiley.

Brandl, J., and R. Brooks. 1982. Public-private cooperation in urban revitalization: The Minneapolis and St. Paul experience. In *Public-private partnership in American cities,* ed. R. S. Fosler and R. A. Berger, 163–99. Lexington, Mass.: Lexington Books.

Browning, R., D. Rogers Marshall, and D. Tabb. 1984. *Protest is not enough.* Berkeley: Univ. of California Press.

Bruce-Briggs, B. 1979. *The new class?* New York: McGraw-Hill.

Carnoy, M. 1984. *The state and political theory.* Princeton, N.J.: Princeton Univ. Press.

Castells, M. 1983. *The city and the grassroots.* Berkeley: Univ. of California Press.

Clavel, P. 1986. *Progressive city: Planning and participation, 1969–1984.* New Brunswick, N.J.: Rutgers Univ. Press.

Cyert, R. M., and J. G. March. 1963. *A behavioral theory of the firm.* Englewood Cliffs, N.J.: Prentice-Hall.

Dahl, R. 1961. *Who governs?* New Haven, Conn.: Yale Univ. Press.

———. 1982. *Dilemmas of pluralist democracy.* New Haven, Conn.: Yale Univ. Press.

Danielson, M. N., and J. W. Doig. 1982. *New York: The politics of urban regional development.* Berkeley: Univ. of California Press.

Elkin, S. L. 1980. Cities without power: The transformation of American urban regimes. In *The ambiguous connection,* ed. D. Ashford. Chicago: Methuen.

———. 1985. Twentieth century urban regimes. *Journal of Urban Affairs* 7 (spring): 1–28.

———. 1987. *City and regime in the American republic.* Chicago: Univ. of Chicago Press.

Emerson, R. M. 1962. Power-dependence relations. *American Sociological Review* 27 (Feb.): 31–40.

Erie, S. 1988. *Rainbow's end.* Berkeley: Univ. of California Press.

Fainstein, N. I., and S. S. Fainstein. 1982. *Urban policy under capitalism.* Vol. 22 of *Urban affairs annual reviews.* Beverly Hills, Calif.: Sage.

Ferman, B. 1985. *Governing the ungovernable city.* Philadelphia: Temple Univ. Press.

Harvey, D. 1973. *Social justice and the city.* Baltimore, Md.: Johns Hopkins Univ. Press.

Hunter, F. 1953. *Community power structure.* Chapel Hill: Univ. of North Carolina Press.

Jones, B. D., and L. W. Bachelor, with Carter Wilson. 1986. *The sustaining hand: Community leadership and corporate power.* Lawrence: Univ. Press of Kansas.

Kasarda, J. D. 1985. Urban change and minority opportunities. In *The new urban reality,* ed. Paul E. Peterson, 33–67. Washington, D.C.: Brookings Institution.

Krasner, S. D., ed. 1983. *International regimes.* Ithaca, N.Y.: Cornell Univ. Press.

Kuhn, T. 1970. *The structure of scientific revolutions.* Chicago: Univ. of Chicago Press.

Ladd, E. C., Jr. 1969. *Ideology in America.* Ithaca, N.Y.: Cornell Univ. Press.

Merton, R. K. 1957. *Social theory and social structure.* Rev. ed. Glencoe, Ill.: Free Press.

Miller, G. 1981. *Cities by contract: The politics of municipal incorporation.* Cambridge, Mass.: MIT Press.

Mollenkopf, J. 1983. *The contested city.* Princeton, N.J.: Princeton Univ. Press.

Molotch, H. 1976. The growth machine. *American Journal of Sociology* 82 (Sep.): 309–31.

Morris, C. 1980. *The cost of good intentions.* New York: W. W. Norton.

Murphy, R. 1971. *Political entrepreneurs and urban poverty.* Lexington, Mass.: D. C. Heath, Lexington Books.

North, D. C. Government and the cost of exchange in history. *Journal of Economic History* 44 (Jun.): 255–64.

Peterson, P. 1981. *City limits.* Chicago: Univ. of Chicago Press.

Peterson, P., B. G. Rabe, and K. K. Wong. 1986. *When federalism works.* Washington, D.C.: Brookings Institution.

Pressman, J. L., and A. Wildavsky. 1984. *Implementation.* 3rd ed. Berkeley: Univ. of California Press.

Rokkan, S. 1966. Norway: Numerical democracy and corporate pluralism. In *Political opposition in western democracies,* ed. R. Dahl, 70–115. New Haven, Conn.: Yale Univ. Press.

Scheppele, K. L., and K. E. Soltan. 1987. The authority of alternatives. In *Authority revisited,* ed. J. R. Pennock and J. W. Chapman, 169–200. *Nomos* 29. New York: New York Univ. Press.

Schultze, C. L. 1977. *The public uses of the private interest.* Washington, D.C.: Brookings Institution.

Selznick, P. 1957. *Leadership in administration: A sociological interpretation.* New York: Harper and Row.

Shefter, M. 1976. The emergence of the machine. In *Theoretical Perspectives on Urban Politics,* ed. W. D. Hawley, et al., 14–44. Englewood Cliffs, N.J.: Prentice-Hall.

———. 1985. *Political crisis/fiscal crisis.* New York: Basic Books.

Simon, Y. 1980. *A general theory of authority.* Notre Dame, Ind.: Notre Dame Press.

Skocpol, T., ed. 1984. *Vision and method in historical sociology.* Cambridge: Cambridge Univ. Press.

Stone, C. N. 1976. *Economic growth and neighborhood discontent.* Chapel Hill: Univ. of North Carolina Press.

———. 1986. Partnership New South style: Central Atlanta progress. In *Public-private partnerships,* ed. P. Davis, 100–110. Proceedings of the Academy of Political Science, vol. 36, no. 2. New York: Academy of Political Science.

———. 1988. Preemptive power: Floyd Hunter's community power structure reconsidered. *American Journal of Political Science* 32 (Feb.): 82–104.

Stone, C. N., and H. T. Sanders, ed. 1987. *The politics of urban development.* Lawrence: Univ. Press of Kansas.

Stone, C. N., R. K. Whelan, and W. J. Murin 1986. *Urban policy and politics in a bureaucratic age.* 2nd ed. Englewood Cliffs, N.J.: Prentice-Hall.

Tilly, C. 1981. *As sociology meets history.* Orlando, Fla.: Academic Press.

Tilly, C., L. Tilly, and R. Tilly. 1975. *The rebellious century.* Cambridge, Mass.: Harvard Univ. Press.

Wolfinger, R. 1974. *The politics of progress.* Englewood Cliffs, N.J.: Prentice-Hall.

Wrong, D. 1980. *Power.* New York: Harper Colophon Books.

Yates, D. 1977. *Ungovernable city.* Cambridge, Mass.: MIT Press.

6. Political Leadership in Urban Politics

Clarence N. Stone

There is no well-developed theory of political leadership, perhaps not even a universally accepted definition.[1] Consequently the treatment of leadership in the urban literature is largely ad hoc, and much of the discussion is embedded in various biographies. Most of the relevant writing concerns the occupants of the office of mayor, but they by no means monopolize the field of urban leadership even in the United States.

Why examine urban leadership as a topic? Why not focus on office holding and study the formal powers attached to elected positions? The answer is that governance is broader than office holding. The actions of office holders *qua* office holders are at most only an anemic version of leadership; these actions give an inadequate account of interactions with followers.

Office holding bestows authority, but the authority conferred is highly limited (Barnard 1968). Particularly at the local level, governmental authority commands only modest resources. Energetic governance requires more than office holding alone can provide. The weakness of formal authority thus gives added importance to the personal leadership of prominent urban actors, especially in the loosely structured context of local politics in America. Elusive as the personal may be as a research target, its importance nevertheless makes leadership a fitting topic of study, more so than the formal structure of government.

This chapter begins with the task of defining leadership and identifying the leadership challenge in the urban arena. Then it moves on to a consideration of existing studies of urban political leadership. Next the chapter turns to the issue of how to assess leadership performance. The chapter concludes with an appraisal of the part that personal factors play in the behavior of mayors and other urban leaders.

DEFINING LEADERSHIP

Aimless interaction requires no leadership. Leadership revolves around purpose, and purpose is at the heart of the leader-follower relationship. Indeed, in some cases a compelling statement of mission not only gives direction to a group, but is its formative experience, shaping the identity of group members by highlighting a shared aim.

Purposefulness does not mean that leaders and followers hold identical goals. While leader-follower interaction centers on purpose, that interaction is quite complex. James MacGregor Burns thus defines leadership as "the reciprocal process of mobilizing . . . various economic, political, and other resources . . . in order to realize goals independently and mutually held by both leaders and followers" (1978, 425; see also 18–19). In this definition, the leader's goals need not be the same as those of followers, and followers themselves may have diverse ends. The effort to realize aims is, however, one that involves an interaction between leader and followers.

For Burns, the leader-follower relationship is central, and it is not one way. Leaders as well as followers engage in an ongoing process of defining and reshaping goals, in part, on the basis of their interaction with one another. What, then, distinguishes leaders from their followers? According to Burns:

> Leaders and followers may be inseparable in function, but they are not the same. The leader takes the initiative in making the leader-led connection; it is the leader who creates the links that allow communication and exchange to take place. . . . The leader is more skillful in evaluating followers' motives, anticipating their responses to an initiative, and estimating their power bases, than the reverse. . . . Finally, . . . leaders address themselves to followers' wants, needs, and other motivations, as well as to their own, and thus serve as an *independent force in changing the makeup of their followers' motive base through gratifying their motives* (1978, 20, original emphasis).

Burns talks about gratifying the motives of followers because he distinguishes between leadership and "naked power-wielding" (1978, 19). Leaders may engage in persuasion, offer inducements, rely on emotional appeals, and even mix coercion with other incentives; but, Burns argues, leaders, in their role as leaders, never lose sight of the fact that their followers are persons who are to be motivated, persons whose wants and needs are to be taken into account.

Although Burns distinguishes between leadership and "naked power wielding," he sees leadership as a form of power. It is a way of making something happen that would otherwise not take place. Hence Burns offers "contribution to change" as a test of leadership (1978, 427).[2] Thus, from Burns, we have a conception of leadership with three essential elements: leadership is purposeful activity, it operates interactively with a body of followers, and it is a form of power or causation. Put succinctly, leadership is "collectively purposeful causation" (Burns 1978, 434).

THE LEADERSHIP CHALLENGE

When difficulties arise, a call for leadership is inevitably sounded. The called-for leader is seen as someone with vision, someone with a plan of action, and perhaps

someone with the ability to summon people to extraordinary effort. Leadership
goes to the heart of politics, that is, to the capacity of a people to act together on
their shared concerns. They act in order to change what would otherwise be the
course of events.

Arendt has explored the matter in depth. Politics, she argues, is about what people can do together. It is a creative process, one in which we "call something into being
which did not exist before" (Arendt 1961, 151). As Arendt sees it, life is enmeshed in
various ongoing processes, and politics—acting together out of shared concerns—
makes it possible to break out of these processes. Such actions constitute what she
terms political freedom; they are "interruptions of some natural series of events,
of some automatic process" (1961, 168). The "automatic process" could be a matter of
convention or established routine or even a large historical trend already in motion.

Sometimes processes take on a crisis-generating character. When people face
increasing difficulties and call for leadership, they are seeking a means to "inter-
rupt" the movement toward greater crisis. They want a way out of what otherwise
promises to be a certain path to disaster.[3] Political leadership is, of course, not
restricted to crisis conditions, but a crisis highlights what in other respects might
not be so plain, that leadership is a means for acting outside routine processes
(Selznick 1957). Moreover, leadership alters events, not as an individual act of hero-
ism, but through interaction with followers. In that context, Burns, as we saw, offers
"contribution to change" as a measure of leadership, but change is not a concept
without ambiguity. I would suggest that we follow Arendt and think of change in
relation to an established course of events. Because a course of events can be threatening, someone who takes the initiative in order to halt a trend or head off an im-
pending threat is no less a leader than someone whose ultimate goal is innovation.
A person does not cease to lead because the goal is one of conserving.

If the test of leadership is one of having an impact on the flow of events, then
leadership is not a mere matter of holding office or even exercising authority. Similarly, speaking for a group does not in itself constitute leadership. The word "pos-
ture" is often used to describe the actions of individuals who speak, sometimes
flamboyantly, but bring about no change. It is helpful, then, to think about leadership in reference to a base point, perhaps a path of least resistance. The leadership
challenge is to produce departures from this base point, to produce, in Arendt's
words, "interruptions of some natural series of events, of some automatic process."

URBAN POLITICAL LEADERSHIP IN ACTION

Let us turn now to urban political leadership in action, looking first at the American experience. Because the American system of government is much more decen-

tralized than the British system, problem-solving responsibilities are more localized than is the case in the United Kingdom. Within the United States and its candidate-centered politics, the office of mayor makes a particularly visible leadership
platform (Svara 1990; Schneider and Teske 1995).

Let us begin by considering two mayors prominent in the first half of the 20th
century, James Curley of Boston and Fiorello La Guardia of New York. Both put
themselves forward as champions of have-nots and had followerships composed
substantially of ethnic minorities. La Guardia, however, is regarded as a highly effective mayor (Kessner 1989; Bayor 1993), while Curley is dismissed as a demagogue
(Beatty 1992; Connolly 1993).

Boston's James M. Curley

By all accounts Curley was an exceptionally skilled politician, an accomplished
speaker, and a figure with extraordinary personal charm. He was quick to offer
assistance and make gestures of concern, especially to Boston's immigrant poor. In
office he raised the wages of ordinary city workers while cutting salaries of higher-
level employees. He expanded hospital facilities, built new schools, increased services, and spent freely on public improvements. He relished being called "Mayor
of the Poor" (Beatty 1992, 297).

Throughout his career, whether as mayor or as a member of Congress, Curley
championed the cause of immigrants and those disparaged for minority status. During World War II, a period in which he was a member of the U.S. House of Representatives, there was an upsurge of anti-Jewish sentiment among the Boston Irish.
While reform Mayor Tobin and Massachusetts Governor Saltonstall remained silent,
Curley took the occasion to make an eloquent defense of American Jews and their
contributions to the country, including service in the military (Beatty 1992, 455).

On what grounds, then, is Curley dismissed as a demagogue? There are two. In
rallying the Irish and other have-nots to his many candidacies, Curley never put
into effect a systematic policy of expanded opportunity for the poor. Mostly he
offered help on an individual basis and favored the kind of public works projects
that would perpetuate a system of patronage. However, lower-level public service
jobs were not an especially effective channel of upward mobility, though they did
provide Curley and other patronage politicians with a secure vote base (Erie 1988).

Even public works were handled in a self-serving manner. Thus, when the New
Deal was in place, Curley was primarily concerned about how to get "his 'cut' from
the federal largesse, and his constant feuding with New Deal officials . . . slowed the
relief effort in Boston" (Beatty 1992, 335; see also 381–82). Under Curley and others,
Boston spent lavishly, but not well. Corruption was widespread, inefficiencies commonplace, and tax favoritism rampant. Curley achieved the worst combination—a

poor climate for business investment and ineffectiveness in redistributing opportunities to the poor. He took a spoils system as given and exploited it ruthlessly for personal gain.

How was Curley able to hold his base of support with so little change in material condition for his followers? Was it patronage alone that sustained him? Curley's biographer answers no. In the first place, Curley's exploitation of the spoils system, especially for personal gain, weakened him as a political figure on a number of important occasions. But more to the point about leader-follower relations, Curley was an adroit practitioner of the "politics of ethnic and religious resentment" (Beatty 1992, 395). He was able to do this because, dating back to the Know-Nothing period of the 19th century, Massachusetts was the scene of intense bigotry on the part of Yankee Protestants toward the Irish and other recent immigrants. Skillful in the exploitation of immigrant indignation, Curley's hold on voters, his biographer argues, had "more to do with the communal resentments he articulated" than with the favors he dispensed (Beatty 1992, 501). When Curley attacked and was attacked by the forces of "good government," led by bankers and other business figures and by such Yankee respectables as Lodge and Saltonstall, he could play the martyr and distract attention from his personal shortcomings as a political leader. The resentments he expressed had a strong basis in reality: "Economic frustration and class hatred, wounded pride and ethnic resentment, thwarted hope and strangled aspiration—these were the mute causes that found their tribune in James Michael Curley. Boston was in decline, the Boston Irish were caught in a spiral of downward mobility, throughout the first half of the twentieth century" (Beatty 1992, 67). Beatty adds: "Curley rose as Boston fell" (67).

How was this possible? Curley's biographer draws a parallel with Peron in Argentina and quotes a Peronist as saying: "Before Peron I was poor and I was nobody; now I am only poor" (Beatty 1992, 501). It is gratifying to a followership when they have someone in a position of authority give voice to their resentments and taunt those they see as their oppressors. It delivers the followers from being nobody. Curley expressed such resentments, but did not restrict himself to negative appeals. One of his tactics was ethnic pride, "to insist that there was an Irishman at the bottom of everything" (Beatty 1992, 168).

While an appeal to ethnic pride and solidarity is not in itself a matter for reproof, Curley comes under criticism for the manner in which he played the "politics of division," pandering to a "conspiratorial worldview" and reinforcing in his followers "the habit of suspicion" (Beatty 1992, 454). "In using 'wedge issues' to split people apart," Curley, it is charged, encouraged the habit of scapegoating (Beatty 1992, 343). That Curley himself encouraged neither the anti-Semitism of the 1940s nor the anti-black sentiments of more recent years is not the point. He fortified a pattern of intergroup resentment and can claim no exemption when the Boston Irish chose targets different from his.

Despite Curley's considerable ability as a political leader, he made little of his talents. He furthered his own career, but left his followers in much the same situation they were in when he entered politics. While he himself traveled widely and became a national figure, Curley reinforced rather than changed the provincialism of his core constituency—the poor and working-class Irish of Boston. Over the many years that he interacted with his followers, there is little evidence that a larger social purpose was advanced in the process. Instead, the energies of his followers were dissipated in intergroup resentments. By playing on these resentments, Curley was able to distract the attention of his followers from the extent to which he was furthering his personal aims instead of meeting the leadership challenge. His innovation was in using the mass media to mold a personal following, not in altering the conditions of his followers (Connolly 1993).

New York's Fiorello La Guardia

La Guardia's career followed a different path. Whereas Curley left a patronage system intact and used it for personal gain, La Guardia not only maintained a record of unassailable personal honesty, he overturned New York's spoils system.

Like Curley, La Guardia related to that followership in a different way and included in his camp of supporters a significant body of good-government reformers. La Guardia expanded New York's merit system, thereby weakening Tammany's base of power and at the same time opening city positions to those who were younger, better educated, and non-Irish. Thus, La Guardia benefited new immigrants eager to use education as a means of upward mobility.

The merit system combined with La Guardia's practice of hiring excellence for top posts and pursuing progressive aims enabled him to bring together followers who were not exactly natural allies, such as the new immigrants and labor along with good government reformers. La Guardia certainly practiced the politics of giving recognition to various groups, but did so in a way that not only "articulated their concerns and shielded them from a sense of isolation," but did so by invoking larger purposes and positioning himself "as a defender of humanity" (Kessner 1989, 400, 403). As a response to frictions between Italian and Jewish workers, La Guardia emphasized "their shared interest in better conditions, breaking down ethnic antagonisms" (Kessner 1989, 29).

In pursuing an activist government, La Guardia lessened the city's financial squeeze by turning to the federal government, working with officials in other cities to encourage new forms of assistance. Whereas Curley's opportunism made federal administrators unwilling to deal with him except in the most guarded terms, La Guardia instilled confidence and enabled New York to receive a generous flow of federal monies (Kessner 1989, 294–95). New schools, parks, infrastructure, low-income housing, relief money, a modern airport, the preservation of free tuition at the city university, and even public art and sculpture became part of an exciting agenda for action. More was involved than just bringing in federal grants. As a biographer observed: "for the first time in a very long while, individuals of goodwill felt that by their efforts, the commonwealth, their city, could be changed for the better, that the good fight had a powerful, decisive leader" (Kessner 1989, 290).

La Guardia's leadership was thus more than assembling a coalition of followers. His leadership energized followers by linking them to purpose and possibility: "His assault on corruption and favoritism raised civic morale and won back for New Yorkers not only the respect of the nation but their own self-respect. By recapturing the charmed capacity of politics to instruct, care, and transform, he attracted to it some of the best-intentioned individuals of his time" (Kessner 1989, 290). In the words of one member of his administration, "his was the most exciting show in town" (quoted in Kessner 1989, 290).

As La Guardia put together his team of talented and highly motivated staff members, he raised expectations and expanded possibilities. He pioneered in appointing women to major city posts, and in putting African Americans into significant and visible posts. In a variety of ways he opened up participation in the governance of the city and did it in a way "that made good government exciting and immediate" (Kessner 1989, 342).

La Guardia's achievements need to be kept in perspective. There is much that he did not accomplish. Genuine reform of the police and law enforcement eluded him. His efforts in expanding affordable housing were tempered significantly by what he saw as "politically possible" (Kessner 1989, 335). Perhaps the clearest example of his acceptance of constraints is his response to the Harlem riot of 1935, during his third year as mayor. Although he was someone on good terms with the major black organizations and an outspoken champion of racial equality and tolerance, La Guardia was nevertheless surprised by the outbreak of disorder and the alienation that it signaled. He responded in constructive ways, appointing a Commission on Conditions in Harlem and initiating new projects in the community, but he was unwilling to give a full public airing to the many deep-seated grievances that the commission gave voice to. "His commitment to correcting the plight of blacks was circumscribed," his biographer argues, because the problems were so large and so intractable—"other problems seemed more promising of solution" (Kessner 1989, 371, 374).

Even though there were substantial gaps in La Guardia's action agenda, his ability to combine good government reform with a progressive program was a considerable accomplishment. He changed what he inherited to fashion a new system of governance. When La Guardia came into office, New York had not yet become a modern city. It was a set of "antiquated boroughs, dingily administered and divided into political and bureaucratic fiefdoms" (Kessner 1989, xii). The city was riddled with corruption and saddled with fiscal crisis. La Guardia led the move to a new way of governing, fashioning a new structure by reorganizing the formal structure and insisting on scrupulous adherence to reform principles and then imbuing the process with a new spirit as well.

Tammany had been little concerned with tangible achievements and was content to rely on the system that Curley relied on in Boston—"an essentially unskilled, labor-intensive system of municipal service made up of political hacks who did loyal party work in return for their patronage appointments" (Kessner 1989, 210). The consequence was to destroy "the delicate fabric of civic virtue that underlies all good government" (Kessner 1989, 237). Restoring civic virtue was, then, a major feat, all the more impressive because in order to do it, La Guardia had to replace an entrenched system of patronage. So while not successful on every count, La Guardia met the challenge of leadership by instituting reformed and progressive governance and initiating a wide range of new programs. In doing so, he energized followers and made them integral parts of the process of change.

Richard Daley and Harold Washington in Chicago

Richard J. Daley was Chicago's chief executive from 1955 until his death during his sixth term in 1976.[4] During that time, he was a force at the state and national levels as well as in city affairs. Daley's style of leadership was mainly to work behind the scenes, presenting himself more as broker than entrepreneur (Banfield 1961). At the same time, he attended to the details of managing the city and promoted the slogan that, under his leadership, Chicago was "the city that works."

In creating a system of personal control, Daley neither overturned the city's patronage system nor created powerful new agencies outside its operation. Instead, by assuming the dual positions of mayor of Chicago and chair of the Cook County Democratic Party, Daley consolidated control of the patronage system under his personal direction. Through an expansive program of infrastructure improvements and downtown redevelopment, Daley successfully courted business support. Since an active program of construction served well the patronage requirements of the Democratic machine, Daley had no need to restructure the city's dominant political organization. His leadership consisted largely of knitting together and working with established centers of power.

In recent years, Daley's leadership record has come under criticism for its unresponsiveness to the changing demography of the city. Even though African Americans provided essential support in his initial capture of the mayoralty, Daley, in office, pursued policies that pandered to his white constituents and restricted opportunities for an expanding black population. Because the city was engaged in an immense program of redevelopment concentrated in the inner city, African Americans were displaced in large numbers at the same time that they were a growing part of the population, even as they were constricted residentially by white neighborhood resistance. Under these circumstances racial hostilities were sure to increase, and Daley had no policy for combating this trend. Though Daley was responsive to the anxieties of his white followership, he did nothing to promote interracial understanding or to expand opportunities for a growing minority population.

Daley's mode of operation was highly paternalistic (Greenstone and Peterson 1973). Indeed, when redevelopment was at work, the Daley machine was as autocratic in dealing with white as with black neighborhoods (Royko 1971, 126). As part of its strategy of holding popular discontent in check, the Daley organization cultivated an image of invincibility. Hence, crushing a white neighborhood was as consistent with Daley's strategy as was the manipulation of representation within the black community (Grimshaw 1992).

Given the tight control that Daley exercised during his 21 years as mayor, one would expect his organization to display considerable staying power. But this was not the case; after his death, the machine incurred a succession of defeats. Harold Washington's election as mayor was a particularly dramatic demonstration of the machine's weak hold in Chicago's African American community. Daley had handled his followership in such a way as to intensify racial polarization and alienate the city's growing black population.

Whereas Daley had tight control of the party and city hall over more than two decades, Harold Washington had firm control of neither and was mayor for less than five years.[5] Much of this short time was spent battling the white majority on the city council. Yet Washington still had a lasting impact on the city's politics. He put together the original "rainbow coalition." Hispanics, liberal whites, middle-class and poor African Americans, the city's small Asian American population, and the city's gay and lesbian community were among those who formed part of what Washington's biographer calls an "improbably broad coalition," the coalition that put him into the mayoralty (Rivlin 1992, 290). Washington even achieved a limited rapprochement with some of the city's white ethnics (Rivlin 1992, 376–77).

The core of Washington's support was in the black community, and it was only through their extraordinary turnout that he was elected mayor. Without being inattentive to this core constituency, Washington put together a diverse administration, including a record number of women in management positions. He also adhered to reform practice by signing the Shakman decree and forgoing patronage as a means for building a council majority.[6] Ward politics did not close down during

Washington's tenure, but he did bring community groups in as an important liaison to the city's neighborhoods and worked with white ethnic groups on policies of mutual concern, such as the home equity proposal (Squires et al. 1987, 90; Rivlin 1992, 248). The new relationship with neighborhood groups was typified in the decision to give citizens open access to public records (Squires et al. 1987, 127). Mayor Washington also facilitated Chicago's venture into school reform and decentralization (Gittell 1995).

Harold Washington offered a different style of mayoralty from Richard J. Daley. Though in office for only a short time and plagued with an enormously high level of resistance to change, Harold Washington pushed his city well along the road to reform, enlarged the role of community groups in the governance of the city, and substantially broadened the city's governing coalition. Considering the short time that he was in office, Washington may have had a more lasting impact than Daley did. For example, the election of Richard J. Daley's son, Richard M., to the mayoralty in 1991 did not end the broader involvement of community groups and others in the governance of the city.

While Richard J. Daley was individually powerful in the sense of exercising considerable personal control, he fell short in meeting the leadership challenge. He took a path of minimal resistance in order to consolidate his personal position, but in doing so, left significant trends unattended. By contrast, Harold Washington had little personal control, especially over the Chicago city council, but he widened participation in city governance and thereby helped set policy change in motion. However, despite his openness and his success at coalition building, Washington created no permanent organization to institutionalize the progressive presence in Chicago.

LEADERSHIP PERFORMANCE

The above sketches offer some indication of leadership impact and how it differs from individual to individual. This is not to suggest that leaders operate in a vacuum or to deny that leadership is situational.[7] Because leadership is interactive, situation is important. But because leadership is also creative, the personal factor is important as well. Leadership study is about human agency and its role in social causation. How, then, do we think about leadership impact? The suggestion earlier was to make use of the notion of change or movement from a base point. While no quantitative measure is available, we can imagine various ways one might be crudely approximated. The total number of policy initiatives enacted might be one alternative, but because such a measure reveals nothing about resistance overcome, it is unsatisfactory. Hence we might employ diving competition as an analogy. In such competitions, each dive has a rating of degree of difficulty so that the score for any one dive is determined by multiplying the performance on that dive by the degree of difficulty. In this way, the disincentive to attempt a difficult dive is taken away.

Although leadership study lacks a comparable rating system, the notion of degree of difficulty can be employed. Consider Hugh Douglas Price's reassessment of Richard Lee's leadership in New Haven. Vastly celebrated by Robert Dahl (1961), Mayor Lee's leadership reputation rested mainly on New Haven's large urban renewal program. Price's response is to suggest that "spending federal funds on a program desired by the economic notables" is not a very "compelling test of ability" (1962, 1594). Significantly, Mayor Daley's policy leadership parallels Mayor Lee's.

In this view, Lee's leadership is not redistributive and thus warrants a modest score because the degree of difficulty is too small. Lee sought no significant concession from the area's business class, from those best able to give but well situated to resist. In short, Lee went for the easy "victory." By contrast, La Guardia took on a number of business interests in New York to negotiate lower interests on long-term borrowing by the city, to keep various prices down for Depression-hit city residents, and to impose higher taxes (Kessner 1989, 270, 343, 390). The redistributive nature of La Guardia's actions provided a more demanding test than Lee attempted.

Promoting change is always difficult because it involves overcoming resistance. Redistribution serves as a gross indicator of the amount of reallocation and therefore of the resistance overcome. Denoting reallocation from haves to have-nots, redistribution is accorded a high degree of difficulty because it is likely to activate the opposition of those especially well positioned to defend the status quo. While promoters of redevelopment, like Lee and Daley, engaged in a form of reallocation in land use, it was from have-nots to haves. Hence, although they were promoting change that involved overcoming resistance, the resistance was relatively minor. Have-nots are poorly positioned to resist changes, especially the kinds that are too piecemeal to affect the whole class of have-nots.

What other criteria might be applied in addition to the nature of policy changes sought? Two seem especially appropriate. One involves the nature of the interaction with followers—the scope of who is involved, the degree to which followers are actively engaged, and the extent to which they are moved by the leader to see themselves in a different and less narrow way. Another test of leadership performance is the extent of institutional change achieved. Note that in all three cases, leadership is being measured by *departure* from an established course, and the change is purposeful whether in policy, follower impact, or institution building.

In interacting with followers, leaders can either seek passive acquiescence or they can attempt to transform followers in some way by engaging them actively in governance or by having followers view themselves and their relations in a new light. The path of least resistance is obviously one of passivity, seeking followers who are compliant and leaving them settled in their long-standing view of the world. As we have seen, Daley pursued the path of minimum resistance, taking part mainly in peak-level bargaining. He insulated decisions from popular discontent rather than undertake the more difficult task of developing a program of citizen involvement. Consequently he found himself poorly attuned to alienation at the grass roots, particularly in Chicago's growing black community. Despite having strong black support initially, Daley concentrated on cultivating the machine's traditional base of white ethnic support.

Curley was more accessible than Daley, but also lacked a program of citizen involvement. His mastery of the mass media was used to reinforce the parochialism and resentments of his largely poor and immigrant followers, making few efforts to enlarge their conception of the purposes they were linked to (Connolly 1993). In contrast, La Guardia and Washington undertook the more challenging task of creating a broad coalition around big causes. Bringing together a broad coalition is a more difficult feat because it requires that followers expand their understanding of who they are. La Guardia and Washington did this in part through opening up the process of governance, not just in a "rainbow" assortment of top appointments, but also in making government more accessible—La Guardia through replacing favoritism with a merit system and Washington by giving community groups an active part in city governance.

Institution building, the third test, is another formidable challenge, and it is also an area of activity in which the mayors discussed above all had an impact, but a limited one. None of the mayoral figures considered here spent much political energy in linking their followers to a set of purposes by means of institutionalized arrangements. For example, while La Guardia left a lasting legacy in the form of New York's expanded merit system, he built no permanent Fusion party to continue the battle against favoritism and corruption. Daley centralized the direction of the Chicago machine by occupying both the office of mayor and the position of chair of the Cook County Democratic organization. Thus the centralization was personal and came unraveled after his death. Harold Washington gave community groups greater access to the governance of Chicago, but failed to institutionalize his "rainbow" coalition. Consequently, with his death, the progressive hold on city hall slipped away.

Curley fares worst in making an institutional impact. He inherited a patronage system and left it unchanged, except for bringing additional discredit to it. The "Mayor of the Poor" provided wide assistance to individuals, but established no plan to alter the long-term prospects for Boston's have-nots. La Guardia and Washington, on the other hand, took on established systems of patronage and replaced them with more open forms of employment and diminished the place of favoritism. Daley engineered a regime change, centralizing control of patronage, perhaps thereby prolonging the life of the Chicago machine. But Daley's efforts

Table 6.1

Mayor	Scope of Policy Impact	Impact on Followers	Institution Building
Curley	Minimal	Little	None
La Guardia	Somewhat redistributive	Significant	Extensive within government but not among citizens
Daley	Reallocative but not redistributive	Little	Some within but not among citizens
Washington	Somewhat redistributive	Significant	Extensive within government including wider access to community groups

rested on his personal control of the offices of mayor and party chair, and his regime did not survive long after his death.

Table 6.1 summarizes the leadership performance of our four mayors. Though all of them exercised significant personal power, Curley falls shortest on the leadership test, while Daley, despite his personal power, had modest success. La Guardia and Washington rank highest, but still had incomplete success.

THE PERSONAL DIMENSION

The four mayors discussed above were all individuals of extraordinary personal ability. Each was a highly visible figure, deemed to be powerful in important ways. Yet all of them, even the dynamic and creative Fiorello La Guardia, operated within very substantial constraints. Many events were beyond their control, their capacity to alter established processes was limited, and each had to contend with other leaders seeking to mobilize support for competing purposes. What, then, does the personal factor of leadership add to our understanding?

By talking about a base point, we have a way of imagining the difference a leader can make. If we take existing conditions (including established trends) as the base point, we can assess the impact of a given individual in bringing about change. Suppose that the office of mayor at a given time in a given city had been occupied by a hypothetical person of ordinary ability, minimal political skill, and little vision. What would have been different? In Curley's Boston, not much. In La Guardia's New York, quite a lot, but in some areas more than others.

Even though Curley and La Guardia represent opposing extremes in leadership impact, we need to remember that even La Guardia faced constraints. The capacity of talented leaders to alter circumstances should not be exaggerated. Jones and Bachelor (1993, 212) offer the term "creative bounded choice" to emphasize that leaders have room to maneuver but within limits imposed by the larger environment. Thus it is not surprising than even La Guardia was selective in the challenges that he undertook.

While it is in order to acknowledge that leaders are constrained by social, political, and economic structures in which they and their followers are embedded, the career of James Curley cautions us not to confine our attention to external constraints. The personal is both a strength and a weakness. Curley, for example, was an individual of extraordinary ability, but his lust for personal wealth undercut his leadership.

The desire for material gain is only one of the personal weaknesses that hampers leadership. The urge to seek revenge, hunger for personal glory, need to be in control, and ambition for higher office also enter the picture, not just for Curley but to varying degrees for most of the mayors considered here. La Guardia's biographer recounts how the New York mayor became increasingly preoccupied with his quest for higher office. La Guardia's unwillingness to tackle intractable problems rested in part on his desire to score quick successes and move onto a larger arena. As mayor, he eventually settled into a caretaker role while pursuing various extra aims (Kessner 1989, 451).

Because leadership is personal, its impact is often transitory. Particularly in the context of America's candidate-centered politics, elected office holders concentrate on personal organization and cultivate personal loyalty. Consequently, the best examples of institutionalizing the connection between followers and causes can be found outside the electoral arena, in community organizations such as the Back of the Yards in Chicago (Slayton 1986; Horwitt 1989) and COPS in San Antonio (Sekul 1983).

The office of mayor is a visible office with access to significant resources, but the personal aims of its occupants often are not conducive to institution building. The personal is a two-edged sword. It can imbue the authority of office with vitality and stimulate follower involvement and growth. But the personal is just that, and the weaknesses and ambitions of individuals impinge on interactions with followers and on the choices of leaders about where and how to direct their energies.

The office of mayor is itself a two-edged sword. Typically the most powerful and visible office in American local government, the mayoralty offers substantial leadership opportunities.[8] At the same time, some of the most capable occupants of the office, La Guardia being a conspicuous example, inevitably aspire to office at a higher level of government.[9] Hence, mayoral goals, leader-follower interactions, and city-level efforts at institution building are often limited by the ambitions of local executives to move into a larger political arena. The professional politician, looking to move up the career ladder, may leave much of the leadership potential of the mayoralty undeveloped.

Career administrators like Robert Moses (Caro 1974) and Austin Tobin (Doig 1987) may find leadership vacuums that they can fill through their longevity and accumulated political and technical skill. They, however, have even less incentive than a mayor like Richard J. Daley to pursue redistributive aims, to develop a mass following with an expansive understanding of the role of citizen, or to institutionalize community involvement in governance. Avoiding high-degree-of-difficulty leadership challenges, administrators tend to cultivate supporting constituencies composed of a select few who are institutionally well connected. So their leadership is limited in scope.

Professional politicians, even those operating at the ward level, also lack a strong incentive to promote an expansive understanding of the citizen role among their followers. A community activist in Baltimore gives this assessment: "Politicians . . . don't do anything to teach people how to be citizens. They teach them how to be consumers. You want something, you go to the organization. . . . But you're not a citizen. You don't know how to do it yourself" (quoted in Crenson 1983, 258).

Operating outside the electoral arena, community organization offers a sharp contrast. In direct opposition to the practice of ward politicians, the Industrial Areas Foundation, started by community organizer Saul Alinsky, embraces the principle: "Never do anything for someone that they can do for themselves" (Greider 1992, 225). Community organizers operate with less visibility and in smaller arenas than mayors, but many of them would score well on tests of leadership performance. It is not incidental that one of the Industrial Areas Foundation organizations is called BUILD—Baltimoreans United in Leadership Development (Orr 1992). Interaction with followers is a central concern.

The irony of the American situation is that the position with the largest potential policy impact, the office of mayor, is greatly underutilized as a leadership post. In the furtherance of their personal and career ambitions, mayors often go after quick successes, insulate themselves from citizen involvement, or indulge in posturing.

A NOTE ON THE BRITISH EXPERIENCE

The leadership profiles above are all of American mayors. The British system of local government provides no counterpart. Though local government in the United States is not uniform, the "strong" mayor form is found in most large cities.[10] It is in some ways a miniature presidency. The "strong" mayor is an elected executive in a separation-of-powers system, and the separation is accentuated by weak party discipline. Electoral politics is candidate centered, and most aspiring big-city mayors must build a personal organization to gain election and maintain support while in office. The popular election of an American mayor thus provides an extraordinary arena for leader-follower interaction and a highly unstructured opportunity to pursue change. The weakness of the party system emphasizes personal leadership in a manner alien to British local government.

In the United Kingdom, with disciplined parties, a strong merit-system tradition with top posts held by career civil servants, and a national context of parliamentary government, there is no twin to the popularly elected executive in the United States. Moreover, the British system is centralized to a degree unimaginable in the American federal system with its tradition of "grassroots" democracy. Local government in Britain thus enjoys neither the institutional foundation nor the problem-solving responsibility that underlies mayoral leadership in the United States.

Cross-national differences mean that personal leadership in British local government is circumscribed to a degree that precludes direct comparison with the American mayor. Local leadership is not missing in British local government, but a "muted leadership style" prevails (Stoker and Wolman 1992, 260). Even before the Thatcher era, policies were "very much laid down by central government" (Game 1979, 402). Local government typically concerns itself with details, and broad policy leadership is uncommon (Gyford 1985, 6). When forthcoming, policy leadership sometimes emanates from councilors who are closely involved with their party groups (Game 1979, 403). Generally, prominent local officials operate quietly in and through official channels. They tend to be concerned mainly with the particulars of policy and to contribute more to stability than change. There are exceptions, of course, but leadership tends to operate more through party channels (including intraparty struggles) or come from independent agencies and professional administrative officers rather than through extensive contact with citizens (Game 1979, 75; Gyford 1985, 8–9; Keating 1988, 63; Gyford et al. 1989; Boyle 1990).

Change does occur, of course. Typically it is mandated by central government, though local officials may contribute to a national-level debate. When not mandated, change may emanate from the crosscurrents of national politics, as in the case of the "new urban left" (Gyford 1985; Lawless 1990). For example, the sharp shifts in policy for Sheffield—first, toward a radical left agenda, and then into partnership with business—involved in neither case a public leader engaged directly in mobilizing popular support (Lawless 1990; Seyd 1990). The first shift represented a response to deindustrialization, and the second shift was a pragmatic adaptation to policies of the Thatcher government.[11] There were significant shifts in key personnel, but they were not central in the changing of policy (Lawless 1990).

The "muted style" of local governmental leadership in the United Kingdom has led to consideration of proposals to move Britain in the direction of an American-style mayor (Stoker and Wolman 1992). The image of the big-city mayor as a dynamic policy entrepreneur, in direct contact with and actively supported by the local citizenry, has appeal as a way of achieving urban revitalization. Especially where existing institutions lack direction and energy, a quest for leadership is understandable. After all, as defined here, a leader is someone who operates beyond as well as within official channels in order to rally followers around a cause and change an otherwise expected course of events. The low level of citizen involvement in the governance of British cities indicates a strong but still latent potential for leadership.

What can the American experience teach about leadership from popularly elected executives? This experience suggests caution and modest expectations. Although the loosely structured context of urban politics in the United States is, in some ways, fertile ground for personal leadership, the personal factor is, as the profiles above show, a complex ingredient. Leadership carries with it personal ambition and individual motives. The opportunity to involve citizens and pursue large policy goals is no guarantee that leadership energies will be used for those purposes. There is an intervening factor of leadership character.

LEADERSHIP CHARACTER

That elected officials engage in ambition-furthering behavior is no great revelation, nor is it the whole story. Mayors do have broad policy goals they advance and rally supporters behind, as is evident in the careers of La Guardia and Washington. Why, then, highlight the personal shortcomings of mayors as political leaders? The answer is that mayoral performance is more complicated than is usually acknowledged. Mayors, for example, are sometimes seen as the embodiment of the corporate interests of cities, personally limited only by their level of skill in pursuing the city's structurally generated needs. Over the past several years, urban political study has given enormous attention to economic imperatives, especially the need to compete for investment in a system of global capitalism. Focusing on structural constraints affects how urban leadership is seen. Peterson, for instance, differentiates urban leaders by their adeptness in pursuing economic growth (1981, 143–48).

Economic competition among cities constrains urban actors, without a doubt— but the quest for business investment is not the complete picture. The point made here, drawing heavily on biographical material, is that, despite the structural constraints imposed by a global economy, mayors pursue a variety of aims; and their relationship to the corporate interests of their cities is extremely complex. The imperative to respond to economic competition is not so all-encompassing or even so clear on many occasions as to dictate a mayor's actions. Thus mayors have room to pursue a variety of aims, *some of which may derive from personal wants and ambitions.* On the citizenry side, they too have a variety of needs and wants, and mayors can be more attentive to their constituents' well-being or less so.

Thus, despite the pressures from a global economy, the interaction between mayor and citizenry can take alternative forms. Consider the following potential mayoral goals:

- Furthering the city's corporate economic interests.
- Seeking to expand life chances for constituents through human investment, especially for the disadvantaged.
- Maximizing the development of constituents as capable, involved, and broad-minded citizens.
- Pursuing easy victories and quick successes in order to enhance appeal in a larger electoral arena.

A mayor can bring more skill and vision or less to these tasks. A mayor can also give overriding priority to any of these goals or achieve some degree of balance among them. The handling of multiple responsibilities, including career aspirations, is a matter of character (see Barnard 1968, 258–84). The variations in performance among the four mayors considered above are not based primarily on unequal abilities, but rather in differences in willingness to incur personal costs and risks in the pursuit of socially worthy aims. As the case of Curley illustrates so clearly, it is not the absence of social aims that is crucial. Rather, it is that social aims have a high degree of difficulty, and Curley lacked the discipline to forgo personal pursuits for socially worthy ones—even though he saw himself as champion of the poor.

Curley differs in degree, but not in tendency, from the others. Because many socially worthy aims have a high degree of difficulty, they tend not to be pursued in a sustained manner because of the personal costs and risks. Interactions between a mayor and the urban citizenry thus leave the city's leadership potential only partially used and significant needs unattended to. Therefore it should not be surprising that community groups may be at cross-purposes with city hall and that community-based organizations can accomplish goals that city hall is often unwilling to attempt (Freedman 1993, esp. 307–44). It is not that community-based actors are necessarily more ethical as individuals. It is that they operate in a different context, one in which aims of personal ambition play a lesser role and the need to energize followers is greater. That changes the claims on a position of urban leadership.

Focusing on the personal dimensions of mayoral behavior is not to deny the importance of structural constraints, but it is to suggest that we look at mayoral leadership in a different way. Skill in dealing with structurally generated demands is not the full story. Biographical material on urban leadership shows that mayors often fail to make full use of the opportunities available. For this reason, the study of urban leadership in the United States needs to look beyond the office of mayor, to look beyond elected office in general and consider other sources of follower activation and development.

In judging leadership performance, we should acknowledge structural constraints. No leader has a blank tablet on which to write at will. At the same time, leadership performances are limited by the personal preoccupations and weaknesses of the individuals who occupy leadership roles. It is appropriate that the negative side of the personal be considered along with the positive side. Success in meeting the leadership challenge is influenced by the balance point between the positive and negative. Mayor Curley's career illustrates how the negative can undermine leadership effectiveness despite exceptional abilities. The other mayors have negatives also, but not so many as to bankrupt their leadership capacity. Elected offices contain great potential and wide opportunity for leader-follower interaction, but the personal ambitions that attach so strongly to elected office are a mixed blessing at most. The careers of big-city mayors remind us that elected offices serve the cause of democracy imperfectly. An open and personal style of leadership by itself is little assurance that policy impact, citizen involvement, or institution building will be substantial.

The British situation presents different issues. Though the circumstances are not static, greater central control and a tighter party system leave less room for personal leadership than in the United States. The level of citizen involvement has been an issue inside the Labour Party, but no basic transformation has occurred. There has been some policy innovation, but initiatives to pursue redistributive strategies, such as those in Sheffield, have not fared well in the face of both interlocal economic competition and counter strategies by the central government. It is not apparent that a shift to an elected chief executive would have substantially altered the British urban experience.

NOTES

"Political Leadership in Urban Politics," by Clarence N. Stone, in *Theories of Urban Politics*, ed. David Judge, Gerry Stoker, and Harold Wolman (London: Sage, 1995), pp. 96–119. Reprinted by permission of Sage Publications.

1. Much of the groundwork for such a theory has, however, been laid in *Leadership* (1978) by James MacGregor Burns—a book remarkable for both its sweep and keen insights. Other especially valuable works are those by Barnard (1968) and Selznick (1957). None of these books has a specific urban focus, and two of the three are focused on organizational leadership.

2. Other things being equal, established ways of acting are easier to maintain than to change. Limited cognition reinforces habit. In addition, an established way of acting provides benefits to an array of people who will resist any change that threatens these benefits. Moreover, as Machiavelli observed, whoever would introduce a new order "has all those who benefit from the old order as enemies," and they are more zealous in their opposition than those who would benefit from, but have yet to experience, a new order (1985, 23–24).

3. Arendt observes that "it is disaster, not salvation, which always happens automatically and therefore always must appear to be irresistible" (1961, 170).

4. Although there is no authoritative biography of Richard J. Daley, there are several major treatments of Chicago politics during his mayoralty: Gleason (1970), Royko (1971), O'Connor (1975, 1977), Rakove (1975), Kennedy (1978), Kleppner (1985), and Grimshaw (1992).

5. There is an excellent biography of Washington by Rivlin (1992). Other treatments of his administration are contained in Alkalimat and Gills (1984), Kleppner (1985), and Squires et al. (1987).

6. In the Shakman decree, a federal judge made patronage hiring and firing illegal, except for a small number of policy-sensitive positions.

7. The search for universal leadership traits long ago gave way to the conclusion leadership is situational (Burns 1978, 79–80). With regard to mayoral leadership, Ester Fuchs makes the essential point that given political personalities could thrive only in certain environments. In comparing politics in New York and Chicago, she observes: "John Lindsay would never have been elected mayor of Chicago, while Richard Daley would never have resided at Gracie Mansion in New York City. The structure of politics in these two cities explains why these men were elected mayor" (Fuchs 1992, x).

8. This applies mainly to "strong" mayor forms of government, and even these mayoral positions have limitations that vary from locality to locality. Some cities, for example, have a term limitation, but there are others as well (Pressman 1972; Preston 1976; Svara 1990). See also Reed (1988).

9. Note that the French system allows a mayor to hold office in the national assembly at the same time; hence the ban on dual office holding is not a universal feature of urban governance (Keating 1991).

10. The "strong" mayor form refers to the scope of administrative control exercised. Under this form, the mayor is a true chief executive, possessing line control of the administrative structure including budgetary power.

11. See also the examples of Glasgow (Keating 1988; Boyle 1990) and Liverpool (Parkinson 1990).

REFERENCES

Alkalimat, A., and D. Gills. 1984. Chicago. In *The new black vote,* ed. K. Bush. San Francisco, Calif.: Synthesis Publications.

Arendt, H. 1961. *Between past and future.* Cleveland: Meridian.

Banfield, E. C. 1961. *Political influence.* New York: Free Press.

Barnard, C. I. 1968. *The functions of the executive.* Cambridge, Mass.: Harvard Univ. Press.

Bayor, R. H. 1993. *Fiorello La Guardia: Ethnicity and reform.* Arlington Heights, Ill.: Harlan Davidson.

Beatty, J. 1992. *The rascal king.* Reading, Mass.: Addison-Wesley.

Boyle, R. 1990. Regeneration in Glasgow. In *Leadership and urban regeneration,* ed. D. Judd and M. Parkinson. Newbury Park, Calif.: Sage.

Burns, J. 1978. *Leadership.* New York: Harper and Row.

Caro, R. A. 1974. *The power broker.* New York: Knopf.

Connolly, J. L. 1993. Reconstituting ethnic Boston, 1909–1925. Paper presented at the Annual Conference of the Social Science History Association, Baltimore, Md.

Crenson, M. A. 1983. *Neighborhood politics.* Cambridge, Mass.: Harvard Univ. Press.

Dahl, R. A. 1961. *Who governs?* New Haven, Conn.: Yale Univ. Press.

Doig, J .W. 1987. To claim the seas and skies. In *Leadership and innovation,* ed. J. W. Doig and E. C. Hargrove. Baltimore: Johns Hopkins Univ. Press.

Erie, S. P. 1988. *Rainbow's end.* Berkeley: Univ. of California Press.

Freedman, S. G. 1993. *Upon this rock.* New York: Harper Collins.

Fuchs, E. R. 1992. *Mayors and money.* Chicago: Univ. of Chicago Press.

Game, C. 1979. Review essay: On political leadership. *Policy and Politics* 7:395–408.

Gittell, M. 1995. School reform in New York and Chicago. *Urban Affairs Quarterly* 30:136–51.

Gleason, B. 1970. *Daley of Chicago.* New York: Simon and Schuster.

Greenstone, J. D., and P. E. Peterson, 1973. *Race and authority in urban politics.* New York: Russell Sage Foundation.

Greider, W. 1992. *Who will tell the people.* New York: Simon and Schuster.

Grimshaw, W. J. 1992. *Bitter fruit.* Chicago: Univ. of Chicago Press.

Gyford, J. 1985. *The politics of local socialism.* London: Allen and Unwin.

Gyford, J., S. Leach, and C. Game. 1989. *The changing politics of local government.* London: Unwin Hyman.

Horwitt, S. D. 1989. *Let them call me rebel.* New York: Knopf.

Jones, B. D., and L. W. Bachelor. 1993. *The sustaining hand.* 2nd ed. Lawrence: Univ. Press of Kansas.

Keating, M. 1988. *The city that refused to die.* Aberdeen: Aberdeen Univ. Press.

———. 1991. *Comparative urban politics.* Aldershot: Edward Elgar.

Kennedy, E. 1978. *Himself! The life and times of Mayor Richard J. Daley.* New York: Viking Press.

Kessner, T. 1989. *Fiorello H. La Guardia and the making of modern New York.* New York: McGraw.

Kleppner, P. 1985. *Chicago divided.* DeKalb: Northern Illinois Univ. Press.

Lawless, P. 1990. Regeneration in Sheffield. In *Leadership and urban regeneration,* ed. D. Judd and M. Parkinson. Newbury Park, Calif.: Sage.

Machiavelli, N. 1985. *The prince.* Trans. H. C. Mansfield. Chicago: Univ. of Chicago Press.

O'Connor, L. 1975. *Clout.* New York: Avon Books.

———. 1977. *Requiem: The decline and demise of Mayor Daley and his era.* Chicago: Contemporary Books.

Orr, M. E. 1992. Urban regimes and human capital policies. *Journal of Urban Affairs* 14:173–87.

Parkinson, M. 1990. Leadership and regeneration in Liverpool. In *Leadership and urban regeneration,* ed. D. Judd and M. Parkinson. Newbury Park, Calif.: Sage.

Peterson, P. E. 1981. *City limits.* Chicago: Univ. of Chicago Press.

Pressman, J. L. 1972. Preconditions of mayoral leadership. *American Political Science Review* 66:511–24.

Preston, M. 1976. Limitations of black urban power. In *The new urban politics,* ed. L. Masotti and R. Lineberry. Cambridge, Mass.: Ballinger.

Price, H. D. 1962. Review of *Who Governs? Yale Law Journal* 71:1589–96.

Rakove, M. L. 1975. *Don't make no waves—Don't back no losers.* Bloomington: Indiana Univ. Press.

Reed, A. 1988. The black urban regime. In *Power, community and the city,* ed. M. P. Smith. New Brunswick, N.J.: Transaction Books.

Rivlin, G. 1992. *Fire on the prairie.* New York: Henry Holt.

Royko, M. 1971. *Boss.* New York: Signet.

Schneider, M., and P. Teske. 1995. *Public entrepreneurs.* Princeton, N.J.: Princeton Univ. Press.

Sekul, J. D. 1983. Communities organized for public service. In *The politics of San Antonio,* ed. D. R. Johnson, J. A. Booth, and R. J. Harris. Lincoln: Univ. of Nebraska Press.

Selznick, P. 1957. *Leadership in administration.* New York: Harper and Row.

Seyd, P. 1990. Radical Sheffield: From socialism to entrepreneurialism. *Political Studies* 38:335–44.

Slayton, R. A. 1986. *Back of the yards.* Chicago: Univ. of Chicago Press.

Squires, G. D., L. Bennett, K. McCourt, and P. Nyden. 1987. *Chicago.* Philadelphia: Temple Univ. Press.

Stoker, G., and H. Wolman. 1992. Drawing lessons from U.S. experience. *Public Administration* 70:241–67.

Svara, J. 1990. *Official leadership in the city.* Oxford: Oxford Univ. Press.

Part Three

Race, Class, and Politics in Atlanta

Since the 1960s, as African Americans attempt to become full partners in the governing coalitions of cities across America, black political incorporation has been an important area of study. In Part 3, Stone examines power and racial politics in Atlanta over a 25-year period, noting factors that were significant to the creation, maintenance, and ultimate decline of its famous biracial governing coalition. In Chapter 6, Stone expands his systemic bias argument by arguing that a "coalitional bias" exists in local governing arrangements—one that is manifested by the predisposition of public officials to work with upper-strata groups. This dynamic is no better explicated than in Atlanta, where African Americans controlled the city's electoral machinery. Stone finds, however, that while African Americans gained the mayor's office and representation in other city offices, it was the black middle class that reaped many of the significant benefits, not the city's black poor. Stone argues that pluralism is less appropriate than "coalitional bias" as an interpretation of race and political change in urban communities. For classic pluralists, class resources are less important than control over the ballot box and thus counterbalance elite characteristics of wealth and status. This, however, is an inaccurate portrayal of Atlanta's political economy. In Atlanta, Stone finds that middle-class African Americans prevail as coalition partners over those in the lower strata because they enjoy a systemic advantage and are insiders in the governmental process. As is evident in Atlanta, even those who owe their election to African American majorities have to respond to the inducements and constraints of privately controlled and unequally distributed resources.

In Chapter 7, Stone illustrates yet another complexity of African American political incorporation in Atlanta. One popular model of minority political incorporation asserts that a shared ideology among coalition members is central. Stone illustrates that shared ideology was not wholly determinative of African American political incorporation in Atlanta. An interplay of ideology, pragmatism, and the particulars of the political setting uniquely situates the political incorporation of African Americans in Atlanta apart from other major cities. Political incorporation, then, is not merely a matter of political ideology, but a pragmatic commitment to change and the particulars of the community setting. An examination of Atlanta's regime illustrates the extent to which African American political incorporation is not a static phenomenon but the result of significant adjustments influenced by African American voter strength and the strength of the business community. In true regime form, what was done in Atlanta was what could be done within the parameters of resources that coalition members brought to bear, as well as within the context of informal arrangements and understandings.

When Clarence Stone came of age as a political scientist, the black-white divide was the major issue confronting most U.S. cities. Stone's analysis of urban politics is based largely on his years of closely observing and writing about an important Southern U.S. city. In Atlanta, race, divisions between blacks and whites, and class were key components of the civic and political landscape. These realities are reflected in the essays that follow. Today, immigration and multiracial/multiethnic themes are increasingly a part of contemporary urban political analysis. Indeed, in the Civic Capacity and Urban Education Project, Stone and his colleagues are attentive to how present-day urban regimes mediate issues like the increase in the number of Latinos and Asians, as well as the increase in immigrants. Multiracial and multiethnic considerations were built into the study (see Part 4 of this volume).

7. Race, Power, and Political Change

Clarence N. Stone

In the past few decades, the politics of race has changed dramatically, and undoubtedly will continue to change in the years ahead. Minorities are a growing force in the electoral politics of U.S. cities. It is in order, then, to ask what changes in policy and political practice increased electoral strength might bring into play. This question is well worth considering for what it reveals about the nature of power in U.S. society. Is change in race relations evidence that the pluralist interpretation is valid after all? Or is there another interpretation that better fits the evolving pattern of race relations in our urban political communities?

The interwoven issues of race, power, and political change addressed here provide a way of examining the workings of democracy at the local level. On the basis of recent research on economic and community development in Atlanta, Georgia, I argue that pluralism is less appropriate than what I term "coalitional bias" as an interpretation of race and political change in urban communities. Atlanta's recent experience illustrates how a reconstituted "mobilization of bias" protects business influence in the face of black electoral power.

COMPETING SCHOOLS OF THOUGHT

Pluralism

Let us begin with a brief review of the pluralist position and how changing race relations might be seen from a pluralist perspective. For pluralists, two features stand out as shaping the character of urban politics. One is the complexity of modern society; the other is the presence of universal suffrage.

The complexity of modern life, pluralists argue, produces a large number of group interests that crosscut divisions of class. According to Polsby (1980, 118), U.S. society is "fractured into a congeries of hundreds of small special interest groups, with incompletely overlapping memberships, widely differing power bases, and a multitude of techniques for exercising influence on decisions salient to them." So strong is the centrifugal force of complexity, pluralists argue, that any coalition is unstable. Polsby (1980, 137) suggested that "the larger the coalition, the more fragile it is and the more limited its political environment." Consequently in the pluralist view, localities are governed "by shifting coalitions of participants drawn from all areas of community life" (Merelman 1968, 451). Influence is particular to the issue and situation; those groups with the greatest immediate stake have the most say in any given decision arena.

Pluralists assume that one group of voters is about as important as another (see, e.g., Dahl 1961, 75). Hence there is no particular affinity among sets of groups; those together on one issue are divided on another. Political entrepreneurs looking for a base of support, pluralists argue, have little incentive to favor one class over another. In this view of modern democracy, because political entrepreneurs are ever in search of a constituency, few groups are without a champion. As pluralists see it, those who are socially or economically disadvantaged find the electoral arena, with the equality of the ballot box, especially attractive (Dahl 1961, 293). Thus numbers supposedly counterbalance such elite characteristics as wealth and status. Because winning elections is ultimately the most important channel to power in a democracy, universal suffrage stands as a counterweight to any tendency toward cumulative inequality.

Numerous groups, fluidity of alignments, and the special usefulness of the electoral arena for those otherwise disadvantaged—these are key elements in the pluralist argument about governing coalitions. This argument recognizes no coalitional bias and, accordingly, assumes that if the disadvantaged continue to be disadvantaged under current policy, their disadvantage can be attributed to the difficulty of modifying a consensus. Veto groups supposedly find it easy to knock down proposals that depart very far from established practice. To the extent there is a bias, it is a bias toward the status quo. Yet change is possible.

Given that line of argument, pluralists naturally see the success of the civil rights movement in the 1960s as ample demonstration that power is dispersed, that inequalities are noncumulative, and that pluralism is vindicated. If blacks were powerful enough to achieve substantial change, they argue, then surely the system must be pluralistic. In a review of Floyd Hunter's *Community Power Succession* (1980), Joseph Gusfield (1982, 86) comments on the transformation of race relations in the urban South and asks, "If the power structure were so powerful, how did this happen?"

Coalitional Bias

Let us now turn to an alternative to the pluralist position, what is called here *coalitional bias*. Before explaining what this term means, I want to lay to rest a couple of misconceptions and indicate why I am avoiding the more familiar term of *elitism*.

In the above-mentioned review, Gusfield (1982, 86) observes that "the history of black relations since [Hunter's] first Atlanta study is as much a study of negotiated settlements as it is one-way monolithic use of power." The dichotomy between negotiation and one-way control, however, is not a useful distinction, though not an uncommon one. Critics of Hunter should put away the straw man of monolithic power. From Hunter on, no one has argued that business elites exercise total domination. What Hunter did describe is a situation in which an active and organized business community used its ample resources to manage the policy agenda in Atlanta.

While agenda management is different from monolithic control, Gusfield's example of race relations is still a telling one. In the 1960s, the business leadership of Atlanta was unable to prevent the opening of the agenda of public debate to a number of new concerns. Elite domination through a closed agenda did not survive the era of direct action. Yet as we shall see, putting an issue on the agenda is not the same as being able to keep an issue on the agenda.

Some groups have more capacity to sustain issues than others do. Some groups encounter more resistance than others. Some groups are eagerly sought out as allies. Some are more formidable as opponents than others are. Because voting strength is only part of a very complicated picture, all groups are not equally attractive as coalition partners.

It helps to remember that important as elections are, governing is different from winning elections. As Stein Rokkan (1966, 106) once observed, "The vote potential constitutes only one among many different power resources . . . what really counts is the capacity to hurt or to halt a system of highly interdependent activities." In a pithy subheading on policy making, Rokkan (1966, 105) offered, "Votes count but resources decide."

Elsewhere I have argued that urban officials are predisposed to cooperate with upper strata interests, disfavor lower strata interests, and sometimes to act in apparent disregard of the contours of electoral power. We have to face the fact that public officials act in a context in which a vast store of strategically important resources are both privately held and unevenly divided. Because this system leaves public officials situationally dependent on the upper strata interests, it is a factor in all they do. Consequently, system features lower the costs of exerting influence for some groups and raise them for others. Thus socioeconomic inequalities put various strata on different political footings, and these different footings represent a systemic dimension of power (Stone 1980).

Dependence on upper strata interests is, of course, not restricted to public officials. Other community actors are also predisposed to seek the cooperation of those who are economically, organizationally, and culturally well off. Lines of alliance, then, are not fully fluid.

Groups are not uniformly valued as partners in governance. Not all have an equal opportunity to become and remain part of the "shifting coalitions that govern communities." Indeed, it seems that some governing coalitions are more durable and resilient than others. Once the political importance of the system of stratification is recognized, we can see the possibility that class position serves as a strong indication of attractiveness as a coalition member. Hence, instead of coalitions being fluid and heavily influenced by the immediate circumstances of an issue, they are a reflection of system biases.

The contrast between pluralism and coalition bias is therefore not one of rule by the many versus rule by the few. Instead, the contrast is over participation in the coalitions that govern communities. According to pluralism, rule—within the constraints of community consensus—is by those groups most substantially affected by the issues at stake. Where those immediately affected interests are in conflict, either compromise or impasse results. The latter possibility tilts decision making toward the status quo, and the overall process gives rise to disjointed incrementalism.

In a system of coalitional bias, some groups prevail consistently, though not totally. Over time, those that prevail do so in part because they enjoy a systemic advantage and are insiders in the governmental process. Other groups lose consistently, though not totally. Over time, those that lose do so in part because they suffer a systemic disadvantage and are outsiders in the governmental process.

Though the counter to pluralism offered here is not the stereotyped contrast between elitism and pluralism, the difference between coalitional bias and pluralism should nonetheless be unmistakable. Pluralism recognizes no particular constraints on participation in governing coalitions. For this school of thought, participation is a matter of motivation; and motivation comes usually from the immediacy of the issue. As an explanation of power and influence, coalitional bias suggests a different dynamic. It recognizes a bias in who is able to participate in governing coalitions and in the terms on which they participate. Because privately held resources are centrally important, that bias reflects the main features of the modern U.S. system of stratification.

RACE AND CLASS

Before looking at particular events in Atlanta, let us consider an additional general factor, namely the contemporary relationship between race and class. Although race and class are analytically separate, they are socially and politically connected in ways that are quite important (see Wilson 1980). For instance, while the civil rights movement was able to bring about important changes, it was greatly limited in its ability to deal with issues that had a class character.

To understand the civil rights movement, it is helpful to keep in mind what did and did not change. A significant transformation did occur. Blacks brought about the end of a Jim Crow system through which they had been relegated by custom and often by the law to an inferior status. Such change is testimony that significant social reform can be achieved in a democratic order, and the importance of this accomplishment of the civil rights movement should not be minimized. Moreover, all can agree that it belies any claim about monolithic control by an established elite.

Even so, it is well to remember that there is much the civil rights movement did not accomplish. For example, it was unable to alter the class character of such matters as residential location, education, health care, and the labor market. But why should a movement based in a concern with racial status also be concerned with class-based opportunities and benefits? The obvious answer is because blacks are disproportionately located toward the bottom of the economic ladder, and economic position has much to do with life chances.

There is, however, another and less obvious dimension to the connection between race and class; for many people race is a shorthand for class. Though it is not always done so consciously, "black" is often equated with lower class and "white" with middle class. Because blacks are poor in larger proportion than whites, statistical association leads to stereotypes, and these stereotypes are hard to displace because they are convenient for making decisions in situations of incomplete information. In many instances, decisions made on the basis of stereotypes are "efficient" for the decision makers, even though highly unfair to the stereotyped population (see Aaron 1978, 47; Thurow 1981, 180–81). The statistical association between race and class thus becomes fixed in mass conduct and has far-reaching consequences. As Schelling (1971, 89), argues, actions based on "minute shadings" of difference in perceived advantage or convenience can be transformed into collective results of which no one approves. Thus, while few people wish for race to continue to be a major factor in community life, it nevertheless is, because of its close association with class.

The great success the civil rights movement had in removing racial identity as a formal barrier to improved opportunity is compromised by the continuing informal barrier that is still in place. The picture is complicated. Ours is presumably an achievement-oriented society in which ascribed statuses such as race no longer have a place. After all, ascribed and achieved status are logically distinct, and race belongs to the former, while class supposedly has more to do with the latter. Yet in social practice achieved and ascribed status are mixed. Even in an achievement-oriented society which gives wide sway to the workings of an impersonal market, the convenience of thinking in categories (for example, racial stereotypes) places all blacks under a disadvantage. As a collectivity—that is, as a category for convenient, quick labeling—blacks are regarded as a low-achievement and therefore lower-class group. A large-scale movement of blacks—even if most are middle class—into a school system, a center of employment, or a residential area gives a signal that the class character has changed. And that subliminal signal is extremely hard to counter publicly. Efforts to do so increase the visibility of the signal and may be self-defeating. Thus middle-class blacks—whether as candidates for public office, potential employees in the private sector, home buyers, or clients for professional service—bear a degree of informal handicap through a subliminal association with lower-class stereotypes.

Let us then consider how the intertwined character of race and class might affect the formation and maintenance of coalitions. Pluralism tends to discount the importance of class (see Polsby 1980, 117–18). By contrast, the coalitional bias argument holds that those with low positions in the system of stratification will not be attractive allies for public officials as these officials confront the task of governance. (Since they may have significant voting power, they may be attractive as a source of electoral support, particularly if that support can be obtained by largely symbolic stances.) The result of this situation is that as political participants, lower-strata groups face high opportunity costs—that is, their "demands" encounter strong resistance (cf. Harsanyi 1962). Consequently they have weak incentives to pursue broad, collective demands; and they have far stronger incentives to pursue particular and immediate benefits. Hence the representatives of lower strata groups are "ripe" for co-optation or for simply giving up the struggle (Stone 1982).

Coalition formation, of course, does not occur in a frictionless world in which information is perfect and past history of no consequence. Coalitional bias thus occurs through a process of learning about and adjusting to systemic factors. As pressures for change interact with systemic resistance, what kind of coalition building might we expect to emerge? The coalition-bias argument suggests that in the process of governing, public officials and others will gravitate toward alliance with upper strata groups. As officials seek to represent their constituents, even those who owe their election to black majorities have to respond to the inducements and constraints of privately controlled and unequally distributed resources. Moreover, although black middle and lower classes have important shared interests for the reasons discussed above, the system of social stratification puts a wedge into their cooperative relationship, as it does in any alliance that bridges class lines. (See, in particular, Chafe 1980 for a detailed account of the experience in Greensboro, North Carolina.)

RACE AND POLITICAL CHANGE IN ATLANTA

Coalitional Bias before the Civil Rights "Revolution"

In the period right after World War II, blacks in several Southern cities, responding to the constitutional demise of the white primary and the signal of greater protection for voting rights, formed issue-oriented political organizations to make greater use of the ballot box as an instrument of influence. This was itself a period in which blacks sought to become part of the ruling coalition in their various communities. It was a period of black political activism as well as continuing caution

(Chafe 1980, 29). But significantly it was a time in which black assertiveness was constrained by a variety of devices and considerations (cf. Matthews and Prothro 1966, 137–46).

Most cities were characterized by a form of paternalism, in which blacks petitioned white benefactors with requests for aid or, in some cases, for approval of modest changes in racial practice. Standard procedure in Atlanta, for example, called for the white business and civic establishment to pass judgment on proposed major changes in community policy—it was this practice that informed Hunter's (1953) notion of community power structure. Typically negotiations between the races did not involve top business leaders as direct participants. Consistently they remained in the background. To illustrate, in Atlanta negotiations generally were between the mayor and the leadership of the Atlanta Negro Voters League or, on some policy issues, between the staff of white civic organizations and officials of the Urban League. Once negotiations at that level were completed, then the agreement was "cleared" with top leaders in the business community.

It should be emphasized that this was not an instance of monolithic control; established leaders did yield to a changing reality of black dissatisfaction, but only if it was not detrimental to collective business interests and the general commitment to economic growth. Further, business leaders did refuse requests.

Even before the college-age generation of the 1960s challenged this pattern of hierarchical decision making, blacks were dissatisfied. Threats of litigation and flexed electoral muscles were part of the negotiation process. But blacks clearly were not an autonomous power group. As Chafe (1980, 37) observes of Greensboro, "blacks had been viewed as dependent extensions of the white community, not recognized as independent people with an agenda of their own."

On what did the political subordination of blacks rest if they had voting power and significant legal protection? There was no single factor, but rather a mixture of material and attitudinal factors, regularized into an ongoing set of arrangements. White business leaders controlled great amounts of money, the major credit sources, and an extensive organizational network. In addition they enjoyed high civic status and favorable standing with the news media. Moreover, the whole of their power position was greater than the sum of its parts. Because the business elite represented an unmatched concentration of resources, subleaders, black and white, were deferential to them. To obtain their active support, many community actors believed, was to go far toward assuring success. To evoke their opposition was not only to run a risk of failure but a likelihood of sanctions. In some cases blacks were beholden to white officeholders, but as Hunter (1953) showed (and Banfield 1965 confirmed), the holders of public office were widely perceived to be subordinate to the business elite. And in those rare instances in which blacks were selected for public office, those who were elected were too constrained to be militant advocates (Chafe 1980, 36). Politics was therefore not a countervailing force against business leadership. It was either subordinate to the business elite or simply not forceful as a means through which blacks could exert pressure.

Black business and professional leaders also fell short of being a significant independent force, partly because blacks were direct recipients of favors from white business leaders. At the time that younger and more assertive black leaders were beginning to emerge, Jack Walker described the older generation of conservative black leaders in Atlanta this way:

> The conservatives feel that their position bars them from taking an active part in protest demonstrations because these public displays of discontent naturally cause bitterness and rancor and tend to destroy the cordial settled atmosphere which they feel is a necessary precondition to effective negotiations. They also worked hard to build institutions such as the Y.M.C.A., the Urban League and many churches which depend heavily on contributions from influential whites. . . . The businessmen among the conservatives have frequent dealings with influential whites in the city; both the bank and the savings and loan association operated by Negroes in Atlanta have very sizable deposits from white customers. In fact, to a large extent, the power of the conservatives depends on their influence with the white community. They are spokesmen for the Negro community primarily because they have gained white recognition and favor, although their own achievements placed them in a position to be chosen for this role (Walker 1963, 116).

Why didn't dissatisfied black leaders go public before the student sit-ins of 1960? Why did they tolerate a situation in which whites largely chose who would represent the black community? It is hard now to recall just how repressive the racial climate was in the pre-1960 South. There was a pervasive fear of white violence, well based in historical fact. In understanding the pre-1960 era, it is important, then, to appreciate the extent to which the white business elite was seen to be a protective force in a hostile racial climate. They were touted as responsible leaders, and, indeed, as proponents and architects of economic growth, they presumably could be counted on to maintain an overall direction of orderly progress. Furthermore, they were not simply people with good intentions; they had the clout to act on their intentions and bring other "less responsible" elements into line.

Fearing that any race-related issue might arouse hostility among the white masses, old-line black leaders had great confidence in the process of quiet negotiations. The head of the Southern Regional Council observed, "Nearly always in Atlanta it's the manipulative adjustment of interests rather than the head-on clash" (quoted in Cater 1957, 18). In this system of quiet and manipulative adjustment, the white business establishment operated with several advantages. Not only did they control enormous resources, enjoy a patron relationship to many black "clients," and stand in very good favor at city hall, but they were regarded as protectors of the public interest. They possessed a form of legitimacy that black leaders lacked.

No one described white business leaders as altruistic, but they were seen as hard-nosed realists—practitioners of "enlightened self-interest"—who had the best interest of the community at heart (cf. Clark 1969). Black leaders, by contrast, were perceived as pleaders of a special cause. They spoke for a factional interest, whereas white business leaders were regarded as representing the well-being of the whole community.

Much of the literature offering a pluralist view of power assumes that the presence of bargaining and negotiation is an indication of some kind of power balance. In one sense it is; power is never completely one-sided even in a "total institution" such as a prison or an asylum (Goffman 1961; Sykes 1958). However, what is important for our purposes is not the absence of complete one-sidedness (that is so universal as to be uninteresting), but the degree of imbalance. Bear in mind that we are not talking about different forms of pluralism—that obscures the issues. Rather our concern is with how much imbalance there is in the bases from which bargaining and negotiation take place (see, e.g., Stone 1976, 74; Chafe 1980, 24).

The student sit-ins in 1960 were an effort to alter the terms under which bargaining and negotiation were conducted. As such, they were part of a political movement concerned with changing a coalitional bias. The civil rights movement sought to shift the position of blacks from that of being an indirect and subordinate member of governing coalitions to that of being a direct and coequal member. That is what the phrase "Black Power" was explicitly about (Carmichael and Hamilton 1967).

The Civil Rights Movement as an Attack on Coalitional Bias

Coalitional bias proved to have multiple layers, and some layers were beyond the reach of direct-action tactics. Let us now consider the impact of the civil rights movement as a frontal assault on the notion that the rights of black people could be guaranteed only by powerful white benefactors. Disdainful of the fears of "white backlash," civil rights activists deliberately made the position of blacks in America into a public issue (see Garrow 1978). In his "Letter from Birmingham Jail," Martin Luther King stated:

> I had hoped that the white moderate would understand that the present tension in the South is a necessary phase of the transition from an obnoxious negative peace, in which the Negro passively accepted his unjust plight, to a substantive and positive peace, in which all men will respect the dignity and worth of human personality. Actually, we who engage in nonviolent direct action are not the creators of tension. We merely bring to the surface the hidden tension that is already alive. We bring it out in the open, where

it can be seen and dealt with. Like a boil that can never be cured so long as it is covered up but must be opened with all its ugliness to the natural medicines of air and light, injustice must be exposed, with all the tension its exposure creates, to the light of human conscience and the air of national opinion before it can be cured (King 1964, 85).

In Greensboro, where King had delivered a sermon credited with being a catalyst for the sit-ins (Chafe 1980, 113), student leaders announced that they would turn their case over to "the reasonable local bar of public opinion" (Chafe 1980, 127). The aim was not to bypass negotiations but to put them on a different footing. As King explained to his fellow ministers, negotiations were needed to resolve the crisis in race relations. Again quoting from his "Letter from Birmingham Jail":

> You are quite right in calling for negotiation. Indeed, this is the very purpose of direct action. Nonviolent direct action seeks to create such a crisis and foster such a tension that a community which has constantly refused to negotiate is forced to confront the issue. It seeks so to dramatize the issue that it can no longer be ignored (King 1964, 79).

But how did crisis generation produce a new bargaining lever? In what way was the bargaining situation different from the past? In its manifest form, the bargaining lever was often the threat of a mass demonstration, with its potential for disorder and a tarnished community image. In scores of cities, white business and political leaders were in fact concerned to prevent repeated demonstrations.

At a deeper level, however, direct action was a demonstration that racial exclusion could be maintained in public places only by "continuing coercion" and "massive repression" (Chafe 1980, 99, 202). When blacks ceased to be compliant with a Jim Crow social order, the "private" decisions of business people to practice discrimination in public accommodations became a threat to community order. As Carmichael and Hamilton (1967, 53) argued, "There can be no social order without social justice."

The civil rights movement thus sought to change the bargaining ground in several ways. New leaders not beholden to white patrons moved to the forefront. Further, instead of retreating into passivity to avoid violence, blacks put the issue of race relations squarely into the public arena, calling for a just as well as an orderly resolution. In this way, they altered the terms of public debate. Moreover, the bugbear of "white backlash" was turned against the community's top political and business leaders. Whereas in the past the possibility of mass violence was used against blacks to urge them onto a path of caution, that same possibility came to be used against established white leaders to urge them into a course of activism.

As new leaders based on a new style of political activism emerged, they put forward a revised agenda of public debate focused on social reform. In contrast with the public passivity of the past, blacks openly sought a direct voice in community governance. What remained to be achieved was an institutionalized basis for such black participation. Protest politics can call attention to the need for change and prompt creative thinking about the need for new political arrangements, but protest politics is not itself a durable base of power (Lipsky 1970). Let us turn to the recent Atlanta experience in altering governing arrangements.

Atlanta and Neighborhood Activism

Atlanta, it is important to bear in mind, is a city with a substantial black middle class and numerous black business and educational institutions. Atlanta also has several significant political features. By 1970, the city had a black majority, and in 1973 elected its first black mayor, Maynard Jackson. After two terms, Jackson was succeeded as mayor by Andrew Young, the city's second black mayor.

Atlanta is the metropolis of the Southeast. Unlike many smaller cities, Atlanta is a place preoccupied with growth and change. Policies to encourage the enlargement and transformation of its central business district have engendered an ongoing conflict between downtown interests and the city's neighborhoods (Stone 1976; Grist, Abney, and Binford 1982; Henson and King 1982). Atlanta's development politics thus offers an opportunity to look at coalition formation in a situation in which several combinations are possible.

Atlanta's housing and redevelopment policy up into the protest era of the 1960s was heavily directed toward revitalization of the central business district and toward the deconcentration of lower-income families from around the center of the city into selected outlying areas. Neighborhood renewal was largely neglected, and residential stability had a lower priority. In one 10-year period (1956–1966), nearly one-seventh of the city's population was displaced by some form of governmental action. This policy was resisted vigorously at several stages over a period of years, but most intensely in the mid-1960s. Citywide, black leaders and both black and white neighborhood groups protested this policy at various times and in the late 1960s era of civil disorder, succeeded for a brief period in committing the city to a new program of neighborhood renewal and improved housing opportunities.

After this brief period of responsiveness in the era of civil disorder, city hall backed away from a neighborhood-based housing and redevelopment policy. By 1969, the last year of his administration, Mayor Ivan Allen had lowered the priority given to his earlier announced slum eradication program and declined to pursue additional local funding for neighborhood improvements. This shift in policy occurred even before federal funding began to diminish. Moreover, Allen moved away from his earlier announced goal of providing new low- and moderate-income housing to a policy of "economic balance." Taking a cue from informal discussions in the business community, Mayor Allen became concerned that subsidized housing would be a "magnet for the poor," concentrating the lower-income population in the city.

Sam Massell succeeded Ivan Allen as mayor, but his electoral base was somewhat different from Allen's. Whereas Allen had come to the mayoralty through the presidency of the chamber of commerce and extensive involvement in civic affairs as a businessman, Massell had served as a vice mayor and had a long history of association with and support by liberal elements in Atlanta's politics. In his mayoral campaign in fall 1969, Massell was opposed by Rodney Cook, a moderate Republican, who had served as chairman of the aldermanic Planning and Development Committee during Allen's mayoralty. Cook was endorsed by Allen, the newspapers, and the business community. Massell—liberal, white, and labor backed—received strong support in the black community and was elected.

Under Massell, conditions seemed propitious for political restructuring. Instead, Massell made an early peace with the business community and centered his program on the development of a mass transit system oriented toward the central business district and funded by a bicounty sales tax acknowledged to be regressive. Neighborhood renewal stayed on the back burner. Massell's electoral base had little bearing on his strategies of governing.

The 1970 Census confirmed that Atlanta had become a black majority city, and Massell put some of his energies into an effort to expand Atlanta's boundaries. While he appointed a number of blacks to high level administrative posts, he also admonished black leaders to "think white" and to represent the general views of all portions of the city, not just those of the black community. During Massell's administration the city officially embraced Ivan Allen's earlier call for a redevelopment policy of "economic balance." As a result, the particular needs of black and low-income people were downplayed in favor of a rhetoric in which programs directed toward business-district growth were assumed to be uniformly beneficial (Stone 1976, 183; see also Peirce 1974, 360–65).

As the era of direct action and civil disorder came to a close, neighborhood groups failed to gain institutionalized access to policy making, and their protest-based influence floundered. Though Sam Massell came into office in 1970 as a candidate opposed by the business establishment, he made no effort to bring together an alternative governing coalition. Even the rhetoric of city policy lost its neighborhood flavor and incorporated terms that were especially congenial to the Atlanta business community.

Atlanta: The Recent Period

While development policy underwent no fundamental alteration, race relations did. The city had a black majority and many of the traditional lines of racial separatism faded. Black business and professional people ceased to be excluded from the associational life of downtown Atlanta. Blacks became members of the chamber of commerce and various other civic organizations. Within the governmental sector, blacks began to hold more elective and appointed offices. Black-white relations were no longer mediated through a few restricted contacts but had multiple channels—both public and private. One, the Action Forum, was almost exclusively private, and was formed to bring black and white business leaders together to discuss and act on community issues. Clearly the Jim Crow system had receded into history, and the black middle class had become part of Atlanta's civic life. But on what terms?

Race remained a central fact in the public life of the city. While appointing blacks to major posts, Mayor Massell, as we have seen, nevertheless urged leaders in the black community to "think white." Blacks were expected not to fill their positions in the city's civic life by being group advocates. Moreover, Massell associated "black" and "low income" and indicated that both were a source of difficulty for the city:

> The 1970 Census showed us that in the decade, 60,000 whites had moved out of the city of Atlanta, and 70,000 blacks had moved in. The average family income of the people who moved out was $13,000 a year; of those who moved in, under $9,000. This is intolerable for a city. It's getting more poor people, which means services have to increase (Quoted in Peirce 1974, 360–61).

In his reelection campaign, Massell warned of "white flight" should a "black takeover" occur, and he used the slogan: "Atlanta is too young to die" (Peirce 1974, 357). While Massell was defeated decisively, the concerns he voiced did not disappear. As Massell's successor in the office of mayor, Maynard Jackson was repeatedly urged by the news media and by white civic leaders to be chief executive to the whole community and not to be narrowly oriented toward the black community. In other words, group advocacy on behalf of the black community was unacceptable.

Business threats to leave the city if the climate became unfavorable served as a further constraint on city hall, and, at one point, representatives of the business community delivered a letter to Mayor Jackson detailing their concerns (see the account in Henson and King 1982, 330–34). Subsequently Jackson arranged a series of "Pound Cake Summit" meetings with the business community. Cordiality between city hall and the business community did not resume, however, until Maynard Jackson was succeeded as mayor by Andrew Young. Young openly and vigorously courted business cooperation.

Given the friction between Maynard Jackson and white business leaders, one might argue that there is prima facie evidence of an alteration in the city's governing coalition—that what direct-action tactics did not achieve in the 1960s, electoral change achieved in the 1970s. Not only did a black mayor assume office in 1974, he did so under a new city charter that made significant change in the city's formal structure of government.

The new charter made substantial accommodations for neighborhood and black representation. Instead of citywide elections for all council members, two-thirds (12 of 18) were elected by district. The new charter also provided for citizen participation in planning and zoning, and an implementing ordinance divided the city up into 24 Neighborhood Planning Units (NPUs) with hearings mandated in each. Minority business and employment opportunities also gained official recognition through the creation of an office of contract compliance and affirmative action, under the new strong executive administration structure (for a discussion of the previous governmental structure, see Stone 1976, 27–30).

From outward appearances, city governance in the 1970s underwent a revolution, but appearances can be misleading. Let us, then, look at the main contours of development policy over the 1970s and early 1980s to see how various group interests have fared. What we find is as follows.

1. There has been no sustained program of neighborhood improvement. Neighborhoods have won some significant, high-visibility victories, particularly in stopping expressways (Grist, Abney, and Binford 1982). But these are essentially defensive actions. Neighborhoods failed to gain a role in setting spending priorities and have encountered substantial resistance from the line agencies of the city (Grist, Abney, and Binford 1982; Stone and Whelan 1979). And neighborhood access to the Planning Department has eroded. The Division of Neighborhood Planning, which once provided planners for each of the NPUs, has been replaced, and the number of neighborhood planners was steadily decreased during the Jackson mayoralty and virtually eliminated under Young.

2. There is no program of targeted employment for minorities or less skilled workers. The city has made efforts to see that business opportunities are provided blacks in construction, at the Atlanta airport, and at such events as the Piedmont Arts Festival. But despite an announced priority for black employment by Maynard Jackson during his mayoralty and despite Andrew Young's emphasis on economic development, neither administration launched a systematic program of targeting jobs. There is not even a study of the impact of development activities on the job market. Consequently there is no firm evidence on the employment effects of the city's economic development efforts. Jackson at one point touted the idea of a 20% guarantee of black employment, but the business community and the Atlanta Economic Development Corporation opposed such a formula on the ground that it would deter businesses from locating in Atlanta. Efforts to negotiate an employment guarantee for neighborhood residents in the redevelopment of the Bedford-Pine renewal area drew strong criticism, and the city failed to back the neighborhood committee on the issue. Further, in response to a study done by Central Atlanta Progress (the downtown business organization), the city changed land use in a section of the Bedford-Pine redevelopment project from light industrial to luxury hous-

ing and no one publicly questioned the employment impact of this decision. A job quota was debated for the proposed redevelopment of Underground Atlanta, but shelved in favor of a resolution "encouraging" the developer to reserve half of the construction jobs for Atlanta residents and give them preference in retail employment. Thus, while there is no shortage of rhetoric on the generation of jobs, concrete efforts to see such jobs are provided to those with the greatest employment needs are noteworthy for their absence (cf. Pressman and Wildavsky 1979, 25).

3. The city, in conjunction with the state and county, has sustained a multi-faceted effort to promote central business district vitality and growth. An illustrative list of projects includes a business-district-centered system of mass transit, expansion of the complex of government office buildings around the southern portion of the business district (an area considered risky for private investment), expanded nonresidential development around Atlanta Stadium, modification of the agreement with the Bedford-Pine neighborhood to provide less subsidized housing and housing preservation, developing luxury housing in Bedford-Pine north of the civic center on the periphery of the business district, use of Community Development Block Grant funds for renewal in the central business district (the Fairlie-Poplar project), creating a historic preservation zone in the central business district in order to provide tax incentives for upgrading, constructing a new library and parks in the heart of the business district, raising the local sales tax in order to cut city property tax, providing bonds to finance economic development in the central business district, building and then expanding a World Congress Center (both state funded) to provide exhibit space, launching an anticrime campaign of intensive police patrolling in the city's central business district to improve the city's image as a tourist and convention site, conducting an antipornography and antiprostitution campaign in the Midtown area just north of the central business district, and planning the redevelopment and expansion of Underground Atlanta. To be sure, business-backed ideas are not always embodied in policy action; for example, the idea of clearing Techwood Homes, the city's oldest public housing project, was entertained but not pursued. Yet despite occasional setbacks, there is an overwhelming pattern of business success in seeing public authority and public funds mobilized behind an ongoing effort to promote the economic vitality of the central business district. In brief, the pattern of the 1950s and 1960s continues through the 1970s and into the 1980s.

Thus, despite a change in the electoral balance and the adoption of a new charter, the business community continues to be a major influence. While the black middle class is now a part of the city's governing coalition, neighborhood and lower-income interests enjoy no such favored position. Institutional rearrangements, such as district elections for city council and the creation of Neighborhood Planning Units, did not alter the class character of coalitional bias. It is in order, then, to ask how business influence is accommodated in a system in which electoral control lies with a black majority.

Let me first make explicit my assumption that business influence occurs in a situation of conflict. While it may be that, in the abstract, business district vitality is in the interest of the whole community (see Peterson 1981), concrete proposals involve trade-offs and competing priorities. Economic growth is not an all-benefit, no-cost policy (see, e.g., the various case studies in Fainstein et al. 1983). There are questions, then, about who will pay the social and other costs and who will garner what share of the benefits. Expressways and redevelopment displacement, tax burdens, spending priorities, targeted employment and housing opportunities, and the compatibility of land use are among specific issues over which the community has been divided. Promoting economic growth in the central business district is thus not a matter of consensual politics, nor one in which popular consent leaves no room for division. It is instead an arena of conflict and its management—an arena in which some contestants have a strong incentive to prevent what Schattschneider (1960) calls the socialization of conflict. Instead, the capacity of corporations to limit popular demands on their conduct is what Lindblom (1977) means by the "privileged position of business" (see also Elkin 1982).

In Atlanta, in the case of economic development, we are dealing not just with the privileged position of individual business organizations but also with the privileged position of the business community. This position is achieved, at least in part, by conscious design. First of all, the major downtown businesses have created in the form of Central Atlanta Progress an organization that plans, acts, and lobbies on behalf of their collective stake in the business district. There are no other interest-group organizations that can match it in finances and professional staff; the one that comes closest is the chamber of commerce, another business organization. In addition, the business community has funded other organizations, such as Research Atlanta, that, because of their private sponsorship, would be able to conduct studies or execute projects without being subject to the "political" pressure of governmental agencies. (By "political" the business community means pressures that emanate from the city's electoral base; "nonpolitical" processes are therefore those which bypass popular control.)

There is, then, a rich network of business-supported organizations that can present themselves as nonpolitical and community minded. They are not departments within individual business enterprises, and they are not a direct part of the profit-seeking activities of any particular business. Consequently, they are not only presented as nonpolitical but also as nonprofit; thus they appear to be less self-serving than most of the organizational actors in city affairs. Their recommendations and actions are therefore not subject to the same kind of critical scrutiny as are the recommendations and actions of business enterprises and more explicitly political organizations.

As a further step toward insulating economic development activities from popular pressures, the business community lobbies for the creation of independent agencies of various kinds to carry on public functions (cf. Friedland 1983). Over time, these arrangements have become more elaborate. For example, during Ivan Allen's mayoralty, the chamber of commerce served as the city's economic development arm (and it still receives city money for promoting development). But under Maynard Jackson, the city created an Office of Economic Development. The business community responded to this step by lobbying successfully for replacing that office under the mayor's control with an independent Atlanta Economic Development Corporation, which is located, not in city hall, but in offices adjoining the chamber of commerce. The corporation board, of course, has heavy business representation.

A variation of this pattern of creating agencies occurred with the redevelopment of Bedford-Pine—the urban renewal area just east of the business district. In this case the connection to city hall was even more remote. The business community lobbied against having the Atlanta Housing Authority, the city's redevelopment agency at that time, deal directly with developers. Instead they called for the redevelopment of a large cleared area through a comprehensive plan controlled by one organization. Central Atlanta Progress, working with several banks, created a subsidiary called Park Central that served as that organization. With its subsidiary, Park Central, in control of redevelopment, Central Atlanta Progress was able to push ahead with its plan for luxury housing—a plan recommended by Central Atlanta Progress's own Task Force on Housing. In the face of neighborhood demands for the inclusion of subsidized housing, Park Central responded that they "did not want to give the impression to developers, lenders, investors, or particularly renters and homeowners that Bedford-Pines was some sort of social experiment" (Henson and King 1982, 324). By gaining control of land disposition through its subsidiary, Central Atlanta Progress "privatized" redevelopment and was able to describe it as an ordinary market transaction—hence not to be viewed as a "social experiment." Pushed into the background was the fact that the land had been acquired through eminent domain and the acquisition had involved the displacement of more than 1,000 low-income residents. At that time there had been a prolonged controversy with civil rights groups and a neighborhood committee that had an agreement with the city to rehouse residents in the area (see Stone 1976, 102–14, 133–64). But Park Central controlled the land disposition and outlasted neighborhood opposition (the Park Central phase is recounted in Henson and King 1982, 319–30).

The recently proposed redevelopment of Underground Atlanta provides a further example of conflict being confined by the city's role being obscured. The redevelopment of Underground is being promoted under the auspices of a task force representing multiple public and private entities. Because the funds involved are not exclusively city funds, the city council after considerable debate concluded that it could not require that a portion of the jobs be reserved for city residents.

In some cases, the insulation from popular pressure is not organizational. Business subsidies, such as development bonds and tax benefits from the historic-preservation designation, are "off-budget" expenditures. Because they don't come through an appropriations process, they don't compete directly with other expenditures. Moreover, they are not subject to the same kind of evaluation. Few officeholders question their impact, their cost-benefit ratio, or even count them as a form of public expenditure.

What can be said of individual phases of the effort to promote business-district vitality can be said with even greater force for the overall effort. Because the individual elements are frequently indirect, are not concentrated at any one time, often are highly technical, and have low visibility, the larger public is not aware of how many resources go into the effort. So, while there are continuing questions about priorities and uncertainties about benefits, in addition to opposition to specific actions, the conflict is too splintered to have much impact. In the meantime the business community has the organization, information, and economic resources to maintain a multifaceted drive to further its interests. And given business's systematic role as revenue provider as well as the amplitude of its resources, few groups, including the mayor's office, are willing to go very far in resisting business influence. Some specific actions are opposed, but no issue is made of how business influence is an integral part of the governance of the community. And since that issue is not raised publicly, there is little opportunity to debate the consequences of business partnership in community governance and to frame questions about how the benefits and costs of business-guided economic development fall on various segments of the community.

Let us now return to our original inquiry about the accommodation between black electoral power and business influence. Inducements to officials to cooperate with business interests are substantial (see Stone 1980) and the risks in excluding them from city governance are great. And, as Maynard Jackson's experience illustrates, should the mayor not be fully attentive to these facts, the business community is quite willing to provide reminders.

The recent Atlanta experience is therefore especially instructive. Despite a shift in the balance of electoral power in favor of blacks and despite modifications in the formal structure of government, the old pattern of business dominance and flagging neighborhood influence reasserted itself. Institutionally this reassertion of business power has occurred through the devolution of planning responsibilities onto quasi-private entities insulated from popular pressure and substantially under the control of the business community.

Why would city officials allow public responsibilities to devolve to quasi-private organizations? Mainly because this was the price of business cooperation and business insisted on it. Seeking the cooperation of business could not be avoided. Prolonged conflict with business would be economically and politically costly, and almost sure to be a losing strategy for any set of local officials. Neighborhoods, especially nonaffluent ones, offer too few resources to provide, by themselves, a substantial base for governing the city. Public officials thus see little to be gained by courting such support at the expense of business disapproval. Hence the constraint on becoming group advocates of lower-class interests is effective. Lacking an alternative base of organizational and economic resources for running the city, public officeholders realize that they cannot govern through an adversary relation to business. Thus they accede to business insistence on working through quasi-private organizations, particularly in promoting economic development.

For its part, the business community is in a good position to play a protected role in governance. Working through a network of seemingly nonpolitical organizations and making use of informal contacts, business is able to remain part of the governing coalition. But it is a low-profile member of the coalition. Business influence is reconciled with black electoral power by the indirect character and low visibility of business influence and the limitations of popular control.

Atlanta Then and Now: A Comparison

Before offering a general conclusion on race and coalitional bias, let me make a brief comparison between Atlanta politics in the years after World War II and Atlanta politics as it took shape in the 1970s. While such matters as the growth of black electoral power and the shift to district elections for the city council are not inconsequential, they are not overridingly important. Consider how business influence has been maintained, while neighborhoods have failed to institutionalize their power. What is significant is how racial and class cleavages are so important in electoral politics but have so subdued a part in the governance of the city. In both the early and the recent period, many policy actions have been insulated from popular pressure and conflict has been scattered among a large number of particular, and usually short-lived, controversies.

I have suggested that, though this pattern represents no one's master plan for ruling Atlanta, it reflects the fact that the business community has worked assiduously to insulate its influence from popular pressure (often labeled as "politics"). While the system of conflict management that surrounds economic development policy has evolved incrementally, it nevertheless represents the superior power position of the business community. There is sufficient authority and control of resources in local government itself for black officeholders to be able to challenge the arrangements through which business protects its position. Black officeholders themselves are constrained to provide a favorable climate for business. To do that, they have to play down racial and class cleavages in the governance of the city. As junior members of the governing coalition, black officeholders find themselves in that classic position— "If you want to get along, go along."

As political officeholders, elected officials (of any race) and their appointees have little opportunity to engage in long-range restructuring. The reelection cycle leaves officials in a situation in which they not only have limited leverage, but they also have little time in which to use that leverage and make their mark. Inextricably officials are led to search for accommodations with established centers of organized power.

RACE, CLASS, AND COALITIONAL BIAS

Even though the Jim Crow system has faded into history, race continues to be a factor in the public life of the United States. Race is intertwined with class, and race is a major factor in public life because class is. While the ascriptive barrier of race is largely gone as an overt feature in public life, the tendency to equate race and class remains.

Middle-class blacks face a dilemma. They can advance individually and secure those advances by associating themselves socially, politically, and economically with their class counterparts who are white. Thus there are strong inducements to become involved in the network of business and civic organizations in which white, upper-strata interests predominate. That is why racial segregation was legally and ethically indefensible in a society committed formally to the equality of citizens and informally to an achievement ethic. But the other side of the dilemma is that racial stereotyping continues, and, until the black community is perceived to be no different in class composition from the general population, blacks will be handicapped by an identification with lower-class status. Consequently blacks of all classes continue to share an interest in group advancement through racial solidarity.

Black political leaders find themselves cross-pressured by the electoral exigency of mobilizing a heavily lower-strata constituency at the same time they need the cooperation of upper-strata interests. Intense concerns with the collective interest of blacks are met with the charge from white business and civic leaders (including the news media) that this is special-interest advocacy. And, indeed, in a real sense it is. However, it is worth remembering that a mayor with a business background, such as Ivan Allen, can promote the collective interest of business without encountering public criticism. Though Allen came to the mayor's office from the presidency of the chamber of commerce, he could work hard for business unity, "a favorable climate for business," and business well-being, and not be regarded as representing a special interest at the expense of the whole community.

Black political leaders lack the same kind of freedom to espouse group well-being. The black politician who works hard for black unity, "a favorable climate for blacks," and the collective well-being of blacks is accused of representing a special interest at some risk to the welfare of the "whole community." In Atlanta, Maynard Jackson encountered this accusation publicly and his leadership was restricted by it.

It might be argued that black political leaders should forego business cooperation and put together an alternative coalition. The left has long urged that class struggle be made manifest by a mobilization of have-nots on behalf of policies of redistribution. But such a strategy has crucial weaknesses. Most obviously, economic competition among cities places institutional constraints on those who would pursue redistribution (Peterson 1981). As we are frequently reminded, business and even nonprofit institutions can disinvest and relocate in other jurisdictions. Affluent individuals are also mobile.

For political leaders, the disincentive to pursue a strategy of redistribution is, however, not exclusively economic. After all, political leaders are not noted for making fine-tuned calculations about the long-term economic health of the jurisdictions they head. Presumably their dominant calculations are political. Let us then put ourselves in the position of a black elected official in a U.S. city.

To launch programs of wide public import and generate activities that can provide particular benefits of the kind that are so useful in coalition building, black political leaders have no place to turn except to white business and civic organizations. We return to Rokkan's phrase, "Votes count but resources decide." White business and civic leaders control the economic and organizational resources essential in undertaking major projects. While federal funds (now diminishing) have provided an alternative source of revenue, many federal programs entail substantial business involvement. It is not that public funds and public authority are inconsequential, but that they often serve as leverage in obtaining private resources for governmental objectives. Public officials have long recognized that efforts to do such things as expand employment, provide job training, and increase the supply of standard housing could be done on a large scale and in a short time period only in partnership with private business. Given a desire for visible action in the short time marked by the election cycle, elected officeholders have little choice but to come to terms with private business and the civic network of which business is an integral part. Class-based mobilization of have-nots on behalf of redistribution cuts off political leaders from economic and organizational resources they sorely need.

It cannot be said too often in the context of U.S. political science: voting strength is a limited base of power (see Keech 1968). Mobilization of mass support can achieve little if it is not connected to some set of arrangements through which social cooperation can be organized and sustained. Without such a set of arrangements, efforts to redistribute benefits will be seen by many people as merely confiscatory. Further, without an institutional base, redistribution efforts can offer at best only short-term gains. Thus leaders who head have-not coalitions and lack an institutional base are not only vulnerable to the charge that they represent special-interest advocacy, they are also unable to bring about substantial improvement in the collective well-being of the lower strata.

In the urban setting, potential leaders of redistributive coalitions thus face awesome barriers. They cannot simply embrace and enact a policy of redistribution. Rather they would have to restructure the associational life of the community and to do so on a time schedule that would not dissipate their support. Moreover, this would have to be done in the face of formidable opposition centered in the economic and organizational power of the business community. It is little wonder that there are few takers. Any major effort to lessen the inequalities of class carries with it all of the costs and risks of bringing about a deep-seated change in the social order itself. It is this stubborn fact that is the underlying foundation of coalitional bias.

What, then, can we say about race, power, and political change? In the civil rights activism of Atlanta and other cities, the politics of race underwent a significant change as blacks made a bid to become part of the governing coalition. By encouraging the neglect of black concerns and by imposing ascriptive considerations widely and blatantly, the Jim Crow system had effectively made all blacks politically subordinate. But not all blacks were "lower strata" in all respects. In Atlanta blacks commanded significant economic, associational, and cultural resources, and it had a sizable black bourgeoisie. From this group came the vision of an ascription-free and more equal society—the dream of which Martin Luther King spoke so eloquently. That mobilizing vision did enable blacks to change the governing coalition in Atlanta as well as in many other communities. However, once blatant racial barriers were removed and the conflict focused more on class inequalities, the staying power of blacks as a mobilized political force weakened. As the resistance to class-oriented demands stiffened, the opportunity costs went up greatly, even in relation to expanded black political resources. Black unity and black activism gave way to a modified governing coalition in which the black middle class was a part. The price of that arrangement was the cessation of the advocacy of lower strata demands by middle-class blacks (cf. Chafe 1980). "Economic balance" and biracial accommodation provided the terms for the inclusion of the black middle class in the governing coalition of Atlanta. Change has occurred, but coalitional bias did not disappear. The lower strata remain outside the governing circle.

NOTE

"Race, Power, and Political Change," by Clarence N. Stone, in *The Egalitarian City*, ed. Janet K. Boles. New York: Praeger Publishers 1986, pp. 200–223. Reprinted with permission of Greenwood Publishing Group, Inc. Westport, CT.

REFERENCES

Aaron, H. J. 1978. *Politics and the professors.* Washington, D.C.: Brookings Institution.

Banfield, E. C. 1965. *Big city politics.* New York: Random House.

Carmichael, S., and C. V. Hamilton. 1967. *Black power.* New York: Vintage Books.

Cater, D. 1957. Atlanta: Smart politics and good race relations. *Reporter* 11 (Jul.): 18–21.

Chafe, W. H. 1980. *Civilities and civil rights.* New York: Oxford Univ. Press.

Clark, P. B. 1969. Civic leadership: The symbols of legitimacy. In *Democracy in Urban America,* 2nd ed., ed. Oliver P. Williams and Charles Press, 350–66. Chicago: Rand McNally.

Dahl, R. A. 1961. *Who governs?* New Haven, Conn.: Yale Univ. Press.

Elkin, S. L. 1982. Market and politics and liberal democracy. *Ethics* 92 (Jul.): 720.

Fainstein, S. S., et al. 1983. *Restructuring the city: The political economy of urban redevelopment.* New York: Longman.

Friedland, R. 1983. *Power and crisis in the city.* New York: Schocken Books.

Garrow, D. J. 1978. *Protest at Selma.* New Haven, Conn.: Yale Univ. Press.

Goffman, E. 1961. *Asylums.* Garden City, N.Y.: Anchor Books.

Grist, M., G. Abney, and M. Binford. 1982. Neighborhood groups: A challenge to the elite theory of Atlanta politics. Paper presented at the Annual Meeting of the Southern Political Science Association, Atlanta, Ga.

Gusfield, J. R. 1982. Review of *Community Power Succession,* by Floyd Hunter. *Society* 19 (Mar./Apr.): 84–88.

Harsanyi, J. C. 1962. Measurement of social power, opportunity costs, and the theory of two-person bargaining games. *Behavioral Science* 7 (Jan.): 67–75.

Henson, M. D., and J. King. 1982. The Atlanta public-private romance: An abrupt transformation. In *Public-private partnership in American cities,* ed. R. S. Fosler and R. A. Berger, 293–337. Lexington: D. C. Heath.

Hunter, F. 1953. *Community power structure.* Chapel Hill: Univ. of North Carolina Press.

———. 1980. *Community power succession.* Chapel Hill: Univ. of North Carolina Press.

Keech, W. R. 1968. *The impact of Negro voting.* Chicago: Rand McNally.

King, M. L., Jr. 1964. *Why we can't wait.* New York: Harper and Row.

Lindblom, C. E. 1977. *Politics and markets.* New York: Basic Books.

Lipsky, M. 1970. *Protest in city politics.* Chicago: Rand McNally.

Matthews, D. R., and J. W. Prothro. 1966. *Negroes and the new Southern politics.* New York: Harcourt, Brace & World.

Merelman, R. M. 1968. On the neo-elitist critique of community power. *American Political Science Review* 62 (Jun.): 451–60.

Peirce, N. R. 1974. *The Deep South states of America: People, politics, and power in the seven Deep South states.* New York: W. W. Norton.

Peterson, P. B. 1981. *City limits.* Chicago: Univ. of Chicago Press.

Polsby, N. W. 1980. *Community power and political theory: A further look at problems of evidence and inference.* 2nd enlarged ed. New Haven, Conn.: Yale Univ. Press.

Pressman, J. L., and A. Wildavsky. 1979. *Implementation.* 2nd ed. Berkeley: Univ. of California Press.

Rokkan, S. 1966. Norway: Numerical democracy and corporate pluralism. In *Political oppositions in Western democracies,* ed. R. A. Dahl, 70–115. New Haven, Conn.: Yale Univ. Press.

Schattschneider, E. E. 1960. *The semi-sovereign people.* New York: Holt, Rinehart and Winston.

Schelling, T. C. 1971. On the ecology of micromotives. *Public Interest* 25 (fall): 61–98.

Stone, C. N. 1976. *Economic growth and neighborhood discontent.* Chapel Hill: Univ. of North Carolina Press.

———. 1980. Systemic power in community decision making. *American Political Science Review* 74 (Dec.): 978–90.

———. 1982. Social stratification, nondecision-making, and the study of community power. *American Politics Quarterly* 10 (Jul.): 275–302.

Stone, C. N., and R. K. Whelan. 1979. Post-reform politics: The changing context of citizen participation. *Midwest Quarterly* 220 (spring): 300–15.

Sykes, G. M. 1953. *The society of captives.* Princeton: Princeton Univ. Press.

Thurow, L. C. 1981. *The zero-sum society.* New York: Penguin Books.

Walker, J. L. 1963. Protest and negotiation: A case study of Negro leadership in Atlanta, Georgia. *Midwest Journal of Political Science* 7 (May): 99–124.

Wilson, W. J. 1980. *The declining significance of race.* 2nd ed. Chicago: Univ. of Chicago Press.

8. Race and Regime in Atlanta

Clarence N. Stone

Blacks hold governmental power in Atlanta. They have a two-to-one majority on the city council, and Andrew Young is completing his second term as the city's second black mayor. Moreover, blacks are a substantial presence in the civic life of Atlanta. They have held the presidency of the chamber of commerce and are to be found among the members of every board and commission in the public life of the community. The political incorporation of blacks in Atlanta is strong enough for Mayor Young to have raised the possibility of city-county consolidation. Even with such a move, blacks presumably would remain at the center of public life in Atlanta.

How such a seemingly strong form of political incorporation came about is in part a familiar story. Key facts in the city's political history are widely known:

1. In 1946, Georgia's white primary was invalidated. A voter-registration drive in the black community brought 20,000 new voters onto the rolls, making the black community more than a quarter of the city's electorate (Bacote 1955).
2. Atlanta's mayor at the time, William B. Hartsfield, recognized the potential for including Atlanta's black community as junior partners in a coalition built around the mutually reinforcing themes of economic growth and racial moderation. He and his successor, Ivan Allen Jr., profited electorally from that coalition over the next 20 years (see Jennings and Zeigler 1966).
3. Atlanta's black community entered a new and more assertive phase in 1960 as direct-action protests signaled the end of the era of quiet accommodation between established black and white leaders (Walker 1963a).
4. The 1970 Census reports showed that Atlanta's population balance had tilted to a black majority, and in 1973 Maynard Jackson was elected as Atlanta's first black mayor. Jackson was reelected by a comfortable margin in 1977, and he has been followed by Atlanta's second black mayor, Andrew Young. Mayor Young was reelected in a landslide in 1985.

Blacks have thus been part of the governing coalition in Atlanta for 40 years, and in that time, their electoral power has steadily enhanced their role within that coalition. As electoral power has grown, the earlier period of mainly symbolic benefits has given way to a situation in which blacks have experienced tangible gains in municipal employment and in the receipt of city contracts (Eisinger 1980).

Electoral mobilization was a key element in black incorporation, and incorporation as a voting majority was central to the ability of the black community to achieve significant policy responsiveness. Clearly elections matter, and majority voting pays real dividends in governmental decisions.

What more is there to say? A great deal, it turns out. Incorporation is a complex phenomenon, shaped by many factors. The ideology of the governing coalition is one factor. A liberal ideology, containing the principle of equality and favoring the redistribution of advantages to promote that principle, paves the way for minorities to be brought into the governing circle (Browning et al. 1984). Ideological opposition to such redistribution is a barrier, and may lead to a struggle between ins and outs over possession of governing power.

But ideology is not the only factor at work. The initial incorporation of blacks into Atlanta's governing coalition occurred under a mayor who held many of the segregationist views prevalent in the Deep South of that time (Martin 1978, 49), but Atlanta's Mayor Hartsfield was first and foremost a pragmatist. He also had strong ties to members of Atlanta's business elite—he was, for example, a former schoolmate and lifelong friend of Coca-Cola's Robert Woodruff. Hartsfield's guiding concern was business progress. He professed deep faith in the enlightened self-interest of top business leaders to act in ways that would promote the city's well-being. Hartsfield looked to the business elite for cues about what was acceptable and unacceptable.

While many of Atlanta's prominent businessmen themselves held traditional Southern views on race, they also were pragmatic. They aspired to see Atlanta grow and become the dominant city in the Southeast and reach the rank of being nationally prominent. Hence they cared about Atlanta's image in the larger world. The last thing they wanted was for Atlanta to be seen as a backwater defender of an old way of life.

The conventional wisdom of the time held that the white working class was the backbone of segregationist resistance to social change and that the educated white middle class, including Atlanta's business elite, was, while not especially liberal on racial matters, at least amenable to a policy of moderation. Certainly throughout the 1950s and 1960s Atlanta's white electorate divided along class lines, as predicted by this conventional wisdom (Walker 1963b; Jennings and Zeigler 1966). But education and social class were not necessarily in themselves the key factors. One active participant in the Hartsfield coalition observed:

> I've found that one of the best ways to anticipate how a man will vote is to ask him where he was born and grew up. If he comes from South Georgia or somewhere else in the Black Belt you can bet he will be against us, but if he's from the Piedmont area or grew up in Atlanta or outside the South chances are he's with us (Quoted in Walker 1963c, 46).

Traditional Southern views on race and an overriding commitment to black subordination, V. O. Key (1949) argued, were politically rooted in the old plantation areas of the Deep South—what is known as the Black Belt. According to Key, what sustained the Jim Crow system was not the racial attitudes of nonaffluent and uneducated whites. Instead, it was the political power and leadership of propertied elites in the rural and small-town South, particularly in the Black Belt. They were committed to a form of social control that centered in the racial subordination of blacks (see also Bartley 1983).

Atlanta's business elite operated on a much different basis. In their change-oriented drive to promote Atlanta, they came into conflict with the tradition-minded in Atlanta, who were less educated and less affluent—and who perhaps felt somewhat threatened by change. In the post–World War II period, the Atlanta business elite also came into conflict with stand-patters in statewide politics, and these included individuals who were educated property holders—this was an elite based economically and socially in the agrarian South.

As mayor, Hartsfield had the foresight to see the possibility of a change-oriented coalition around the twin themes of economic growth and racial moderation. Atlanta's electorally mobilized black community provided the numbers for swinging the balance of city voting power toward the forces of change. The state struggle was a different and more complicated matter.

Significantly, when black college students began their sit-ins protesting segregation in Atlanta in 1960, the reaction of the mayor and the governor were diametrically opposed. Hartsfield characterized the statement of the protesting students as "the legal aspirations of young people throughout the nation and the entire world" (*Atlanta Journal*, March 9, 1960). He immediately sought a negotiated settlement. The governor, Ernest Vandiver, characterized the student statement as "anti-American propaganda" and as a "left-wing statement . . . calculated to breed dissatisfaction, discontent, discord, and evil" (*Atlanta Journal*, March 9, 1960). In the face of a threatened student march to the state capitol grounds in Atlanta, Governor Vandiver deployed state highway patrolmen, who were armed with nightsticks, tear gas, and fire hoses—a preview of the coming reaction in Alabama (Walker 1963c, 88).

A predisposition about the political incorporation of racial minorities is therefore complicated. In the case of Atlanta, the predisposition to favor incorporation was based not on pure political ideology so much as on a pragmatic commitment to change. Whether or not the political incorporation of minorities occurs, what kind of incorporation takes place, and when it occurs are matters influenced by the particulars of the community setting.

As an illustration of how setting matters, consider the Atlanta situation. By the time World War II ended, Atlanta had become a "good government" city, with nonpartisan elections, extensive civil service coverage, and minimal patronage. Hartsfield used a public relations firm to guide his campaigns, and he was sensitive to mass media coverage. No precinct network was available to mobilize voters; electoral mobilization was based on group appeals. Without a quantity of jobs, contracts, inside tips, and the like to distribute, Hartsfield had little choice but to make broad group appeals. This need to make broad group appeals may very well have enhanced city hall's willingness to embrace policies of change.

With the "good government" reform context in mind, we can see that the incorporation of blacks into Atlanta's governing coalition is most readily explained by a somewhat unique conjunction of factors. Incorporation is indeed a complex phenomenon. In postwar Atlanta, a key element was the congruence of black interests and white business interests around the policies of change. To be sure, there were conflicting interests between these two segments of the community as well, but Mayor Hartsfield was able to see the congruence and was skillful in mediating the conflicts that otherwise would have made coalition difficult.

It is also important to realize what was not present in Atlanta. As a "good government" city, Atlanta lacked ward-based patronage politics. Within the black community, the absence of machine-style politics made it easy for the black middle class to assume political leadership, and do so on the basis of group appeals. The presence of the Atlanta University complex and a sizable black business class (Alexander 1951) provided the black community with a body of organizational skills and resources that facilitated organization around group claims. The role of black business and professional people also facilitated communication with the white business elite. Furthermore, black business and professional leaders were not demanding a class-based redistribution of benefits. They were simply asking that doors closed on a racial basis be opened.

The congruence of black interests, especially black middle-class interests, with those of the white business elite has yet another dimension. Atlanta provides a vivid example of the interplay between electoral and economic power (see Jones 1978). As a city that has come to have a black majority, that has had a significant black middle class of business and professional people all along, and that has also had all along a white business elite broadly active in political and civic affairs, Atlanta represents a case well worth examining.

In particular, Atlanta illustrates the worth of a political economy perspective. Consider Stephen Elkin's (1985) concept of an urban regime. A regime, Elkin explains, turns on the need to bridge the division of labor between state and market, to reconcile the principle of popular control with the community's need for private investment in business activity. In Atlanta, with its black electoral majority and its still preponderant white control of economic institutions, the dual character of an urban political economy is plainly visible, and black political incorporation occurs in that context. Congruence of interest in Atlanta rests on the fact that blacks have numbers and substantial voting power but limited economic resources. The business elite controls enormous economic resources, but lacks numbers. That blacks could supply needed numbers paved their way into incorporation initially, and as those numbers reached an electoral majority, they took on added weight.

Black political incorporation therefore has been no static phenomenon. Instead, incorporation has entailed a series of adjustments in the regime, adjustments influenced by several factors. Not only has black voting strength increased over time, but the national climate for black political mobilization has undergone important changes. Furthermore, the Atlanta business community is no passive partner in devising arrangements through which economic power and voting strength are reconciled. That interests are congruent is no guarantee that a coalition is forthcoming. Divisive forces are also at work, and tendencies toward political fragmentation are never to be overlooked. Atlanta's business elite has understood that point and built bridges to overcome the racial divide. They have seen the need for accommodations between the economic sector of community life and the political-electoral sector. They have also realized that there is nothing automatic about achieving accommodation and nothing certain about the terms on which it is achieved. Much is at issue. Thus, while any urban regime is constrained by the necessity of achieving accommodation between popular control of elected office and private control of investment, community actors can envisage a variety of arrangements through which that accommodation is made. Accommodation is necessary, but the specific terms of accommodation are matters of choice and judgment. Often they rest largely on informal arrangements and understandings.

The character of an urban regime is influenced by more than the fact that blacks or other minorities are incorporated or not. As the Atlanta experience illustrates, the terms by which incorporation is achieved and maintained matter greatly. Furthermore, the case of Atlanta illustrates that as communities change, their urban regimes change. Neither the composition of a governing coalition nor the relationship among its members is static.

PHASE ONE: WEAK INCORPORATION

As argued in the last section, incorporation is shaped by the political character of both the group achieving incorporation and the coalition into which it is being incorporated. The coalition into which Atlanta's black community sought incorporation with its 1946 voter registration drive had its roots in the city's experience with the Great Depression. During that time, patronage-based organization ceased to be a major factor in the city's politics. Beginning nearly a quarter of a century of service as Atlanta's mayor, William B. Hartsfield was elected in 1936 with business support as a reform mayor, promising to replace spoils politics with efficient government. With insufficient revenue to cover the city's debts when he took office, Mayor Hartsfield turned to the city's business community for help and to the banks in particular for loans. Hartsfield thus had an especially close tie with Atlanta's downtown businesses and financial institutions from the beginning. He ran on a business-backed platform of reform, received business support during the mayoral campaign and afterward, and he depended on business-extended credit to meet city financial obligations and carry out his personal program of reform.

Without a patronage base through which to mobilize mass support, Hartsfield needed to maintain a good-government image, and he saw the city's daily newspapers as vital in projecting a favorable image. He also realized that the newspapers were an integral part of the business community, even holding membership in the downtown business association. Hartsfield tended to check out policy decisions with business leaders, and he was open to their initiatives. He also appointed major business figures to important posts such as the Board of the Atlanta Housing Authority (which also served as the city's redevelopment agency beginning in the 1950s).

Black voter mobilization in the 1940s therefore occurred in a context of a close and ongoing alliance between city hall and main street. Hartsfield saw how black electoral support could be added to that alliance without disrupting the alliance. Blacks were incorporated, but as clearly subordinate members of the governing coalition. In 1952, a Plan of Improvement was put through in order to add a large amount of new land and population to the city, a step that was in part an effort to counterbalance increased electoral participation by blacks. The inclusion of Atlanta's black community in the city's governing coalition thus proved to be a weak form of incorporation in which even their use of electoral power was closely watched.

The reasons for black subordination within the governing coalition are several, but two seem especially significant. First, there was a multifaceted process of co-optation. White business leaders made large donations to black organizations and placed substantial deposits in black financial institutions (Walker 1963a). Churches and other nonprofit organizations that undertook projects such as the building of subsidized housing found white business elites to be invaluable as allies, not only as a sources of credit and expertise but also for their prestige and connections. In addition, city hall and the Atlanta Housing Authority were sources of particular benefits to blacks. As the city launched redevelopment, black real estate companies and builders were provided with major business opportunities in land acquisition and in relocating and rehousing those displaced. The colleges in the Atlanta University system also benefited materially from white patrons, and they also were provided with land acquisition opportunities under the city's redevelopment program

(Stone 1976). The go-along-to-get-along system is known too well to require elaboration. The point is that strategically important and co-optable black organizations and institutions were brought into the system of insider cooperation and negotiation, but they came in largely as clients of white patrons. The result was that the moderate Urban League was an effective link; the more militant (by pre-1960 standards) NAACP was not. The benefits of going along were fully understood in both the black community and the white business and civic network. However, there were costs as well. In the 1950s, despite opposition from black neighborhood leaders, Atlanta's governing coalition inaugurated a redevelopment program that displaced at least one-seventh of the city's population.

To understand why co-optation was possible and the costs were borne, we need to see those practices in the larger racial context. That brings us to the second element underlying the subordinate role of blacks in the governing coalition. White business leaders controlled more than material benefits. Initial black incorporation into the governing coalition occurred in a political climate and political circumstances that are quite important. *Brown v. Board of Education* had not yet put national authority behind the disestablishment of the Jim Crow system. The United States Congress had proved unwilling to enact anti-lynching legislation, much less stronger civil rights measures. Georgia's county unit system exaggerated the voting influence of the state's more tradition-bound elements, and racial demagoguery was rampant (Key 1949). In that racial context, white business leaders stood out as a moderating influence, and they had enough clout in state affairs to be recognized as an element capable of holding in check violence-prone whites.

Hence, in 1961, with the state government prepared for a campaign of massive resistance to even token school desegregation, the business elite, under the leadership of Atlanta banker and lawyer John A. Sibley, pressed for a shift in state policy (Homsby 1982). Reluctantly, the governor and the legislature yielded to the argument that the state's economic future required acceptance of social change. As a major source of campaign funds for the state's small-county "court house gangs," Atlanta business leaders had additional leverage that could be used to counteract traditionalism (Key 1949, 123).

In the years following World War II, Atlanta's business elite, with their overriding concern about economic growth and their sensitivity to national image, served as a check on the most volatile elements among traditional whites. At that time, before strong civil rights legislation had been enacted, black voting strength was inconsequential in Georgia politics, tilted as it was so heavily toward rural domination. The economic power of an urban business elite, however, was transferable to some degree into political influence, and it could be used to moderate what V. O. Key (1949) called the "rule of the rustics."

EFFORTS TO STRENGTHEN INCORPORATION

As the 1950s gave way to the 1960s, Atlanta's system of quiet, behind-the-scenes negotiations fell into disrepute in the city's black community. Following the Supreme Court's *Brown* decision ending constitutional protection for racial subordination, a new generation of civil rights activists emerged, and they were willing to challenge both the leaders and tactics of the past. The 1960 sit-ins represented more than an effort to end the exclusion of blacks from Atlanta's public accommodations. They represented an effort to end the white-patron, black-client relationship and enable blacks to be assertive in making a wide array of claims.

Eventually that assertiveness spilled over into the electoral arena as Atlanta moved toward becoming a city with a black majority. In 1969, the black community successfully supported a white mayoral candidate, Sam Massell, in opposition to the candidate backed by the white business community and endorsed by the outgoing mayor, Ivan Allen. Four years later, Maynard Jackson was elected Atlanta's first black mayor. Jackson's assumption of office also coincided with the institution of a new city charter in which the executive power of the mayor was strengthened, two-thirds of the city council were elected by district, and major steps were taken to incorporate neighborhoods into the city's planning process.

Seemingly, a peaceful revolution had occurred. New leadership and new bases of leadership within the black community had emerged. Neighborhood groups had also developed into significant actors in the city's politics, and the new city charter provided access for their participation. The city council enacted a citizen-participation ordinance, dividing the city up into Neighborhood Planning Units and calling for advisory committees to represent each. Mayor Jackson restructured the Planning Department to create a Division of Neighborhood Planning and designated twelve staff members as neighborhood planners to work with the citizen advisory committees.

Atlanta's ballot box "revolution" was not the whole story, however. A number of crosscurrents were at work. Once Sam Massell was in office, for example, he sought to realign his political base by working closely with the business community on its policy agenda, in particular the launching of the rapid transit system (MARTA). While unable to ignore a large black constituency, Massell sought to mobilize a white base of support. To try to tilt the population balance, he backed an unsuccessful measure in the state legislature to enlarge the city limits and bring in an additional 50,000 people. He also shifted rhetoric. He cautioned about the long-term consequences of white flight and urged blacks to "think" white and to reflect the general views of all portions of the city, not just a distinctly black viewpoint (Stone 1976, 183). In his unsuccessful bid for reelection in 1973, he campaigned on a "Save Atlanta" theme and attacked Maynard Jackson for being race minded.

He charged Jackson, the incumbent vice mayor, with having "always taken the black position," and added that he couldn't recall anything that Jackson had favored "that wasn't initiated by a racial viewpoint" (*Atlanta Constitution*, October 9, 1973). Bear in mind that at this time, though blacks were a slight majority of the city population, differences in age composition gave whites a slight edge in registered voters. Attacking Jackson for "reverse discrimination" while linking the prospect of black control with city decline, Massell heightened race consciousness. Nevertheless, Jackson won the election.

Maynard Jackson came into office in an atmosphere highly charged with racial feeling. While Massell had lost the election, the concerns he had raised about city hall favoritism toward black interests and about white flight were kept alive by the city's newspapers. Jackson's efforts to see that the city government and its contractors increased their minority hiring thus met with considerable criticism and resistance. Responsiveness to neighborhood groups, particularly in opposing expressway proposals, also generated concern among white business elites.

Before he had been in the mayoralty a full year, Jackson received a letter from the president of Central Atlanta Progress, the association of major downtown businesses, citing the danger of business disinvestment in downtown Atlanta, complaining about the lack of business access to the mayor, and telling the mayor he was perceived as being anti-white (Jones 1978, 111–12). Criticism of the mayor was also voiced in a business forum on the future of the city and given big play in the newspapers. Jackson avoided confrontation by beginning a series of "Pound Cake Summit" meetings, in which he conferred with business leaders every two or three weeks to discuss issues of concern. By the time his second term of office was over, central business district revitalization once again dominated the city's development agenda, and the number of neighborhood planners had dwindled. When Andrew Young assumed office, he somewhat reluctantly kept a single planner assigned to the neighborhoods—apparently as a symbolic gesture—and committed himself strongly to a development program backed by Central Atlanta Progress. Young stated openly that he could not "govern without the confidence of the business community" (*Atlanta Constitution*, July 24, 1983). While affirmative-action guarantees and joint-venture contracts continue to be occasional friction points, the white business community has ceased to oppose them in principle. A large measure of cooperation and goodwill between city hall and Central Atlanta Progress marks the emergence of a revamped but apparently stable urban regime, as in the past devoted mainly to promoting economic development, especially in Atlanta's central business district.

This account is of necessity much abbreviated, but it bears out the soundness of the comments made by Mack Jones several years ago when he observed that black officeholders were devoted mainly to "guaranteeing for blacks a more equitable share of existing governmental benefits and services within existing priorities" (1978, 99). Still, Atlanta's politics are not conflict free. Members of an unsteady, and now it seems dwindling, city council bloc, which fluctuates from an occasional majority to a minuscule two or three, oppose particular development projects; but without a helping hand from the city administration, they have no program of their own and they make no systematic oversight effort. And, while Atlanta's neighborhoods are not politically quiescent, they have become a fragmented and somewhat dispirited force.

Thus, despite a variety of efforts extending from the 1950s to the present, no one has been able to keep neighborhood development and housing improvements on the city's policy agenda or undertake a searching examination of how widely the benefits of downtown development are distributed. There is an acknowledged split within the black community between haves and have-nots, but no concrete program to bridge that gap (Clendinen 1986). Atlanta's urban regime is therefore built around accommodations between the black middle class and white business elites. However, there is more to the Atlanta arrangements than officeholder attentiveness to the need for business investment. Let's look more closely at the specifics of Atlanta's contemporary urban regime.

ATLANTA'S CONTEMPORARY URBAN REGIME

It would be too simple to say that the present arrangements in Atlanta prevail because they are what is economically best for the city. In the first place, the present arrangements came about through a process of conflict and negotiation. Black political leaders, dating back to the 1960s, have struggled to garner a significant share of the city's jobs and contracts (Stone 1976, 142–43). As we have seen, white business leaders have resisted those demands, at one point in effect threatening disinvestment. The present allocation of affirmative-action benefits is by no means guaranteed for the future. Decreasing judicial support for minority set-asides could weaken the bargaining position of black officeholders, perhaps in the process making more difficult their task of politically mobilizing the black middle class.

In the second place, there is a continuing concern in the black community that the benefits of Atlanta's economic growth are not widely enough shared. While this concern is not embodied in a specific program, it is a recurring issue. The white business community for its part is in search of ways to buffer investment activity, even that subsidized by the city, from social-justice demands.

Evolving over time, the strategy of the white business elite has had several facets. As it became increasingly evident that the city would have a black electoral majority, an effort was made to bring the black middle class into the mainstream of civic

life of the Atlanta business community. There was, after all, a long history of negotiation and accommodation between the white business elite and the black middle
class. In the late 1960s, two new organizations—Leadership Atlanta and Action
Forum—were formed to provide means through which black and white business
people could be brought together to consider various civic issues and seek common ground. Concurrently the chamber of commerce moved to integrate blacks
into its membership and activities. At the same time, while black demands for affirmative action were being resisted, the white business community did not reject
those demands totally. Subsequently it came to accept the idea that city employment and city contracts would carry affirmative guarantees. However, the white
business community has sought to promote development and the public subsidy
of development in ways that are insulated from city hall control. Examples of the
kind of arrangements the business community has promoted that reduce city hall
control over development activities include nonprofit corporations formed under
private auspices (Park Central to oversee redevelopment east of the central business district, Underground Festival Development Corporation to bring into being
the city's proposed new entertainment district, Atlanta Economic Development
Corporation to oversee generally the facilitating of economic development); state
rather than city subsidy (the building of an enormous convention facility in downtown Atlanta—the Georgia World Congress Center); and the issuance of tax-free
development bonds by an independent authority (Atlanta Downtown Development Authority).

One of the current policies being promoted is, in effect, a privatization of the
city's revenue capacity. State legislation allows for the creation within cities of special tax districts through which increased revenue from development in that district can be earmarked for infrastructure expenditures in that district. The business
community is urging that the city's posh Buckhead area, currently a site for intense
development activity, be designated as such a district. Additional legislation provides for the creation of special service districts through which *the property holders* in such a district can agree to levy a special tax on themselves in order to pay
for increased services, such as extra policing, within that district.

Over time, the white business elite has thus made use of the carrot and the stick.
It has sought to integrate the black middle class into the network of civic and business associations (formal and informal) that has throughout the postwar years been
central in the political life in Atlanta. At the same time, it has been critical of various city efforts to assure a black share in the economic life of the community, but
still willing to go along in practice with a number of measures guaranteeing city
jobs and contracts for blacks. All the while, business has lobbied for procedures
whereby economic activity would be insulated from city hall control. Blacks therefore have achieved a strong form of political incorporation, but their control is over

an increasingly limited sphere of economic activity—even though much of that activity is publicly subsidized.

The current urban regime seems to be stable but not static. Neighborhood development and housing improvements occupy no major position on the city's policy agenda and show no signs of gaining such a position. Neighborhood activists have been forced to rely mainly on litigation in what may be losing efforts to stop proposed expressway projects. Benefit from the city's "supply-side" development strategy has accrued to the black middle class, but there is not much evidence the lower class has gained. Atlanta is second only to Newark, New Jersey, among American cities in its poverty rate.

CONCLUSION

The present state of affairs in Atlanta is very much a reflection of prevailing political arrangements. However, it is significant that the city election of 1973 and the initial actions under the new city charter in 1974 seemed to point to a different scenario. Why was the black middle class incorporated but working class and neighborhood groups not? One answer is that the white business elite worked hard to bring about that outcome. But the issue is more complicated than that. Various nonbusiness groups have weaknesses and liabilities they have not been able to overcome.

Neighborhoods are not easy to work with as development partners. They are not usually organized in ways and equipped with resources that enable them to achieve highly visible successes. The same disadvantages are apparently true for other nonbusiness groups as well. For example, when city hall disregarded the wishes of the white business elite in selling a West End site to a black church association (the National Baptist Convention) for redevelopment, the association was unable on its own to put together a successful project. While they had financial capacity, they lacked the kind of organizational and technical experience needed for development projects. By contrast, the business community pulls city hall in the direction of its agenda because business is able to fill an action vacuum with its highly useful policy expertise and its practical experience in development projects.

Other forces also pull the city's black middle-class political leadership toward tight alliance with the white business elite. The black middle class and the white business elite have accumulated a long history of successful and productive backstage negotiations. It is an alliance that works. It has members who have learned the lessons of bargaining and accommodation. One activist in city politics emphasizes the city's "mercantile ethic" and is reported to have said that a room full of black and white leaders in Atlanta "is nothing but a roomful of people trying to cut a deal" (*Atlanta Constitution,* August 11, 1987).

Wanting to cut a deal is, however, not enough to forge a cohesive coalition. Distrust, particularly across racial lines, is to be expected among individuals who are unaccustomed to interacting with one another and have had little opportunity to build a compact of mutual support (on the importance of repeated transactions and the chance to develop norms of mutual support, see Hardin 1982; Axelrod 1984). But Atlanta provides a situation in which interaction across racial lines is a deep and constantly renewed tradition. Newcomers learn from old hands, and organizations such as Action Forum are structured to maintain that tradition. Although the habit of trust does not come easily, the leaders in Atlanta's governing coalition realize that; and they take deliberate steps to preserve the city's tradition of biracial cooperation. This tradition makes possible an accommodation between the city's economic sector and its political-electoral sector. Tight cross-sector cooperation gives the regime a powerful capacity for governing the community.

Yet despite the presence of a biracial governing coalition, Atlanta is no paragon of democratic practice. The city's version of biracial cooperation leaves out a variety of interests. Neighborhood organizations, historic preservationists, and a range of groups interested in maintaining a supply of affordable housing are outside the governing coalition. They are not part of the community of mutual accommodation. Development policy takes little heed of their concerns. Within the black community, not only are neighborhood concerns neglected, but class tension is significant. Mayor Andrew Young's personal appeal and his position as a principal in the civil rights movement of the 1960s attenuates the conflict, but the issue keeps bobbing to the surface. And Young himself comes under sporadic criticism for a system in which the same few black contractors garner a large share of the city's construction contracts (*Atlanta Constitution,* August 14, 1987; September 6, 1987). Significantly, the city's program of expanded opportunities for minorities calls for primary emphasis on the development of minority business enterprises. Jobs for the working class are not a direct target, and no systematic monitoring of job creation is in evidence.

What lessons do we draw from the Atlanta experience? We have long looked on democratic politics as the process that equalizes opportunities and redresses imbalances. The evolution of Atlanta's urban regime suggests a different conclusion. To a considerable extent, democratic politics mirrors resource inequalities. When the white primary was declared illegal, Atlanta's black middle class, with its rich network of organizations and its substantial store of civic skills, was able to bring off an immediate and substantial voter mobilization. That voting power was converted into policy gain for blacks as a group. But as the Jim Crow system was disassembled, class differences within the black community became more salient. The skills and resources of the black middle class enable its members to take advantage of opportunities that come from a place in the city's governing coalition. The black lower class lacks comparable opportunities.

198 CLARENCE N. STONE

Numbers alone amount to little. The Atlanta experience also suggests that loosely organized voting carries small weight. Consider the overall picture. Atlanta is a city with weak unions. They are not a central part of the civic and political life of the community, and job creation takes a back seat in policy deliberations. Many neighborhoods are organized, but interneighborhood cooperation across class and racial lines is limited. Furthermore, neighborhoods practice primarily an adversarial form of politics—each mobilizes best around its own immediate crisis; and that seems weak ground from which to try to gain a position in the city's governing coalition. As Atlanta's politics is now organized, neither specifically working class nor neighborhood organizations are essential in mobilizing an electoral majority. Nor do they control other resources essential in community activities. Consequently these groups have no irresistible claim on membership in the city's governing regime, and policy is not responsive to the kinds of interests they represent.

Atlanta offers a sobering lesson. Instead of electoral power serving to equalize resource capabilities, we see that a substantial store of resources is essential in order to make a telling use of the vote. Groups cannot simply make demands on city government; they must be in a position to enhance a city's capacity to govern. At the very least they must be able to deliver a dependable *and needed* block of votes. All groups face that test of whether they can contribute something essential to a community's capacity to govern: economic resources, mobilization of electoral majorities, promotion of civic cooperation, and engagement in the building of durable alliances. Atlanta's black middle class has the resources to pass that test; its lower class does not. Even in a formally democratic system where racial exclusion has been successfully combated, it is difficult to have an inclusive governing coalition. That is a challenge that remains before us.

NOTE

"Race and Regime in Atlanta," by Clarence N. Stone, in *Racial Politics in American Cities*, ed. Rufus Browning, Dale Roges Marshall, and David Tabb (New York: Longman, 1990), pp. 125–39. Reprinted with the permission of Pearson Education, Inc.

REFERENCES

Alexander, R. J. 1951. Negro business in Atlanta. *Southern Economic Journal* 17 (Apr.): 451–64.
Axelrod, R. 1984. *The evolution of cooperation.* New York: Basic Books.
Bacote, C. A. 1955. The Negro in Atlanta politics. *Phylon* 16(4): 333–50.
Bartley, N. V. 1983. *The creation of modern Georgia.* Athens: Univ. of Georgia Press.
Browning, R. P., D. Rogers Marshall, and D. H. Tabb. 1984. *Protest is not enough.* Berkeley: Univ. of California Press.

Clendinen, D. 1986. In Black Atlanta, affluence and sophistication are for the few. *New York Times* (Jan. 20): 10.

Eisinger, P. K. 1980. *The politics of displacement.* New York: Academic Press.

Elkin, S. L. 1985. Twentieth century urban regimes. *Journal of Urban Affairs* 7 (spring): 11–28.

Hardin, R. 1982. *Collective action.* Baltimore: Johns Hopkins Univ. Press.

Hornsby, A., Jr. 1982. A city too busy to hate. In *Southern businessmen and desegregation,* ed. E. Jacoway and D. R. Colburn. Baton Rouge: Louisiana State Univ. Press.

Jennings, M. K., and H. Zeigler. 1966. Class, party, and race in four types of elections: The case of Atlanta. *Journal of Politics* 28 (May): 391–407.

Jones, M. H. 1978. Black political empowerment in Atlanta: Myth and reality. *Annals of the American Academy of Political and Social Science* 439 (Sep.): 90–117.

Key, V. O., Jr. 1949. *Southern politics in state and nation.* New York: Alfred A. Knopf.

Martin, H. H. 1978. *William Berry Hartsfield: Mayor of Atlanta.* Athens: Univ. of Georgia Press.

Stone, C. N. 1976. *Economic growth and neighborhood discontent.* Chapel Hill: Univ. of North Carolina Press.

Walker, J. L. 1963a. Protest and negotiation: A case study of Negro leadership in Atlanta, Georgia. *Midwest Journal of Political Science* 7 (May): 99–124.

———. 1963b. Negro voting in Atlanta, 1953–1961. *Phylon* 24 (winter): 379–87.

———. 1963c. Protest and negotiation: A study of Negro political leaders in a Southern city. Ph.D. dissertation, State Univ. of Iowa.

Part Four

Power, Politics, and Urban Social Reform

The most salient issues in the urban education arena are funding, privatization, and reform. Much of the literature on these issues sets forth dire predictions about the prospects of reforming urban education, the limited resources available to do so, or the futility of attempting to do so. Stone leads us in a different direction by asking us to alter our understanding of power and civic capacity in order to solve some of the challenging issues related to urban education.

Stone's conception of civic capacity goes beyond voting, volunteering, and participating in public hearings. It encompasses efforts beyond business as usual or routine governmental action. For Stone, civic capacity is measured by the extent to which a community is involved in concerted efforts to address major community problems. The major community problem that Stone is most concerned with is education, and by extension the ability of traditionally excluded groups to have their interests met.

Throughout Chapters 9–11, there is an explicit understanding that education is class based, and that affluent parents bring to bear resources that are typically unavailable to poor and uneducated urban parents. Educated and affluent parents are able to provide their children with greater academic readiness and opportunity because they are generally able to supplement school resources, they have the time to volunteer, they have higher expectations, they have access to the leaders in the community, and they possess the skills needed to effectively engage school officials. Middle- and upper-class families have a range of resources that lower the opportunity cost to resolve education-related issues.

On the other hand, poor urban parents face systemic bias and an often unresponsive school bureaucracy in their attempts to address policy issues related to the low academic achievement of their children. In this environment, distrust is pervasive, educator expectations of children are low, and little gets resolved. In order to surmount these obstacles, Stone demonstrates the need to bring together different sectors of the community, including business, parents, educators, state and local officeholders, nonprofits, and external funding sources together around a shared purpose: to resolve issues related to poor performance, curriculum development, professional development, and standards-based schooling.

In Chapter 9, Stone summarizes the findings of the Civic Capacity and Urban Education Reform Project. In this 11-city study of school reform politics, Stone and his colleagues consider the question of why, in their efforts to revitalize central cities, American cities have not put forth a sustained effort at urban school reform. The Civic Capacity and Urban Education Reform Project, which included cities from all regions of the United States, addressed the difficulty of developing and sustaining concerted action around urban education. Although it is easier to build capacities around urban redevelopment—an issue area that does not typically involve the concerted action of the masses—it is much more difficult to build civic capacity in the educational arena.

In Chapter 10, Stone addresses an alternative to the typical conception of power and preferences. Normally interest groups are viewed to have fixed preferences. Politics is seen of as a matter of one preference defeating another, or of one interest group or set of preferences assuming power over another. Stone expands this power concept to provide us with an alternative understanding of the ideal environment to advance civic capacity and lasting school reform.

In Chapter 11, Stone chronicles the school reform efforts of four very different local communities—Kent County, Maryland; El Paso, Texas; Boston, Massachusetts; and Philadelphia, Pennsylvania. In all four communities, educational achievement had reached crisis proportions, and there was a general recognition that something needed to be done. However, in contrast to routine school reform efforts that are typically created and implemented in a top-down fashion, Stone describes how those communities that exhibit a high level of civic capacity bring key stakeholders together in the process of pursuing and implementing a shared plan of action.

Because it is a dominant theme in his other work, Stone recognizes that government cannot go it alone in the educational arena, but that it requires the resources and cooperation of nongovernmental actors. Civic capacity enhances the ability and opportunity to contribute to the policy-making process. If democracy is about having a role to play in shaping public policy, various segments of the community need to be mobilized in order to develop and utilize a shared framework of action. Stone's work can be subsumed under the "breaking the stalemate of local politics" category. His scholarship broadens our routine conceptions and serves as a guide beyond the realm of routine interactions in order to promote sustainable and viable school reform in a manner consistent with democratic values.

9. Civic Capacity and Urban Education

Clarence N. Stone

Norton Long (1958) once described the urban community as an "ecology of games," in which few players display a sense of responsibility for the locality's common well-being. As Long saw it, the usual form of civic life little suits concerted action on community-wide problems. Banks play the financial game, politicians serve mainly as brokers and focus narrowly on the reelection game, unions engage in their individual collective bargaining games, developers play the land-use game, and so it goes. According to Long, the "protagonists of things in particular are well organized and know what they are about; the protagonists of things in general are few, vague, and weak" (255).

In Long's (1958) account, broad topics of concern receive occasional attention at civic club lunches. From time to time, civic staff prepare task force reports on community-wide issues, but, Long argued, civic life is not geared to wide and sustained engagement in big problems. Mostly people deal with issues that are immediate in their daily lives, not wider concerns of the community. Yet Long suggested, most citizens feel a vague need for some group to take charge and bring the resources of the city to bear on its major problems.

In the decades since Long's (1958) article appeared, metropolitan areas have become increasingly fragmented, and within cities, functional specialization continues to be a powerful force. Thus urban civic life has not changed drastically. Still, what Robert Salisbury (1964) once called "the new convergence of power" has swung into action on significant occasions. In many places, public-private partnerships took shape, and over time they contributed greatly to remaking the physical character of the contemporary city.

It is not surprising, then, that as the performance of urban schools has come to be a matter of rising concern, calls for civic action have spread. A few cities have held "education summits" but not always with effective follow-through. Education is different from urban redevelopment, and concerted action around schools appears much harder to develop and perhaps even more difficult to sustain.

With this consideration in mind, in 1993, a team of political scientists launched a study, funded by the National Science Foundation, under the title of "Civic Capacity and Urban Education."[1] One of our working assumptions was that even though talk about civic action was plenteous, cities differ substantially in ability to mobilize around education; therefore, it is important to gain a better understanding of the nature of this varying capacity and what it looks like at different levels of development.

Although the overall project has explored the politics of urban school reform from a variety of angles, the purpose of the present report is less far ranging. It is to hold up for consideration the concept of civic capacity, with specific attention to urban education. With this groundwork laid, it is then possible to differentiate between civic capacity and social capital. Though the two terms have some kinship, they represent quite distinct perspectives on the urban community and how to respond to its problems.

Civic capacity concerns the extent to which different sectors of the community—business, parents, educators, state and local officeholders, nonprofits, and others—act in concert around a matter of community-wide import. It involves mobilization—that is, bringing different sectors together but also developing a shared plan of action. Much of the school reform literature talks about the need to assemble stakeholders and develop a common agenda, but language about stakeholders assumes that different elements of the community see themselves as having a stake in something they hold in common. Long's (1958) concept of the local community as an "ecology of games" cautions us that the role of stakeholder is not necessarily foremost for many community actors. For civic capacity to become a reality, "protagonists of things in particular" must come to view themselves as participants in a wider "game."

In taking a cue from Norton Long, as we looked at 11 cities (Atlanta, Baltimore, Boston, Denver, Detroit, Houston, Los Angeles, Pittsburgh, St. Louis, San Francisco, and Washington, D.C.), our research team did not presuppose that various sectors of the community routinely see themselves as stakeholders in urban education. Indeed, we assumed that acting around a shared purpose would be atypical, and therefore it is important to explore the nature of city coalitions and the varying degrees to which they came together *around the issue of urban education*.

As indicated above, school reform is a distinctive kind of process, with a dynamic different from redevelopment or other processes centered on changing urban land use. Moreover, our research taught us quickly that whatever might be the case with various forms of social capital, civic capacity is not a generic quality that is easily transferable from one issue to another. An ability to address educational improvement is not simply an application of a general community capacity to solve problems but requires its own particular development. A brief account of selected cities will illustrate.

ATLANTA: A CASE OF WEAK CIVIC CAPACITY

Over a period of many years, Atlanta has demonstrated its considerable capacity to pursue a policy of urban redevelopment, centered on the city's main business district (Stone 1989). Yet Atlanta has consistently failed to draw key sectors of the community together around an agenda of educational improvement. Consider Atlanta in 1993, a decade after the publication of *A Nation at Risk* (National Commission on Excellence in Education 1983). By the early 1990s, the national call for education reform had been made and remade in several forums. The state of Georgia had initiated its Quality Basic Education Act and had taken other initiatives. Yet none of this determined what the local response would be. Despite weakly performing schools and widespread worry about the situation, Atlanta did not come together around a comprehensive and sustained move to reform its educational system. The city shows what a low level of civic capacity looks like, significantly, not because various sectors of the city were indifferent but because diffuse concerns and scattered activities never generated a community synergy.

In 1993, however, Atlanta seemed ripe for a thoroughgoing reform effort. Schools were performing at an abysmal level, with test scores lower even than some of Georgia's rural counties. Moreover, the longer Atlanta students were in the education system, the worse they performed; high school scores were even more dismal than scores in the elementary grades. The dropout rate was high, at an estimated 30%. Even with per pupil expenditures higher in Atlanta than in many of the surrounding suburbs, enrollment in city schools had gone down at an astonishing rate. From 1975 to 1993, enrollment halved, declining from 119,000 to 60,000.

Atlanta's elected school board was scandal ridden and rife with conflict, leading one observer to characterize it as "the most criticized and ridiculed" body in the city government (Holmes 1993). One member had been removed for channeling funds at questionable payment levels to favored contractors, and another board member was under fire for accepting funds from the board's highly paid ($300,000 per annum) attorney. The board was sharply split along racial lines, and personal disputes within and across racial lines heightened the conflict level. Civility was at a low level, and an argument between a member of the board of education and the school superintendent nearly turned violent. Though school board proceedings were televised and therefore viewed by the public, questions of education policy took a backseat to personal disputes about who was in charge of what and who was to get which contracts and jobs.

With school board elections upcoming, the time seemed right for coalition building around a fresh start. If Atlanta were to build civic capacity around educational improvement, 1993 would seem to have been the time to do so.

Obstacles stood in the way, however. Racial tension was not confined to the school board but extended throughout the education arena and beyond. Furthermore, 20 years earlier, under the auspices of a federal district court judge hearing Atlanta's school desegregation suit, a biracial group signed an agreement known as the Atlanta Compromise (Jackson 1978; Fleishman 1980). Though the signatories were biracial, the agreement essentially ceded control of the school system to the African American community, thereby eroding ground on which the interaction between the races could occur around issues of education.

In this earlier era of jurisprudence, when racial balance was a consideration, Atlanta, with a school system already heavily African American, posed the possibility that litigation could turn down the path of a metropolitan solution. White business leaders were eager to avoid that turn of events for fear that it would torpedo an ongoing effort to gain suburban support for a regional mass transit system. Leaders in the African American community were unsure that they could achieve a workable agreement centered on racial balance, and some had doubts that racial balance should be the top education priority in any case. With that background, a biracial committee reached an agreement to forgo the busing of students for racial balance and instead to alter the racial balance of power in the administrative control of the school system. An African American would be named to replace the white superintendent, who was stepping down, and black representation would be increased throughout the upper ranks of school administration. Informally, black and white leaders understood the arrangement to be one of shifting control of the schools from white hands to black.

Subsequently, business involvement in education virtually disappeared. In 1993, two decades after the Atlanta Compromise, one observer noted that until the chamber of commerce's newly awakened interest in education that year, business leaders made no effort to be a voice in the deliberations of the city's school board.[2]

Nevertheless, for 1993, business put aside its practice of disengagement and created a campaign organization, EDUPAC, to support a new majority on the nine-member school board. In an environment of rising opposition, four members of the board chose not to seek reelection. A biracial coalition came together in another organization, Erase the Board, and it was seeking a completely new school board. Erase the Board was led by the president of Concerned Black Clergy, and it enjoyed biracial support spanning a diverse set of groups: the Atlanta Council of PTAs (a racially mixed but majority black organization), 100 Black Men, Atlanta Parents and Public Linked to Education (Apple Corps, a small but well-organized group then headed largely by white women professionals), the education division of Jimmy Carter's Atlanta Project (a group with strong business connections), the teachers' union, and the Council of In-Town Neighborhoods and Schools (another racially mixed group).

Whereas Erase the Board sought a complete ousting of incumbents, EDUPAC supported three incumbents, and those three were reelected. But two other incumbents were defeated, and the postelection board of education had six new members. The school superintendent also resigned, and the stage was set for a new era in Atlanta's education politics. For a time, racial division had taken a backseat to a move for change.

With business having a renewed interest in education, the chamber of commerce formed a committee on public education as an organization to bridge the gap between business and schools. Already in place at that time was the Atlanta Partnership of Business and Education, concerned with matters such as adopt-a-school programs and teacher-of-the-year awards. In addition, like most cities, at this time, Atlanta had a number of advocacy groups for children as well as organizations concerned with various aspects of youth development. Overall, there was no shortage of actors interested in education and related matters.

Diffuse concerns provide useful raw material, but in and of themselves, they do not generate synergy. Someone has to see and act on a big picture of community-wide purpose and cooperation around that purpose. In Atlanta, that did not happen.

ATLANTA'S ROAD NOT TAKEN

With schools desperately in need of attention, with the education issue prominent in public discussion, with a diverse set of players coming together to elect a new school board, and with an opening to bring in a new school superintendent, Atlanta could have come together to build a high level of civic engagement around improving its education system. Stakeholders, however, did not join their efforts, even though a high level of interest in school reform was clearly in evidence. Civic energy was scattered among several organizations, each of which continued to pursue its particular agenda. No one came forward to summon the disparate players to join efforts and form an encompassing coalition with a comprehensive program of action.

Perhaps it is not surprising, then, that during the school board election there were two separate campaign organizations despite the fact that their aims coincided closely. When the election was over, the two organizations folded and made no effort to join in a common cause of school reform. Instead, potential partners went their separate ways.

The business sector started 1993 off with a resurgent interest in education and an encouraging chamber of commerce study, and the Committee on Public Education held promise of an institutionalized commitment. The chamber of commerce study sounded a supportive note for the public schools, and it engaged in self-reproach over lack of business involvement in education. The study touched on the issue of workforce development and criticized business reliance on the graduates of suburban schools to meet labor needs.

Once the election was over, however, these broad concerns faded, and the business sector once again narrowed its focus to the conventional issues of containing costs, unbusinesslike practices such as tenure (subsequently eliminated by state legislation), and excessive bureaucracy. The new school board and new superintendent embraced a kindred outlook and soon occupied themselves with various financial matters such as the underfunded pension plan and with economy measures such as school closings. Issues such as the use of closed schools, underused space for prekindergarten programs, and services for families and children were not pursued.

Among advocacy and social service organizations, no move toward a comprehensive approach emerged. In some cases, the staff of such agencies, what Floyd Hunter (1953) called "under-structure professionals," seemed, as one observer noted, to spend much of their time and energy in meetings with other professionals. In the eyes of some, the most effective groups in the city were the smaller and often unfinanced groups such as 100 Black Men of Atlanta and Apple Corps. With small resource bases, these organizations have an impact through a sustained but narrow focus. Without major allies, they simply cannot afford a wider approach.

Overall, volunteers and social service organizations have nothing within their own dynamic that would lead them to generate a broad vision of community needs and how to meet them. The one move toward a comprehensive approach was the Atlanta Project of Jimmy Carter. Launched during the city's preparation for the Summer Olympics, this was a business-backed and nongovernmental effort to address poverty and show the world that Atlanta possessed a social conscience. It was a five-year program intended to spur volunteerism in Atlanta to new heights, but it came under criticism for its lack of focus, its paternalistic approach, and the unrealistic expectations it fostered (Stone and Pierannunzi 2000). It was weak on community consultation, and after its planned five years, the Atlanta Project closed shop, leaving only a few of the initiatives it launched still operating. With open-ended aims but a firm promise to business to remain unconnected to local government, the Atlanta Project lacked sustaining power and possessed no institutional capacity to design broad programs to combat poverty and improve city schools.

Perhaps as an unintended legacy of the Atlanta Compromise, education has proved to be highly resistant to civic mobilization. During the 1990s, the school system had four different superintendents (the fourth continues in office at this writing), and many of them have shown little inclination to court business involvement. Moreover, subsequent to the 1993 chamber of commerce study mentioned above, business has mainly been critical of Atlanta schools and their management practices.

To complicate matters further, the city and its schools have come under sharp attack by political representatives from the surrounding and overwhelmingly white suburbs. It is not surprising, then, that the Atlanta Project shared with many lesser initiatives an inability to overcome barriers of race and class and to genuinely engage Atlanta's nonaffluent African American population. To many residents, the city's civic climate is highly uninviting.

The depth of distrust can be seen in reactions to a 1999 proposal to convert Grady High School to charter status. Grady has a magnet program and is one of the few high schools in the city to have a racially mixed enrollment. As discussion proceeded, it became clear that black parents, particularly those whose children were not part of the magnet program, strongly opposed change and distrusted the motives of those backing the charter move. In a series of meetings, these parents registered the following objections:

1. Governance of the charter school would be dominated by magnet parents and white parents generally.
2. In a charter school, programs for students not in the magnet program would be underfunded.
3. Many parents would not be able to express their views because they could not attend governance meetings due to work and family commitments.
4. Nonaffluent parents would be better able to protect their interests by working through the elected board of education than through an autonomous board for a charter school.[3]

Anxieties about white dominance served to undermine support for change. Distrust at various levels and across lines of race and class gives rise to Atlanta's weak form of civic capacity. With distrust widespread, actors tend to carve out small bits of turf and defend them. In the education arena, coalitions are ad hoc and short lived. What should be noted, however, is how little effort is devoted to altering the situation. Broad-vision leadership is in short supply. Perhaps still operating in the shadow of the Atlanta Compromise, business ventures little. Activity lies largely in the hands of "under-structure" personnel, and they carry little credibility as "movers and shakers." Yet although civic elites can make change believable, the Atlanta Project reveals how shallow their legitimacy is. As the Grady High School experience illustrates, unless parents and other community-based actors can be engaged in the cause, resistance to reform may run deep. The striking feature of the Atlanta scene is the scarcity of people either seeking to enlist elites to come together on the education issue or to overcome the distrust among the masses. Despite the city's long history of biracial governance around urban redevelopment, Atlanta's education arena provides a striking example of weak civic capacity. As an issue, education remains tellingly disconnected from economic development, general worries about the quality of city life, or other concerns that might power a reform-minded coalition willing to tackle school reform.

The other 3 cities with low civic capacity in the 11-city study are St. Louis, Denver, and San Francisco. Significantly, all three were under court-directed orders for school desegregation, and an unintended effect was to discourage the building of civic capacity—many stakeholders saw education as the court's responsibility, not theirs (Stone et al. 2001).

LOOSELY CONNECTED CIVIC CAPACITY

Atlanta represents a stubbornly low level of civic capacity around the issue of school improvement. Contrast Chicago's widely written about experience with school reform.[4] After *A Nation at Risk* and other reports put the spotlight on public education, the weak performance of many school districts came under close scrutiny. During a 1987 visit to Chicago, then U.S. Secretary of Education William J. Bennett labeled the city's school system the "worst in America" and said to Chicagoans, "You've got close to educational meltdown" (Vander Weele 1994, 3). Bennett lent drama to what the city's research and advocacy groups had already documented: A high dropout rate and low test scores were damning proof of the failure of Chicago schools.

In 1987, the same year that Bennett's comments caused a stir, a prolonged teachers strike (the ninth in 18 years) brought matters to a head, and Mayor Harold Washington initiated a summit process, bringing major sectors of the community together to address the need for school reform. The mayor had already taken a preliminary step to draw Chicago business into a more active and open role (Shipps 1998). After the strike settlement, Mayor Washington arranged for an all-day, open meeting on the city schools. "Attended by thousands," this meeting led the mayor to appoint a parent community council, and he asked it to sponsor "parent and community forums throughout the city" (Bryk et al. 1998, 19). Though Harold Washington's death a short time later weakened the effort to create a tight-knit coalition around school reform, the process had nevertheless been set in motion, and the reform coalition achieved far-reaching legislation to create decentralization and parent participation through a system of powerful local school councils. Subsequently, however, with a shift in party control of the Illinois legislature, a business-dominated coalition gained state authorization for an additional form of restructuring superimposed on the recent decentralization. It provided for business-style management, controlled by city hall, to guide and monitor the school system overall. Mayor Richard M. Daley embraced this version of school reform and put in place a management team to operate it.

Chicago illustrates not a highly developed form of civic capacity but rather a loosely connected form. Short on continuity, it nevertheless represents a markedly higher level than the diffuse and fragmented capacity Atlanta displays. From the outset, Chicago possessed research and advocacy groups able to focus attention on systemwide problems. Chicago business has a long record of involvement in education, and its concerns are broader than the low-taxation, economy-and-efficiency concerns that Atlanta business displays. In addition, first under Mayor Harold Washington and later under Mayor Richard M. Daley, city hall has played an active role of a more facilitative kind under Washington and of a more top-command kind under Daley. Significantly, however, parent- and community-based groups have also played an important, albeit uneven, part, first in shaping the reform agenda and later in implementing decentralization. Though the major players have not always formed a tight-knit coalition, they have cohered to a significant degree around sundry efforts to improve schools.[5] Chicago shows, however, that civic capacity is not constant and does not always build cumulatively. Civic capacity can and does sometimes regress.

Among our 11 cities, Baltimore's experience provides a rough parallel to that of Chicago in that a wide array of players have engaged to varying degrees in the furtherance of a school improvement agenda, but over time, one sees only a loose joining of efforts.[6] In Baltimore, at roughly the same time as the Chicago summit, BUILD (an Industrial Areas Foundation affiliate) put school reform on the city's action agenda, pressing for site-based management (decentralization) and also for the creation of an agreement between the schools and the city's major business organization, the Greater Baltimore Committee, to deal with school-to-work and school-to-college issues. Unlike many cities, Baltimore organizes its school system as a department of the city government. And when Kurt Schmoke became mayor in 1987, city hall became an active participant in the reform coalition. Though Baltimore has never had the kind of citywide forums, "attended by thousands," that Chicago has had, the city does have a rich array of neighborhood organizations. Over the years, several of them have taken up the school reform issue—some of them stimulated by Baltimore's Citizens Planning and Housing Association, a significant citywide actor (Orr 1999). Moreover, another organization, Advocates for Children and Youth, monitors key aspects of school performance in the city. Sundry state officials have also been part of the loose coalition concerned to improve schools in Baltimore.

Chicago and Baltimore are alike in that business, community and advocacy groups, and public officials became loosely allied to improve public education. In both cities, administrators and teachers have offered resistance, and racial divisions over employment have hampered cooperation. The main difference between the two is the central role assumed by Chicago's mayor, whereas the restructuring in Baltimore created a peculiar state-city partnership, in which the school system continues to enjoy a degree of autonomy. At the same time, the state set a short deadline for a master plan, and this worked against the engagement of parents and community groups in the planning process. Baltimore thus has a stronger base of school reform than Atlanta but falls short of the scope of community engagement that Chicago has had.

Among the 11 cities, aside from Baltimore, 3 other cities fell into the middle category in the level of civic capacity for the 1993–1994 period covered in the National Science Foundation project: Houston, Detroit, and Washington, D.C. At the time of the fieldwork, civic capacity in Houston was limited by conflict between Latino and African American communities (Longoria 1998; McAdams 2000). Since then, although Houston has moved forward in building civic capacity, Detroit and Washington, D.C., have experienced takeovers of their school systems and accompanying setbacks in community engagement.[7]

HIGH CIVIC CAPACITY

If neither Baltimore (among our 11 cities) nor Chicago (as a well-publicized case nationally) represents a top level of civic capacity, is there an example? One strong candidate for that rating is El Paso, Texas (Navarro and Natalico 1999). In the early 1990s, confronted, as were many other cities, by weakly performing schools, El Paso moved to foster community-wide collaboration around educational improvement. Following extensive discussion among a cross section of city leaders, a small group came together to form the El Paso Collaborative for Academic Excellence. The key figures were the superintendents of the three school districts that serve El Paso: the president of the University of Texas, El Paso; the president of the El Paso Community College; the executive director of the Texas Education Agency's regional service center; the lead organizer of the El Paso Interreligious Sponsoring Organization (an affiliate of the Industrial Areas Foundation); the president of the Greater El Paso Chamber of Commerce; the president of the El Paso Hispanic Chamber of Commerce; the mayor of the city; and the county judge. Unlike the loosely connected reform movement in Baltimore or the totally scattered activity in Atlanta, El Paso formed and still maintains (unlike Chicago's short-lived summit effort) a tight-knit organization around a set of agreed-on concerns. The collaborative has a professional staff, and it pursues activities that involve parents and the broader community and has embarked on a project to develop "a cadre of community leaders and parents who are willing to support educational renewal for the long term" and help "keep the public engaged in the endeavor" (Navarro and Natalico 1999, 599).

The business sector has played a major part. In February 1998, city leaders came together in an economic summit identifying education and workforce development as a top priority for the city. The Greater El Paso Chamber of Commerce followed this summit with a business/education white paper, including a series of recommendations for how businesses could address the concerns identified (El

Paso Collaborative for Academic Excellence 2000). Another period of community consultation followed, and in February 2000, the city held an education summit to move on a wide array of specific recommendations.

Several things are noteworthy about El Paso's experience. One is that all sectors of the community are represented, and this includes the leadership of the city's three school districts. Moreover, not only is there a major community-based organization involved, but the development of parent and community leadership and the promotion of grassroots engagement are also part of the ongoing activity of the collaborative. Another feature is the strong representation of the institutional basis of power and resources: the three school districts, the state, the city, the county, two chambers of commerce, the university, and the community college. The durable character of the collaboration is another notable feature. Significantly, it is formally organized and staffed, and it maintains a high level of visible activity. Perhaps related to this feature of El Paso's experience is the fact that collaboration focuses on concrete and specific courses of action; it is no mere expression of general sentiment. Furthermore, grassroots- and elite-level consultation and deliberation are ongoing activities. Finally, it should be noted that the collaborative has received important material and intellectual support from extralocal sources: the National Science Foundation (the Urban Systemic Initiative); the Pew Charitable Trusts; the Education Trust, headed by Kati Haycock; and John Goodlad's National Network for Educational Renewal.[8]

What is relatively easy to trace, especially for a formally organized entity such as the El Paso Collaborative for Educational Excellence, is the extent to which various segments of the community are mobilized to take part. Less easy to track is the interaction among those mobilized and the consequences of interaction for a shared understanding. However, it should be noted that El Paso uses a highly planned form of consultation. For most cities, the process is more casual and even incidental. Yet although the process sometimes breaks down, as it has on occasion in Baltimore (typically along the fault line of race), there is an identifiable path of development that can take place. It has to do with an enlarged understanding, a widened perspective on what is at issue. A simulation exercise on school reform generated the observation that the "importance of a mixed group of people considering what to do cannot be overstated" (Hill, Campbell, and Harvey 2000, 58). Most people start with what they know personally, from what they do and experience in everyday life. But when given a collective commitment to solve a problem, they often find a need to listen to one another and consider what observations each has to offer. In the above simulation exercise, participants found themselves weighing a wide array of viewpoints and "attributed their expansive thinking to the ideas of other panelists who brought a variety of perspectives to the table" (Hill, Campbell, and Harvey 2000, 58).

A summit consultation can operate in just that manner. First, it focuses attention on the community-wide dimensions of a problem. It is not a matter of addressing particular problems on an individual basis but of considering a broad issue from the combined concerns and insights of a variety of participants. In short, it is a form of public deliberation, and it is this form of consultation that El Paso has intentionally cultivated. As we saw earlier, however, Chicago followed quite a different path, even though it started reform through a summit. Chicago's process later gave way to a more restricted form of consultation, as the traditional alliance between business and city hall displaced a more inclusive form of community engagement. Significantly, Chicago, unlike El Paso, did not institutionalize community-wide consultation as an integral part of school reform.

PITTSBURGH, BOSTON, AND LOS ANGELES

None of our 11 cities has as refined a form of civic capacity as El Paso displays, but 3 of them—Pittsburgh, Boston, and Los Angeles—achieved relatively high levels of civic capacity. Each reached that level in a somewhat different manner. At the time of our collective field research, 1993–1994, Pittsburgh had the highest level of civic capacity, though it was experiencing some significant transitions (Portz, Stein, and Jones 1999). Civic capacity in Pittsburgh's education arena grew out of the desegregation struggles of the 1960s and 1970s. Key leaders came together around the idea of school improvement as a way to transcend battles over racial balance. The Allegheny Conference on Community Development (ACCD), the business sector's voice on major civic issues, made some vital moves. First, it created the Allegheny Conference Education Fund to support innovative projects within the school system, and it brought in national experts to foster school-business partnerships. Second, the ACCD provided leadership for a citizens' advisory committee formed in 1980, and that committee developed a school improvement plan and launched a "community dialogue" to engage neighborhood leaders. The committee also sponsored a public information campaign along with a series of troubleshooting meetings to emphasize the strengths of the school system.

The president of the teachers' union was an important member of the school improvement coalition, providing a critical base of support for the reform process. In 1980, Richard Wallace was hired as superintendent, and he further shaped reform around an "excellence agenda" and brought the education-research community in as participants in reform. During his 12 years as superintendent, Pittsburgh acquired a reputation as "a national model of urban educational reform" (Portz, Stein, and Jones 1999, 56). Wallace's successor, Louise Brennan, continued an activist agenda. Moving in the new direction of decentralization, she used a series of broad-based task forces to develop a strategic plan of action. The plan provided for an expanded and formally recognized role for parent and community involvement, and she also inaugurated a program of training for parent involvement in the new structure. Thus Pittsburgh established and made strong use of a tradition of civic collaboration in education, but ongoing events show that even such a tradition may rest on a tenuous basis, as a financial squeeze, the redirection of business attention to issues of regional economic decline, and continuing tensions over racial balance versus neighborhood schools have taken a toll on civic cooperation. The ACCD provided crucial institutional support for collaboration around education, and with that organization now less focused on city issues than regional ones, civic cooperation is today less firmly anchored than at any time since the 1960s and 1970s.

Whereas Pittsburgh built civic capacity to avert a major battle over school desegregation, Boston built civic capacity amid the ruins left by one of the nation's bitterest struggles over busing. For a time, the Boston business community kept a distance from education, and at one stage, a corporate executive in Boston told the U.S. Civil Rights Commission that business did not see itself as "a major actor" in public education (Portz, Stein, and Jones 1999, 87). Yet during the time that Federal District Court Judge W. Arthur Garrity presided over the desegregation process in Boston, unlike some of his judicial colleagues in other communities, he took steps to head off civic disengagement. Judge Garrity developed a number of initiatives to involve business and higher education in the Boston schools (Portz, Stein, and Jones 1999). He also formed a citywide coordinating council to monitor school compliance with desegregation orders, and he created district advisory committees along with racial-ethnic parent councils at each school. As the 1970s gave way to the 1980s, three networks emerged, perhaps facilitated by Judge Garrity's moves to enlist involvement in Boston education. In 1982, the Boston Compact became the channel for a partnership in which the school system would pursue improved learning outcomes and business would provide jobs to graduates. Subsequently, the Boston Building and Trades Union joined the partnership, as did institutions of higher education, thereby expanding the job base and including postsecondary education opportunities for graduates. Boston's Private Industry Council provided an additional institutional base for school-business partnership. Boston Compact II followed in 1989, with an expanded agenda of school reform, and in 1994, Boston Compact III brought the teachers' union into the partnership.

A second network, the Boston Plan for Excellence in Education in the Public Schools, was a spin-off of the compact. It provided a means whereby corporate and foundation grants could be provided to further innovation in the school system. The third network was the Citywide Educational Coalition. It stemmed from a human services collaborative concerned with children and youth and became a nonprofit entity with membership, including parents, educators, and community organizations as well as business, foundations, and higher education. It assumed the important role of sponsoring public forums and disseminating information on the school system. An advocate of greater community involvement, it established parent councils at each school.

Even with these overlapping networks and their expanding memberships, civic cooperation often came in second to community conflict until a mayoral-appointed school board replaced the elected board. This was much more than a formal reorganization of school governance; it represented a strong commitment by city hall to add its weight to the coalition seeking school reform.

Thus neither Pittsburgh nor Boston created a single encompassing organization such as the El Paso Collaborative for Excellence in Education, though the Boston Compact was a significant move in that direction. Pittsburgh was more dependent on informal civic cooperation, and as business attention came to focus on regional economic issues, the city's civic capacity around school reform weakened. On the other hand, the involvement of the teachers' union and the parent and community base in Pittsburgh are features of that city's civic capacity that many places cannot match.

Though Boston has not completely overcome its history of community discord, it experienced a remarkable turnaround in civic cooperation. Despite an unsteady start, the institutional networks mobilized resources, offered channels of discussion and deliberation about the city's schools and about the school-community interface, and furnished a wide base of support for school reform. The mayor's leadership provided a centripetal force that counterbalanced a history of civic discord and helped put school reform on track, but a history of community conflict is not easily put aside.

Among our 11 cities, Los Angeles is the third community that ranks high on civic mobilization behind school reform. Like Pittsburgh and Boston, however, it shows that civic capacity can be tenuous. Our field interviews in 1993–1994 caught Pittsburgh just before a weakening of its school reform coalition. They caught Boston on the rise, just as mayoral leadership clinched the coalescence of reform forces. In Los Angeles, 1993–1994 found the city at the point where its newly formed coalition had momentum, but before budget problems; the death of the president of the teachers' union and other changes reduced that momentum.

The key event in Los Angeles was the creation of LEARN (Los Angeles Educational Alliance for Restructuring Now).[9] It was preceded by two organizations that came together to form LEARN. One of the predecessor organizations was the Los Angeles Educational Partnership, a business-formed organization to promote reform and arrange for consulting by corporate management with selected schools. The other predecessor organization was Kids 1st, a grassroots coalition representing Latino, African American, Jewish, and other ethnic neighborhoods. Its cochair was Richard Riordan, subsequently mayor, but in the early stage a crucial link between Kids 1st and the business sector. He thus became a key figure in the creation of LEARN. In forming LEARN, the two predecessor organizations forged an alliance with the teachers' union and the school superintendent. To increase involvement, LEARN organized seven task forces covering various aspects of educational improvement. With broad backing, LEARN gained school board acceptance of its plan.

LEARN clearly was a formidable organization, with the chief executive of Atlantic Richfield Corporation as chairman and a former state legislator as the president and principal action person. However, city budget problems, resistance to the reform agenda among secondary school teachers, and strong political crosscurrents, combined with the loss of some central players, narrowed the number of schools LEARN targeted. It continues as a force and is now allied with the Los Angeles Metropolitan Project, the channel for the Annenberg Challenge Grant funds for Los Angeles.

Missing, however, is the kind of solidified or expanding base of collaboration achieved in El Paso and that held sway for many years in Pittsburgh. Also missing is the kind of citywide deliberation and consultation that other reform coalitions have set in motion to try to ensure that they have a continuing base of grassroots support. In the massive Los Angeles school district, LEARN has narrowed its focus to a relatively small body of pilot schools, and it is no longer the force it once promised to be.

OVERVIEW

In a recent examination of school reform, Hill, Campbell, and Harvey (2000, ix) offered the telling observation that "the normal politics of school systems cannot support fundamental reform." Such reform never comes from people who are engaged in running routine operations. It comes, instead, only when the members of a community acknowledge that they have a problem in need of the attention of the community as a civic body. The ability to give that attention is what we term *civic capacity.*

Significantly, Hill, Campbell, and Harvey (2000, 107) argued that even a highly innovative superintendent is unlikely to have an enduring impact without a strong foundation of community support: "Leadership must come from a longer-lasting source and one that is both more deeply rooted in the community than a superintendent and less protective of the status quo than a school board or district central office."

Consider what is implied in this statement. School boards and school administrators tend to focus on the immediate responsibilities of running a system, and because they are an integral part of that system, their reflexes are to defend it (Rich 1996). They do not ask fundamental questions about how effectively the community is being served. For those questions to be raised and pursued, people need to embrace a special kind of civic-mindedness. They do that by being brought together on a community-serving basis to confront a common need. This is what theorist Hannah Arendt (1968) regarded as politics. For her, politics is not the everyday pushing and shoving around particular interests but an activity *out of the ordinary* in which people become conscious of their common welfare and act on it. In this light, civic capacity has two facets: assembling in recognition of a problem to be tackled and developing an understanding from a community-wide perspective. With these two facets in mind, let us look again at the varying levels of civic capacity displayed among sundry cities.

Atlanta provides an example of a community not totally lacking in civic spirit around education but one in which concerns about improving schools are scattered among a variety of groups with no organized means of coming together, discovering and expanding their shared concerns, and developing an overall strategy of action.

El Paso falls at the other end of the spectrum. Here a conscious effort brought all segments of the community together, drawing on the major institutional bases of power and resources, to form an organization and sponsor efforts to keep all sectors of the community involved and indeed to widen and deepen that involvement. Actions have both fostered wide-ranging consultation and also moved from discussion to concrete action.

Among our 11 cities, Pittsburgh, Boston, and Los Angeles created versions of comprehensive coalitions in different ways, and they engaged in wide consultation around issues of fundamental reform. None has achieved quite the same high level of civic action that El Paso has, but each has demonstrated a capacity for community-minded deliberation and action. Less cohesive efforts in Chicago and Baltimore set these cities apart from the scattered activities of Atlanta. Both represent loosely connected capacities, with mayoral leadership giving school reform in Chicago a centripetal force missing in Baltimore. However, as Chicago's top-down leadership emerged, wider consultation weakened. Consultation in Baltimore has simply been more loosely joined throughout.

Drawn partly from our 11-city study, but in the cases of El Paso and Chicago from a broader base of experience, these examples show significant variation. Some cities move more haltingly toward school reform than others, and the role of business and other stakeholders is irregular across cities and over time. Moreover, race and ethnicity are often significant barriers. The public character of civic capacity is itself a two-edged sword. On one hand, bringing representatives of various sectors of the community together to consider a community-wide problem has the potential to expand understanding and move people out of their pattern of narrow, everyday thinking. On the other hand, the process is public, and the actors are on a public stage. It is never simply a matter of stimulating particular individuals to think more broadly. Players in a reform process perform in an arena in which the public is not an undifferentiated mass but a public sometimes deeply divided by group differences.

Baltimore's experience with a pilot project—the contracting out of the management of nine schools to Education Alternative, Inc.—illustrates the problem (Orr 1999, 143–64). When Kurt Schmoke was elected mayor, he was eager to turn around the performance of Baltimore city schools but found the central school bureaucracy to be a formidable force of resistance. Even though BUILD, a community-based organization, and the Greater Baltimore Committee, an organization of major businesses, had already done groundwork for school reform, there was little forward momentum. With a new school superintendent of his choosing in place, Mayor Schmoke sought an innovative way of moving the school system toward greater decentralization and improved academic performance. Supported by a local foundation, the mayor had the school superintendent and union officials make site visits and consider a private company, Education Alternatives, Inc., for a pilot project of managing nine of the city schools. The teachers and principals in these schools would be kept in place if they so chose, or they could transfer to other positions in the system. The teachers' union president endorsed the idea. However, once the project was put in place and the company transferred teachers' aides out of the nine pilot schools and replaced them with college-educated interns, apprehensions about job security rose. This transfer of teachers' aides helped foster unease within the African American community about privatization and contracting out. It set off alarm bells about a potential threat to the school system as a source of employment for the city's African American community. The school system was the city's largest employer, and more than 70% of the jobs in the system were held by African Americans (Orr 1999, 149).

As the contracting-out pilot moved to implementation, BUILD and the city's black clergy criticized Mayor Schmoke for acting without consultation, and the president of the teachers' union shifted from support to opposition. Limited consultation was a major hindrance to continued momentum toward school reform, but it is also significant that an initial focus on what was "good for kids" (as phrased by the teachers' union president) gave way to concerns about race and employment as the proposal became public and a wider array of players added their voices (Orr 1999, 143–64).

Whether Education Alternatives, Inc., was a sound project to pursue is not the issue. The point is that agreement among a small number of individuals, even though they held key institutional positions and even though they enjoyed support from the newspaper and the greater Baltimore community, did not constitute strong civic capacity. The larger racial context asserted itself, reversed momentum toward school reform, weakened the mayor's standing as a leader in education, and heightened community tensions. Civic capacity proved highly fragile, and earlier experiences of working together quickly lost their weight. A wider form of deliberation might have maintained momentum behind reform, but in the mayor's judgment, it would simply have cut off a chance to pursue an experiment and left him still stymied by an uncooperative school bureaucracy. Subsequently, a reform alliance has been reassembled, but it is more narrowly based than the earlier coalition. As a result, civic capacity in Baltimore remains at an intermediate level, loosely connected in form and still hampered by the city's racial divide.

DISCUSSION

From this brief look at civic capacity, we can offer a couple of observations. One is that civic capacity works in quite a different way from our conventional understanding of social capital. In Robert Putnam's (1993) treatment, social capital comes about as people learn to work with one another, practice reciprocity, and develop trust. In this view, social capital does not become depleted from use. Quite the contrary, use strengthens it. The more people work with one another and practice reciprocity, the greater the trust among them. And greater trust encourages more working together and wider practice of reciprocity. This view of social capital contains valuable insights about human behavior, but it seems to apply most readily to microbehavior—informal kinds of helping among people engaged in everyday activities. Repeated interactions provide opportunities for people to become comfortable with one another, develop understanding, and cooperate with minimal negotiations. Yet useful as they may be for some purposes, such microbehaviors do not yield civic capacity.

In education especially, civic capacity is about mobilizing various segments of the community to become engaged in considering and acting on a problem in a way that is out of the ordinary. To the degree that such a mobilization is successful, it takes people outside the channeled thinking that normally prevails. Hill, Campbell, and Harvey (2000) reminded us that fundamental reform in education requires that "normal politics" be bypassed or overcome in some way. They cautioned that "school boards are not good forums for creating integrated strategy, but they are excellent platforms from which reform initiatives and their leaders can be destroyed" (111). In many ways, civic cooperation is inherently unstable, especially when it operates out of the ordinary. Unlike the conventional social capital described by Putnam (1993), civic capacity may not be self-replenishing. The public nature of civic capacity and its connection to issues that are potentially controversial mean that a spirit of cooperation can be speedily eroded. To the extent that civic capacity rests on a narrow foundation of elite cooperation, it is vulnerable to quick collapse. Though representatives of institutional interests and group leaders may develop good interpersonal relationships, they are never simply individuals learning to cooperate with one another. The public stage on which they perform is centrally important. The Baltimore experience shows that simply having a few key actors embrace a reform idea may only invite opposition from those not part of the deliberation and fearful of its consequences. For a mayor or teachers' union president to get out of line with important constituencies may thus set back the whole process of moving toward fundamental reform.

Yet El Paso, Pittsburgh, Boston, and even Los Angeles are examples of something much more potent than fragile coalitions around particular initiatives. As examples of strong civic capacity, they represent an ability to bring diverse elements and resources together in a sustained effort to meet a major community challenge. The highest levels of civic capacity rest on an ability to engage not just an array of strategic elites but also a broad base of ordinary participants. To withstand the corrosive power of public contention, civic capacity needs strong pillars of support.

Informal alliances are relatively weak pillars; formal and fully staffed collaboration is stronger. Informal alliances are by definition dependent on continuity among central players, and as Los Angeles demonstrates, such continuity may be hard to come by. The reform coalition in Los Angeles has survived changes in key actors and a climate of strong contention only because LEARN was in place.

All of this is a difficult set of arrangements to maintain, and if these arrangements break down at some point or never quite gel, then there is a risk that misunderstanding and mistrust will carry the day. That civic capacity centers on community problem solving means that major public issues are considered, and these are matters always apt to become contentious. Any civic consensus is far from stable, and therefore the process of building support for a program of action around one problem is not easily transferred to (or borrowed from) another exercise in problem solving. Civic capacity is therefore not akin to the microlevel social capital described by Putnam (1993) and others. That kind of social capital is largely the unconscious by-product of everyday interactions. Civic capacity is the conscious creation of actors seeking to establish a context in which extraordinary problem solving can occur. As such, it is always across the grain of what Hanna Arendt (1968, 169) called "automatic processes" and therefore subject to erosion. Civic capacity is neither easy to establish nor easy to maintain once it is set in motion. For that reason, institutionalization is a surer foundation than informal understandings among select individuals.

APPENDIX

The Civic Capacity and Urban Education Project (including its planning stage) involved both a long time span and a large number of participants. Started informally in 1991 with a two-day brainstorming session involving 11 scholars, the project over time added several members and lost a few to moves, shifting research obligations, and in the case of Byran Jackson, the death of one of our most valued and beloved teammates.

With funding from the National Science Foundation, the study officially launched in May 1993. I served as principal investigator (PI), and Jeffrey Henig and Bryan Jones served as co–principal investigators. Field research for the 11 cities was divided as follows:

* Atlanta—Carol Pierannunzi, Desiree Pedescleaux, and John Hutcheson.
* Baltimore—Marion Orr.
* Boston—John Portz.
* Denver—Susan Clarke, Rodney Hero, and Mara Sidney.
* Detroit—Richard Hula, Richard Jelier, and Mark Schauer.
* Houston—Thomas Longoria.
* Los Angeles—Fernando Guerra and Mara Cohen.
* Pittsburgh—Robin Jones.
* St. Louis—Lana Stein.
* San Francisco—Louis Fraga and Bari Anhalt Erlichson.
* Washington, D.C.—Jeffrey Henig.

Bryan Jones, Whitney Grace, and Heather Strickland did all of the steps in the coding of the 516 interviews across 11 cities. Jeffrey Henig and Mark Kugler, assisted by Cheryl Jones, Connie Hill, and Kathryn Doherty, collected and analyzed a large body of demographic, program, and financial data.

In addition to these contributors to the project, several other individuals also helped shape the research design and the field research protocol. These include the late Byran Jackson, Alan DiGaetano, Barbara Ferman, Valerie Johnson, Katherine McFate, Timothy Ross, Jorge Ruiz de la Vasco, and Marta Teilado.

The overall research protocol included a guide for data collection, a template for case narratives, interview schedules for three categories of respondents (general influentials, community advocates, and program specialists), and a designated set of interviewees. Over a three-year period, the team met annually for a two-day workshop on issues of research and analysis, and we also put on a number of panels at various professional conferences and piggybacked additional team meetings on these conferences. Subgroups of the overall team also met for workshops.

Intellectually, the project was rooted in work on issue definition and urban regimes. Methodologically, it represented an effort to combine the case study approach with comparative analysis. The 11 cities were chosen to extend across the nation's major regions and to make use of in-depth knowledge that participating scholars had of various cities. The team members were diverse in race and ethnicity, gender, and age, but all shared grounding in the discipline of political science, albeit representing sundry approaches. Though there were notable exceptions, many of us came into the project with limited research experience in education. All of us shared a strong interest in public policy. Collectively, we benefited from the advice and suggestions at various stages of a number of fellow scholars: Marilyn Gittell, Jennifer Hochschild, Michael Kirst, Kathryn McDermott, Dorothy Shipps, Stephen S. Smith, Margaret Weir, Frederick Wirt, John Witte, and

Kenneth Wong, each of whom has enormous depth in the politics of education. As PI, I benefited especially from the advice and suggestions of three colleagues in education: Edward Andrews, Betty Malen, and Sylvia Rosenfield.

Some might view the research team as so large as to be cumbersome. In many ways, they would be right. Yet the process worked. Three books out at this writing are a direct result of the project: Stone (1998), Henig et al. (1999), and Portz, Stein, and Jones (1999). In addition, Marion Orr's *Black Social Capital* (1999) draws partly on the project as well as on his individual research work on Baltimore. Two additional books are in production: Stone et al. (2001) and Clarke et al. (forthcoming). The listing of book authors reveals a significant point. A large team has to subdivide into small groups to remain viable. Yet there are advantages in scope of understanding that come from deploying a large team, so long as the tasks of collaboration are kept manageable. The more the large team comes together for joint deliberation, the more understanding can be expanded.

Though there are advantages to the assemblage of a large team, centrifugal forces are strong. Our team held together (with the significant reinforcement of summer stipends) for two years of field research, 1993 and 1994. Data collection and case narratives reached back to encompass the period from 1989 to 1994. Analysis and writing continued after 1994, but this work fell mainly to subgroups. And even the maintenance of subgroups presented challenges. Thus, even though much would have been learned by sustaining field research over a longer span of time, a large research team cannot expect to hold in place for such an effort. For comparative case analysis of the kind undertaken in the Civic Capacity and Urban Education Project, scope of study necessarily trades off against coverage over time. Although the trade-off was highly useful, it was nonetheless a trade-off. Education politics is a volatile and ever-changing arena. For that reason, important work remains to be done by individuals and small research teams and, yes, at some point again by a large research crew. Large as it was, the Civic Capacity and Urban Education Project can only be seen as a step in an ongoing research process. In a long tradition, it has raised more questions than it has answered.

Urban education is too important for the future of cities to deserve anything less than a strong and varied field of researchers. I can only hope, then, that the Civic Capacity and Urban Education Project will encourage research to continue at a pace and in forms that will prove fruitful both for scholars and for those who seek to put policy ideas into practice.

NOTES

"Civic Capacity and Urban Education," by Clarence N. Stone, *Urban Affairs Review* Vol. 36 (May 2001), pp. 595–619. Reprinted with permission of Sage Publications.

1. Funding came from the Education and Human Resources Directorate of the National Science Foundation (grant RED 9350139). For a listing of the research team, see the Appendix.

2. Off-the-record interview by Carol Pierannunzi.

3. From personal notes by Carol Pierannunzi, who attended several meetings in the spring and fall of 1999 leading up to a parent vote against charter status.

4. Hess (1991), Shipps (1997), Bryk et al. (1998), Wong (1998), and Shipps, Kahne, and Smylie (1999).

5. Significantly, however, the creation of the local school councils had the unintended effect of focusing attention on individual neighborhood schools to the detriment of citizen concerns about citywide education policies and issues (Shipps 1998, 179).

6. On Baltimore, see various works by Marion Orr, especially his book-length study *Black Social Capital* (1999). See also Henig et al. (1999) and Baum (1999).

7. On Detroit and Washington, D.C., generally, see Henig et al. (1999). On the takeover in D.C., see Henig (1998).

8. On the importance of external organizations as sources of ideas and support for local initiatives, see Schorr (1997).

9. For a brief but recent account of the formation and evolution of the Los Angeles Educational Alliance for Restructuring Now, see Annie E. Casey Foundation (1999, 22–25).

REFERENCES

Annie E. Casey Foundation. 1999. *Improving school-community connections.* Baltimore: Annie E. Casey Foundation.

Arendt, H. 1968. *Between past and future.* New York: Penguin.

Baum, H. S. 1999. Education and the empowerment zone. *Journal of Urban Affairs* 2 (3): 289–307.

Bryk, A. S., P. B. Sebring, D. Kerbow, S. Rollow, and J. Q. Easton. 1998. *Charting Chicago school reform.* Boulder, Colo.: Westview.

Clarke, S. E., R. Hero, M. Sidney, B. A. Erlichson, and L. Fraga. Forthcoming. *The new educational populism: Multi-ethnic politics of school reform.* Durham, N.C.: Duke Univ. Press.

El Paso Collaborative for Academic Excellence. 2000. *El Paso education summit: Building the best El Paso.* El Paso, Tex.: El Paso Collaborative for Academic Excellence.

Fleishman, J. L. 1980. The real against the ideal—Making the solution fit the problem: The Atlanta school agreement of 1973. *In Roundtable justice: Case studies in conflict resolution,* ed. R. B. Goldmann, 129–80. Boulder, Colo.: Westview.

Henig, J. R. 1998. *Building conditions for school reform in the District of Columbia.* Washington, D.C.: Woodrow Wilson International Center for Scholars.

Henig, J. R., R. C. Hula, M. Orr, and D. S. Pedescleaux. 1999. *The color of school reform.* Princeton, N.J.: Princeton Univ. Press.

Hess, G. A. 1991. *School restructuring, Chicago style.* Newbury Park, Calif.: Corwin Press.

Hill, P. T., C. Campbell, and J. Harvey. 2000. *It takes a city.* Washington, D.C.: Brookings Institution.

Holmes, R. 1993. *The status of black Atlanta.* Atlanta, Ga.: Southern Center for Studies in Public Policy, Clark Atlanta University.

Hunter, F. 1953. *Community power structure.* Chapel Hill: Univ. of North Carolina Press.

Jackson, B. L. 1978. Desegregation: Atlanta style. *Theory into Practice* 17 (1): 43–53.

Long, N. E. 1958. The local community as an ecology of games. *American Journal of Sociology* 64 (Nov.): 25.

Longoria, T., Jr. 1998. School politics in Houston. In *Changing urban education,* ed. C. N. Stone, 184–98. Lawrence: Univ. Press of Kansas.

McAdams, D. R. 2000. *Fighting to save our schools . . . and winning: Lessons from Houston.* New York: Teachers College Press.

National Commission on Excellence in Education. 1983. *A nation at risk.* Washington, D.C.: Government Printing Office.

Navarro, M. S., and D. S. Natalico. 1999. Closing the achievement gap in El Paso. *Phi Delta Kappan* 80 (Apr.): 597–601.

Orr, M. 1999. *Black social capital.* Lawrence: Univ. Press of Kansas.

Portz, J., L. Stein, and R. R. Jones. 1999. *City politics and city schools.* Lawrence: Univ. Press of Kansas.

Putnam, R. D. 1993. *Making democracy work.* Princeton, N.J.: Princeton Univ. Press.

Rich, W. C. 1996. *Black mayors and school politics.* New York: Garland.

Salisbury, R. H. 1964. Urban politics: The new convergence of power. *Journal of Politics* 26 (Nov.): 775–97.

Schorr, L. B. 1997. *Common purpose.* New York: Doubleday.

Shipps, D. 1997. The invisible hand: Big business and Chicago school reform. *Teachers College Record* 99 (1): 73–116.

———. 1998. Corporate involvement in school reform. In *Changing urban education,* ed. C. N. Stone, 161–83. Lawrence: Univ. Press of Kansas.

Shipps, D., J. Kahne, and M. Smylie. 1999. The politics of urban school reform. *Education Policy* 13 (Sep.): 518–45.

Stone, C., and C. Pierannunzi. 2000. Atlanta's biracial coalition in transition. Paper presented at the annual meeting of the American Political Science Association, Washington, D.C.

Stone, C. N. 1989. *Regime politics.* Lawrence: Univ. Press of Kansas.

———. 1998. *Changing urban education.* Lawrence: Univ. Press of Kansas.

Stone, C. N., J. R. Henig, B. D. Jones, and C. Pierannunzi. 2001. *Building civic capacity: The new politics of urban school reform.* Lawrence: Univ. Press of Kansas.

Vander Weele, M. 1994. *Reclaiming our schools: The struggle for Chicago school reform.* Chicago: Loyola Univ. Press.

Wong, K. K. 1998. Transforming urban school systems. Report prepared for the cross-Atlantic conference, A Working Conference on School Reform in Chicago and Birmingham, University of Chicago.

10. Powerful Actors Versus Compelling Actions

Clarence N. Stone

The term *interest group* is closely associated with the idea that politics is fundamentally about struggle among contending collectivities. We understand such struggle as a form of power in which a group's effort to dominate or get its way is often met by countereforts. The struggle to gain one's way and the resistance it engenders put on center stage what may be called *power over*. But a center stage position for "power over" is worrisome. The "interest" in interest group is also troubling because it implies something fixed and largely determined by one's place in the socioeconomic order. Below, I will explain why these two points are significant for those concerned with such topics as urban school reform.

Though the term interest group has a ring of realism about it and it directs attention to part of what we experience, I maintain that it is not the whole story. To treat it as such is therefore to miss part of what is going on. Politics, political theorist Hannah Arendt (1977) reminds us, involves constructing how we relate to one another. Similarly, activist Ernesto Cortes and the Industrial Areas Foundation make use of the idea of "relational power" and how it enables us to see our interest, that is, our stake in public policy, in a different way (Cortes 1993).

These disparate thinkers are alerting us to an aspect of politics we ignore at some risk. In a process different from the ongoing struggle among groups, relationships form and structure how we understand who we are. If we pay no attention to this process, we miss an opportunity to shape our political future. Thus, we need a complex way of thinking about politics. For this reason, I advocate treating power as having a second and not necessarily benign dimension. It turns on what I term the *social production model of power*, though the shorthand version involves *power to* as contrasted with *power over* (Stone 1989).

Unlike power over, power to is not about will (as in willpower), but about discovering or, sometimes, happening into relationships that take hold, relationships that, whether originally intended or not, prove attractive and viable. The interactions that go along with these relationships often determine policy practice, sometimes simply filling a void left by legislative enactment, but sometimes overriding or redefining what was officially mandated. In other words, interactions follow a rule of viability with which officials' mandates may or may not accord.

For this reason, we need to consider compelling actions as well as powerful actors. With this in mind, we also need to think about reform—lasting reform—as more than an act of bringing down the walls of the status quo, which is often a willful act of "power over." Beyond contention between the old and new, lasting reform entails a set of workable arrangements to replace the old order. This calls for a different way of thinking about politics. The new order that replaces an old order is often not something that willful actors design, negotiate, and put into place. Sometimes, the compelling actions of a new order simply emerge from the chaos of change, or they may come about as the unintended side effects of an outwardly orderly process of change. If human reflection and deliberation are to have a role in shaping the course of change, we need to think about what relationships and which forms of interaction are compatible with the outcomes we want and seek to nurture those relationships and interactions. This is political activity quite different from the combat between organized interest groups.

I will elaborate below, starting with power and identifying the theory behind the notion of compelling actions. Next, I will focus on why relationships are important and discuss those features of relationships that make some more durable (i.e., more compelling) than others.

POWER

Politics can be explained in two fundamentally different ways. One is the powerful actors scenario. In this version of the story, politics is a contest of wills. Those who prevail are powerful. They prevail either because they can mobilize more resources or because they use their resources with more skill.

The story can be told at various levels. The contending actors can be individuals—the chair of the school board versus the president of the taxpayers association. The contenders can be institutions within the system of government—mayor versus the city council. Alternatively, the contenders can be collectivities—interest groups, political parties, factions within parties, economic classes, or racial groups. On the international stage, the struggle may be between nation-states or even multinational alliances. Let us stay close to home and concentrate on the local community.

Urban school reform is certainly in part a battle between powerful actors. Consider a Thomas B. Fordham Foundation report on the Annenberg Challenge grants. Seeing a largely Hobbesian war of all against all, author Raymond Domanico (2000) sets great store by conflict and confrontation, and he notes that "political change is seldom polite." He argues that systemic reform "requires political action," and

It is not collaborative; it is confrontational to a point and then negotiable. The outcome is determined not by the merit of the ideas but by the relative strengths of the negotiators. Governance reform, charter schools, and the abolition of principal tenure came about in New York because strong-willed politicians, namely Governor Pataki and Mayor Giuliani, chose, by whatever political calculus, to challenge the existing system head on (18).

The contest of wills, the conflict between powerful actors, is unquestionably real. It is not to be dismissed. But it is not the whole political story. There is another dimension less obvious but no less important. Thus, we need to move away from thinking about power exclusively as a contest of wills between actors with preset preferences. The social production or power to model provides an opportunity to consider how actors come to embrace and stay with some courses of action rather than others. Regardless of initial sentiment about the relative worthiness of various aims, some purposes seem to have a capacity to crowd or even replace others. Some ways of acting tend to prevail over others, and they do so almost regardless of the personalities involved. Why?

Let us return to power over and power to. Bear in mind that, even when looking at power over, we may not find relationships that are highly asymmetrical. Sometimes such power is not one sided, and the contestants in a struggle may be evenly matched. Efforts to dominate (A trying to get B to do what B would not otherwise do) are met by counterefforts to resist and may result in negotiation and compromise. Power and dependence theory teaches us that mutual vulnerabilities are especially conducive to negotiated settlements (Blau 1964; Emerson 1962).

If we move from the notion of mutual vulnerability to that of mutual dependence, then we have a segue into the alternative conception, power to. Individual actors often find that they can accomplish little on their own. It is in concert with others that they enjoy a power to act that they would not otherwise have. To be part of the political community is, then, to have an enhanced capacity to pursue collective aims. This is to be empowered, and it is a fundamental part of the political experience. It is a reason we talk about community power rather than confining ourselves to power as a relationship between individuals.

Such empowerment is, however, complicated. To become part of a political community or a coalition is also to take on certain responsibilities. These might include an obligation to refrain from harming other members of the community or to avoid raising divisive issues that weaken the solidarity of the community. Or the obligation might entail joining with other members of the community to meet some external threat or challenge. Membership in a political community thus has a dual character; as with any structure, it is both enabling and constraining.

The same might be said about membership in a profession or mastery of a discipline. It enables the actor to do things that otherwise would be unattainable, but the fact of membership in a profession or immersion in a discipline shapes how matters are seen and what one feels obligated to do about them.

POWER AND PREFERENCES

In some ways, power over and power to are not radically distinct phenomena; they shade into one another. However, there is a point at which the two are sharply at odds, and that is the place of preferences in a relationship. As a contest of wills, power over assumes that preferences are fixed; the contest is about the extent to which A's preference to impose a change on B would be accommodated and the extent to which B's preference to resist this change will prevail.

Power to works from somewhat different premises. Though an actor may carry a set of strongly held preferences into the formation of a community or association or into the joining of such a collectivity, preferences are most appropriately seen as a work in progress. To some extent, progress is a matter of refinement. It may be a matter of discovering trade-offs. Pursuing a goal or forming an affiliation may, as it unfolds, involve unforeseen sacrifices. For instance, joining a group brings to the surface hidden costs in the form of obligations to others. Hence, the joiner learns that membership in a community, association, or coalition provides a capacity to achieve ends that was not there before affiliation, but that capacity also involves responsibilities not fully anticipated. Yet the responsibilities may be embraced as appropriate to the new identity as a member of the collectivity.

Affiliating into a capacity to act jointly opens new possibilities. These can be thought of in two ways. One is the awakening of a preference kept dormant by the previous lack of feasibility. Awakening can occur as awareness grows that a goal becomes achievable as sufficient support and cooperation are brought together. Hence, Dennis Chong (1991) talks about a social movement as a context in which preferences are dynamic. As the assurance of wider support for a movement grows, the attractions of a movement expand and do so for a variety of reasons.

One important reason support may increase is an enhanced sense of feasibility. In discussing the French Revolution, historian Robert Darnton (1989) suggests that there are events that release "utopian energy." He uses the term *possibilism* to denote a "sense of boundless possibility." Darnton views the French Revolution as a succession of events in which there were "moments of madness, of suspended disbelief, when anything looked possible and the world appeared as a tabula rasa, wiped clean by a surge of popular emotion and ready to be redesigned" (10). Revolutionary moments are rare, of course, but times when credible choices simply widen are more common. They, too, awaken inert preferences.

Beyond the rousing of latent preferences lies the possibility of discarding old preferences for new ones or of simply discovering entirely new preferences. March and Olsen (1986) discuss two kinds of behavior involved in making choices. One is what they call a theory of children and the other a theory of adults. They remind readers that though the adult model is one of fixed preferences (concerned with the best way to achieve an already determined goal), there is a child in all of us. As the "child" is exposed to and drawn into activities—perhaps even activities initially resisted—he or she discovers and acts on new preferences. They may simply become new habits of mind. Thus, in various ways, power to relationships reshape an individual's preferences and certainly modify them in significant ways.

If preferences are not fixed but can modify on the basis of experience, then we can turn to the question of why some interactions and relationships crowd others out. Why are some more sustainable than others? Bear in mind that sustainable does not mean normatively superior. That is a different issue.

SUSTAINABLE INTERACTIONS

One of the continuing puzzles in politics is why seemingly popular ideas sometimes have little lasting impact. Reformers win elections but falter in their efforts to bring about change. Frequently, they are, as Plunkitt of Tammany Hall observed, "mornin' glories"—they tend to wilt as the political day wears on.

The Plunkitt perspective invites us to think about political change in a particular way. How does reform become institutionalized? Once we ask this question, we are no longer concerned only with how reformers mobilize opposition to an existing order. We shift attention to the question of how a reform agenda plays out in practice. Even if a challenge is victorious, the challenge itself is not the end of the process. Some form of political settlement follows a successful challenge. The lasting terms of a settlement may differ from the counterpart elements of a political challenge. Why? This is a question well worth pondering. It may help us understand why reformers are so often "mornin' glories."

One explanation for the weak staying power of reform is that although reformers may capture high-visibility offices, other strategically important positions are outside their control. But, on close examination, this argument begs the question. If reformers have popular backing, why don't the high-visibility offices they hold become beachheads for long campaigns to bring about reform? What is it that works against extended efforts? This is where we need to be mindful of power to and the malleability of preferences. As we are drawn into forms of interaction that are doable with an acceptable level of friction, we may embrace them because they are doable. They become part of who we are. Consider the opposite case. We may be compelled to undertake some worthy activity, or we may attempt such activity because we believe it to be worthy. Suppose, however, that the pursuit of this activity thrusts us into difficulties that we may master only with great effort, and our endeavors encounter much friction. Soon, the activity loses appeal, and it is repelling instead of compelling. Preferences modify accordingly.

Education historians make the telling observation that Edward Thorndike proved to have greater influence over education practice than did John Dewey because Dewey's ideas, though intellectually more appealing, were harder to implement. Thorndike's ideas translated into practice easily and met practical, everyday needs (Lagemann 1989; cf. Tyack and Cuban 1995). In this sense, they were more compelling.

Mark Moore (1988) makes a parallel point about why some ideas carry more weight than others. It is not, Moore argues, the intellectual properties that carry the day. Instead, "contextual properties" provide a guide in organizing activities, and they may make some compelling but others not. He notes,

> Thus, to the extent that ideas distinguish heroes from villains, and those who must act from those who need not, and to the extent that these distinctions fit with the aspirations of the parties so identified, the ideas will become powerful. If powerful people are made heroes and weaker ones villains, and if work is allocated to people who want it and away from people who do not, an idea has a greater chance of becoming powerful (80).

Let us be clear about what is being said. The connection of an idea to a socially worthy purpose, the novelty of an idea, its catchiness, or its internal logic may give it appeal as a topic for discussion and even promote popular approval, but such an idea may still fail to become a framework for action. It is not compelling in an everyday way in that it does not bring us into a productive relationship with others. That role may fall to ideas with less glitter but greater ease of execution. As Richard Elmore reminds us, "few visionary leaders have any effect on the dominant institutional patterns of American education" (2000, 2). Visionary ideas may lack appeal in the cold light of day-to-day interaction with others.

What is it, then, that makes an idea or a policy goal sustainable as an organizing factor? There is almost certainly no single answer to this question, but there are several possibilities worth considering.

Moore (1988) argues that consistency with established practices should receive major attention. What is already in place has passed a test of workability. Certainly Moore's reminder about the test of experience predicts the low batting average for reforms. By its very nature, reform calls for overturning existing practices and putting in place new ones. Reform, then, always operates at a disadvantage in competition with the status quo. And bounded rationality helps account for these patterns. The limited capacity of human beings to envisage new relationships in new modes of operation serves to advantage established ways of doing things.

The point can be elaborated. Purposes that are consistent with established lines of cooperation are easier to pursue than those that cut across deeply felt lines of cleavage. Not only do past antagonisms not die easily but also past relationships of cooperation contribute to social capital and facilitate future cooperation.

Yet, another elaboration of the point is that redistributive measures are a more formidable challenge than those that simply allocate a limited amount of new cost and benefits. Because redistribution is unsettling to a higher degree and involves more players, it is a more difficult process to bring off. In short, putting a redistributive policy into place represents a huge organizational challenge.

The first principle offered is, then, that (other things being equal) change, as Moore (1988) suggested, is more difficult than working with established arrangements. The greater the change, the more difficult it is. As the amount of change required decreases, the task becomes more manageable. Change versus the status quo is, however, only one dimension.

ADVANCING LARGE-SCALE CHANGE

Because policy change does occur, we can probe further about what makes some changes easier than others. Following the guidance of Herbert Simon (1969), we can distinguish between different versions of large-scale change. Simon reminds us through the parable of the two watchmakers that equally large and complex entities can be constituted in alternative ways (90–93). An entity can be composed of a single set of interlocking parts or of an assemblage of subsets. In Simon's fable, the two watchmakers assemble watches of 1,000 pieces each, but one makes use of 10 subassemblies of 100 pieces each. In the case of the watchmaker proceeding by a process of single, interlocked assembly, every time there was an interruption, the whole effort came apart. For the other watchmaker who made use of subassemblies that could stand alone, an interruption only set back the operation to the beginning of the subassembly in process. Hence, an interruption did not mean that the whole effort of watchmaking had to begin from scratch. Simon thus offers the lesson that, in a complex task, an assemblage of subsets is easier to work with than a single interlocked set.

Simon's (1969) parable can be applied to policy change. Like watches, policy efforts can take the form of interconnection without benefit of subtasks that can be handled independently of one another, or they can take the form of independently viable subtasks. In a study of the civil rights movement, Dennis Chong (1991) considers problem solution over time, and argues that a sustained effort is more likely if it can be made piece by piece. Chong elaborates the point by saying, "problems with long-term solutions do not lend themselves to the short-term reinforcement schedule that is often required to nurture large-scale political activism" (240).

The degree of change enters the picture again. Consistent with the contemporary concept of bounded rationality, Machiavelli (1985) argues,

> Nothing is more difficult to handle, more doubtful of success, nor more dangerous to manage, than to put oneself at the head of introducing new orders. For the introducer has all those who benefit from the old orders as enemies, and he has lukewarm defenders in all those who might benefit from the new orders. This lukewarmness arises . . . partly from the incredulity of men, who do not truly believe in new things unless they come to have a firm experience of them (23–24).

Seemingly, the possibility of a broad and long-term change has less capacity to engage human motivation than smaller and more immediate steps. If so, large-scale change can be built more readily on a foundation of assembled parts than on a foundation of one grand action. Cumulative small opportunities sustain political activity more readily than a single grand opportunity. One might argue, of course, the best of all is a grand opportunity built of many small opportunities.

If we apply this argument about segmented task to the urban policy experience, we can see it is supported in the pattern that planned physical change is easier to promote than planned social change. Physical change lends itself more readily to a step-by-step process. Hence, the "unheralded triumph" of an earlier era, celebrated by historian Jon Teaford (1984), was largely an engineering triumph, a triumph wrought project by project—projects that could be advanced step by visible step. Planned social change, as a more holistic enterprise, was thus not part of the unheralded triumph Teaford highlighted.

For more recent times, we can compare efforts to redevelop the city physically with efforts to reconstruct the city socially. Physical redevelopment wins going away as a sustained policy effort—not because the physical reconstruction of the city has been uncontroversial. Whether in the form of urban renewal, expressway development, or the building of large sports facilities and convention centers, redevelopment has encountered enormous opposition. Changing land use, providing relocation, and committing big tax dollars are all matters that have generated intense community conflict, whereas, by contrast, improving schools and fighting crime are highly popular, at least as broad policy aims to pursue. Yet, physical redevelopment has been at the top of the action agenda for cities throughout the postwar decades. Hence, as we look at the policies around which sustained efforts have been made, we do not see policies that enjoyed wide popular support but policies that could be divided into small segments for piece-by-piece action and the kind of short-term reinforcement highlighted by Chong (1991).

MARKET EXCHANGE

As we take stock of the argument presented above, we can see that some kinds of inter-actions (hence the courses of actions compatible with them) might be more potent than others. Specifically, market exchanges seem to have strong capacities for estab-lishing and maintaining relationships. At first glance, this may seem counterintuitive. On the surface, markets are impersonal forms of interaction that seem to provide only limited bonds between parties to a transaction. But that is only part of the story.

Consider two starkly different processes. One is typified by a market transaction. Two parties engage in a very narrow exchange. No broad area of agreement is needed, and the behavior of third parties typically has small, if any, relevance. The transaction may require little trust between the two parties; but when such transaction is repeated many times between the same parties, a relationship of trust can grow. Repeated trans-actions appear to facilitate a relationship of cooperation (Axelrod 1984).

The contrasting process is that of generating agreement to act on behalf of a social purpose. Two parties may cooperate because they agree on the purpose to be fur-thered. Shared purpose seemingly provides a common bond. But any broad purpose has built into it numerous smaller issues the nuances of the purpose, the level of pri-ority it holds, acceptable trade-offs, how relations with others are affected, and partic-ulars of implementation (Pressman and Wildavsky 1984). Therefore, mutual acceptance of a social purpose as a basis for cooperative action requires broad agreement not only on the purpose itself but also on numerous accompanying issues as well. In sum, act-ing on social purpose can be very cumbersome compared to a simple market exchange. Thus, transaction costs surrounding the pursuit of social purposes are often quite high.

The contrast between transactions and social purpose mobilization enables us to see why marketlike relationships might take hold readily and flourish widely. This con-trast also suggests that the durability of capitalism may be less a matter of hegemonic ideology and more a matter of transaction-cost efficiency. Capitalism may hold sway not because people believe markets serve their needs better but because markets have a flexible capacity to organize and sustain cooperative relationships. Here, I am not referring to society-wide cooperation but rather small and autonomous intercon-necting modes of cooperation. Market transactions and social-purpose mobilization resemble the contrasting approaching of Herbert Simon's (1969) two watchmakers.

POWER TO

To understand fully the "power to" dimension of politics, we must move away from the assumption that preferences are fixed. Cohen and March (1986) reject the notion that people have preferences first and then act to satisfy those preferences: "human choice behavior is at least as much a process for discovering goals as for acting on them" (220). According to Chong, "people want what they get" as well as "get what they want" (1991, 143).

In this way, some courses of action are more compelling than others; people are thrust into activities (what they get), and these often carry with them rules for conserving effort (what they want). For that reason, activities may give rise to policies and practices that tend to prevail. They represent purposes that are achievable. In short, prior preference does not necessarily guide everyday behavior; sustainable interactions may carry that behavior in a new direction, and alternative purposes may gather support.

We have now left the realm of power over, of *A* getting *B* to do what *B* would not otherwise do. In the realm of power to, the preferences of *A* and *B* may give way to involvement in activity *X*. What often carries the day is not that one actor prevails in a contest of wills through superior resources or, alternatively, greater skill and shrewdness. Instead, actors are drawn together into noncumbersome interactions around practicable purposes. In this scenario, sustainable interactions explain more than powerful actors. Initial intention is not the guide to action; indeed, they may give way to subsequent intentions that are discovered in the activity. Hence, we can no longer characterize the prevailing activity in terms of power over. As presented here, it is not, then, a matter of one side prevailing over the another but one course of action proving to be more viable than others because cooperation developed along a path strewn with fewer obstacles.

A CAUTION

I want to emphasize that power to is not necessarily benign. Compelling actions can take us down a road not considered desirable. It is important, then, to take stock of where we might be drawn.

Consider what is happening in school reform today. As Richard Elmore (2000) argues persuasively, standards-based reform is undermining the role and legitimacy of central-office direction of school affairs. Performance assessments put the spotlight on school-level action. Parent concern readily focuses on the individual school rather than the school district. Elmore sees a possible scenario in which educators try to hang onto the past (believing that this too will pass) while losing legitimacy. A possible result is that "the public purposes of public education drift away into matters of individual taste and preference" (Elmore 2000, 11). Elmore adds,

> I frequently tell my students that, if they want to see a possible future for the public
> schools, they should visit the public hospital system—a subsystem in a largely capitation-

based healthcare market, that specializes in clients no one else wants to serve, a subsystem that is also chronically underfinanced, and one in which the costs of serving clients bear little or no relationship to the reimbursements the hospitals receive through the capitation grant system. Such systems exist to catch the overflow of the unchosen from market-based capitation systems that work pretty well for active choosers (11).

The caution is that as public education undergoes change, the future shape of American schools may turn out to be one favored by neither reformers of the right nor reformers of the left. Consider what is likely to emerge in a highly fluid situation as the old order fades away. Given a market society with a highly uneven distribution of wealth, one can see that Elmore's (2000) public hospital scenario is not improbable.

More is at stake than a potential misstep in policy that could be corrected by later legislation. There is no backing up, saying, "Oops, that is not what we wanted." The structure of public education is not simply a product chosen from an array of alternatives with the option of simply reverting to the earlier product if the new one proves undesirable. The citizen is not a mere consumer; the citizen is not someone who merely selects from a menu from which policy dishes are to be served. Instead, politics is a process of choosing and acting on relationships, of determining which relationships will be established and nurtured and which ones will be neglected. It is a process of fostering some forms of cooperation while rejecting or neglecting others. The selection need not be a conscious one. It may grow out of what seemed to be purely routine, day-to-day choices.

What grows out of those routine, everyday choices shapes preferences and determines who we are as a people. For now, most people would like to maintain a system of public education, a system composed of common schools. Yet that preference is not fixed. After all, we are a highly individualistic society, especially in rhetoric. It would be easy to overlook our high level of interdependence and imagine ourselves as simply consumers, complete with our individual set of preferences, operating independently of the preferences of others. There is no strong barrier to seeing ourselves that way.

However, from Aristotle on, there are those who would remind us that, in reality, our preferences are shaped and expressed by our relationships. We discover who we are and what we are about through our actions together. One might say that each of us is what we do in relationship with others. That is roughly what Aristotle had in mind when he said humankind is a political animal. He is suggesting that our true nature is developed socially, not individually.

Much is at stake, then, in the reshaping of education. My argument is that the outcome of this reshaping will be only partly determined by struggles between powerful actors. Lobbying and election campaigning are part of the picture, but only part. For those who want a society of citizens, acknowledging their interdependence and interacting around their shared concerns, it is not enough to win a succession of legislative battles. It is possible to prevail in many such battles and still lose the war.

If we are not to have a society of people adjusting to one another individually on the basis of their differing amounts of market power and acting without public deliberation, then it is urgent that those who see the citizen as more than a consumer act to develop viable relationships around a common stake in public schools. This will not be easy, but at this point, public schools still have the advantage of being the established pattern. A needed step to preserve genuinely public schools is to mobilize communities around the goal of their collective improvement (Elmore 2000; Stone et al. 2001). Selected examples, such as El Paso's Collaborative for Academic Excellence, show this can be done (Navarro and Natalicio 1999).

For such efforts to take hold, we must move beyond the notion of politics as interest groups pressing decision makers. Politics is more than the clash of powerful actors. We need to take seriously the idea of relational power, of power to, and its implications. The relationships we build now will shape preferences for the future.

Power-over struggles often yield mandates, but those mandates may or may not take hold and become practice. Moreover, practice sometimes develops not because it is mandated, but because it meets an everyday need. In some cases, such practice stems from patterns of interaction by people coming together to form structures of mutual assistance. Thus, power to may rest on foundations shaped in part by acts of power over, but not necessarily so. Sometimes, people come together as an act of political creativity.

CONCLUSION

At one level, conflict between powerful actors is a central part of the political process. But if we think in terms of "power to" and acknowledge that preferences are not always fixed, then we are led to think about politics in a different way. Thus, Cohen and March (1986) invite us to be attentive to goal-finding behavior, what they term "sensible foolishness" or "playfulness" (223, 225). Rightly so, they call for greater attention to openness to discovery.

The consideration I want to offer is, however, a different one from that. Too little reflection on direction may mean that we become prisoners of what Hannah Arendt (1977) calls automatic processes, some of which have damaging social consequences. Because intentions are susceptible to shifting winds of experience, it is easy for social reforms to be blown off course. Even reforms that have strong electoral backing may prove to be short lived. Despite widespread popular support, reforms may nevertheless yield to policies and practices that rest on dubious principles.

Power to provides a reminder that because some kinds of interactions are more sustainable than others, we may drift away from a desirable course of action. As we think through the implications of power to, we can see that planned change (reform) may be inherently disadvantaged. Machiavelli (1985) cautioned that people are reluctant to embrace a new order because they have difficulty envisaging how it would operate. The more fundamental and far reaching the change, the harder it is to envisage.

Bounded rationality means that we are in some sense captives of immediate considerations—what it is easy for us to grasp, especially as we engage in everyday routines, is compelling. But we are not totally captive. Following Herbert Simon's (1969) parable of the two watchmakers, we can devise a strategy for increasing the viability of reform. The watchmaker lesson is to design ways to subdivide broad reform into components, each of which has interactive characteristics that can be readily sustained.

Herbert Simon's (1969) parable does not teach us to go it alone. After all, "power to" means that we gain a greater capacity to act by coming together in ways that make collective action possible. Because some forms of interaction are more sustainable than others, reform efforts do not succeed merely because they represent legislative victories or even popular ideas. Successful reform must rest on a foundation of sustainable interactions. Discovering constructive forms of everyday interaction may be at least as important as mobilizing to take part in group struggle.

NOTE

"Powerful Actors Versus Compelling Actions," by Clarence N. Stone, *Educational Policy,* Vol. 15 (January/March 2001), pp. 153–67. Reprinted with permission of Sage Publications.

REFERENCES

Arendt, H. 1977. *Between past and future.* 1961. New York: Penguin Books.
Axelrod, R. 1984. *The evolution of cooperation.* New York: Basic Books.
Blau, P. M. 1964. *Exchange and power in social life.* New York: John Wiley.
Chong, D. 1991. *Collective action and the civil rights movement.* Chicago: Univ. of Chicago Press.
Cohen M. D., and J. G. March. 1986. *Leadership and ambiguity.* Boston: Harvard Business School Press.
Cortes, E. 1993. Reweaving the fabric. In *Interwoven destinies,* ed. H. G. Cisneros, 294–319. New York: Norton.
Darnton, R. 1989. What was revolutionary about the French Revolution? *New York Review of Books,* 311. Jan. 19.
Domanico, R. 2000. A small footprint on the nation's largest school system. In *Can philanthropy fix our schools?,* ed. R. Domanico, C. Innerst, and A. Russo, 5–18. Washington, D.C.: Thomas B. Fordham Foundation.

Elmore, R. F. 2000. *Building a new structure for school leadership.* Washington, D.C.: Albert Shanker Institute.

Emerson, R. M. 1962. Power-dependence relations. *American Sociological Review* 27:31–41.

Lagemann, E. C. 1989. The plural worlds of educational research. *History of Education Research* 29 (2): 185–207.

Machiavelli, N. 1985. *The prince.* 1513. Trans. H. C. Mansfield. Chicago: Univ. of Chicago Press.

Moore, M. 1988. What sort of ideas become public ideas? In *The power of public ideas,* ed. R. Reich, 55–83. Cambridge, Mass.: Harvard Univ. Press.

Navarro, M. S., and D. S. Natalicio. 1999. Closing the achievement gap in El Paso: A collaboration for K-16 renewal. *Phi Delta Kappan* 80 (Apr.): 597–601.

Pressman, J. L., and A. Wildavsky. 1984. *Implementation.* 3rd ed. Berkeley: Univ. of California Press.

Simon, H. A. 1969. *The sciences of the artificial.* Cambridge, Mass.: MIT Press.

Stone, C. N. 1989. *Regime politics.* Lawrence: Univ. Press of Kansas.

Stone, C. N., J. R. Henig, B. D. Jones, and C. Pierannunzi. 2001. *Building civic capacity.* Lawrence: Univ. Press of Kansas.

Teaford, J. C. 1984. *The unheralded triumph.* Baltimore: Johns Hopkins Univ. Press.

Tyack, D., and L. Cuban. 1995. *Tinkering toward utopia.* Cambridge, Mass.: Harvard Univ. Press.

11. Civic Capacity
What, Why, and from Whence
Clarence N. Stone

Some observers think of a community's civic capacity as level of voting, volunteering, and participating in public hearings. In this essay, I put forward a different view, that of civic capacity as concerted efforts to address major community problems. By "concerted" I mean special actions to involve multiple sectors of a locality, governmental and nongovernmental. The label "civic" refers to actions built around the idea of furthering the well-being of the entire community not just a particular segment or group.

Bringing a locality's civic capacity into play represents a deliberate attempt to move beyond business as usual. Because the community faces an out-of-the-ordinary challenge, solving the problem will require a great deal more than routine governmental action. As a concept, civic capacity rests on the assumption that government and civil society are not discrete spheres of activity. They connect and merge in myriad ways. It follows, then, that what we call public policy is in fact the joint product of governmental and nongovernmental action. Put another way, the character and effectiveness of governmental activity depends substantially on how it combines with related nongovernmental activity. The relationship is particularly important in public education, and education puts democracy in a revealing light.

Education is not so much a service delivered to the public as an aim that is served by the combined efforts of educators and members of the community. Thus, whereas many analysts treat electoral accountability as central, the democratic system allows for a wide enlistment in efforts to solve or ameliorate the major problems faced by a community. In this view of democracy, citizens are not a passive audience that approves or disapproves of the performance of public officials, but rather needed contributors to community efforts. To the extent that citizens are passive, democracy falls short of its full measure. Since public-policy results are the product of both governmental and nongovernmental action, a process such as school reform is democratic only to the extent that the community is broadly engaged.

Below I present four cases in which localities have participated in extraordinary efforts to turn school performance around. First, however, consideration is given to the nature of the education problem and why the mesh between schools and community is so important.

THE PROBLEM OF PUBLIC SCHOOL PERFORMANCE

Disappointing academic achievement is found primarily in areas where low-income populations are concentrated. Research has shown that the performance of individual schools is greatly influenced by the family background and community environment of the students in attendance. The education problem is thus closely linked to poverty. When the school community is affluent and the parents themselves are well educated, there is an easy fit between what public schools do routinely and the population served.

The education problem is class based for several reasons. First, better-educated parents provide their children with greater readiness for conventional academic learning. Moreover, affluent parents provide home advantages and auxiliary resources for the schools their children attend. Children of the affluent middle class exist in an environment of high expectations, reinforced by abundant examples of realized opportunities. Support, encouragement, and aspirations are not missing from households of low and modest means, but they are harder to come by, more difficult to sustain, and face more barriers.

Schools themselves play a major role in shaping expectations. As early as the mid-1960s the psychologist Kenneth B. Clark (1965), in the book *Dark Ghetto: Dilemmas of Social Power,* identified a pattern of low regard for poor and minority students, lax standards, and an undemanding curriculum. A destructive cycle of low expectations feeding low achievement has long been at work. Throughout much of the 20th century, urban schools faced little pressure to change their approach.

Educator expectations and performance, along with student response, do not occur in a vacuum. They take shape in an environment of school-community relations, with social, political, and economic dimensions. Contrast the experience of schools serving the poor with an account of school-community relations in a setting of affluence. A former school board member from Houston, Texas, says this of the parents in his middle-class district:

> Most volunteered some time in their neighborhood school. Some, the school activists, were exceptional. I called them the PTO mothers. They were usually wives of professional men with excellent incomes. Some had professional degrees themselves. They had put their careers on hold to be full-time homemakers. And as their children grew older, some became practically full-time, unpaid school employees.

The PTO mothers volunteered time to chaperone students on field trips, assisted teachers in the classroom, worked in the office, and managed events like fall concerts, show choirs, carnivals, auctions, Christmas programs, and fundraising walkathons. Some programs attracted nearly 1,000 parents. These PTO mothers (and sometimes fathers) helped raise $30,000, sometimes up to $100,000, per year for teaching materials, computers, stage curtains, or whatever the school needed. And they didn't just serve their own children. . . .

These PTO mothers made schools successful. They demanded effective teaching, high academic standards, and strong leadership. They were towers of strength to effective principals. But if principals were ineffective or the bureaucracy did not respond to programmatic or facilities needs, they took action. They called their [school board member], took him out to lunch, organized letter-writing campaigns or circulated petitions. They knew how the system worked, and they got results (McAdams 2000, 60–61).

In concrete and direct ways, schools and community formed an integrated system. Parents volunteered and raised money privately for extras, thereby enhancing school resources. They not only had the time and inclination to be involved, they also made demands on the schools directly and through the school board. And in some matters they were allies of principals and the school board. Parents possessed a high sense of political efficacy on school matters to go along with the fact that they were organized and had resources and connections. Almost certainly, students in these schools came from households in which academic achievement was expected and college attendance was the norm. Parental engagement was a powerful signal to children about the great importance of education. Family and friendship connections provided concrete reinforcement for aspirations that linked academic achievement with personal career goals and the promise of a satisfying life. These connections also provide detailed information about how to pursue paths of educational advancement. As the psychiatrist and education reformer James P. Comer (1993) would argue, school and community outlook and expectations were aligned around academic achievement. What Comer (1993, viii) in his book *School Power* called "the hand of hopelessness" that grips many urban schools posed little threat to this affluent corner of Houston, where school and community formed a productive partnership.

Consider now the contrasting situation in many schools serving lower-income neighborhoods. Distrust is pervasive—in the words of Charles M. Payne (2001, 243), "The basic web of social relationships is likely to be severely damaged." Instead of home and school reinforcing one another, they may be in conflict, and teacher-parent tension may run at a high level. In such circumstances, Comer (2003, 39) argues in *School Power*, students have unfulfilled needs and become negative about their school experience. He observes: "The power of all involved is amorphous, fragmented, and tenuous. Thus nobody is able to address the school mission in a cooperative, systematic, sustained way. . . . Administrators, teachers, and parents are paralyzed." Instead of promoting an effective collaboration between school and neighborhood, community conditions and household vulnerabilities conspire to promote disappointment and defensiveness.

By no means do all schools in lower-income neighborhoods perform weakly, and some educators are quite skillful in mobilizing resources from the larger community and enlisting constructively the support of parents. Still, the pattern is clear; schools in poor neighborhoods face greater challenges—parents have fewer material resources, they tend to be less strongly organized, external assistance is often scarce, central offices often seem overwhelmed, union officials may be unhelpful, and the struggle to combat low expectations is unending.

When schools are predominantly middle class and affluent, public and private efforts often cohere without extraordinary mobilization. The private (that is, the nongovernmental) contribution to a joint effort is not always appreciated by the casual observer. Yet the closer one looks, the more the nongovernmental part stands out, and the private infusions include intangible matters of outlook and aspiration as well as tangible forms of assistance. In nonaffluent areas, school and community can come together, but the pull of centrifugal forces is strong, and good intentions are hard to sustain.

The mesh between school and community depends on both what the households of students bring to the engagement and what schools provide. Under terms of strong fiscal constraints, traditionally, public schools provide a set of standardized education practices. These are adjusted to the particular situation of the community they serve, but schools have a much more difficult time responding effectively to the circumstances of students from backgrounds scarce in privileges and opportunities. In a predominantly middle-class society, educators have no built-in propensity to reach out to and meet the needs of families at the poverty level. To do so likely means extraordinary effort. The school-community relationship often turns on the stubborn fact that much of society's investment in children and youth occurs through the household, and some households are able to invest a great deal more than others.

The American dream pictures schools as the great equalizer (Hochschild and Scovronick 2003). Yet an accompanying belief sees performance as a matter of individual effort, leaving one with little inclination to look widely for systemic forces at work. Without a larger sense of direction and purpose, individuals tend to make what they can of the immediate situation.

The impetus for big-picture reform seldom comes from professionals on the inside, operating as insiders. It almost always involves the entry of a new and more wide-ranging set of actors. Once education became a national concern, reform and reexamination of schools became matters of widening public debate. With a national movement under way, communities were in a better position to challenge the traditional position of schools as insulated from external scrutiny and establish education as a problem that could be tackled as a local issue of wide civic importance. Reform-minded educators could search for allies, and civic and political leaders could put forward their concerns without being rebuffed by claims that they were intruding into matters best left to educators. Contemporary local efforts thus operate under an umbrella of a national movement that has made it easier to identify education as a problem for community-wide action. The ongoing national movement for education reform has activated crucial state players, but even combined federal and state action has limited impact without local enlistment in the effort.

Turning the situation around involves intentional and concerted efforts to move beyond the usual state of affairs and create a new set of conditions. At the local level, it means making moves to bring a community's civic capacity into operation. The national climate is important but in itself amounts to little without local communities taking concrete action. Let us turn now to the local process of building civic capacity around school reform.

BUILDING CIVIC CAPACITY: FOUR CASES

Kent County, Maryland

Kent County is a small, nonmetropolitan jurisdiction on Maryland's Eastern Shore. It is a place neither of great affluence nor of high poverty. Of the county's 2,795 students, 38% are eligible for federally assisted meals, and the racial breakdown is 30% African American and 70% white.[1]

When the state's education department first put into operation its Performance Assessment Program, Kent students scored quite low. Reflecting community concern, the elected school board moved immediately to address the problem by hiring a new school superintendent who could be a strong instructional leader. Board members decided on Dr. Lorraine Costella, who had previously served as assistant superintendent for curriculum and instruction for the state. Costella had a reputation as an innovator, and by hiring her, this rural county showed its willingness to pursue a new path to school reform. Urgency to move beyond business as usual came from the disappointing scores on the state test.

The new superintendent immediately laid the groundwork for a cross-sector coalition. Including key stakeholders from the very beginning, she started by holding an all-day strategic planning forum that included teachers, principals, school board members, and community leaders. The forum refined the school system's goals into a list of five, headed by academic achievement. The main activities were curriculum development, which included aligning curriculum with state standards and tying these aims to professional development. Superintendent Costella tackled the difficult work of building an organizational infrastructure by devising multiple ways to involve principals and teachers, relying particularly heavily on principals rather than central office staff to implement reforms. She followed through on the strategic planning forum by turning to a school board member for guidance in adopting a special management process, designed for education—the Baldrige in Education approach. Involving all stakeholders in devising an implementation plan, this process was initiated by creating a Baldrige Leadership Team to begin the planning and to oversee its implementation. This team included members from the school board, the union, principals, teachers, parents, and the community. The approach involved a year's training and led to a classroom compact through which teachers could work with students in determining goals and defining how those goals would be met. As part of the process, there were also site teams in each school.

What is striking about the Kent County experience is that the initial involvement of multiple stakeholders was followed by extensive continuing engagement. The superintendent also adopted the practice of meeting regularly with the union president, and those meetings yielded concrete results such as decentralizing professional development to the school level and shifting responsibility for it to the faculty.

Dr. Costella created a Professional Development Council, again made up of multiple stakeholders. Professional development included sending teachers and principals to other school districts to observe their practices and also putting them into special summer training programs. These extraordinary measures cost money, and the superintendent used her expertise in proposal writing to bring external funds into the district from the state, federal government, and private sources. That too became a collective enterprise as the superintendent trained staff at all levels in grant seeking.

Professional development also served to create networks of teachers to support professional growth and to link new teachers with mentors. Collaboration occurred at the top as well. The superintendent met regularly with the board chair and distributed a weekly newsletter to board members. Relationship building thus included the superintendent's high accessibility to school board members, as she sought to keep all elements closely involved.

A process of setting goals and measuring progress on those goals can be unsettling to members of an organization. Superintendent Costella's strategy for easing this transition was to create structures and informal practices to encourage collaboration and innovation. These efforts worked, and three years after Dr. Costella became superintendent, Kent County moved to the top in performance on the state's tests. How did such a quick turnaround happen? Togneri and Lazarus (2003, 28) explain: "Only by building internal leadership capacity at the school level were district leaders able to infuse improvement throughout the district." Kent County provides an example of reform based on clear goals with detailed attention to creating a sense of inclusion in planning and implementation. Partnership and pursuit of shared understanding were not confined to an initial exercise but very much a continuing part of the reform process. The superintendent took little for granted and made Kent County into a clear case of a locality that "worked on working together" (Togneri and Anderson 2003, 32).

A superficial observer might take Kent County as evidence that school systems need only try harder. However, the multifaceted approach pursued in Kent was not done within the confines of the ordinary budget. Moreover, Dr. Costella developed the professionalization of her staff in such a way that they put in long hours and extra effort. They did so because they felt valued and saw themselves as respected members of a team. Teachers and principals also found themselves under a heavy workload. The superintendent's approach was to distribute leadership throughout the district, but not without making changes. During her eight years as superintendent, she replaced a majority of the school principals as she reshaped the system into one in which principals are instructional leaders.

As a small school district, Kent County is administratively simpler than large urban districts. But small rural districts are not known for being especially open to change. The superintendent managed the feat of shaping a highly innovative system by clear direction from the top, legitimized by extensive consultation not just with the school board and community leadership but also with the professional staff through multiple channels of interaction. She balanced direction from the top with dispersing leadership responsibility throughout the system. And by combining careful orchestration inside the system with added resources from outside, she engendered an ethos of professional pride that nurtured a willingness to make extra efforts.

El Paso, Texas

El Paso, Texas, is a border city, with a population of more than a half million. In Texas, school districts do not match city or county boundaries. The city is served by three districts, two of which spill outside the city limits. The three urban districts in combination contain 163 schools and enroll 135,000 students, of whom 85% are Hispanic. Two-thirds of the students are low income, and about half begin school with limited proficiency in English.[2]

Whereas Kent County is small enough for most exchanges to occur between individuals personally connected, El Paso's route to school reform involved significant interaction among people possessing important institutional bases. And while reform in Kent County took place primarily in a single small school system, reformers in El Paso established an education intermediary, the El Paso Collaborative for Academic Excellence, housed on the campus of and supported by the University of Texas at El Paso (UTEP). Launched in 1992, the collaborative originated in discussions around education and a changing economy.

As a border city with a low-wage economy, El Paso is highly vulnerable to the forces of globalization. In this context, a conversation opened up between the chamber of commerce and Sister Maribeth Larkin, lead organizer for the El Paso Interdenominational Sponsoring Organization (EPISO), a community-based organization and the local affiliate of the Industrial Areas Foundation. The recently inaugurated president of UTEP, Dr. Diana Natalicio, joined the discussions as someone interested in seeing the university take a larger role in the community.

President Natalicio also brought into the discussions Dr. Susana Navarro. A native of El Paso, Navarro had just returned to the city after involvement in education reform in California. From this experience Navarro had a clear vision of the need to combine standards reform with a closing of the achievement gap, and she had a firm idea of how to go about it. President Natalicio agreed to base an initiative at UTEP, and Navarro was named executive director. The collaborative thus became an autonomous unit on the UTEP campus, headed by a broadly representative board with President Natalicio as chair. Joining her on the board were Larkin of EPISO, representatives of the business sector (the presidents of the Greater El Paso and El Paso Hispanic Chambers of Commerce), major local-government officials (the mayor and the county chief executive), and key education figures (the three school superintendents, the executive director of the regional service center of the Texas Education Agency, and the president of the community college).

Larkin, Navarro, and Natalicio formed an inner core of actors with a close harmony of vision and complementary roles to play. As a highly regarded university president, Natalicio could bring key people to the table. Larkin provided an important community base of support, and Navarro gave the initiative a concrete form that had strong appeal to the three school superintendents. In bringing to fruition the collaborative, its architects made use of a network of existing organizations and specially created task forces. Taking a cue from an approach Navarro had developed in her earlier work, they used education data to highlight the problem of weak academic performance, especially its equity dimension. State testing added urgency to the picture.

The collaborative represented a response to the concerns of educators, the community, and the business sector. Heading an organization with a distinct and appealing mission, Navarro recruited a dedicated and focused staff. She also made good use of her connections to the foundation world. Although a small operation at first, the collaborative got off to a fast start and, with the backing of the superintendents, established momentum early on.

The approach of the collaborative resembles the systemic effort that Kent County followed. It included close attention to curriculum, extensive use of data, and the involvement of parents and other members of the community to foster support for standards-based schooling. The central activity, however, was teacher training and professional development for administrators, teachers, and staff. Like Kent County, El Paso's schools have experienced significant increases in test-score performance. In addition, growing percentages of students enroll in and pass demanding math and science courses.

The launching of the collaborative coincided with a state mandate for site-based management, and the initial effort of the collaborative was to encourage teachers, administrators, and parents to work together at the school level to develop a team approach. Thus a Teams Leadership Institute held a central place in the work of the collaborative from early on, and professional development for principals enjoyed high priority. Principals provide a vital link to parents and community, and they have been a key to building and maintaining school-level support for standards-based reform.

With teacher quality a critical concern, the collaborative worked closely with the College of Education to align teacher preparation with school reform. UTEP became a member of John Goodlad's National Network for Educational Renewal, and the college restructured its teacher preparation to a field-based program, working more closely with and in the area's public schools. Collaboration is by no means restricted to matters of curriculum. The university's Center for Civic Engagement seeks to help area schools foster parent involvement.

In working with the three urban school districts (and then extending some of its activities to the smaller districts in the county), the collaborative wanted the schools to be active partners. As a manifold force, the collaborative offered technical assistance in various forms, tangible resources through its success in grant seeking, an accessible fount of ideas, and a communication link to various elements of the wider community. The collaborative also has operated a series of yearlong seminars and offers follow-through sessions as part of a Parent Engagement Network. The meetings of the collaborative's board provided a way to disseminate ideas and lay groundwork for high-profile work. Because the board meets on a regular basis and deliberates about priorities, it can orient newcomers, whether they be school superintendents, the lead organizer for EPISO, the chamber of commerce president, or the new head of the community college.

The collaborative and its goal of systemic reform have been backed by major centers of institutional power in the community. Its board members are top officials in various organizations and institutions; in February 2000, the executive director of the collaborative and a leading business figure cochaired an Education Summit to bring together more than three hundred participants—educators, parents, businesspeople, government officials, and community representatives—to discuss ongoing challenges and consider steps for the future. Several task forces were created to pursue specific aims identified in summit discussions. With the collaborative as a continuing source of ideas, activities, and outreach, educational achievement remains a focal concern in the community and the collaborative has fostered initiatives, encompassing EPISO, UTEP, and the business sector, such as one to increase college enrollment in the community.

In a large and diverse community like El Paso, building civic capacity is no easy matter. For action to take place, someone needed to identify a crisis and frame it as a specific problem in need of urgent action. The convergent concerns of Natalicio, Navarro, and Larkin provided that framework, and data on student performance, dropouts, and low college enrollment made the problem specific and concrete. With Navarro's prior experience to draw on, the collaborative provided a proven solution to fit the problem. As in the case of Kent County, state actions provided important context. Skillful framing is thus one important step—identifying a problem broad enough to address concerns of a wide cross section of civic and other community actors, while specific enough to show that planned actions could make a difference.

Second, the initiating actors had high civic standing. It made a difference that the president of UTEP was not only head of a major institution in the city, but also someone of stature, widely recognized for her leadership and accomplishments. That the governing board of the newly formed collaborative was both broadly representative and composed of important figures in the locality reinforced the credibility of the initiative.

Significantly, the El Paso Collaborative for Academic Excellence has enjoyed substantial corporate and foundation support that enables it to employ full-time professionals and offer high-quality and focused professional development. Local nonprofits dealing with education and other issues of children and youth are often shoestring operations in which the staff finds itself having to cut corners and raise funds just to meet the payroll. By contrast, the collaborative operated from the beginning in a secure position with ample backing. Furthermore, being housed at a university highlighted the collaborative's professionalism and expertise. Following through on initial support from Coca-Cola and Pew Charitable Trusts, funding from, among others, the National Science Foundation (NSF) has provided resources and additional credentialing.

Developing civic capacity is a dynamic process that, at any given time, can break down. Personal misunderstandings, the allure of new and different calls for action, the coming and going of central figures, or simply the erosion over time of important connections among people or between organizations can cause an initiative to lose force. It is important, therefore, to display continuing momentum. The collaborative benefited greatly from the fact that its first program effort was fully embraced by one of the area's school superintendents, who committed his entire system to taking part from the beginning. That contributed to early drive, and substantial NSF funding along with such events as the Education Summit sustained momentum to give the collaborative a recognized place in the community.

Boston

In the same population category as El Paso, Boston also has a sizable poverty population among its schoolchildren, with 71% eligible for federally assisted meals. But that figure derives partly from the fact that one-quarter of the school-age children in Boston attend private schools or schools in the suburbs. Whereas El Paso is overwhelmingly Hispanic, Boston has a diverse school population and runs programs for a total of seven language groups. Combined with a school population made up mainly of children of color, Boston has a white-majority electorate. It also has a history of racial tension.[3]

For much of the latter half of the 20th century, Boston, with its changing student demography, provided an example of low civic capacity with respect to education. In the post–World War II era, Boston schools were noted first for their isolation from the community they served. The school system next went through a prolonged battle over school desegregation and busing, and, as a result, a federal judge assumed control.[4] Racial and ethnic conflict, patronage and scandal, demagoguery by members of the city's elected school committee, and an inwardly focused school administration helped keep business at a distance and academic achievement levels in the background.

A mix of racial discord and public cynicism gave Boston's school system an unpromising heritage to overcome. Yet several factors converged to turn around school politics and make possible the building of civic capacity. First of all, with desegregation at an impasse in 1974, when Judge W. Arthur Garrity took charge, he formed community support structures, including a Citywide Coordinating Council, to monitor compliance with the desegregation order, but also district advisory councils, racial-ethnic parent councils for each school, and an extensive set of school-college and school-business partnerships.

In a second significant turn, Boston's business sector recognized its growing need for a workforce of high-tech employees. However, business needed a comfortable platform for its involvement, and that came through its participation in job training. The Boston business group the Vault had no infrastructure of staff and programs. But its involvement in the Private Industry Council (PIC), created under the federal Job Training Partnership Act, led to the development of business-school partnerships. The PIC did possess staff, and it became the entity for creating and housing the Boston Compact, initially an agreement between the school system and the business sector involving a pledge by business to provide summer jobs and hire graduates in exchange for a promise by the school district to bring about educational improvement. Although the Compact has had a somewhat rocky history, it has focused attention on academic achievement and enlisted a growing number of partners—higher education, labor organizations, the local public education fund, the Boston Human Services Coalition, and the Boston Cultural Partnerships.

Business funding helped initiate the public education fund—the Boston Plan (short for the Boston Plan for Excellence in the Public Schools)—as a spin-off of the Compact. Among other activities, it was initially home to a scholarship and mentor program to boost college attendance among high school students, and that program—ACCESS—was in turn spun off as an autonomous operation.

It is not clear how much business involvement would have taken place anyway, but Judge Garrity played a key role, not only in bringing about a desegregation plan and ending that impasse, but also in helping spur the process of building civic capacity by pressuring "businesses, higher education institutions, community organizations, and parents to become more involved" (Portz, Stein, and Jones 1999, 89). Regardless of the initial motivation, business proved to be a willing participant and became increasingly important as the federal presence diminished.

However, even with an expansive business role, the enlistment of other partners, and the growth of the local education fund into one of the premier intermediaries in the nation, Boston's education politics still had to overcome a difficult history. Conflict centered in the elected school committee and frequent turnover in the office of superintendent. In reaction, business played a major role in the move to replace the elected body with one appointed by the mayor. The move to an appointed school committee began with Mayor Raymond Flynn and was carried forward eagerly by his successor, Thomas Menino.

Although the emergence of mayoral leadership is the most visible change to occur in Boston, it was but one of a series of moves to replace an older system of provincial politics centered in the city's Irish Catholic population. A turn to strong, professionally minded superintendents was a key factor in the transition, and creation of the Boston Plan as reform intermediary was a parallel move. It too has given focus to reform, as business began to support systemic change. The Boston Plan's leadership and the superintendent's office, backed by a sizable Annenberg grant, thus give the city a scope of professional capacity and vision, without which the mayor's leadership would amount to little. Further Mayor Menino's recruitment of Thomas Payzant in 1995 was an important step. From previous service as U.S. assistant secretary of education and before that superintendent of San Diego schools, Payzant had a reputation as eminent education administrator, and his professional standing contributed to the reform alignment.

With the mayor's office as a pivot around which change was accomplished, it is significant that the appointed school committee was overwhelmingly affirmed in a 1996 referendum. Nevertheless there is criticism that the school committee is not as attuned as it should be to the city's grassroots groups and to the African American community particularly. Be that as it may, the mayor provided political protection for the school committee and the superintendent, claiming that the mayor wanted to be judged by what happened with the city's schools.

Professional development (largely school based) around standards-based reform and improved classroom instruction are central activities. Parent and community engagement are recognized goals, and the system makes use of part-time liaisons in an effort to build a parental network. Extra resources have come through foundation and private and public sector grants. A thriving economy in the 1990s enabled the state to increase its education funding and add momentum to school reform. (A prolonged downturn in the national economy after 2000 took a toll on funding.) More than most places, Boston under mayoral leadership has linked schools with health, youth development, and other social services. The elements of mayoral leadership, business support, a top-notch education fund, and varied forms of parent and community involvement along with a respected superintendent and a teachers' union that is (for the most part) an ally of school reform provide a good base on which to build civic capacity.

Still, the legacy of the past remains and the foundation of collaboration is less than rock solid. In Boston, as in Kent County and El Paso, state testing is an important feature of the context, and time is a scarce commodity. A high level of commitment to raising academic achievement puts large demands on staff, and, as Michael Usdan and Larry Cuban (2003, 46) have observed, "There persists the feeling that the school system is 'drowning' with all it has to do to improve instruction and student achievement." High school test scores have proven stubbornly static, even as elementary scores rose, and the school system continues to receive criticism for the slow pace of reform. Despite an unpromising legacy, Boston has moved on a variety of fronts, but success remains uneven.

Philadelphia

Although its population had declined to a million and a half by 2000, Philadelphia remains one of the nation's largest cities. As in El Paso and Boston, the school population is preponderantly children of color and poor. Like Boston, Philadelphia received an Annenberg grant, and launched school reform with backing from the business sector. From there the similarity breaks down. Whereas Boston eventually worked its way through intergroup conflict and public cynicism to get on track,

Philadelphia saw its reform initiative derail. The damage may not be permanent, as a reform effort continues to be mounted, but the civic disrepair was serious.[5]

The context is important. Since 1950, Philadelphia has lost about one-third of its population and four-fifths of its manufacturing jobs. The city also has a high tax burden and receives a low level of assistance from the state, Pennsylvania being one of the weakest states in the nation in efforts to equalize expenditure on education. Suburbs around Philadelphia offer higher salaries to teachers than the city does and spend considerably more per pupil. The teachers' union is strong and not averse to strikes, and the school bureaucracy and union displayed strong resistance to a major reform initiated under Constance Clayton, Philadelphia's superintendent of schools from 1980 to 1992.

In 1994 a city newspaper series highlighted dismal performance by the school system. Finger-pointing was commonplace. Business saw a weak school system as a major cause of the city's economic decline, but some community-based leaders, in the words of Jolley Christman and Amy Rhodes, "resented what they perceived as unrealistic expectations for public education" and "were angry that school bore the blame for deep-seated social ills." A foundation study characterized the city's civic leadership as "disengaged" and caught up in a "pervasive defeatist mentality" (Christman and Rhodes 2002, 14–15).

Yet the story is not entirely one-sided. Business and philanthropy established an important education intermediary, the Philadelphia Education Fund. Numerous other education and youth-related organizations populate the civic landscape, and business leaders have long been concerned about school performance. Moreover, under Mayor Edward G. Rendell's tenure from 1992 to 2000, the city experienced a modest economic resurgence.

Into this mix of forces came David Hornbeck, appointed superintendent of schools in 1994. That event came very shortly after a 1993 state legislative decision to freeze the funding formula for local school districts. Adjusted for inflation, state assistance to Philadelphia schools declined by 5.9% over the next five years, one study found (Christman and Rhodes 2002, 11). In the fall of 1994 Republican Thomas Ridge was elected governor, and he quickly proved to be an unsympathetic participant.

Hornbeck was not a professional educator by background, but he had served as state school superintendent in Maryland and as a consultant to the state of Kentucky in implementing the widely touted Kentucky Education Reform Act in 1990. Drawing on his experience in Kentucky, Hornbeck initiated his reform plan, Children Achieving, in February 1995, and Philadelphia received a $50 million Annenberg Challenge grant for a five-year period, matched by $100 million from Philadelphia businesses and foundations and from federal grants.

Children Achieving was a comprehensive approach aimed at reforming the system around the twin aims of achievement and equity, very much in line with the aims identified in Kent County, El Paso, and Boston. It was standards based, embracing the principle that all children can achieve at a high level with appropriate learning opportunities. Ongoing assessment and accountability, professional development, and, at least in rhetoric, parent and community engagement were important elements, again closely similar to the three communities described above. However, a close examination of parent engagement in Philadelphia showed that pursuit of parent and community involvement was quite limited, with the superintendent preoccupied with mobilizing support behind his effort to obtain greater funding from the state. Staff development was a part of the "Action Design" of the initiative, but, given scarce resources, it also failed to get full attention. Indeed, earlier work in professional development through teacher networks was largely ignored.

Corporate and other civic leaders saw Hornbeck's initiative as an important vehicle for improving schools, and they provided not only matching funds for the Annenberg grant but a business-created entity, Greater Philadelphia First, that served to administer the grant. Initial corporate enthusiasm was high, and Philadelphia moved quickly to raise the matching funds. Early support, however, was not sustained. Five years after the launching of Children Achieving, as the Annenberg grant period was coming to a close, Superintendent Hornbeck resigned when he faced the prospect of his initiative being dismantled. How did reform get off track? An important fact is that school performance did improve initially in that five-year period. Test scores went up, and there was greater public attention to education. In the aftermath, some observers complained that test scores did not go up fast enough and far enough. Yet an analysis of test results showed that Philadelphia's performance not only went up, but city schools also made more progress than other districts. On the face of it, Philadelphia's performance was for a time stronger than Boston's in test-score improvement.

Philadelphia's coalition of business and philanthropic interests and the school superintendent was not in itself a sufficient base from which to launch and sustain comprehensive school reform. There were two main sources of conflict, one involving the city and the state. In Kentucky, where Hornbeck had promoted comprehensive reform with considerable success, the state made major increases in funding. In Pennsylvania, Governor Ridge proved totally unresponsive to city pleas for more money. A board member of Greater Philadelphia First recounted his conversation with the governor, in which he asked Ridge how they could "link arms" in reforming Philadelphia's schools. The response was that the governor saw the existing system as something that could not be fixed and that energy should go into "building an alternative system" (quoted in Boyd and Christman 2002, 111). Ridge twice introduced but failed to get enacted statewide voucher plans. The funding impasse held throughout Ridge's tenure as governor.

Teachers and principals also failed to join the reform coalition and widely resisted accountability provisions. Some observers fault Hornbeck's approach. His version of systemic reform avoided incrementalism, going after everything at once. Even though this approach put everyone under pressure, a sustained effort to bring teachers and principals along did not materialize. As some saw it, the architects of change tended to fault teachers rather than working with them to gain support for reforms. For their part, school officials viewed the teachers' union, the Philadelphia Federation of Teachers (PFT), as adversarial and intransigent, often either unwilling to take part in meetings or obstructionist in those they did attend. In turn, PFT saw Children Achieving as a threat and strongly objected to its accountability provision. The researcher Ellen Foley (2001, 30–31) reported that during "four years of meetings with and interviewing central office staff and PFT representatives, we did not hear a single positive comment from either group about the other." When Hornbeck attempted to reconstitute two poorly performing high schools, school staff challenged the move and, according to Foley (2001, 30–31), an external arbitrator found the process faulty because "the District failed to engage in the necessary consultation with the PFT."

Further, flawed implementation included awkward sequencing, with the accountability mechanism put in place before curriculum and professional development were established as support. Indeed, even though the Philadelphia Education Fund persuaded the central office that a capacity-building role was needed, scarce resources meant that teachers were given little time for professional development, to develop curriculum, and to build relationships with colleagues. Insufficient classroom materials aggravated the situation further. Much of the professional development effort that did take place focused on informing staff about Hornbeck's ambitious program of reform. With little input from teachers and principals, the experience came across more as mandates from the central office than as something related to classroom experience.

In a climate of friction and misunderstanding, many principals and other administrators resisted various parts of the initiative and held back support during Hornbeck's clash with the state over additional funding. The teachers' union, in particular, made relations with the state and the business sector more difficult by giving no ground on key changes sought, from a longer school day to pay for performance. Failing to gain such concessions, the school district saw its standing with the business sector nosedive.

Instead of moving toward calibration, the planets of reform stayed in serious misalignment. As the Annenberg grant approached its close, Governor Ridge proved to be ideologically unbending, and Hornbeck by many accounts was undiplomatic and confrontational. When Ridge yielded nothing as state education aid continued to decline, school and city officials along with community leaders filed a lawsuit against the state (a successful suit in Kentucky had been a precipitating event in that state's embrace of school reform). The case in Pennsylvania was dismissed by the state supreme court, which held that funding decisions must be made by the legislature. The next year, Hornbeck threatened to adopt an unbalanced budget unless the state provided more money, and he and city officials filed a federal civil rights suit against the state, contending that its funding practices discriminated against school districts with large numbers of nonwhite students. As the conflict began to take an increasingly personal form, the chances of resolution faded away. For its part, the state responded by passing a takeover law aimed at Philadelphia.

Further adding to the isolation of city and school officials, business support for Children Achieving eroded badly, and the makeup of the Greater Philadelphia First board changed—by 2000 only 4 of the founding 23 CEOs remained. The days of early enthusiasm for Hornbeck's initiative gave way to a new political era; in March 1999 board members of Greater Philadelphia First endorsed Governor Ridge's second attempt to enact a statewide voucher plan. One observer offered this comment: "David [Hornbeck] believed you could make a social contract with the business community, but he looked up and they were gone. I don't think the corporate community is playing a healthy, visible constructive role in public education. But they carry tremendous weight. It's a combination of factors. So few businesses are local now. And there are some leaders who came through the Archdiocese system. They want to keep taxes down and have vouchers" (quoted in Boyd and Christman 2002, 109).

A study by the Philadelphia-based Consortium for Policy Research in Education offered a mixed assessment of Hornbeck's superintendency. He brought significant strengths to his position: "David Hornbeck was an attractive candidate for Philadelphia's superintendency. He brought star power as a national educational reform figure, and a passionate commitment to improving both urban schools and the life chances of poor students of color. He also had a strong belief that his systemic approach to school reform could turn around a poorly performing urban school system" (Christman and Rhodes 2002, 57). Yet the study also found contradictions in Hornbeck's approach, and the superintendent's effort to be truly comprehensive and move on all fronts at once meant that building broad support and achieving a shared understanding suffered.

Business proved to be an unreliable ally, reluctant to do battle for enhanced state funding and easily attracted to such marketlike solutions as vouchers. Against a backdrop of the city's fiscal squeeze, the launching of something as ambitious as Children Achieving was, in the words of Foley (2001, 26), "a calculated risk that the Annenberg Challenge grant could be used to improve performance, and that improved performance would generate the political will to obtain increased funding either through the city, the courts, or the legislature." The gamble failed, even with early test score gains.

Although the presence of parochial schools may have weakened the support of the city's business leadership for sustained reform of the public school system, the Boston example shows that the presence of parochial schools is not a sufficient stumbling block to account for the failure of civic capacity to be sustained behind reform. No single factor stands out as the source of the demise of Hornbeck's initiative. The superintendent's political skill can be faulted, but there is also no doubt that sustaining a coalition around school reform is particularly difficult when financial resources are lacking.

Declining assistance from the state was a major obstacle, and that has to be understood against the background of the political isolation of the city. Hornbeck may have played that isolation badly, even worsening it, but the friction between Mayor John F. Street, who took office in 2000, and Governor Mark Schweiker, who succeeded Ridge in 2001, suggests that the problem was more than a clash of personalities. It had deep partisan roots in the state-city relationship between Pennsylvania and Philadelphia. Race also played a part.[6] When Hornbeck arrived, the city's voluntary desegregation plan had already given rise to explicit concerns about equity and inadequate school finance. Yet Governor Ridge and Republican legislative leaders proved unresponsive to calls to address the city's funding situation; and they also ignored a referendum call for Mayor Street to assume a leadership role in education parallel to that of mayors in Boston and Chicago. Still, Hornbeck made significant missteps. Frustrated over an extremely difficult financial position, Hornbeck found himself consumed by conflict. Promising initiatives, such as those on parent engagement, lost priority standing as the superintendent became preoccupied with his fight over state funding.

For Philadelphia, the resignation of Superintendent Hornbeck brought an end to Children Achieving, but one community activist saw a silver lining: "I think the ability to have a running conversation about achievement for all kids for 4 years running is a huge accomplishment. I think that people on the street have something to say about the education crisis we're facing because of David's efforts. It gives us something to build on, but we have to remember that it takes a long time" (quoted in Boyd and Christman 2002, 114). Yet there is no avoiding the harsh reality that, even though Hornbeck brought powerful ideas to bear, they proved not to be enough to carry the day.

The derailment of Hornbeck's Children Achieving is one part of the story but not the final word. Immediately following Hornbeck's resignation, his program was dismantled as the state exercised its takeover option. A proposed broad-gauge privatization in school management set off another round of conflict. Subsequently the election of a Democratic governor opened a new episode in state-city relations and gave fresh footing for the challenge of building civic capacity. The story continues to unfold.

CIVIC CAPACITY AND LOCAL DEMOCRACY

In school reform, local action is a complement to, not a substitute for, national and state action. Still, local action is necessary. Federal- and state-initiated reforms are not self-executing. Across the four jurisdictions examined here, significant actors set in motion out-of-the ordinary processes to tackle the problem of weak academic achievement. Many other places have experienced ferment around education, but the nature and scope of activity vary greatly, with some communities still largely attached to business as usual. One purpose of civic capacity as a concept is to provide a framework for assessing the degree to which business as usual has been surmounted by a wider engagement in reform of public education.

Skeptics, particularly those who believe that improved academic achievement is strictly a matter of proper classroom technique, question whether wide engagement is really a positive factor. Given that reform, particularly systemic reform of the kind promoted in the four communities covered here, is multifaceted, and given that reform efforts face a certain amount of lag time, we can hardly expect an authoritative resolution of the issue to happen overnight. What we can observe is that Kent County and El Paso did show substantial test-score improvement. In addition, El Paso students have greatly increased enrollment in demanding math and science courses (Stone 2003). Philadelphia showed some short-term improvements, but, as might be expected, they tailed off as Superintendent Hornbeck and his initiative became increasingly enmeshed in conflict. Of the four considered here, Boston is the unclear case. Elementary scores went up, but high school scores did not. Yet Boston is unquestionably a different school system from the one described in telling detail by observers in the prereform days (Schrag 1967; Kozol 1967). Moreover, high school improvement has now moved to center stage, and the final chapter of reform has yet to be written.

Two big questions remain: First, what is the logic behind viewing civic capacity as a useful response to school reform? Second, how does civic capacity relate to democracy?

The logic is embedded in the Houston example cited at the beginning of this essay. The basic premise is that policy results such as educational achievement derive from the dual impact of governmental and nongovernmental actions. In the case of affluent, middle-class communities, the mesh of these two forces is usually academically productive because parents and their networks furnish academic readiness and reinforcing support to students, contribute supplementary resources to their schools, and provide monitoring of school performance. In lower-income and less-educated communities, the mesh between these two forces is not as smooth. Despite individual exceptions, these communities provide weaker readiness and support to students, contribute fewer supplementary resources, and are less able to monitor school performance. This pattern has a long history, based in racial stereotyping and discrimination, multigenerational confinement to low-wage work, and a general position of marginality.

For much of the 20th century, schools serving the nonaffluent were politically insulated enough to cope with and even foster low expectations without pressure to perform effectively on counts of academic achievement. But now a new political climate has emerged. Within a larger national context of concern and action, civic capacity focused on education problems can provide a means whereby school isolation is ended and expectations of effective academic performance are brought to bear. When conditions are favorable, civic capacity brings additional resources (tangible and intangible) into play, and it provides a broad political framework within which school performance is scrutinized.

The full civic capacity of a community is a highly complex matter and may be only partly realized even when strong efforts are made to mobilize it, particularly in communities with large populations of lower-income and minority students. Mobilization is an effort to compensate for the consequences of the usual course of affairs in a stratified society, but those consequences have multiple aspects that are not easily overcome. Immediate matters such as curriculum and teacher preparation are most readily identified, but much more is at stake. That is why parental engagement is important, though not easily achieved. Parent involvement is itself a form of resource, but, as is often the case, it takes resources to generate resources. And it requires looking beyond the classroom.

Overall, it is important to remember that not all resources are of a material kind. The expertise of educators, the political skill of central figures, proficiency in specialized matters such as proposal writing, and legitimacy and credibility generated by reform coalition membership are also important elements. In the overall mix, the effort and insight that parents can contribute, though not easy to enlist, have a potential to deepen the impact of school reform. The observers Cuban and Usdan (2003, 160) caution against the "shallow roots" of top-down reform, pointing out that because the aim is to enhance "classroom teaching and learning, securing teachers' endorsement and parents' support for changes are essential." Thus civic capacity itself is not a particular blueprint for how schooling should take place, but a way of realigning how the community supports its education effort.

Important as civic capacity may be to school reform, it is also part of a larger story about democracy. It provides an important perspective on the practice of local democracy. To be true to the ancient understanding of a form of governance in which all rule and are ruled in turn, democracy must be differentiated from majoritarianism. Democracy precludes practices by which any group is relegated to the position of permanent minority either by the ballot box or other means.

Local democracy involves much more than holding periodic elections or town hall–style meetings. If having a role in shaping public policy is integral to local democracy, then voting or even a chance to voice opinions falls short of what is needed. Full citizenship means contributing to major areas of public policy, particularly those that bear directly on daily life. From the Houston vignette, we can see what is missing when educators are isolated from their communities. For good reason, Joel Handler, in *Down from Bureaucracy* (1996), speaks of "service engagement" rather than service delivery.

The quality of citizenship can be affected in various ways. Some observers equate democracy with the sounding of diverse voices without regard to what follows and how talk connects to action. Yet to the extent that democracy is about problem solving, the community in its various segments needs to develop and utilize a shared framework of action. If the populace is so divided that no common framework of action can be devised, then the chance to contribute to problem solving is diminished and so is the quality of citizenship. Conciliation, not impasse, is at the heart of democratic politics. Philadelphia during the Hornbeck era is a telling example of how deadlock constricts the practice of democracy.

Thus building civic capacity involves developing a shared understanding, even if loose in significant details and even if coexistence is part of the understanding. With the importance of a shared understanding in mind, we can see why professional development occupied such an important place in Kent County, El Paso, and Boston, and why in Philadelphia the relative neglect of professional development left deadlock undiminished. In short, when professional development gives educators a shared understanding of their task, augments their capacity to perform that task, and opens them to greater interaction with parents and other community members, then it is an effective, indeed much needed, contributor to civic capacity.

In full measure, building civic capacity also involves enhancing the abilities and opportunities to contribute of those previously excluded. To the extent that segments of the population continue to fall into a pattern of noninvolvement, then the principle of no permanent minority is violated and democratic practice falls short.

For lower-income parents, often unaccustomed to asserting themselves with professionals in positions of authority, an unwelcoming manner by educators can end the process. Barriers of mutual mistrust and apprehension can be substantial. A twofold process may be needed—one to orient parents toward participation in broader ways and the second to direct educators along the path toward embracing new modes of practice. However, in Philadelphia, top school officials failed to incorporate into professional development the practice of working with parents and viewing them as assets in the education of children. In some cases intermediaries have at least partially filled that gap. El Paso's collaborative, for example, has included parent engagement in its agenda, and the Boston plan also works on parent-educator collaboration. Significantly, despite overall weaknesses, Philadelphia had two intermediaries, the Alliance Organizing Project (AOP) and Teachers and Parents and Students (TAPAS), working to establish new relationships between parents and schools, and these organizations had some successes. However, these were selective instances in which not only were school-site educators receptive but special external funding provided support for outreach and organizing. This scope of effort is rare, and it had no large role in any of the four communities examined here.

An analysis of one such experience in Philadelphia, that of the Watkins Elementary School (a pseudonym), is nevertheless revealing. AOP provided a community organizer to work with the school as part of a broader strategy of strengthening lower-income neighborhoods. The school was performing relatively well, but the principal, after some initial reluctance, proved open to the idea that parents might provide him, as he put it, "with another level of support" (Gold et al. 2001, 23). With assistance from the school counselor, the organizer found a small group of parents as a starting base, and then used one-on-one meetings to expand the circle of participants. When these parents talked about their concerns, safety emerged at the top of the list. And restoring some of the crossing guards cut in recent budgetary moves became the solution they settled on and around which they worked with parent groups at other schools. A few teachers joined the "public action" as well. With success on that matter, the parents moved on to the issue of an after-school program. Initially rebuffed by a no-resources response from the principal, they turned to the idea of an after-school parent-run homework club. The aim was academic enrichment, and the principal consented to the use of school facilities. The Philadelphia Education Fund provided training and assistance in writing what proved to be a successful funding proposal. Some teachers began to cooperate by offering their classroom materials for use and by referring students with need for assistance, and soon teachers and parents were working together for the benefit of children. Parents gained skill and confidence working with the students, and teachers saw the parents in a new light. Although coming from a background of exclusion and marginality:

> parents learned how to research an issue of concern; they were trained in classroom management, instruction, and curriculum; they learned to write funding proposals; they gained the confidence to interview public officials; they led public meetings; and they created a political campaign to focus attention on their children's needs. The AOP organizing process provided parents the opportunity to learn the skills of civic participation (Gold et al. 2001, 23).[7]

The example is a small and unrepresentative one in the large picture of Philadelphia schools, but it shows that participation by parents can make substantive contributions to academic achievement, not just for their own children, but in shaping the climate for learning at the schoolwide level. In addition, parent engagement brings a broader set of concerns to bear and can contribute needed "local knowledge." Moreover, "questions of societal inequities are often pushed to the surface" (Gold 2001, 47). Wider participation expanded the scope of concerns considered.

The promise of building civic capacity is that, when carried through thoroughly, it can both serve instrumentally to advance school reform and at the same time strengthen democratic practice. The task of school reform is formidable; it involves changing expectations, increasing commitment, and expanding efforts all around. For local democracy's part, understood as containing a contributory dimension, it is no starry-eyed luxury. Rather, it is essential if school reform is to be achieved in full measure.

Although the four cases in the condensed versions provided here can give only brief illustrations of civic capacity at work, they do show something of what is possible and of the dynamics of the process. At an abstract level, key elements in building civic capacity may sound formulaic: a shared definition of a problem as an agenda for action, combined with cross-sector mobilization of a coalition, yielding a proper mix and amount of resources, and executed through an appropriate and detailed plan. However, the process is more organic than this statement conveys. A community's problem-solving capacity has to do fundamentally with relationships—with who is included and on what terms. Moreover, for education particularly, a full capacity rests on what is in reality a democratic foundation; that is to say, a full capacity includes all stakeholders, parents and front-line educators among them. Thus, building civic capacity typically involves more than employment of existing relationships. As the AOP example illustrates, it sometimes means shaping new relationships, particularly in communities with sizable lower-income and minority populations.

NOTES

"Civic Cacpacity—What, Why, and from Whence," by Clarence N. Stone, in *Institutions of American Democracy: Public Education*, pp. 206–34, ed. Susan Fuhrman and Marvin Lazerson (New York: Oxford Univ. Press, 2005). Reprinted with permission from Oxford Univ. Press.

1. The account of school reform in Kent County, Maryland, is based on a study for the Learning First Alliance by Togneri and Lazarus (2003). Kent County was one of five districts studied by the Learning First Alliance, each of which had measurable success in pursuing systemic reform focused on instructional improvement. An overview of findings from all five districts is presented in Togneri and Anderson (2003).

2. The account of El Paso's experience draws heavily on a case study conducted by the author

for the Annenberg Institute for School Reform; see Stone, *Civic Cooperation in El Paso* (2003). Other sources include Navarro and Natalicio (1999); and Parra (2002). I am also indebted to Professor Kathleen Staudt for her invaluable observations about El Paso.

3. The presentation of Boston's experience is based mainly on: Portz, Stein, and Jones (1999); Gary Yee (2003); Usdan and Cuban (2003); Boston Plan for Excellence in the Public Schools (2001); and Portz (2004). John Portz also kindly read a draft of the chapter and provided comments.

4. Useful accounts of the Boston busing crisis can be found in Lukas (1986); Lupo (1988); and Formisano (1991).

5. The Philadelphia case narrative is based mainly on research reports by Foley (2001); Gold et al. (2001); and Christman and Rhodes (2002). See also Boyd and Christman (2003); and Christman et al. (2003). Personal communication with Ellen Foley, Eva Gold, Elaine Simon, and Jolley Christman also helped refine the author's understanding of Philadelphia's experience.

6. Useful background on this issue can be found in Birger (1996).

7. For parallel instances, see Shirley (1997) and Warren (2001).

REFERENCES

Birger, J. S. 1996. Race, reaction, and reform: The three R's of Philadelphia school politics, 1965–71. *Pennsylvania Magazine of History and Biography* 120 (Jul.): 163–216.

Boston Plan for Excellence in the Public Schools. 2001. Triennial report 1998–2001. http://www.bpe.org/.

Boyd, W. B., and J. Christman. 2003. A tall order for Philadelphia's new approach to school governance. In *Powerful reforms with shallow roots: Improving America urban schools,* ed. L. Cuban and M. Usdan, 96–124. New York: Teachers College Press.

Christman, J., and A. Rhodes. 2002. *Civic engagement and urban school improvement: Hard-to-learn lessons from Philadelphia.* Philadelphia: Consortium for Policy Research in Education and Research for Action.

Christman, J., et al. 2003. Philadelphia's Children Achieving initiative. In *A race against time: The crisis in urban schooling,* ed. J. G. Cibulka and W. L. Boyd, 23–44. Westport, Conn.: Praeger.

Clark, K. B. 1965. *Dark ghetto: Dilemmas of social power.* New York: Harper and Row.

Comer, J. 1993. *School power: Implications of an intervention project.* Reprint. New York: Free Press.

Crick, B. 1993. *In defense of politics.* 4th ed. Chicago: Univ. of Chicago Press.

Folley, E. 2001. *Contradictions and control in systemic reform: The ascendancy of the central office in Philadelphia schools.* Philadelphia: Consortium for Policy Research in Education.

Formisano, R. P. 1991. *Boston against busing: Race, class, and ethnicity in the 1960s and 1970s.* Chapel Hill: Univ. of North Carolina Press.

Gold, E., et al. 2001. *Clients, consumers, or collaborators? Parents and their roles in school reform during Children Achieving, 1995–2000.* Philadelphia: Consortium for Policy Research in Education.

Handler, J. F. 1996. *Down from bureaucracy: The ambiguity of privatization and empowerment.* Princeton, N.J.: Princeton Univ. Press.

Hochschild, J. L., and N. Scovronick. 2003. *The American dream and the public schools.* New York: Oxford Univ. Press.

Kozol, J. 1967. *Death at an early age: The destruction of the hearts and minds of Negro children in the Boston public schools.* Boston: Houghton Mifflin.

Lukas, J. A. 1986. *Common ground: A turbulent decade in the lives of three American families.* New York: Vintage.

Lupo, A. 1988. *Liberty's chosen home: The politics of violence in Boston.* 2nd ed. Boston: Beacon Press, 1988.

McAdams, D. R. 2000. *Fighting to save our urban schools . . . and winning!* New York: Teachers College Press.

Metz, M. H. 1990. How social class differences shape teachers' work. In *Contexts of teaching in secondary schools: Teachers' realities,* ed. M. McLaughlin, J. E. Talbert, and N. Bascia, 40–107. New York: Teachers College.

Navarro, M. S., and D. Natalicio. 1999. Closing the achievement gap in El Paso. *Phi Delta Kappan* 80 (Apr.): 597–601.

Parra, M. A. 2002. A case study of leadership in systemic education reform: The El Paso Collaborative for Academic Excellence. Ph.D. diss., Univ. of Texas at El Paso.

Payne, C. M. 2001. So much reform, so little change. In *Education policy for the 21st century,* ed. L. B. Joseph, 239–78. Chicago: Univ. of Chicago.

Portz, J. 2004. Boston: Agenda setting and school reform in a mayor-centric system. In *Mayors in the middle: Politics, race, and mayoral control of urban schools,* ed. J. R. Henig and W. C. Rich, 96–119. Princeton, N.J.: Princeton Univ. Press.

Portz, J., L. Stein, and R. R. Jones. 1999. *City schools and city politics: Institutions and leadership in Pittsburgh, Boston, and St. Louis.* Lawrence: Univ. Press of Kansas.

Schorr, L. B. 1997. *Common purposes: Strengthening families and neighborhoods to rebuild America.* New York: Doubleday.

Schrag, P. 1967. *Village school downtown.* Boston: Beacon Press.

Shirley, D. 1997. *Community organizing for school reform.* Austin: Univ. of Texas Press.

Stone, C. N. 2003. *Civic cooperation in El Paso.* Report to the Annenberg Institute of School Reform. http://www.schoolcommunities.org/Archive/index.html.

Stone, C. N., et al. 2001. *Building civic capacity: The politics of reforming urban schools.* Lawrence: Univ. Press of Kansas.

Togneri, W., and S. Anderson. 2003. *Beyond islands of excellence.* Washington, D.C.: Learning First Alliance.

Togneri, W., and L. Lazarus. 2003. *It takes a system: A districtwide approach to improving teaching and learning in Kent County public schools.* Washington, D.C.: Learning First Alliance.

Usdan, M., and L. Cuban. 2003. Boston: The stars finally in alignment. In *Powerful reforms with shallow roots: Improving America's urban schools,* ed. L. Cuban and M. Usdan, 38–53. New York: Teachers College Press.

Warren, M. R. 2001. *Dry bones rattling: Community building to revitalize American democracy.* Princeton, N.J.: Princeton Univ. Press.

Yee, G. 2003. From Court Street to city hall. In *A race against time: The crisis in urban schooling,* ed. J. G. Cibulka and W. L. Boyd, 82–105. Westport, Conn.: Praeger.

Part Five

Conclusion: Reflections and Prospects

In *Regime Politics,* Stone offered the "urban regime" as an "illuminating concept" that was potentially useful for opening up comparative analyses of governing arrangement in local communities. Stone, however, acknowledged that he did not expect the regime concept "to be frozen at the version" he presented in 1989. He anticipated that there would be some challenge, responses, and refinements to his conceptualization of urban politics. Interestingly, over the past nearly two decades, no one has been more significant in the continuing evolution and refinement of urban regime analysis than its principal creator. Stone has been willing to continue to develop regime analysis despite its overwhelming success—and in the face of the American politics subfield's general resistance. This evidences his iconoclasm and avid analytical mind. He is dissatisfied with the original framework and has continued to modify it. We see some of that in the next chapter, an essay expressly written for this volume.

In Chapter 12, Stone provides some reflections on urban political science scholarship, considering his own views of urban politics alongside two significant studies in the field, Paul Peterson's *City Limits* and Robert Dahl's *Who Governs?* Stone highlights the weaknesses in these studies and the faulty assumptions on which their theoretical models are derived. A perennial issue confronting Stone's use of the regime concept as a framework for examining Atlanta has been whether the conceptualization sheds light on political change and regime continuity. In this new essay, Stone sketches what he calls a "new urban agenda." Drawing on experiences from several U.S. cities, Stone identifies emerging patterns in the areas of affordable housing, crime prevention, and school reform. He sketches out what is required to expand and sustain them.

In the final chapter, Jennifer Hochschild locates Stone's scholarship within political science, pointing out many of its strengths. Hochschild also provides some points of omission in Stone's work. She provides insights into urban political analysis, suggesting avenues of research that could potentially reconnect urban politics to mainstream American politics. Hochschild believes that much can be learned by cross-fertilization with subfields.

12. Urban Politics Then and Now

Clarence N. Stone

In *Regime Politics* I offered the view that, in a fragmented world of the kind we have today, the paradigmatic issue is "how to bring about enough cooperation among disparate community elements to get things done—and to do so in the absence of an overarching command structure or a unifying system of thought" (Stone 1989, 227). At this writing, Atlanta's biracial coalition has been at the heart of the city's governing arrangements for well over a half century. During that time, despite a disjoined structure of local government, Atlanta has been highly successful in getting a number of big and important things done. The pattern continues, but there is an unevenness to it that warrants close attention.[1]

After the publication of *Regime Politics* in 1989, the city's most visible accomplishment was becoming the host city for the 1996 Summer Olympics. Although the actual running of the Olympics was through an independent authority, ACOG (Atlanta Committee on the Olympic Games), the biracial coalition was an integral part of the event from its inception to its close. Significantly, Atlanta's current mayor, Shirley Franklin, was a vice president of ACOG.[2]

As the Olympics approached, former President Jimmy Carter took a keen interest in the city's poverty problem. Atlanta had (and continues to have) a high rate of poverty. Carter launched a major effort to ameliorate conditions for the poor through a voluntary effort called TAP (The Atlanta Project). This was a multimillion-dollar effort intended to draw heavily on volunteers, involve the business sector, and give voice to neighborhood concerns. By design, the role of government was to be minimal. Although the project had some modest successes, notably a child-immunization effort, the official evaluation noted the initiative's failure to address issues in a systematic, long-term manner. In a reporter's assessment, the main lesson learned was about "the inherent limits of private charity" (Kurylo 1996). The project failed to take hold as a sustained endeavor, and after an initial phase of activity, it receded into a token remnant.

A major government initiative fared even worse. Under President Clinton, the city received an Empowerment Zone Award, but subsequently found itself enmeshed in an extended experience of mismanagement along with a high level of friction between then Mayor Bill Campbell (mayor from 1993 to 2001) and neighborhood representatives (Rich 2003). The program never enlisted Atlanta's major businesses as participants and yielded little beside bad publicity.

In 1996, with yet another initiative, the biracial coalition seemed to kick into motion. Ostensibly building on the momentum from hosting the Olympics, Mayor Campbell, with strong backing from the business sector, assembled a blue-ribbon commission called the Renaissance Program. Its announced aim was to take on a far-reaching program for addressing city problems, including major attention to neighborhood development. At one hearing, representatives of the city's Concerned Black Clergy called for programs to address the city's social needs, such as expansion of preschool opportunities. Yet despite the outward markings of the biracial coalition at work and various reports over a two-year period, the project gradually faded from the civic scene. After Campbell's reelection in November of 1997, the initiative lost focus, and no significant programs came out of it.

The Olympics notwithstanding, Campbell's mayoralty overall was a difficult time for the biracial coalition, with widespread instances of poor management and problems of corruption. Municipal affairs have righted under the current mayor, Shirley Franklin, and the biracial coalition seems back on even keel.[3] On becoming mayor, Franklin's signature initiative was, however, not to address the poverty but to launch a major upgrade in the city's water and sewer system. Atlanta's biracial coalition handles some matters well, but not others. The above are only illustrative episodes, but they raise the question of how to account for the city's uneven policy experience. Much more is involved than succession in the mayor's office.

If a city's politics does not center on who holds its top electoral posts, what is it about? If we look below the outer layer of formal office holding, what do we find? Although Atlanta is by no means typical, the long run of its biracial coalition is instructive. Atlanta's experience shows that the presence of a regime effective in pursuing some policy aims is no assurance that it can accomplish others. *A regime is not a generic capacity to govern.* For instance, even policy goals widely deemed worthy may languish while others beset by intense opposition may move ahead. Public sentiment is a poor guide to what is doable.

What, then, is the political foundation for a city's action agenda? Important as voting is, politics is not election centered. Although the enfranchisement of black Atlantans made the city's biracial coalition possible, elections are not the pivot on which politics turns. Voting power can help bring about change, as it did in Atlanta, and on the surface, much politics has to do with elections.[4] Yet political life has an understructure that must be reckoned with.

I started the research for *Regime Politics* from a political-economy perspective by considering how business control of investment is reconciled with popular control of elected office. Quickly, however, I learned that not only are there many ways these two elements of modern life can be linked, but also that the linking occurs through a rich and complex civic sector.[5] Politics in Atlanta is not a highly autonomous activity. Instead the city's politics is interwoven in myriad ways with civil society—with civic organizations that consider and weigh issues, provide training for civic life, promote a form of community-mindedness, supply not just volunteers but a pool from which political activists emerge for varying stints of service (paid and unpaid), and above all furnish a setting in which informal and interpersonal networks take shape. In Atlanta, civil society, far from being autonomous itself, is something profoundly shaped by the business sector and the resources, connections, and concerns that it brings to bear.[6]

Governing, market processes, and civil society are woven together in intricate ways.[7] The operational autonomy that each sector enjoys is but one level of political life. Operational autonomy is heavily mediated through the reality of interdependence. Urban regime analysis is therefore an effort to go beneath the surface of legal form and learn how these various sectors are woven together. Thus, although it was important that black leaders in Atlanta used electoral clout as leverage with city hall, they also had to be able to form bridges across the city's highly segregated civic life. Their subsequent success in penetrating the inner circles of business in Atlanta had a profound influence on the policy direction pursued. Thus, gaining position within the chamber of commerce, forging connections around business partnerships, and establishing Action Forum as a communication link between private elites were all important steps in the kind of incorporation achieved.[8] Cumulatively, these and related steps changed the city's civic life, and did so in a way that is more than a simple addition process. The sum—that is, the evolved configuration of relationships—is greater than the parts.

The Atlanta configuration—that is, the regime—is not a static phenomenon. And it has evolved in such a way as to make it difficult for the city to address in a sustained way the concerns and challenges faced by Atlanta's lower-income population. The wider metropolitan order, with its antipathy toward the city, particularly its African American citizens, only compounds the problem (Kruse 2005). Within the city, the configuration that makes up the core of the governing arrangement represents an important capacity to take on challenges, but as President Carter's TAP, the Empowerment Zone, and then Mayor Bill Campbell's Renaissance Program all show, the regime is much better positioned to pursue some aims than others.

To address poverty, the challenge is not simply to come up with new program ideas and have them enacted. The essential task is to reconfigure relationships so that a different mix of players is engaged, drawing on a different corpus of resources and addressing a different body of concerns. As typified by African American incorporation into the chamber of commerce and the establishment of Action Forum,

Atlanta's regime has evolved away from anything more than a superficial concern with poverty and instead has fixed firmly on expanded business and professional opportunities for the black middle class.

Once we look at politics as involving configurations of how government, the business sector, and civil society are conjoined, then we can begin to appreciate why change is much more complicated than pressuring those in office, electing a new set of leaders, or "throwing the rascals out."

LOOKING BACK

Thinking about Assumptions

What makes politics configurative rather than election centered?[9] A useful starting assumption is that of bounded rationality. We are creatures of limited cognition, able to comprehend the world incompletely and focus attention on only a narrow piece at any given time (Jones 2001). We are very much creatures of the institutions and networks in which our lives are immersed (Steinmo, Thelen, and Longstreth 1992; Hall and Taylor 1996). It is hard for us to imagine vastly different arrangements. Social inertia in the form of established relationships has a cognitive foundation, and it is rooted in microbehavior.

Macro-level forces are also at work. In more thoughtful instances, they are treated as a matter of structure and agency,[10] but in many urban analyses, complex structures tend to be reduced to an economic imperative, often given little scrutiny beyond the obligatory obeisance to global capitalism.[11] By assuming that politics is highly autonomous, classic pluralism largely took socioeconomic structures as exogenous. Primary attention went to elections, party competition, and practices within the political arena narrowly understood.[12] As a consequence, socioeconomic inequalities were treated mainly as factors that might influence level of voting and other forms of explicitly political participation.

Two decades after the publication of *Who Governs?*, Paul Peterson's *City Limits* (1981) discounted such participation. Peterson posited a form of local politics dominated by an overriding economic imperative to promote growth and enhance economic well-being. Yet because any given structure involves a degree of looseness as it is reproduced, and because even the mode of economic production is only one of multiple structures at work, agency has room to maneuver. Hence reconfigurations of governing arrangements are not precluded, though some are much easier to bring about and perpetuate than others. For example, given that in Atlanta labor unions are a feeble force, philanthropy of the kind inclined to support community-based organizing has historically been weak, city elections are nonpartisan, and political parties are largely absent in the city's internal politics, leverage points for recasting the city's civic life are scarce. Business-centered civic life enjoys a huge preemptive advantage.

Thus, in contrast to Peterson, regime analysis operates within a Tillian tradition of not assuming that a single structure is dominant (Tilly 1984; Stone 1989, 226–27). Still, any current configuration is difficult to change. Established arrangements have great staying power (Clarke et al. 2006). With narrow cognition at work, there is virtually no chance in contemporary Atlanta that, under current arrangements, mass discontent could turn into sustainable change. In short, broad structures—whether capitalism or the idea of popular consent—do not work in an unmediated fashion. They operate through organizations, particular practices, alliances, networks, and understood channels of activity. Hence it is no incidental matter that students of movement politics swung away from explanations based on social strains and mass discontent to explanations based on resource mobilization, intermediary organizations, and political opportunity structures.[13]

The details of how arrangements are put together and maintained matter greatly. Take, for instance, the evolution of the channels of interracial communication within Atlanta's governing arrangements. On the black side, what originally rested on the electoral process, operating on a mass basis mobilized primarily through churches (organizationally the bipartisan Atlanta Negro Voters League) with an important operational role for the Atlanta Urban League, evolved over time into an arrangement centered on regular interaction between top business and professional people through Action Forum. Behind-the-scenes communication prevailed at both times, but the operating base from which interaction took place changed tremendously. This shift is not a trivial factor in Atlanta's ineffectiveness at addressing the conditions of the poor. The stumbling block is not lack of awareness, but rather weakness in the arrangements to frame an appropriate agenda, supply that effort, refine its application, address operational flaws, and see that the agenda enjoys priority attention.

Policy initiatives take place in a structured context, but the structures need to be understood at an operational level where contending structural forces are adjusted to one another. This is politics in a guise far more complicated than the specifics of who won the last mayoral election. Such elections are not insignificant, but their consequences take shape through a complicated interweaving of forms of interdependence. When Maynard Jackson became Atlanta's first African American mayor, he found in place black-white connections far wider than those that ran through city hall. Race was an enormously significant factor in his election, but in office, Jackson could not count on African American solidarity in dealings with the city's white business elite.

With Atlanta as a background for making some key assumptions explicit, I want to turn now to showing in detail how regime analysis differs from alternative approaches and build toward an examination of a nascent urban agenda and what the politics of this new agenda might look like. Much of my understanding of urban politics has come through a career-long dialogue with Robert Dahl's *Who Governs?*. Admirable as that book is on many counts, ultimately it offers a fundamentally flawed understanding of how the politics of cities operates. It is important to see why.

My aim here, then, is to explain why an alternative model is in order. In doing so, I have to confront another influential book as well, and that is Paul Peterson's *City Limits* (1981). It poses the important question of how much political agency is possible in the face of the structural force of place competition in a capitalist order. By no means is this structural force to be minimized. It affects who is involved in politics, how coalitions are put together, and what has a claim on priority. Yet an assumption of structural determinism is not a suitable foundation for constructing a model of politics.

As an alternative, think about the paramount importance of political interdependence in a setting of multiple structures. Instead of taking it as given that government officials are in charge or that business can exact compliance, let us suppose that the crucial issue is about how state, market, and civil society intersect. Regime analysis assumes that although government enjoys a high degree of autonomy in day-to-day operations (i.e., it has a differentiated role), it does not operate with a high degree of independence from other sectors of society. It is profoundly affected by all that is entailed in a system of social stratification. Contrast this with Dahl.

Who Governs? begins with this question: "How does a 'democratic system' work amid inequalities of resources?" (1961a, 3). Dahl's answer is that competitive elections in a context of consensus on fundamentals yields a system of "dispersed inequalities"—dispersed in such a way as to make politics relatively open and inclusive. I argue that this endpoint remains a hope, not an achieved reality. A harsh fact of the 20th century is that segments of the urban population found themselves disconnected from the mainstream and thus were served badly by the institutions that govern and provide important services. Hence political reconfiguration is in order. Even though politics reflects social and economic inequalities, political patterns are not predetermined. Because multiple tendencies are at work, the social-justice challenge is to find leverage points to lessen the impact of socioeconomic inequalities. Normatively, this underlies regime analysis. First, however, we need to clear a path.

Two post–World War II scenarios spread long shadows over the study of local politics. One is the Atlanta scenario, in which a mayor somewhat reluctantly supports an agenda of large-scale redevelopment and reordered land use. He does so because the redevelopment agenda has the insistent backing of a civically active and cohesive business elite.[14] The other is the New Haven scenario, in which an entrepreneurial mayor enlists a somewhat reluctant and not always united business sector to support his agenda of large-scale redevelopment and reordered land use.[15]

How to reconcile these two scenarios has been at the center of an intensely waged debate about the very nature of local democracy. The puzzle is that radically different forms of surface politics serve to advance essentially the same agenda. *City Limits* offers one view.

Urban Politics as Servant to the Economic Imperative

Paul Peterson's *City Limits* puts front and center the possibility that local politics amounts to little, that the politics of cities is mainly a matter of their position in a market system.[16] In focusing on the fact that cities face economic competition, Peterson invokes the idea of the interest of the city as a whole.[17] Building on the idea that "policy structures political relationships" (1981, 131), Peterson develops a threefold typology around the economic well-being of the city. *Developmental policies* are those that enhance the economic position of the city through upgrading land use, improving transportation, and providing opportunities for economic development. *Redistributive policies* shift benefits to the less well-off but put the city at risk because capital is mobile, and the well-off can easily move to an adjoining locality. A flight of capital or of affluent residents would leave the city in a worsened economic position.

The residual category is *allocational policies,* those that have neither positive nor negative effects on the economic position of the city. Given the logic of the city's structural position, Peterson argues that cities heavily favor developmental policies, tend to stifle redistributive proposals, and have only the allocational arena as a place for pluralist bargaining. Effect on economic position defines the character of a policy and thereby determines the character of the politics surrounding the policy. Using his typology, Peterson recharacterizes the community-power debate by offering a grand synthesis. Because, as Peterson sees it, developmental policies enjoy a broad consensus within the city but are pursued under conditions of competition with other localities, they are marked by closed decision making in the hands of a few, typically policy specialists within local government in consultation with major business figures. These are the people with expertise and the ones who command the needed resources. Developmental politics is thus a neutered form of elite rule, treated in effect as a depoliticized activity, guided by technical considerations rather than competing priorities, clashing judgments, and contending group interests.[18]

The stifling of redistributive demands, when they are occasionally raised, corresponds to nondecision making, and according to Peterson, they never amount to much because they enjoy little or no popular support. Allocational policy serves as the arena of pluralist bargaining, but the stakes are deemed modest (contrast Kaufmann 2004). What the elitists characterized as behind-the-scenes manipulation by business leaders to alter land use and promote downtown redevelopment along with keeping redistributive matters off the agenda turns out, in Peterson's hands, to be simply a matter of a consensual adjustment to the city's economic position. Business executives benefit, but that is because what they want corresponds to the interest of the city as a whole. In Peterson's judgment, policies are driven not by group struggle, but by reasonable and intelligent people concerned about the city's well-being (Peterson 1981, 133).

The internal logic of Peterson's argument may seem solid, but it is a poor fit with the real world of politics. Highways, land use, and redevelopment—Peterson's examples of developmental policy—have been among the mostly intensely contested issues on the urban landscape. Yet working from the logic of his analysis, Peterson depicted local politics as "generally a quiet arena of decision making where political leaders can give reasoned attention to the longer range interest of the city, taken as a whole" (Peterson 1981, 109).

Centered on system-based determinism, Peterson's model of urban politics is flawed. Several complications stand in the way of translating a structural force unproblematically into specific policy measures.[19] *Uncertainty* tops the list. Consider, for example, the question of whether a new stadium or convention center is justified. Planners can make cost-benefit calculations, but they are bedeviled by uncertainties, and when choosing one priority over another, the uncertainties multiply. Technical calculations are seldom beyond dispute. Meaningful market feedback is a long time coming, and even then may not be entirely clear.

Trade-offs are a second complicating factor. Building casinos, for example, may increase local revenue, but they may also change the quality of life and affect the level of public safety. Development may expand employment opportunities, but it may also tilt the local culture in a new direction (Ramsay 1996). Because judgments about trade-offs often involve competing values, they don't lend themselves to technical resolution.

Time horizons are a third complicating factor. Political time is different from policy time, and politicians generally prefer quick returns to those over a longer time span (Erie 2004). By some calculations, investing in preschool programs for disadvantaged children yields important long-term economic benefits, but the politics of that kind of developmental policy is quite different from questions about land use and redevelopment.

Diffuse general benefits versus concentrated particular costs are yet another complication. Many city actors are not the kind of consistently public-spirited citizens whom Peterson sees in a leading role. Tension almost always surrounds a call to forego the immediate benefits for some in favor of the broad, long-term good of the community. Consider, for instance, unionized teachers. It may be widely agreed that reform of the school system would be good for the city, but if that means modifications in tenure and seniority rules, then change faces likely resistance.

As these various considerations come into play, we encounter *ambiguity about policy types.* It becomes important to distinguish rhetoric from reality (Pagano and Bowman 1995). Proponents of an initiative are apt to promote it as being in the interest of the city as a whole. But the very nature of a policy may be at issue politically. What is touted by one faction as good for the whole city may be labeled by another as a crass case of rewarding one's allies. In Atlanta, minority set-asides were initially attacked by the white business sector as reckless redistribution (Reed 1999). Black political leaders insisted it was allocational (i.e., did not harm the city economically) and equity serving (overcoming past discrimination). Over time, as the program came to be appreciated for its contribution to coalition building in support of developmental projects, the white business sector became strong defenders of minority set-asides. The argument about redistribution faded away.

Because initiatives may have mixed features that unfold in different ways over time, the apparent character of a policy may look different as the times and context change. In addition, once the full array of policy initiatives comes under consideration, the line between even the opposites of developmental and redistributive becomes fuzzy. For example, a below-market loan fund can assist in the conservation of older neighborhoods and bolster the value of housing therein.[20] Is that redistributive or developmental?

Public safety has a close connection to economic development, especially when it is tied to the tourist industry. Many police officials are staunch advocates of youth programs because they see them as contributing to crime prevention.[21] Are such programs developmental or redistributive? Or consider intergroup relations. With its slogan, "the city too busy to hate," Atlanta made a connection between race relations and economic development. Examples of complex mixes of policy features are legion.

Policies may help shape politics, but it is also clear that politics has much to do with how policies are understood.[22] City politics often fits poorly within the boundaries of logically constructed typologies. Many policies, with a myriad of consequences, extend beyond Peterson's typology. Efforts to promote economic well-being are characterized by varying forms of uncertainty, an inescapable element of subjectivity, a need to accommodate multiple considerations, and anything other than a low-key, technically guided process of consensus building. Peterson got a major structural force right but neglected the politics that surrounds its translation into concrete policy.

Misreading the Power Map

It is now widely recognized that Dahl's account of New Haven politics was inadequate in particular ways (see, e.g., Fox 1988). Yet the internal logic of Dahl's argument and its historical foundation rarely receive close scrutiny. Though Dahl himself acknowledges that he should have paid greater heed to the "limiting factors" that surround local decision making, he offers no elaboration (1986, 192). We should note, then, that the claims of classic pluralism involve much more than the absence of a controlling elite. They form an argument that politics is an accessible channel for expressing discontent even for those of modest position.[23]

Dahl posits three interrelated processes through which rule by an oligarchy of wealth and social standing gave way to a more open and inclusive form of governing. In Dahl's hands, the shift is from an arrangement of cumulative inequality to one of dispersed inequalities. One process was the development of universal suffrage, with an accompanying decline in traditional forms of deference. A second process was that of a functional differentiation of roles that took place as the preindustrial town gave way to the growth and then decline of the industrial city. The third process was one of assimilation in which a diverse immigrant population evolved beyond divisions of class and ethnicity toward a widely shared consensus about the broad features of the social and economic order and the values embodied in this order.

The historical portion of *Who Governs?* traces a transition from a beginning point where a small elite sat at the peak of an order that combined the role of governing with a top economic position and high social standing. Over time, these various roles are differentiated and occupied by different segments of society: "Wealth was separated from social position by the rise of industry, and public office went to the wealthy. Later, popularity was divorced from both wealth and social position but had the advantage of numbers" (Dahl 1961a, 11).

Note the evidence Dahl relies on to show the movement from oligarchy to democratic pluralism. His method of historical inquiry simply assumes that holding electoral office is the chief power position for which various elements of society contend. Relying on the social background of the city's mayors provides a succinct indicator of change, but it assumes that contending for electoral office is the central power process in governing the city. It also enables Dahl to downplay the significance of an additional role differentiation: that of the policy expert. In his analysis, the emergence of what Dahl calls "the new men" further disperses power, but it poses no threat to the role of the mayor as the linchpin in the city's politics.

Dahl's understanding of power assumes that wills clash and that in its purest form, power consists of the ability to prevail in such a clash. This understanding of power also puts legal authority at the center of power wielding: "No group of people in the United States has ever succeeded in imposing its will on other groups for any significant length of time without the support of law—without, that is to say, the acquiescence of government officials and the courts" (Dahl 1961a, 246). Hence Dahl deemed the increasing inability of New Haven's social and economic notables to contend for the city's top elected office to be an enormous factor in ending cumulative inequalities.

If Dahl's understanding of power—the capacity to command compliance in a system in which its various parts presumably have a high degree of autonomy— were the full story, then Dahl would indeed have a case for dispersed inequalities. However, let us look at New Haven's role differentiation in another way. As a form of complexity, role differentiation involves a high degree of interdependence. Against that background, if power is more than an ability to exact compliance from unwilling subjects, how do we think about power?

Without denying that "power over" (control) is an important facet of human relationships, let us think about "power to" (moving from an incapacity to act toward enjoying such a capacity) and consider its implications. Interdependence becomes a central fact. Indeed, New Haven's Mayor Lee reflects the usual political condition of an inability to do much of consequence without the cooperation of others. We need, therefore, to understand how actors come to establish relationships of cooperation, particularly for big and complicated undertakings (such as urban redevelopment). Alignments compete indirectly, and in that competition, some actors enjoy systemic advantages because they embody or command useful resources.

Interdependence is not a basis for an unceasing war of all against all—quite the contrary, it is a foundation for seeking workable alignments. Attraction is a field force, akin in some ways to gravity. The more actors have to offer as potential coalition partners, the greater their attraction. Hence there are many potential partnerships, but some are easier to put together than others. Still, none is foreordained to take shape, and many potentially workable partnerships may go unassembled. This is, in fact, an underdeveloped subtext in *Who Governs?*. Dahl sees Mayor Lee as an embodiment of political agency in shaping an arrangement that otherwise might not have come into being (on such political entrepreneurship, see Schneider, Teske, and Mintrom 1995). Dahl also recognizes that organization is important, but he has little to say about the inequalities that impinge on the ability to organize. And despite some tentative steps in this direction (1961a, 282–93), he fails to confront the ways in which socioeconomic inequalities confer systemic advantages to some and disadvantages to others. Thus, he gives little attention to forces that favor clustered rather than dispersed inequalities.

By focusing heavily on the mayoralty, Dahl slips into the assumption that the ballot is the great equalizer. Elections, however, suffer significant handicaps as means for public engagement. This does not mean elections are inconsequential. They can register demographic change and help put new policy agendas into motion, but elections are an imperfect form of popular control.

Because control of elected office constitutes only a limited part of governance, even issue-oriented elections fall well short of full democratic accountability. European scholars especially point to the growth of special service districts, QUANGOs (quasi-autonomous nongovernmental organizations), partnerships, central government inspections and audits, contracting out, vouchers, and such devices as complicating the link between citizens and governing officials (John 2001; Stoker 1998; Cochrane 2007; but see Jordan, Wurzel, and Zito 2005). Even before the recent proliferation of entities involved in governing, a pure line of accountability connecting citizens to councilors and on to the government service was compromised by functional (and professional) specialization and the workings of the committee system (Stewart 2000, 43–59). Indeed, one scholar has argued that the sheer scope and complexity of modern government makes traditional ideas about representative democracy obsolete (Hirst 2000).

A stubborn reality is that without the compliance and cooperation of nongovernmental actors, elected officials have limited capacity to achieve their policy aims. By itself, public authority is inadequate as a foundation for governing. Any significant problem-solving effort necessarily rests on both the exercise of public authority and the mobilization of nongovernmental actors. Whether the arrangements are old-style machine politics (Shefter 1976; Erie 1988), an executive-centered coalition as highlighted in *Who Governs?* (Dahl 1961a), or Atlanta's biracial coalition (Stone 1989), a governing arrangement requires multiple resources, some of which come from the private and voluntary sectors.[24] Therefore, by itself, winning an election is not a sufficient basis for putting together a governing arrangement (Thompson 2006).

For Dahl, the point that every socioeconomic elite is "automatically outnumbered at the polls" (Dahl 1961a, 248) is only part of his argument about dispersed inequalities. The second element in Dahl's classic pluralism is that complexity operates in such a way that any given policy initiative mostly affects only a restricted segment of the population.[25] That view, however, is embedded in a wider argument about assimilation, the expansion of the middle class, and the role of consensus.

Assimilation and Consensus versus Race and Complexity

Historically, in New Haven, with its sizable immigrant population, political mobilization followed ethnic and racial lines.[26] Because new immigrants mainly filled manual and low-skilled jobs, class and ethnicity coincided closely—sometimes dividing old-stock and immigrant populations into sharply antagonistic forces (on parallels in neighboring Boston, see O'Connor 1995). Dahl, however, posits a three-stage process of assimilation in which, as immigrant groups settle in politically and then gradually acquire a better economic position and increased levels of education, the fit between class and ethnicity fades away (see also Rae 2003, 288–94). By the time Richard Lee became New Haven's mayor in the 1950s, most immigrant groups had reached the third stage. Dahl (1961a) saw only the city's then-small African American population as in the second stage. Whereas conflict in stage one had often been sharp and persistent, in stage three, conflicts moderated (236). By the mid-20th century, New Haven, in Dahl's eyes, lacked "great cleavages" (198).

With assimilation and the growth of the middle class, Dahl saw a shift in the nature of issues: "The new issues did not so much emphasize divisible costs and benefits—either to an ethnic group or a class—as shared costs and benefits diffused across many different groups and strata" (1961a, 60). Patronage did not disappear, but increasingly policies "emphasized shared benefits to citizens in general rather than specific categories" (61). Moreover, Dahl described redevelopment in New Haven as being pursued in an "aura of nonpartisanship" (133), and as he saw it, muted conflict allowed policy experts to play a major role.

Dahl's New Haven study preceded the period of urban civil disorder, and it was completed before protest against urban renewal and expressway displacement reached its peak. He thus did not anticipate the intensity of resentment unleashed by displacement. Instead, he saw Mayor Lee's redevelopment program as growing from what he regarded as a latent form of support among both business leaders and voters (1961a, 115–40).

However, there is more at work in *Who Governs?* than a simple misreading of a trend. Even though conflict is central to Dahl's understanding of power, *Who Governs?* comes across largely as a testament to the role of consensus (Judge 1995, 15).[27] To Dahl, the major features of the socioeconomic order form boundaries within which conflict is waged. There were factional tiffs but not class battles. Dahl believed that policy activity in New Haven occurred "within the vague political consensus, the prevailing system of beliefs, to which all major groups in the community subscribe" (1961a, 84).[28] Thus "common values and goals" linked the "apolitical strata" to the "members of the political stratum" (92). Even during the previous period of intense ethnic conflict, Dahl says that the "socioeconomic order was not considered illegitimate; discrimination *was*" (33; emphasis in original). For the mid-20th century, Dahl took outward quiescence as a sign that the fundamentals of the American system enjoyed solid support and that assimilation had softened the edge of earlier conflicts. Redevelopment appeared mainly to be a coordination challenge. *Who Governs?* interprets the decreasing overlap between class and ethnicity as an indication that broad conflict had less political space in which to operate and consensus had more room to take hold.

Only a few (but highly eventful) years separate the publication of *Who Governs?* from the issuing of the report of the National Advisory Commission on Civil Disorders (1968). Among its many points, that report rejected the notion that

African Americans were in the second stage of an encompassing process of assimilation, tracking the same path followed by European immigrants. As the report emphasized, race was a profound division—a far deeper divide than Dahl realized.[29] In retrospect, we can see that Dahl seriously misread the role of consensus. Agreement about a general idea tells us little about the scope and intensity of conflict that may occur under its umbrella. The specifics of socioeconomic differentiation may matter more than abstract beliefs about such things as democracy, individualism, and capitalism.

Looking back to mid-20th century, we can see that, far from bringing about the "shared costs and benefits diffused across many different groups and strata" (Dahl 1961a, 60), heightened social and geographic mobility may have accentuated differences in how various segments of the population experienced societal changes and the policy initiatives that address those changes.[30] For instance, we should understand that Dahl was looking back on the Eisenhower years, when the interstate highway system and the vast network of expressways now in existence were just beginning. Geographic segmentation, as we now know it, was still at an early stage. Divisions of race and class appeared less acute then than they openly became later. Immigration law was yet to be changed, and the issue of undocumented immigrants had not assumed the dimensions that it now has.[31] In addition, the contemporary version of "culture war" had not surfaced as a challenge to the notion that American politics is essentially consensual (Sharp 2007).

In addition to consensus, we need to rethink immediacy. As put by Dahl in *Who Governs?*: "Most decisions have strong and immediate consequences for only a relatively small part of the population and at best small and delayed consequences for the rest" (1961a, 297). Immediacy, however, needs to be handled with care. "Strong and immediate consequences" greatly outweigh "small and delayed consequences" as a motivating force, but if one extends the time frame and scope of consequences, allowing that small and indirect consequences may build cumulatively, then the picture takes on a different appearance.[32] Interdependence comes into play, and delayed consequences sometimes accumulate into large consequences (Pierson 2004). Acquiescence by the many may mean not indifference, much less consensus, but rather that a pattern of actions and consequences was not evident at the beginning stage. A series of short and confined battles may be only the tip of the iceberg of larger struggle, a struggle not fully comprehended until profound change has taken hold.

With the benefit of hindsight, we can see that in New Haven and many other places, redevelopment did not grow from an underlying consensus about the need for progress, but rather was a process in which an executive-centered coalition muscled through a controversial and contested agenda. Nor did the redevelopment experience consist merely of narrow, disjointed conflicts over particular aspects of redevelopment. As urban historians have shown, the struggle ran deep, with far-ranging consequences.

From the perspective of the late 1950s, it may have seemed that we had the best of all possible worlds, where those most significantly affected by policy initiatives could defend their interests. In the pluralist view, the public is divided into many small segments, and the domain of each is seen as tiny and of little consequence to others. Yet the notion of a world highly segmented so that activities do not impinge on one another greatly underrates the class and racial character of society. Consider the alternative view that American society is deeply divided along racial lines, with blacks occupying a position of "a weak political minority in a majoritarian white society" (Thompson 2006, 232). The emergence of a multiracial society does not displace the racial past so much as add another dimension of colliding interests (Clarke et al. 2006).

The pluralist model of politics posits a loosely joined world in which each group is able to defend its own bit of turf. This is a key aspect of dispersed inequalities. Because most people can claim superior influence in the small arena they care the most about, pluralists do not see inequality as a fundamental problem. If ordinary citizens have little influence on most issues, that is not a matter of worry. In *Who Governs?*, Dahl recounts how Mary Grava successfully organized against metal houses, thereby bolstering a key pluralist claim: that ordinary citizens may have little influence in many matters (in which their resources remain politically slack), but in a system of dispersed inequalities, they nevertheless can protect themselves quite adequately.

The difficulty with the pluralist account is not that it misportrays behavior—people often focus on matters close at hand. Rather, it mischaracterizes the workings of complexity. It mistakenly treats consequences of policy actions as of limited reach. Dahl wrote as the 1950s came to a close, so he saw urban redevelopment as a generally beneficial policy for New Haven with harm to very few. In a pluralist perspective (foreshadowing *City Limits*), the struggle was over how the mayor, as leader of an executive-centered coalition, could overcome the centrifugal forces of narrow and short-sighted concerns to pursue a policy of broad and lasting good.

To protect against centrifugal and short-sighted forces, the redevelopment agency was not only given an aura of nonpartisanship by the accompanying Citizens Action Commission (containing, in the mayor's words, "the biggest muscles in New Haven" [quoted in Dahl 1961a, 130]),[33] but it was also insulated from the board of aldermen and others. As Douglas Rae reports, the redevelopment agency was known as "the Kremlin" (2003, 318), thus indicating that the populace understood its penetrability to be quite limited. On big questions with far-reaching consequences, the kind that enlisted New Haven's biggest muscles, it appears that inequalities were not so widely dispersed after all.

During Richard Lee's mayoralty, New Haven underwent a transition from an old-style, neighborhood-based politics to one in which professionalization and policy expertise played an increasingly large part.[34] Dahl recognized this change in his treatment of the "new men," but he saw this change as no great shift in power. As Dahl recounts, Lee was pushing for greater formal authority by the executive branch, but the mayor suffered a setback in the campaign to adopt a new city charter, so change was halting and uneven. Another proponent of the pluralist view, Edward Banfield (1961), saw Richard J. Daley's mayoralty in Chicago as caught in similar crosscurrents between shifting styles of political operation.[35] Both Dahl and Banfield resisted the idea of a controlling group because clearly no element was able to command the scope and pace of the change taking place. These two leading proponents of pluralism mistook the absence of a controlling elite for something more profound. They saw the circumstances of a halting but fundamental change in political style as signs of pluralism. Dahl equated the weakness of top-down control with an accessible and inclusive system. That no one was "in charge" of the change process is, however, not the same as having a penetrable system of dispersed inequalities.

Complexity poses a special analytical challenge (Simon 1969). It involves arrangements that in an immediate sense seem loosely joined, giving the impression that interdependence is quite limited. However, spillover effects are considerable, even though many are sufficiently indirect to be delayed. As Dahl observes in work after *Who Governs?*, complexity hinders the openness and accessibility of politics (1982). The practical knowledge of ordinary citizens lacks the scale of the more formal and expert knowledge of professionals. Those who can operate through highly professionalized channels thus enjoy an advantage of greater comprehension of interdependence and its indirect and delayed consequences. But technically derived knowledge offers limited insight into the concrete experiences of various sectors of the community. This means that the "interest of the whole city" is a highly fugitive matter. It also means that the vote of the ordinary citizen lacks the countervailing force that Dahl posits.

An Interdependence Perspective on Public Policy

Regime analysis starts from the view that governing is enmeshed in socioeconomic inequalities. The public is much more than an aggregation of voting blocs. The market resources that individuals control, the human capital they develop, the civil society aptitudes and connections they possess, and the skills and inclinations they accumulate through their various relationships—all enter the picture as elements of systemic power.

At the same time, it is important to remember that people are not locked into an endless set of zero-sum relationships in which all aims are necessarily at cross-purposes. Attraction and competition are both at work, and they spring partly from position in the social and economic order. Systemic power concerns the advantages that some actors enjoy over others as potential allies. Still, relationships are matters of ongoing construction, involving the purposes to which actors become attached and how those attachments are understood. How an agenda is framed makes a difference, but the concept of systemic power reminds us that framing does not occur in a vacuum.

In a capitalist system, economic development is a joint product of government and business, but the complexity of policy does not end there. Policy goes far beyond rhetoric and enactment. Policy is that which is actually put into operation. In its full reality, policy consists of the mesh between the actions of agents of the state and the behaviors of the various segments of the public in response to those actions. Policy making is a diffuse process involving significant co-construction by a varied public, often taking shape in sundry ways (Honig 2006).

Consider the important part that the community plays in law enforcement and crime prevention. If, for example, local stores do a thriving business in selling "don't snitch" T-shirts, then law enforcement is a handicapped process that spills over into and shapes policing policy, just as police practices can provide fertile ground for "don't snitch" sentiments. For local governance, coproduction occupies a prominent place—not only in such routine areas as education and law enforcement, but also in nonroutine areas such as AIDS prevention (Brown 1999; Cohen 1999).

Historically, much redevelopment took place with very limited understanding of what it meant concretely in the lives of directly affected segments of the population (Gans 1962). Atlanta's early urban renewal experience provides a pointed example. A 1958 housing study showed that government action would displace more than 10,000 families, mostly low income and black. However, one of the commissioners of the Atlanta Housing Authority discounted the seriousness of the relocation problem with the statement that "experience in other cities shows that some, especially those who are renting slum dwellings, will just fade away as the deadline for moving nears. In many cases this group prefers to quietly get out of the picture" (quoted in Stone 1976, 69). Subsequent federal regulations provided some check on that kind of callous misunderstanding, but during the period of large-scale urban redevelopment, massive dislocation, friction-laden racial transitions in neighborhoods, and rehousing those who had been displaced in projects that concentrated the very poor had devastating consequences for segments of the population. In addition, the politics of many cities continues to be marked by resentments that grew out of that period (see, e.g., O'Connor 1993; Self 2003; Kruse 2005;

Gillette 2007). When governing coalitions were put together around redevelopment and related efforts to remake the city physically, they operated with incomplete understandings of what they were bringing about. They had neither the firm grasp of the well-being of the whole city that Peterson attributes to them, nor the effective kind of political feedback that Dahl, generalizing from the "metal houses" controversy, assumed to be in operation.

Let's revisit the two redevelopment scenarios sketched early in this essay and apply regime analysis to Mayor Lee's executive-centered coalition as an arrangement with substantial staying power. In his analysis, Dahl attributed this stability in New Haven's governing arrangements to Mayor Lee's political skill and the mayor's ability to discern and activate a broad base of "latent support" for urban redevelopment. A regime analysis of Mayor Lee's New Haven would highlight a different mix of factors, specifically that stability of arrangements rests on a cohesive mix of the following: (1) an agenda to address a distinct set of problems, (2) a governing coalition assembled around that agenda and containing nongovernmental as well as governmental members (a majority of the Lee-appointed Citizens Action Commission were business figures, most of whom lived in the suburbs), (3) resources to pursue the agenda (drawn from members of the governing coalition and involving such matters as governmental authority, skill in obtaining external funding, and command of investment capital), and (4) a scheme of cooperation to bring those resources together (mainly by insulating urban redevelopment with its need for business investment from the everyday give and take of New Haven's ward politics). Seen through a regime lens, the New Haven and Atlanta redevelopment scenarios are not radically different.

The surface push for redevelopment was different, but the underlying dynamic was similar. The issue in both cities was to frame the agenda and its pursuit in such a way as to join the institutional capacities and resources of city hall and the business sector. In the urban regime model, a workable set of arrangements rests not on a foundation of mass support, but on a strategic set of connections. Continuity comes about through recognition by a set of resource-commanding actors that they need to act together in order to take on problems and pursue goals.

If we think about pursuit of an agenda in this way, then the electoral connection recedes in importance. It does not disappear by any means, but is less central. Effective pursuit of a social reform agenda does not then become, contrary to Kingdon (1995), a fortuitous confluence of problem recognition, policy response, and favorable audience politics (e.g., public mood, mass opinion, electoral outcome). Rather, it requires framing an agenda that is attentive to the city's economic standing and therefore is not in defiance of the economic imperative. It also calls for building a civic-political infrastructure that engages previously disconnected and alienated populations in such a way that it embraces their concerns and thereby enhances their contributory capacity. Is such a political reconfiguration possible?

LOOKING AHEAD

Urban Politics: Is a New Era in the Making?

The study of urban politics is not a matter of identifying a static body of forces, whether business elites operating behind the scenes or political entrepreneurs fixed on the electoral connection. Instead, it is a matter of understanding how a changing mix of forces is related to an evolving urban condition. If we look back at the period when the community-power debate first took shape, we can see that American cities faced a fundamental transformation. Partly driven by technology and partly by public-policy choices, economically vibrant central cities of the first half of the 20th century faced significant change and potential decline. The centrifugal forces of deindustrialization and suburbanization had "urbanization" in full retreat (Rae 2003; Dreier, Mollenkopf, and Swanstrom 2004). The scope of this change was beyond what traditional and neighborhood-based actors were capable of responding to.[36]

Though there was slight variation from place to place,[37] the problem-solving vacuum was filled by what Robert Salisbury called the "new convergence of power" (1964). Across a range of places, city hall and the business sector formed alliances to address redevelopment in the form of a large-scale restructuring of land use and economic purpose. The partners in this alliance are what Paul Peterson saw as the trustees of the "interest of the city as a whole."

An account written in this period bears the telling title of *Cities in a Race with Time* (Lowe 1967). Although some urban observers viewed cities as aggregations of neighborhoods, with special qualities of life worth protecting (Jacobs 1961; Gans 1962), others were of a different mind. Those with big economic stakes, major institutional and financial resources, and a sense of change in the making indeed envisioned themselves in a race against time to bring about transformation. Players centrally engaged in engineering a transition were, however, inattentive to the depth of the social and demographic change occurring.[38] The "new convergence of power" left large segments of the population weakly connected politically, economically, and socially to the restructured city and its region, as evidenced most dramatically in outbreaks of civil disorder in the 1960s.[39]

The current period offers a much different pattern of urban politics. Two things have changed. One is that the industrial city has largely given way to a new urban form, and the period of racing against time to bring about a thorough overhaul is mainly over. Although restructuring is an ongoing process that continues to be fueled by economic competition within and between metropolitan regions (Schneider 1989), much of the redevelopment dust of the latter half of the 20th century has now settled. Even though important sites of change and transition remain, that collective sense of urgency among powerful elites has eased.[40] The second thing is that the nature of the civic landscape itself has altered, and this changing civic terrain warrants attention (Sirianni and Friedland 2001).

A Possible Emerging Agenda

If the redevelopment agenda of the "new convergence of power" has aged, is a new agenda taking shape?[41] If so, how inclusive will it be? What might its accompanying political configuration look like? As we reexamine the era of redevelopment, we can see that it rested on a very narrow understanding of the well-being of the city and its population. A new and inclusive agenda would give a prominent place to two major responsibilities cities share with the larger society. One is the education of children and bringing them as maturing youth into the embrace of adult responsibilities. That, after all, is how society perpetuates itself. The second is the promotion of social cohesion. This aim serves the cause of social peace, and inattention to it poses obvious dangers. The redevelopment agenda neglected the one and, no matter if unintentional, actively undermined the other. Today's urban condition is a legacy of a narrow agenda. It is in order, therefore, to consider how a widened policy agenda might be put into motion. This means thinking anew about local democracy.

Much debate about democracy revolves around the tension between majority rule and minority rights. Important as that tension is, the discourse around it often assumes that voting is the central process.[42] I have argued above that elections are only one thin layer of politics and that democracy involves deeper issues of inclusion. Holding a position within the operational fabric of how society is governed is the ultimate test of inclusion, but one that gets too little attention. Closer examination of the redevelopment agenda along that line would have exposed the inadequacy of how urban communities were governed in the post–World War II period. As we look to the future, the issue of inclusion needs to be brought into the spotlight.

With that in mind, three lines of inquiry merit attention. First, is there change in focal concern? Has preoccupation with the future of the central business district yielded to an awareness of a wider challenge? Confronted with prospects of population losses and the realization that even lower-income communities have an economic capacity, neighborhoods have come in for fresh attention. It is noteworthy that turning around the South Bronx, for example, doubled the yield in real estate taxes from the area even though the poverty level remained essentially the same (Grogan and Proscio 2000, 28). There are indications, then, that some local decision makers now see a need to hold onto the residents they have and attract new ones, even those of modest income and wealth. In some places, property abandonment has become a major concern. In contrast with the early days of redevelopment, driven by concerns over the future of the central business district, today a number of city halls have gravitated to the idea that older neighborhoods are assets to be preserved and even enhanced. Growth on the urban fringe continues and poses an ongoing threat of residential disinvestment. Hence sundry city actors see that encouraging home ownership, promoting improvements in older homes, countering any tendency toward rising vacancy rates, and in general promoting neighborhood stability can be sound social and economic practice.

A second and related line of inquiry is whether the city's economic imperative has come to be seen in a different light. Awareness has grown that, far from standing apart, the economic imperative spills over into questions about social cohesion. After all, city dwellers not only want a prosperous economy, they also want safe streets. And it is not difficult to see that these two aims are intertwined. The character of the social order and therefore its ability to affect public safety are shaped by multiple factors, among them the performance of schools,[43] the level of residential stability, the process of youth development, and the training and placement practices surrounding the workplace. Connections are interactive. Economic decline weakens the social order, but a high rate of crime and other signs of a weakened social order hamper economic growth and harm the quality of urban life generally. Connections between social disorder and disinvestment offer grounds for thinking anew about the strength of local democracy. Might a more inclusive, and therefore more democratic, politics put the city's economic footing on a sounder long-term basis? Are there arrangements that might support a broadened and more nuanced understanding of the economic imperative?

Related to the substantive features of a new urban agenda is a third area for inquiry, one about who is to carry out this agenda. Redevelopment was the special province of what was then a new breed of policy professionals and administrative entrepreneurs, but the bloom is now off such expertise. Whereas the redevelopment agenda often involved insulating policy decisions from the populace, there is now a view that we need to open up new avenues of citizen engagement.[44] Whether it is someone advocating expanded partnerships in education (Waddock 1995), Lisbeth Schorr highlighting the "new professionals" (1997, 12–15), or cities searching for ways of aligning community-based efforts with municipal government (Stone and Worgs 2004), one can detect a call to restructure the relationship between local government and the populace it serves.[45] In this fresh appreciation of the role of the populace, people are viewed both as having useful insights through their firsthand experience of matters and as serving as a source of efforts to solve city problems (Fung 2004, but contrast Goldberger 2007). This goes to the heart of the operational fabric of how society is governed and whether governance passes the test of democratic inclusion (Sirianni and Friedland 2001).

None of these three areas promises to be a complete turnaround from the redevelopment era, but all three offer signs of change. None of the three ignores the city's need to attend to its economic position, but all three represent new thinking about how to go about fostering that position. All three point to a fresh way of viewing the well-being of the city and its populace.

With new thinking afoot, what about the politics of moving to a new urban agenda? Setting priorities, deciding on a level and form of taxation, and devising a mix of efforts across sectors and policy functions are matters that do not lend themselves to consensus or technical calculation. They come from a political settlement. We can look back at the era of redevelopment led by "the new convergence" and see that action rested on a political base that was much too narrow. Governing groups had a constricted view of the conditions for economic growth. Similarly, they saw the poor and near-poor only in terms of redistribution, without considering issues of social investment and capacity building.[46]

At this stage, the problematic issue is about governing arrangements. If a new agenda is emerging, it is unlikely (even should it reach a mature form) to generate the tight form of collaboration that came together so often around the post–World War II redevelopment agenda. But what would it look like? For several years, we have had piecemeal reform, parts of it with more staying power than others. In his study of community policing and school reform in Chicago, Archon Fung found that the city's associational life, though rich in some ways, was not robust enough to provide an institutionally stable foundation for sustained reform (2004). Neighborhood-based community development also suffers from a tendency to rest on a narrow, close-to-home view, and it seldom has a capacity to operate on more than a small scale.[47] As one observer said of neighborhood actors, "it is often difficult to discern in their work a long-term, coherent city-wide strategy" (Krumholz 1996; see also Burns 2006). If inclusion does not also widen perspective and increase awareness of how well-being rests on a foundation of interconnectedness, then democratic governance will suffer accordingly (Smock 2004).

From where is a new and more inclusive policy direction likely to come? A mayor could play an important role, but only as part of a horizontal rather than pyramidal network. At this stage, new agenda efforts have limited cohesion but involve a political mix quite different from the narrow, top-down version of an earlier era. Let's consider some concrete experiences.

In the past, redevelopment was often dominated by an entrepreneurial figure, such as Edward Logue, a policy czar who combined personal influence with institutional position to push a program along despite substantial resistance. Contemporary initiatives assume a much different character. Efforts to provide affordable housing and encourage neighborhood regeneration stem from more diffuse processes, involving the nonprofit sector—including local CDCs and various regional and national intermediaries—and in select ways the business sector, along with a variety of government-based incentives such as those found in federal tax law, various historic preservation provisions, and the Community Reinvestment Act. In several large cities, philanthropic foundations are key players, as are financial intermediaries, who provide information and technical assistance as well as money. Moreover, in contrast with the frequent reliance during the urban-renewal era on big-time developers, one of the lessons learned in New York City about affordable housing was the important role of small businesses. Indeed, small property holders own many of the buildings in inner-city New York, and, as providers of housing, they can operate more cheaply than big companies can (Von Hoffman 2003, 51). Rather than a few large companies building huge complexes for the city's housing authority, an alternative approach has emerged through which intermediary organizations operate to connect small businesses to city government and CDCs in the housing field. Community development thus has often become a matter of orchestrating the work of many small-scale actors (Von Hoffman 2003, 255).[48]

The process has not been top down, but rather has come through a latticework coordinated from several angles. Having a capacity such as CDCs at the grassroots level is important, but they can operate most effectively when large-scale intermediaries such as LISC and the Enterprise Foundation can be brought into the picture. City hall can be a significant player as well, as in the case of the huge housing-investment program of New York's Mayor Koch (Grogan and Proscio 2000, 164).[49] CDCs by no means obviate an active role for local government, but instead they provide means by which a new role can be defined.

Boston's campaign to prevent youth violence similarly emerged from a variety of sources and was sustained by contributions from many different sources, including city hall.[50] Police and probation officer collaboration provided a street-level source, and after a dramatic course of events, the Ten-Point Coalition emanating from the city's black clergy established cooperation with the police department. A special report followed by the selection of a new police commissioner and reinforced by federal money for community policing brought about changes in police training and police practices, and included a community-consultation and strategic-planning process by the police department. State and federal prosecutors and the federal Bureau of Alcohol, Tobacco, and Firearms along with the Drug Enforcement Agency contributed their efforts. The business sector added a summer-jobs program for youth as carrots to complement the stick of strict enforcement against those deemed to be incorrigible. The mayor's office contributed youth workers, but no policy czar presided over the operation. Starting with Raymond Flynn and continuing with Thomas Menino, the mayor met regularly with black clergy, but that was not central to the antiviolence campaign.

The heart of the antiviolence coalition was informal cooperation between law-enforcement officials and black clergy to get violence-prone offenders into prison, but also to open up pathways of opportunity to other youth to dissuade them from lives of gang banging. While the Ten-Point Coalition provides an institutional base in the community, much of the effort behind the campaign within the government sector rests on personal commitments, subject to change as holders of various positions rotate into new places and assignments. Moreover, the antiviolence campaign has proved to be difficult to import to other cities (Tita et al. 2003, but see McClanahan 2004). The Boston experience shows that multisector collaboration can be brought together around an important social aim, but it is not clear how durable such arrangements are. They point to a significant potential but questions of detail remain unanswered.

Boston's school-reform experience is also instructive.[51] Although Boston may appear to be a case of mayoral-guided reform (the mayor now appoints the school board), mayoral leadership is only part of a long process of reconstituting a civic foundation for the city's schools. Starting under Judge Arthur Garrity's desegregation plan, the city initially had a Citywide Coordinating Council to help monitor school desegregation. However, Boston also soon formed a Citywide Educational Coalition to serve as a clearinghouse of information and an advocate for change. In addition, Judge Garrity created advisory councils in each community school district along with racial-ethnic parent councils for each school. To lessen the isolation of the schools, the judge brought about a number of business and college partnerships (one participant described the process as "being dragged into the arena by court order"[52]). Other bodies, such as a Critical Friends group, were subsequently created. As business came to be involved more in the schools, they worked initially through the city's Private Industry Council to create what became the Boston Compact, a coalition whose membership has expanded over time to include the teachers' union and others. A vital step was creating the Boston Plan for Excellence, an important intermediary that works closely with the school system.

Mayor Menino has made education a city priority. He has been a strong backer of after-school programs and has linked schools with health, youth development, and social services, including family resource centers. Clearly, education in Boston is embedded in an elaborate network of civic organizations and supported with a variety of related public programs. There is now a Boston Parent Organizing Network, and it has successfully lobbied for the creation of the position of Deputy Superintendent for Family and Community Engagement. Yet with all of this, a recent report notes a concern about inclusiveness, "a sense that the city's elites—the political leadership, the business community, and the universities—have greater access to decision-making authority than other groups," and "many city residents and grassroots groups feel . . . [they] are not at the table when decisions are made" (Aspen Institute 2006, 15, 16).

A shift in agenda does not guarantee that all affected by the shift will feel included. The depth and scope of associational connections is clearly a matter of enormous importance.[53] They determine the degree to which politics is inclusive and thus bear greatly on the extent to which local politics is genuinely democratic. Still, to move from hope to reality on a large scale, it helps to have a big-time organizational player involved, whether it is city hall, a university, or some other major institution based in the locality.

Questions about Emerging Patterns

Although each of the three sketches above suggests an emerging pattern of urban politics, each is also consistent with the imperative that cities attend to their economic position. The role of CDCs in affordable housing bolsters the city against residential disinvestment. An antiviolence campaign helps make a city a more inviting place to live, transact business, and spend leisure time. Likewise, school reform can heighten the attractiveness of life in the city and serve the aim of workforce development.

However, none of the three fits Peterson's treatment of developmental politics. They are not policies pursued by a small insider group of city officials and business executives—quite the contrary. All three are policy efforts in which city hall is central only on occasion, and the role of business is less one of agenda setting than of selective support. Concurrently, it may be that advocacy organizations have come to play a considerable role (McLaughlin et al., forthcoming). New and explicit multiissue organizing has also become a larger presence (Sirianni and Friedland 2001; Orr 2007). Financial institutions have an important part to play, particularly in housing investment, but so does small business. Even large development projects may have shifted toward wider consultation and involvement.[54]

In each of the above three cases, the shape of the effort is largely determined by the civic sector, how it is organized, and how it meshes with the actions of public agencies. CDCs, the Ten-Point Coalition, and such nonprofit and advocacy groups as the Boston Plan for Excellence are essential actors. Although it is not clear to what extent these three policy efforts incorporate the most marginalized elements of urban society, they represent a wider body of concerns and actors than was earlier the case with the redevelopment agenda.

Because the three sketches above do not represent an integrated agenda, there is no reason to regard them as springing directly from an awareness of what is good for the city as a whole. Although there is recognition that the policy actions involved are socially and even economically beneficial, they are not *driven by* a shared commitment to the city's unitary interest. Mobilizing behind policy purposes involves much greater particularity than that. At the same time, specific purposes can provide a framework within which public-serving networks can be constructed (Schneider, Teske, and Mintrom 1995; Stone, Orr, and Worgs 2006). It matters

greatly who is in a position to assert a claim and how particular claims are reconciled. To the extent that there is a guiding sense of the well-being of the city, it
comes out of struggles around particular issues and the dialogues that those struggles engender.

To draw a parallel from the redevelopment era, Atlanta's coalition framework of
"the city too busy to hate" was not a proposition from which particular actions could
be deduced. Instead, it was a shared understanding, itself born of struggle, providing
a context within which specifics could be worked out. Similarly for the emerging
new urban politics, there is no action-determining consensus with particulars about
what best serves the city. Rather, there is an ongoing process of realization through
bargaining, negotiation, and discovery of mutual aims. In Madisonian fashion,
breadth and diversity of constituency voices move deliberation toward a wider
understanding of what is at stake for the city. The drawback is that at this stage, the
scope and depth of support for the new agenda remain quite limited.

Two questions stand out. One is about according priority. Are actors in pursuit
of a loosely defined agenda able to give their policy efforts priority standing? The
second is a related question about the ability of such assemblages to persist over
time—to persist long enough to constitute a durable restructuring of how local
governments and their citizenries relate.[55]

The answer to neither question is certain, but an outline of significant considerations can be identified. At this stage, we know too little about local agendas,
though we can be sure that they involve more than a Downsian attention cycle
(Downs 1972). We can also put aside the garbage-can metaphor (Kingdon 1995). A
better starting point is Mark Moore's (1988) argument that we heed the *context* of
policy ideas—how ideas fit into institutional arrangements, what interests and new
responsibilities they identify, and what power relationships they make salient.
Urban regime analysis adds an emphasis on resources and modes of coordination.

In thinking about the emerging agenda, it is important to see resources as more
varied than money and credit. Interpersonal and organizational skills as they relate
to specific bodies of people, local knowledge from and about citizens, and social-
action energy within local communities are among the resources needed for the new
urban agenda (cf. Krumholz 1996, 217). These in turn may depend on training and
development, technical assistance (especially given the complexity of some incentive provisions), and a supportive associational network (Cohen 2001; Fung 2004).

Because agenda setting is context dependent, it is not enough to talk at a general
level about ideas and policy entrepreneurs. As a recent study of urban school reform
cautions, a more complex congruence of factors is at issue (Clarke et al. 2006). Ideas
amount to little unless they come to be embedded in institutions with substantial
resources and aligned with players able to sustain their involvement in the face of
competing demands on their time and energy. Chicago's experiences with school

decentralization and community policing show the fragility of the new urban agenda (Fung 2004; Shipps 2006). As long as associational life among the non-affluent remains anemic, alignment of policy effort between government and citizenry will surely fall far short of robustness.[56]

A true priority agenda is not something short-lived. It is about guiding actions over a period of time. The redevelopment agenda of yesteryear brought together two important centers of power: executive authority (often but not always in the form of the office of mayor) and major downtown businesses (sometimes supplemented by hospitals, universities, or other large institutions tied spatially to the central city). The resources for action—the power of eminent domain, investment capital, policy expertise, and a huge early (but over time decreasing) flow of federal money—combined with insider collaboration among a select few to constitute a durable arrangement of action, even in the face of substantial popular opposition.[57]

The three examples sketched above show that cooperation can be achieved. The question is about the durability of these arrangements and their capacity to take hold on a wider basis than selected enclaves of activity. What we can learn from the redevelopment era is that the sustainability of an agenda depends on the establishment of political relationships consistent with its program. Can an agenda with elements such as affordable housing, community-based law enforcement, youth development, and community-anchored school reform cumulatively bring about a realignment of government-citizenry relationships needed for the pursuit of this agenda?[58] The answer is currently unclear, but we can identify significant considerations.

One concerns a favorable meso level of policy thinking, a level broader than particular initiatives.[59] Social peace and constructive youth-to-adult transition are public aims that are not readily served by automatically and uncritically turning to market solutions. Such matters are more likely to be advanced if policy discourse includes awareness of interdependence and a place for long-term thinking. Family-owned newspapers once could contribute to such discourses, but they have become a rarity, and civic responsibility has become a weaker force in the mass media. Community foundations represent one such contemporary potential, but they are underresearched. Organizations such as Coleman Advocates for Children and Youth, the force behind San Francisco's Children's Amendment, is another potential channel for social-mindedness. In short, the climate of ideas is a significant factor, but it is not something separate and distinct from a community's civic institutions. It is worth remembering that the post–World War II redevelopment agenda was tirelessly promoted by an extensive network of national and local organizations (Crowley 2005, 38–42). As we assess the direction a new urban agenda might take, the presence of civic and advocacy organizations with professional staffs is an important indicator to track. Is there such a cadre of professionals creating a framework for thinking about long-range responsibilities toward the city and its people?[60]

A second factor is the need to hold at bay the demands of patronage-based politics.[61] In many American cities, it is a pervasive factor, but it can undermine the legitimacy of a policy effort in the eyes of both business elites and the general public. It can be checked (Grogan and Proscio 2000, 90–92),[62] and nonprofit intermediaries may offer better protection than central reliance on governmental channels. At the same time, it is difficult to see how adequate funding of an agenda involving social investment and capacity building can occur without substantial government monies. The redevelopment agenda of mid-20th century was heavily subsidized through urban renewal and federal highway funds. Nothing comparable is in sight for such concerns as social cohesion and other matters bearing on the urban quality of life.[63] Federal support for community policing, for example, was modest to begin with and has been cut rather than increased. The current national priority is homeland security rather than bridging the police-community divide. There is thus a twofold challenge: to find monetary resources, and then protect those resources from a politics of patronage and corruption.

A third significant factor is the building of associational bridges between disconnected populations and mainstream institutions. Among the disconnected, norms such as "no snitching" provide an indication of continuing weakness in the populace–public authority relationship.[64] Distrust, often intensified by middle-class resistance to altering the opportunity structure, sustains social division (Oakes and Rogers 2006). The disconnection may not be absolute, but observers in such areas as workforce development and juvenile corrections talk about the "two worlds" phenomenon (Stone and Worgs 2004). While skeptical of the notion of a dual city, Castells and Mollenkopf (1991) point to structural conditions that are conducive to "the formation of subcultures of survival and helplessness" (410).[65]

To what extent can connections be established with such populations? Examples such as the Dudley Street Neighborhood Initiative suggest a fruitful path to follow (Medoff and Sklar 1994). Yet even though postpatronage, community-based organizations have grown significantly in recent years, it is still the case that the affluent middle class is able to "exert a strong economic, cultural, spatial, and political impact on the city, while the constellation of subordinated or marginal groups is fragmented and disorganized" (Castells and Mollenkopf 1991, 415). Until that pattern of skewed representation is modified, the new urban agenda faces a major obstacle.[66]

A fourth area of consideration involves the inclinations of personnel in public agencies, both at the street level and at the upper level of administration. The civil rights and other movements have brought us beyond the point of seeing "neutral competence" as sufficient to answer the problems we face. That insight has yet to be brought fully into professional practice. Thus the relationship of policy and

administrative professionals to lower-strata communities holds uncertain possibilities. There are inherent tensions but also shared interests (Fung 2004; Shipps
2006). Professionalism can serve as a means by which expertise forms a wall against
public engagement, but there is an alternative view of professionalism as servant
of the public good and as protector of social equity (Marquand 2004). Moreover,
Lisbeth Schorr's "new professionals" are sensitive to the wisdom and contribution
that can come from those who have firsthand, experience-based knowledge.[67] In
this vein, new and explicit forms of coproduction have emerged, such as Baltimore's
Community Law Center, with its community-based approach to code enforcement
and drug-nuisance abatement (Blumenberg, Blom, and Artigiani 1998).

Professionals can play an active role in facilitating the organization of communities, and their openness to interaction with lay people is a key determinant of
whether organization for coproduction succeeds or fails (Epstein 2001; Baum 2003).
Training and professional development can thus greatly affect the connections
between professionals and laypeople.

Much depends on the dynamics at city hall and how these dynamics interact
with the world of community-based organizations. Does the mayor see such organizations as allies to be worked with or forces to be ignored and worked around?
School reform in Chicago illustrates the point. As a populist-style mayor, Harold
Washington sought to integrate neighborhood organizations into the city's governance. In such matters as school reform, he sought "to balance power between
poorly resourced low-income communities and much better resourced business
executives" (Shipps 2006, 124).[68] In contrast, neighborhood groups found themselves marginalized later, when Richard M. Daley became mayor and gravitated
toward a managerial style by such steps as naming his budget director, Paul Vallas,
as head of a restructured school system. Vallas received praise in business circles,
and in those circles, he acquired a reputation as someone who liked to operate with
"as little democracy as possible" (Shipps 2006, 156).

As a highly visible office with command of an array of executive powers, the
mayoralty can be a valuable ally in giving an agenda priority status. But mayors are
not inclined to take on a long-term perspective on their own, especially when the
office is term limited. Resort to managerial slight of hand offers a quick alternative
to the more consuming task of building and maintaining an inclusive coalition.
Harold Washington's fatal heart attack brought to a premature close what would
have been an important test of the inclusive-coalition approach (Clavel and Wiewel
1991). Under Mayor Menino, Boston may afford an alternative example, but it is
also a reminder that a city's associational life provides an important context in
which mayoral leadership takes shape.

With the urban political and civic landscape undergoing transition, lines of
both conflict and cooperation have emerged that differ from those prevalent in the

era of redevelopment. Ward politics may not have completely disappeared, but there are new and more vigorous forces at work. Community organizing is more evident than precinct workers attached to political machines.[69] The unfolding of new political patterns depends greatly on how issues are framed, how their legal and technical features are coped with, and what institutional structures are activated around those issues.

At this stage, urban political development can move in any of several directions. Such areas as education and policing have gained prominence, but there are widely differing views about both crime prevention and educational improvement. Still actors from varied sectors of the city, from law-enforcement to business, see the opportunities available to the young as an important concern. Positive valences such as "children" and "neighborhood" could become forces at the heart of a new urban agenda,[70] but only if relevant civic connections expand as well. For such connections to help shape the urban agenda, an appropriate frame of reference also has to be brought into play. Treating the future of the city as primarily a matter of economic development versus redistribution needs to give way to a broader viewpoint. Economists like to think in terms of equality versus efficiency (Okun 1975), a trade-off not highly conducive to giving consideration to social investment. Hence it is worth bearing in mind that there is a near-term/long-term trade-off as well. Thinking only in the near term limits options. A city's civic infrastructure and the intergovernmental connections that feed into it should be attuned enough to the long term to be accommodating to the idea of social investment and how it can serve the future well-being of the city. How do we get to that stage?

Social Reform: Urban-Regime Analysis and Beyond

The democratic ideal calls for no permanent minority, for those who lose on one occasion to have a potential to become a force for change in the future (cf. Thelen 2004; Pierson 2004).[71] Given that ideal, we need to ask why is it that some actors are able to overcome resistance and implant a path to policy change, but others have great difficulty in doing so. Although path dependence is a factor to be reckoned with, it seems not to affect all segments of society equally.

Path dependence is about how policy choices made at one time generate feedback that makes it easy to continue that policy direction. Important as this insight may be, the concept of path dependence does not tell us why some choices give rise to weaker supportive feedback than others, or why in some cases initial positive feedback proves not to be durable because delayed resistance builds gradually. Policy choices are made in a context, and, among choices pending at a given time, more is at issue than what gets tried first. Some initiatives have a lesser capacity than others to engender a supportive network of interests and organizations. Sequencing is important, but it is not everything.

The paths of change at the local level may be less open than they appear from a national perspective. The reason is not about path dependence itself, but that local politics is more embedded, spatially and otherwise, in the system of social stratification than is apparent from a national viewpoint. In the local context, it takes a "full court press" to make even incremental differences in expanding opportunity for those at or near the bottom of society. The kind of policy feedback that enables a middle-class innovation to be surrounded and supported by a thick collection of durable connections is hard for the lower strata to come by. Moreover, for those in the lower reaches of the ladder of social stratification, forms of resistance are manifold (Oakes and Rogers 2006), as are the disadvantages to be overcome (Henig and Stone 2007, 126–28).

Take the example of urban school reform. Proponents of change are fond of asserting such bold sentiments as, "We will no longer describe failure as the result of vast impersonal forces like poverty or a broken bureaucracy."[72] Nonetheless, the reality is that "vast impersonal forces like poverty" are at work, even more so as students reach adolescence and become aware of the life chances they face. And broken bureaucracy is partly a product of conditions of poverty and frustrations those conditions give rise to. Reformers like to talk about changing the "culture" of a school, as if that culture were somehow separate from the community and all those factors that separate the life of the poor from the life of the middle class.

Many specifics could be cited, from inadequate health care to a history of unfulfilled promises (Payne 2001; Rothstein 2004; Gordon, Bridglall, and Meroe 2005; Fruchter 2007). The teachers' union is typically more concerned about protecting seniority rights than placing qualified and committed teachers in the poorest schools, and the principals' association may be more focused on protecting tenure than assuring job performance. Directing additional resources into low-income neighborhoods encounters opposition on the grounds that it disregards competing claims based on merit and takes away from programs for talented and gifted students (Oakes and Rogers 2006). Aside from "merit" claims, there is the attraction, as some see it, to "teach the teachable" (Milloy 2007, B10). The triage practice of special attention to a selected few serves for business and others as "evidence" that the poor can make it without large investments of resources (Suskind 1998). Explanations consistent with low taxation have a short-term appeal not readily repelled. Reform efforts rarely tackle more than a handful of the obstacles faced, but regardless of how incomplete the effort may have been, failed reforms reinforce a sense of futility and make it even harder to turn matters around.

In the face of so many obstacles, how can social reform be advanced? The task is formidable. At some level, we have long known that the underlying challenge is an ecology of disadvantage and that the appropriate response needs to be both comprehensive and sustained. Yet the key constituency for social reform is too disconnected from mainstream activity to press for change of this scope. Many in society's lower strata hold a high level of distrust for mainstream institutions and processes because they have served the poor and near-poor so badly in the past (Cohen 1999). Further, because lower-strata social needs are experienced in a particular and immediate form, this population constitutes a constituency not readily mobilized around a broad vision for the future (Henig 1982; Smock 2004). In any case, *lasting* reform is not simply a product of pressure on a set of community arrangements. Instead, it is a matter of creating path dependence by altering arrangements, by steps that in broad terms would have the following features:

- Encourage a long-term approach to problem-solving.
- Encourage a wide-vista approach to problem-solving.
- Provide resources sufficient to go beyond pilots and sustain full-scale efforts.
- Work actively on enlistment and engagement of the lower-strata population.

Because the lower-strata population is only weakly connected to mainstream activities and on its own possesses no tendency toward unity, even within the bounds of a single racial group (McRoberts 2003), urban social reform is no simple matter of mobilizing the discontented, nor is it mainly a matter of bringing together the elites who head major city institutions. To fully grasp the big picture, it would be productive to think in terms of a local political order with a significant vertical dimension (intergovernmental and philanthropic), and with significant constituencies that are only weakly linked to society's mainstream institutions and that are internally splintered, often by race and ethnicity (Kaufmann 2003). Local social reform thus includes the challenges of how to tap the vertical dimension more effectively and how to build bridges to those now experiencing disconnection. A plan of action might include:

- Federal funding on a substantial scale, comparable to what went into the post–World War II redevelopment agenda.
- Some form of permanent community forum, with the mission of promoting long-term thought about the city and its future.[73]
- An array of intermediaries, other nonprofits, and related entities through which community organization and interorganizational connections among the nonaffluent can be promoted.
- A body of programs aimed at broadening the foundations of coproduction, such as community schools, community policing, CDCs, and community law centers.

One observer has expressed concern that globalization pushes urban governance in the direction of a "technocratic-managerial-entrepreneurial" mind-set (Garcia

2006, 748). This caution should be well heeded. But at some point institutional arrangements become malleable, and with a productive mix of political representation, grassroots engagement, philanthropic support, and professionally staffed civic bodies, an alternative mind-set can be encouraged. It would consist not of some evanescent sense of the public interest, but rather a pragmatic realization that the fates of city dwellers are intertwined. Reform-minded actors can most effectively advance the well-being of the community by combining efforts in ways to be determined by ongoing conversations and negotiations. The aim is to attach people to concrete purposes, but to do so in a manner that draws them into a wider understanding of what those purposes are about.

In order to understand better the prospects for reform, the research task needs to range widely. We no longer live in the era of a single-peaked city hall–business convergence of power. Instead, we are part of a loosely assembled political order that includes not just city hall and business leadership, but foundations, intermediaries and other nonprofits, and grassroots people with whom service agencies are often not constructively aligned. The ways in which neighborhood groups are organized (and sometimes splintered), the varied concerns they harbor, and the tensions and frustrations they experience are all part of the political order and bear on how the city will develop.[74] From the fugitive possibilities for wide cooperation that occasionally surface, research needs to glean what it can about potentially workable paths of reform.

CONCLUSION

Looking back now, we can see that such benchmarks in the study of urban politics as Robert Dahl's *Who Governs?* and Paul Peterson's *City Limits,* along with Floyd Hunter's *Community Power Structure* (1953), were efforts to understand a particular era in the ongoing evolution of city political life. They are about what I call the redevelopment era, and they offer competing views of the "new convergence of power" characteristic of that era. But all three interpret a body of relationships now giving way to something new. The times have changed—perhaps not in a dramatic, punctuated-equilibrium way (Baumgartner and Jones 1993), but changed nevertheless.

Scholars thus face the question of how best to analyze a new and still evolving urban reality. Political science could usefully follow the example of urban historians and concern themselves with how the larger political order is intertwined with the local setting. Cities and their regions are not simply convenient laboratories for testing general propositions. In reality, they are an integral part of the overall political experience of the nation, and as urban historians have convincingly shown, the urban part of that encompassing experience has contributed mightily to the reshaping of national political issues and alignments (Sugrue 1996; O'Connor 1993; Nicolaides 2002; Self 2003; Kruse 2005; Lassiter 2006; and Kruse and Sugrue 2006).

This change is still in process. With what lens, then, should we view the arena of urban politics? Useful as the urban-regime concept has been to me in such matters as understanding the importance of a stratified distribution of resources, rethinking the nature of community power, and reassessing the role of ideas (Stone, Orr, and Worgs 2006), there are various reasons to explore alternative lenses. For some, the regime concept is tied too closely to a political-economy perspective (Brown 1999; Bailey 1999). Others see the concept as unduly limited to the dynamics of coalition formation and insufficiently linked to the wide array of forces that shape governance (Crowley 2005; Pierre 2005; Gendron 2006; and Hackworth 2007). Still others argue that the concept has done its creative work and it is now time to consider a broader range of perspectives (Sapotichne, Jones, and Wolfe 2007). Some years back, Gerry Stoker cautioned that urban-regime analysis focused attention on elite interactions to the neglect of "wider relationships between government and its citizens" (1995, 60). Today, even the concept of citizen is proving unduly narrow, given the phenomenon of transnational immigration (Olivera and Rae forthcoming).

It is appropriate, therefore, to put aside constricted arguments about what is or is not an urban regime and consider an expansive framework for thinking about relationships. The polity-centered approach of Orren and Skowronek, with its emphasis on the nexus between state and society, might be a fruitful frame of reference (2004, 80; see also Mollenkopf 1992). This points us toward a notion of the political order, though one in need of being refined.[75] With refinement it can accommodate both normative and empirical elements, and it provides ample room to consider the ramifications of race and class at the grassroots level.

Because the redevelopment agenda, combined with a narrow form of professionalization, did considerable damage to civil society, particularly to traditional neighborhood links to governing arrangements, scholars should think anew about local democracy and how to construct inclusive arrangements for governing. Building a more inclusive form of governance faces two systemic hurdles. One is the challenge of preemption. Existing arrangements are not easy to change; this fact places a special burden on those who seek change (Trounstine 2006). This burden is perhaps a little less currently than it was in some past times because an older order of governance seems to have lost some of its vigor, and we find ourselves in a period of transition.

From experience, we know that preemption is by no means insurmountable. In its opening phase, the redevelopment agenda required a significant reconstitution of arrangements, but reconstitution could be brought about then because those seeking to remake the economic purpose of the central city had substantial resources and, particularly in the case of the business elite, considerable civic prestige (Clark 1969). Social reform starts from a much different position; it faces the challenge of a stratified society and the unequal hand it deals for gaining a place in governing arrangements. Thus, as the second systemic hurdle, the politics of social reform has to work around the stubborn reality of socially embedded inequality.

Though there are indications that a fresh agenda is taking shape, it is unclear what its priorities will be. Whether a more inclusive politics is evolving remains to be seen. That depends on several factors—among them how large a place advocacy and community-based organizations are able to occupy politically; whether business and civic elites are engaged in such a way as to take a wider and longer-term perspective on the future of the city and their stake in it; the scope of activity subsumed intergovernmentally under a broad version of professionalism; and above all, the extent to which service-providing professionals are inclined and able to connect more constructively with lower-strata populations, including immigrants.

An analytical challenge we face is that of trying to figure out what makes some things into a durable part of a shifting political order while other things fade away. Social reform today is a matter of taking advantage of a period of relative political fluidity to see what can be done to connect the lower strata of society to mainstream institutions. The logic of what I have argued here is that this task is not a matter of finding a single key lever, be it ideology, more CDCs, or something else. Transformation comes when interests, ideas, resources, and institutions are understood and operate in a substantially congruent fashion (Clarke et al. 2006).

For reformers, political transformation means constructing arrangements in which the lower strata are an integral part of how things operate day to day. It is not a simple matter of mobilizing outsiders to pressure the established order, but of opening a way for disconnected populations to become part of the established order. For social reform, a central relationship is that between service providers and the lower strata. Can they become constructively aligned coproducers? That is partly a matter of how the two principals engage one another.

It is important that we not view the task of social reform in such totally immediate terms that we lose sight of the need for a favorable frame of reference. Although street-level engagement is crucial, it can be encouraged by propitious terms of policy thinking. As Schattschneider argues, "*Whoever decides what the game is about decides who can get into the game*" (1975, 102). That is why I have suggested a policy framework of social investment.

Urban scholars have become so imbued with thinking in terms of redistribution that they have neglected other dimensions of the policy picture. One is about time—hence the need to bring the idea of social investment into consideration. Social-investment framing thus calls for incorporating a longer time perspective into policy thinking, and it means bringing the reality of interdependence front and center. There are collective stakes in such policies as those that smooth the path from childhood to adult responsibility and that promote an increased degree of social cohesion. Because these are matters of long-term and complex consequences and the relevant decisions often offer few immediate payoffs, it becomes important in a city's civic and governmental network to have some institutional voice explicitly concerned with the community's future well-being. Such a voice is hardly sufficient for bringing about social reform, but it may be a necessary contributor to the process.

Scale is also a significant dimension. Neighborhood concerns got pushed aside in the redevelopment era in part because, on their own, neighborhood actors operate on a very limited scale and are easily overrun by forces well beyond their coping capacity. Simply devolving decision making to a neighborhood level is not a promising path to community empowerment. If neighborhood-based actors cannot operate with the assistance of intermediaries, public agencies, and research allies on a wider scale, they are likely to find themselves pushed aside once again as city hall and other big institutional actors respond to change and react to potential disinvestment in the city.

A social-reform perspective calls for more than examining the pressure that groups can exert. It means thinking about capacities to become part of large-scale operations, whether they involve neighborhood regeneration, campaigns against youth violence, or the education and incorporation of young people into mainstream society. As a term of reference, scale, combined with time and capacity, places the equality-efficiency trade-off in a whole new framework. As scholars address these terms, they need to put aside the myth of fundamentally disassociated spheres of modern life. In pursuing social reform, the voice of civil society is much needed, and it would also be helpful if the business sector were brought to have a greater appreciation of the fact that it operates within, not outside, society (Granovetter 2005). The notion in some business circles that profit-seeking has to be sheltered from social responsibilities surely has the matter backward. Such thinking is a denial of the reality of interdependence.

My recurring argument in this essay has been to the need to heed the ways in which state, market, and civil society intersect and impinge on one another. That intersection is the true realm of politics. It is not surprising that two of the scholars most attentive to problems of inequality and the fragility of representative government are Theda Skocpol (2003) and Robert Putnam (2000), and both have given close attention to civil society, and specifically to the dangers that attach to a weakening of local civic life and to the shortcomings of highly centralized civic activity. Carmen Sirianni and Lewis Friedland sound a similar theme, adding a special caution about the corrosive impact of the market (2001, 12). Members of the political science discipline need to look more closely at how civil society interlocks with the institutions of local governance, see where the disconnections are, and suggest constructive ways of filling those gaps. Some scholars are uncomfortable with mixing social science and reform. Others of us are equally uncomfortable trying to separate them. As someone once said, there is no better way to understand the world than by trying to change it. It is useful to think about how to change the political order, bearing in mind that we are indeed all in this together.

Advanced modernity provides little immediate consciousness of a widely shared fate. In a superficial sense, life is highly segmented, but the reality is that of profound interdependence. It should not fall to natural disasters such as Hurricane Katrina to teach us that. Political science has a special responsibility to cultivate awareness of underlying reality. Campaigns and elections may be a highly specialized activity worthy of close analytical attention, and the formal institutions of government may enjoy a high degree of operational autonomy, also worthy of scholarly attention. But at some point, we must reckon with the functioning actuality that policy is constituted by how state, market, and civil society are interwoven.

Martin Luther King Jr. reminded us: "We are caught in an inescapable network of mutuality, tied in a single garment of destiny. Whatever affects one directly affects all indirectly" (1986, 290). The local community is where a "network of mutuality" is ultimately worked out. Understanding how to work that out more democratically is a challenge that the discipline of political science should make every effort to meet.

ACKNOWLEDGMENTS

I thank the following for their comments, suggestions, and questions: Peter Burns, Jennifer Hochschild, Valerie Johnson, Ira Kowler, Marion Orr, Mary Stone, and Matthew Thomas. And special thanks to G. William Domhoff more broadly for his ongoing challenges to the orthodoxies of American political science.

NOTES

1. On the post-1989 period, see Stone and Pierannunzi (2000). Other accounts of Atlanta extending beyond the 1980s include: Pomerantz (1996); Allen (1996); Bayor (1996); Holmes (1999); Keating (2001); Newman (1999, 2002); and Owens and Rich (2003). To put Atlanta's experience into a longer time perspective, drawing on the pre-1946 experience, readers can turn to Kuhn, Joye, and West (1990); and Ferguson (2002).

2. Franklin, a longtime insider in the biracial coalition, began her public-service career early on as a member of Mayor Maynard Jackson's cabinet and later served as chief administrative officer for Mayor Andrew Young.

3. The city charter imposes term limits on the mayoralty, but no drastic political change appears in the offing. The current city council president, Rita Borders, an African American with

close business ties, is also very much part of the biracial coalition. She is a senior vice president for an Atlanta-based real estate investment trust.

4. It is noteworthy, however, that recent research suggests that in the case of immigration professionals in education and law enforcement may be more responsive to change than are elected officials (Jones-Correa 2004; Lewis and Ramakrishnan 2007). These scholars identify a significant form of bureaucratic incorporation identified, separate from the electoral incorporation identified by Browning, Marshall, and Tabb (1984).

5. On this point, consider also the pioneering work of Barbara Ferman (1996).

6. It is on this point that U.S. and European experiences differ so sharply. Variation from place to place notwithstanding, historically, the larger role of labor unions and of the political party system in "strong state" Europe yielded a civil society legacy much different from the one in the "weak state" United States. Although Atlanta's business elite may play an atypically large role within the city's civic life, the variation within the United States is largely a matter of degree. Robert Crain's study of school desegregation, for example, yielded this observation: "one of the most complex issues in the study of American local government [is] . . . the phenomenon of the businessmen and others who, without holding formal office, make up a civic elite that influence the government's actions" (1968, 356).

7. For an interesting comparative perspective on this point, see Clark and Southern (2006).

8. Action Forum is a biracial organization formed in 1971 (the time when the population balance within the city tilted from white to black majority) to provide a channel of communication between upper-level holders of business and professional positions. It operates in the tradition of closed-door negotiations, with no public record.

9. For another use of configurative analysis, one looking at urban school reform, see Clarke et al. (2006).

10. Although not urban specific, see Abrams (1982); Sewell (1992); and Hay (1995).

11. For an exception, see the probing analysis centered on the European experience in Brenner (2004).

12. After *Who Governs?*, Dahl did acknowledge that in his New Haven study, he could have paid more attention to the capitalist system as a limiting factor in public decision making (1986, 192). But it was his colleague and sometimes coauthor, Charles Lindblom, who made a major structural argument about "the privileged position of business" (1977).

13. See, e.g., the pathbreaking work of Eisinger (1973).

14. At one point, the mayor sent a message to the chair of the aldermanic committee handling urban redevelopment. In it, he said, "our downtown citizens, together with the newspapers," would "go to the extent of rooting the entire government out if they feel we have been remiss in the face of federal opportunities to make progress" (quoted in Stone 1976, 66).

15. In addition to Dahl (1961a), see Rae (2003); and Wolfinger (1974). The experience in Boston is also closely parallel (O'Connor 1993).

16. See also Mark Schneider's *The Competitive City* (1989). Schneider's analysis is less encompassing (and perhaps for that reason less influential) than Peterson's, but it has the virtue of paying closer attention to the metropolitan setting.

17. Readers might note that in *City Limits*, the language of "the city as a whole" replaces the language of a "unitary" interest used in Peterson's earlier book on school politics (1976).

18. On the dangers of treating politics as consensual and technical, see Crick (2000); and Barber (1984). For an interesting case of conflict between competing versions of downtown development, see Crowley (2005).

19. In examining various forms of the new institutionalism, Hall and Taylor cite a trend away from functionalist explanations (1996, 937). See also March and Olsen (1989).

20. On programs in the California cities of Berkeley, Oakland, and Richmond, see Browning, Marshall, and Tabb (2003, 31–32); and in New York and Boston, see Von Hoffman (2003).

21. Consider the area of law enforcement and the importance of community cooperation. Indirect considerations come into play as well. See, for example, the Web site of Fight Crime: Invest in Kids (http://www.fightcrime.org/). Noteworthy as well is a study done under the auspices of the Federal Reserve Bank of Minneapolis, which concludes, "Many of the financial benefits of early childhood interventions come out of reductions in criminal justice system use" (Burr and Grunewald 2006, 34). The general implications of cross-sector interpenetration are wide ranging. On New Labour's approach to this point, see Newman and McKee (2005).

22. It is worth remembering Schattschneider's maxim: "the definition of the alternatives is the supreme instrument of power" (1975, 66).

23. *Who Governs?* posits that those who are well off have little incentive to be heavily engaged in public matters and that those with fewer private advantages have a stronger incentive. See the discussion of African American involvement (Dahl 1961a, 293–96). Moreover, Mary Grava's battle against metal houses is highlighted to show that ordinary citizens can mobilize and win significant victories (Dahl 1961a, 192–99). In a conference discussion of power and democracy, Dahl argued, "any group that feels itself badly abused is likely to possess both the resources it needs to halt the abuse and the incentive to use those resources at a high enough level to bring about changes" (1961b, 89).

24. On the way in which a corporatist system involves dependence on the nongovernmental sector, see Rokkan (1966).

25. For example, Dahl says of New Haven's redevelopment program, "Those who suffered directly were a handful of small businessmen and several hundred slum dwellers without much political influence" (1961a, 244). For a much later and carefully weighed assessment, see Rae (2003, 332–46).

26. But see Shefter (1976) and Katznelson (1981) for interpretations less benign than Dahl's as to how that came about and what its consequences were.

27. But note the important role attributed to conflict in Dahl's later work (e.g., 1989, 209).

28. Later, Dahl distinguishes "between political conflicts over particular issues and conflicts over the regulative structures and principles of society" (1982, 160). New Haven, as he saw it, had plenty of the former but little of the latter, as evidenced in widespread acceptance of "the democratic creed."

29. Consider two telling critiques of the applicability of classic pluralism to the experience of African Americans, one centered on Chicago (Pinderhughes 1987) and the other on New York City (Thompson 2006). Both reject the idea that notions of assimilation and consensus apply to racial politics in the United States. On New Haven for a more recent time than the period treated by Dahl, see Cohen (2001) and Summers and Klinkner (1996). See also the recent study of Chicago and its neighborhoods by Wilson and Taub (2006).

30. See especially the treatment of regional development in Self (2003), a matter also addressed, though less centrally, in Rae (2003).

31. The literature on immigration is now vast and growing. Especially useful guideposts are early treatments by Smith and Feagin (1995) and Jones-Correa (1998).

32. In this vein, historians have provided extraordinarily thought-provoking analyses of the urban experience: Kruse (2005); Kruse and Sugrue (2006); Lassiter (2006); O'Connor (1993); and Self (2003).

33. The extended quote is informative about the affinity between executives and those who control strategically important resources: "They're muscular because they control wealth, they're muscular because they control industries, represent banks. They're muscular because they head up labor. They're muscular because they represent the intellectual portions of the community. They're muscular because they're articulate, because they're respectable, because of their financial power, and because of the accumulation of prestige which they have built up over the years as individuals in all kinds of causes, whether United Fund, Red Cross, or whatever" (Dahl 1961a, 130).

34. The fading of the old order in Boston was caught in the fictionalized account of James Michael Curley's mayoral defeat in Edwin O'Connor's novel, *The Last Hurrah* (1954). See also Lukas (1984).

35. Along with Edward Banfield's treatment, see the astute characterization of the Chicago machine under Richard J. Daley by Paul Peterson (1976, 12–18).

36. It is significant that in both Atlanta and New Haven, as well as many other cities, redevelopment was highly insulated from the politics of ward and neighborhood. In Atlanta, the informal rule of "ward courtesy" was changed and the city's redevelopment agency, the Atlanta Housing Authority, was thoroughly buffered from the city's electoral politics (Stone 1976). In New Haven, an independent redevelopment agency, chiefly financed by external funds, was largely unanswerable to the city's ward politics (Rae 2003). On the general pattern, see Friedland and Palmer (1984). In short, new-convergence alliances made moves to keep neighborhood-based political channels on the periphery of redevelopment decision making, and that was the case whether the redevelopment initiative lay with city hall or business.

37. Comparative studies include Mollenkopf (1983); Ferman (1996); and Portz, Stein, and Jones (1999).

38. For a telling account from that period, see *Dark Ghetto* (1965) by Kenneth Clark.

39. In its report, the National Advisory Commission on Civil Disorders found that many residents of the urban core felt "a profound sense of isolation" and that to them "city government appears distant and unconcerned" (1968, 284, 288).

40. Various authors have observed a parallel shift in the level of business engagement as corporations have become increasingly absentee-owned and executives less attached to the local community: Savitch and Thomas (1991); Gurwitt (1991); Lemann (2000); Hanson (2003); and Hanson and Norris (2006). However, the extent of the pattern should not be overstated; see, e.g., Shipps (2006). Furthermore, in some places, downtown development has become institutionalized through the creation of independent agencies. For example, BDC (the City of Baltimore Development Corporation) is a 501(c)(3). It was established "to provide economic development services." The BDC Web site states: "Our job is to ensure that Baltimore is meeting the needs of its business community to the greatest extent possible every day" (http://www.baltimoredevelop ment.com/). And in one version, the influence of the bond-rating system puts the contemporary city under unrelenting pressure to accommodate to business friendly versions of economic development (Hackworth 2007).

41. Thought-provoking works include: Goetz (1993); Clarke and Gaile (1998); Grogan and Proscio (2000); Florida (2002); Varady (2005); and Gillette (2007).

42. An election-centered understanding is what Archon Fung calls "minimal democracy" (2007); see also Barber (1984) and Imbroscio (1999).

43. With its dual concern about equity and economic performance, No Child Left Behind is one indicator of new thinking that bears importantly on urban areas. A caution, however, is that Tyack and Cuban remind that "the utopian tradition of social reform through schooling has often diverted attention from more costly, politically controversial, and difficult social reforms" (1995, 3).

44. Significantly, the struggle in Pittsburgh over redevelopment in the business district turned, in part, on the issue of openness and inclusion (Crowley 2005, 112–39).

45. Concerns about the soundness of representative government are not restricted to the local level. See, e.g., Dalton, Scarrow, and Cain (2003); Hirst (2000); Jacobs and Skocpol (2005); Macedo et al. (2005); Norris (1999); and Pharr and Putnam (2000). Note that I use the word *citizenry* rather than *citizens* to emphasize that citizenship is not an individual matter subject to simple aggregation, but necessarily a collective matter with a foundation of interdependence.

46. For a discussion of the need for social investment as a policy consideration, see Giddens (2000).

47. I am indebted to Matthew Crenson for directing my attention to this point and to a related study by Eric Friedman (2003).

48. For an interesting treatment of the role of CDCs in industrial development, see Rast (2007) and his earlier work cited there.

49. Edward Koch was mayor of New York City from 1978 to 1990.

50. Important sources include: Pruitt (2001); Nelson (2000); Kennedy, Braga, and Piehl (2001); Berrien and Winship (2002, 2003); Winship (2002, 2006); McRoberts (2003); Jackson and Winship (2006); and Braga and Winship (2006).

51. Pertinent sources include Portz, Stein, and Jones (1999); Usdan and Cuban (2003); Yee (2003); Portz (2004); and Aspen Institute (2006).

52. Quoted in Portz, Stein, and Jones (1999, 90).

53. On the importance of associational life as a channel of representation, see Burns (2006).

54. Note, for example, Baltimore's biomedical initiative, which is being carried out by East Baltimore Development Incorporated, a nonprofit financed by a combination of funders, including Johns Hopkins University, the public sector, and several foundations. It works with one community-based organization, but it faces a more adversarial relationship with a second.

55. One of the significant factors to consider is the unionization of municipal workers. Because unionization can pull front-line employees and their immediate supervisors into a zero-sum view of proposed changes, it can limit the leadership potential of the mayor's office. For that reason, some observers see no hopeful path to reform without breaking up the large service-providing bureaucracies that Lowi (1967) once referred to as the "new machines." For a contemporary view, see Grogan and Proscio (2000); and Rae (2006).

56. In his study of the shortcomings of black churches as a force for revitalization in a poor Boston neighborhood, McRoberts asks, "Who will advocate for neighborhood interests in the near absence of secular institutions such as CDCs?" (2003, 148).

57. Variations of this theme can be seen in a huge number of sources, in addition to Salisbury on St. Louis (1964), including those for: Atlanta (Stone 1976); Baltimore (Stoker 1987); Boston (O'Connor 1993); New Haven (Dahl 1961a; Wolfinger 1974; Rae 2003); New York (Caro 1974); Newark (Kaplan 1963); Detroit (Mowitz and Wright 1962); Philadelphia (Lowe 1967); Denver (Judd 1986); San Francisco (Fainstein, Fainstein, and Armistead 1986; Hartman 1984); Oakland (Self 2003); Chicago and Pittsburgh (Ferman 1996).

58. A somewhat different but overlapping framing of this agenda is presented in Grogan and Proscio (2000).

59. This is not a question of a consensus about what to do. Rather it is a matter of an often implicit frame of reference for thinking about how to solve problems. Consider the discussion of schemas in Sewell (1992).

60. A San Francisco organization, Coleman Advocates for Children and Youth, is a high-visibility example of such an entity, which, through its success in pushing the Children's Amend-

ment and related efforts, has managed to penetrate the city's agenda and shape budget priorities. Significantly, Coleman Advocates started as an organization with narrowly bounded concerns about the juvenile justice system and care for foster children, but over time, it took on a much broader agenda.

61. To the extent that public employee unions fixate on such matters as job protection and privileges, particularly for those with senior standing, and are inattentive to issues of performance, then they are indeed the "new machines" oriented toward the spoils of office. See Rae (2006); Rich (1996); and Stone (1998).

62. For consequences of not doing so, see the discussion of Naples, Italy, in Savitch and Kantor (2002).

63. For an assessment of the limited scope of the Great Society programs, see Jackson (1993).

64. For an example of a community-based organization attempting to counteract a broad and therefore highly permissive form of the "no snitching" norm, see the article on Washington, D.C.'s Peaceoholics (Pierre 2007).

65. See also Gaventa (1980); and Wilson (1996).

66. Consider the quite differently tempered, but parallel, arguments put forth in Sirianni and Friedland (2001, 234–80) and Hackworth (2007, 188–204).

67. *New professionals* is also a term used in the development literature to underscore the point that international experts need to listen to local people in order to obtain a better understanding of the problems of poverty and how to respond to them in constructive ways; see Chambers (1995). There is a parallel argument that schools and other local agencies in the United States can learn from and should engage youth (Ferman 2005, 2007).

68. On the counterforce to city hall–CBO alignment, note the examples of the tension between a social-reform mayor and the business sector: Hollander (1991); and Hanson and Norris (2006).

69. The literature on community organizing is vast and growing. Important studies include Gittell and Vidal (1998); Warren (2001); Shirley (2002); Smock (2004); and Orr (2007).

70. If housing, policing, and educating the young were to become the foci of a new urban agenda, that would not mean an absence of conflict in relations between homeowners and renters, or between those who advocate more patrols and strict enforcement in policing versus those who emphasize more extensive youth programs (Peterman 2000; Freeman 2006). The presence of issues on an agenda does not mean that conflict is precluded; it simply means that the issues are not ignored. There is opportunity to deliberate about them and negotiate points of difference. A democratic process would mean no permanent minority in this process—that is, no group that is consistently bypassed or rebuffed (Fung 2004).

71. Cathy Cohen directs attention to an alternative pattern of response: "Recognizing the inaccessibility of dominant systems, marginal groups often turn inward, redirecting their resources, trusts, and loyalty toward community-based institutions and relationships that more directly address their needs. They rely upon indigenous organizations, leaders, networks, and norms to provide some version of the resources and information that are unavailable from dominant institutions and relationships" (1999, 51). See also Gaventa's argument about how powerlessness can be self-perpetuating (1980).

72. This is a quote from Washington, D.C.'s newly appointed school chancellor, quoted in Milloy (2007, B1).

73. There are several ad hoc instances of education summits and community-wide planning processes that have managed to generate some sense of acting on behalf of the well-being of the whole community. Relevant instances include the summit organized by Mayor Harold Washing-

ton (Shipps 2006); Hampton, Virginia's community planning process (Stone and Worgs 2004); El Paso's Collaborative for Academic Excellence (Stone 2003); mobilization for school improvement in Mobile, Alabama (Akers 2005); and school-reform mobilization in Hamilton County—the consolidated district—which includes Chattanooga, Tennessee (Fruchter 2007).

74. For examples of recent neighborhood research that is highly informative in a policy-relevant way, see McRoberts (2003); Peterman (2000); and Small (2004).

75. One path of refinement might be to rework the concept of political incorporation, taking into account not just politics centered on city hall but how groups (including various categories of immigrants) fit into the wider picture. In what ways are they connected and in what ways disconnected?

REFERENCES

Abrams, P. 1982. *Historical sociology.* Ithaca, N.Y.: Cornell Univ. Press.

Akers, C. 2005. Developing a civic infrastructure. *Voices in Urban Education* 9 (fall): 14–23.

Allen, F. 1996. *Atlanta rising.* Atlanta, Ga.: Longstreet Press.

Aspen Institute. 2006. Education and Society Program and Annenberg Institute for School Reform at Brown University. *Strong foundation evolving challenges: A case study to support leadership transition in the Boston public schools.* Washington, D.C.: Aspen Institute; Providence, R.I.: Annenberg Institute for School Reform. http://www.eric.ed.gov/ERICDocs/data/ericdocs2sql/content_storage_01/0000019b/80/1b/c6/53.pdf.

Bailey, R. W. 1999. *Gay politics, urban politics.* New York: Columbia Univ. Press.

Banfield, E. C. 1961. *Political influence.* New York: Free Press.

Barber, B. 1984. *Strong democracy.* Berkeley: Univ. of California Press.

Baum, H. S. 2003. *Community action for school reform.* Albany: State Univ. of New York Press.

Baumgartner, F. R., and B. D. Jones. 1993. *Agendas and instability in American politics.* Chicago: University of Chicago Press.

Bayor, R. H. 1996. *Race and the shaping of twentieth-century Atlanta.* Chapel Hill: Univ. of North Carolina Press.

Berrien, J., and C. Winship. 2002. An umbrella of legitimacy: Boston's police department—Ten Point Collaboration. In *Securing our children's future: New approaches to juvenile justice and youth violence,* ed. G. S. Katzmann, 200–228. Washington, D.C.: Brookings Institution.

———. 2003. Should we have faith in the churches? The Ten-Point Coalition's effect on Boston's youth violence. In *Guns, crime, and punishment in America,* ed. B. E. Harcourt, 222–48. New York: New York Univ. Press.

Blumenberg, A., B. Blom, and E. Artigiani. 1998. A co-production model of code enforcement and nuisance abatement. *Crime Prevention Studies* 9:261–90.

Braga, A., and C. Winship. 2006. Partnership, accountability, and innovation: Clarifying Boston's experience with pulling levers. In *Police innovation,* ed. D. Weisburd and A. Braga, 171–87. New York: Cambridge Univ. Press.

Brenner, N. 2004. *New state spaces.* New York: Oxford Univ. Press.

Brown, M. 1999. Reconceptualizing public and private in urban regime theory. *International Journal of Urban and Regional Research* 23 (Mar.): 70–87.

Browning, R. P., D. R. Marshall, and D. H. Tabb. 2003. Mobilization, incorporation, and policy in 10 California cities. In *Racial politics in American cities,* 3rd ed., ed. R. P. Browning, D. R. Marshall, and D. H. Tabb, 17–48. New York: Longman.

Burns, P. F. 2006. *Electoral politics is not enough.* Albany: State Univ. of New York Press.

Burr, J., and R. Grunewald. 2006. Lessons learned: A review of early childhood. *Development Studies* (Apr.). Federal Reserve Study.

Caro, R. A. 1974. *The power broker.* New York: Knopf.

Castells, M., and J. Mollenkopf. 1991. Conclusion: Is New York a dual city? In *Dual city: Restructuring New York,* ed. J. H. Mollenkopf and M. Castells, 399–418. New York: Russell Sage Foundation.

Chambers, R. 1995. Poverty and livelihood: Whose reality counts. *Environment and Urbanization* 7 (Apr.): 173–204.

Clark, D., and R. Southern. 2006. Comparing institutional designs for neighborhood renewal: Neighborhood management in Britain and the *régies de quartier* in France. *Policy and Politics* 34 (1): 173–91.

Clark, K. B. 1965. *Dark ghetto.* New York: Harper & Row.

Clark, P. B. 1969. Civic leadership: The symbols of legitimacy. In *Democracy in urban America,* ed. O. P. Williams and C. Press, 350–66. Chicago: Rand McNally.

Clarke, S. E., and G. L. Gaile. 1998. *The work of cities.* Minneapolis: Univ. of Minnesota Press.

Clarke, S. E., R. E. Hero, M. S. Sidney, L. R. Fraga, and B. A. Erlichson. 2006. *Multiethnic moments.* Philadelphia: Temple Univ. Press.

Clavel, P., and W. Wiewel, eds. 1991. *Harold Washington and the neighborhoods.* New Brunswick, N.J.: Rutgers Univ. Press.

Cochrane, A. 2007. *Understanding urban policy.* Oxford: Blackwell Publishing.

Cohen, C. J. 1999. *The boundaries of blackness.* Chicago: University of Chicago Press.

———. 2001. Social capital, intervening institutions, and political power. In *Social capital and poor communities,* ed. S. Saegert, J. P. Thompson, and M. Warren, 267–89. New York: Russell Sage Foundation.

Crain, R. L. 1968. *The politics of school desegregation.* Chicago: Aldine.

Crick, B. 2000. *In defence of politics.* 5th ed. London: Continuum.

Crowley, G. J. 2005. *The politics of place.* Pittsburgh: Univ. of Pittsburgh Press.

Dahl, R. A. 1961a. *Who governs?* New Haven, Conn.: Yale Univ. Press.

———. 1961b. Equality and power in American society. In *Power and democracy in America,* ed. W. V. D'Antonio and H. J. Ehrlich, 73–89. Notre Dame, Ind.: Univ. of Notre Dame Press.

———. 1982. *Dilemmas of pluralist democracy: Autonomy vs. control.* New Haven, Conn.: Yale Univ. Press.

———. 1986. Rethinking *Who governs?:* New Haven revisited. In *Community power: Directions for future research,* ed. R. J. Waste, 179–96. Beverly Hills, Calif.: Sage.

Dalton, R. J., S. E. Scarrow, and B. E. Cain. 2003. New forms of democracy? In *Democracy transformed,* ed. B. E. Cain, R. J. Dalton, and S. E. Scarrow, 1–20. New York: Oxford Univ. Press.

Downs, A. 1972. Up and down with ecology—The issue-attention cycle. *Public Interest* 28:38–50.

Dreier, P., J. Mollenkopf, and T. Swanstrom. 2004. *Place matters.* Lawrence: Univ. Press of Kansas.

Eisinger, P. K. 1973. The conditions of protest behavior in American cities. *American Political Science Review* 67 (Mar.): 11–28.

Epstein, J. 2001. *School, family, and community partnerships.* Boulder, Colo.: Westview Press.

Erie, S. P. 1988. *Rainbow's end.* Berkeley: Univ. of California Press.

———. 2004. *Globalizing L.A.* Stanford, Calif.: Stanford Univ. Press.

Fainstein, S. S., N. I. Fainstein, and P. J. Armistead. 1986. San Francisco: Urban transformation and the local state. In *Restructuring the city,* rev. ed., ed. S. S. Fainstein, N. I. Fainstein, R. C. Hill, D. R. Judd, and M. P. Smith, 202–44. New York: Longman.

Ferguson, K. 2002. *Black politics in New Deal Atlanta.* Chapel Hill: Univ. of North Carolina Press.

Ferman, B. 1996. *Challenging the growth machine.* Lawrence: Univ. Press of Kansas.

———. 2005. Youth engagement in practice. *Good Society* 14, 3:45–50.

———. 2007. Reclaiming democracy through civic society: The role of education, local institutions, and community organizing. Paper prepared at a symposium on Global Look at Urban and Regional Governance: The State-Market-Civic Nexus, sponsored by the Claus M. Halle Institute and the Department of Political Science at Emory University, Atlanta, Ga.

Florida, R. 2002. *The rise of the creative class.* New York: Basic Books.

Fox, K. 1988. Who can govern? Dahl's *Who governs?* revisited. In *Power, inequality, and democratic politics,* ed. I. Shapiro and G. Reeher, 123–31. Boulder, Colo.: Westview Press.

Freeman, L. 2006. *There goes the 'hood: Views of gentrification from the ground up.* Philadelphia: Temple Univ. Press.

Friedland, R., and D. Palmer. 1984. Park Place and Main Street: Business and the urban power structure. *Annual Review of Sociology* 10:393–416.

Friedman, E. 2003. Vacant properties in Baltimore: Strategies for reuse. Paper submitted to the Abell Foundation Award in Urban Policy. January 18.

Fruchter, N. 2007. *Urban schools, public will.* New York: Teachers College Press.

Fung, A. 2004. *Empowered participation: Reinventing urban democracy.* Princeton, N.J.: Princeton Univ. Press.

———. 2007. Democratic theory and political science. *American Political Science Review* 101:443–58.

Gans, H. 1962. *The urban villagers.* New York: Free Press.

Garcia, M. 2006. Citizenship practices and urban governance in European cities. *Urban Studies* 43 (Apr.): 745–65.

Gaventa, J. 1980. *Power and powerlessness.* Urbana: Univ. of Illinois Press.

Gendron, R. 2006. Forging collective capacity for urban redevelopment. *City and Community* 5 (Mar.): 5–22.

Giddens, A. 2000. *The third way and its critics.* Cambridge, UK: Polity Press.

Gillette, H., Jr. 2007. Urban renewal revisited. *Journal of Urban History* 33 (Jan.): 342–50.

Gittell, R., and A. Vidal. 1998. *Community organizing.* Thousand Oaks, Calif.: Sage.

Goetz, E. G. 1993. *Shelter burden.* Philadelphia: Temple University Press.

Goldberger, P. 2007. Eminent dominion: Rethinking the legacy of Robert Moses. *New Yorker.* Feb. 5.

Gordon, E. W., B. L. Bridglall, and A. S. Meroe, eds. 2005. *Supplementary education: The hidden curriculum of high academic achievement.* Lanham, Md.: Rowman and Littlefield.

Granovetter, M. 2005. The impact of social structure on economic outcomes. *Journal of Economic Perspectives* 19 (winter): 33–50.

Grogan, P. S., and T. Proscio. 2000. *Comeback cities.* Boulder, Colo.: Westview Press.

Gurwitt, R. 1991. The rule of the absentocracy. *Governing Magazine* (Sep.): 52–58.

Hackworth, J. 2007. *The neoliberal city.* Ithaca, N.Y.: Cornell University Press.

Hall, P. A., and R. C. R. Taylor. 1996. Political science and the three institutionalisms. *Political Studies* 44:936–57.

Hanson, R. 2003. *Civic culture and urban change.* Detroit: Wayne State Univ. Press.

Hanson, R., and D. F. Norris. 2006. Corporate citizenship and urban governance in Baltimore. A case study prepared for the Brookings Institution Metropolitan Policy Program (September).

Hartman, C. 1984. *The transformation of San Francisco.* Totowa, NJ: Rowman & Allanheld.

Hay, C. 1995. Structure and agency. In *Theory and methods in political science,* ed. D. Marsh and G. Stoker. New York: Palgrave.

Henig, J. R. 1982. *Neighborhood mobilization.* New Brunswick, N.J.: Rutgers Univ. Press.

Henig, J. R., and C. N. Stone. 2007. Civic capacity and education reform. In *City schools: Building smart education systems,* ed. R. Rothman, 117–36. Cambridge, Mass.: Harvard Education Press.

Hirst, P. 2000. Democracy and governance. In *Debating governance,* ed. J. Pierre, 13–35. New York: Oxford Univ. Press.

Hollander, E. 1991. The Department of Planning under Harold Washington. In *Harold Washington and the neighborhoods,* ed. P. Clavel and W. Wiewel, 121–45. New Brunswick, N.J.: Rutgers Univ. Press.

Holmes, B. 1999. Atlanta politics on the eve of the millennium. In *The status of black Atlanta, 1999,* 1–39. Atlanta: Southern Center for Studies in Public Policy, Clark Atlanta University.

Honig, M. I., ed. 2006. *Confronting complexity.* Albany: SUNY Press.

Hunter, F. 1953. *Community power structure.* Chapel Hill: Univ. of North Carolina Press.

Imbroscio, D. L. (1999) Structure, agency and democratic theory. *Polity* 32:45–66.

Jackson, R., and C. Winship. 2006. *Race relation in Boston: A tale of two mayors, Raymond L. Flynn and Thomas M. Menino.* Cambridge, Mass.: Hauser Center for Nonprofit Organizations. http://www.innovations.harvard.edu/showdoc.html?id=13705.

Jackson, T. F. 1993. The state, the movement, and the urban poor: The war on poverty and political mobilization in the 1960s. In *The underclass debate,* ed. M. B. Katz, 401–39. Princeton, N.J.: Princeton Univ. Press.

Jacobs, J. 1961. *The death and life of great American cities.* New York: Vintage Books.

Jacobs, L. R., and T. Skocpol, eds. 2005. *Inequality and American democracy.* New York: Russell Sage Foundation.

John, P. 2001. *Local governance in Western Europe.* London: Sage.

Jones, B. D. 1994. *Reconceiving decision-making in democratic politics.* Chicago: Univ. of Chicago Press.

———. 2001. *The architecture of choice.* Chicago: University of Chicago Press.

Jones-Correa, M. 1998. *Between two nations.* Ithaca, N.Y.: Cornell University Press.

———. 2004. Racial and ethnic diversity and the politics of education in suburbia. Paper presented at the annual meeting of the American Political Science Association. Chicago.

Jordan, A., R. K. W. Wurzel, and A. Zito. 2005. The rise of "new" policy instruments in comparative perspective. *Political Studies* 53:477–96.

Judd, D. R. 1986. From cowtown to sunbelt city: Boosterism and economic growth in Denver. In *Restructuring the city,* rev. ed., ed. S. S. Fainstein, N. I. Fainstein, R. C. Hill, D. R. Judd, and M. P. Smith, 167–201. New York: Longman.

Judge, D. 1995. Pluralism. In *Theories of urban politics,* ed. D. Judge, G. Stoker, and H. Wolman, 13–34. London: Sage Publications.

Kaplan, H. 1963. *Urban renewal politics.* New York: Columbia Univ. Press.

Katznelson, I. 1981. *City trenches.* Chicago: University of Chicago Press.

Kaufmann, K. M. 2003. Cracks in the rainbow. *Political Research Quarterly* 56:199–210.

———. 2004. *The urban voter.* Ann Arbor: University of Michigan Press.

Keating, L. 2001. *Atlanta: Race, class and urban expansion.* Philadelphia: Temple Univ. Press.

Kennedy, D. M., A. Braga, and A. Piehl. 2001. *Reducing gun violence: The Boston Project's Operation Ceasefire.* Washington, D.C.: U.S. Department of Justice, National Institute of Justice.

King, M. L., Jr. 1986. *A testament of hope.* Ed. J. M. Washington. New York: HarperCollins.

Kingdon, J. W. 1995. *Agendas, alternatives, and public policies.* New York: HarperCollins.

Krumholz, N. 1996. Metropolitan development and neighborhood revitalization. In *Revitalizing urban neighborhoods,* ed. W. D. Keating, N. Krumholz, and P. Star, 211–21. Lawrence: Univ. Press of Kansas.

Kuhn, C. M., H. E. Joye, and E. B. West. 1990. *Living Atlanta: An oral history of the city, 1914–1948.* Athens: University of Georgia Press.

Kruse, K. M. 2005 *White flight.* Princeton, N.J.: Princeton Univ. Press.

Kruse, K. M., and T. J. Sugrue, eds. 2006. *The new suburban history.* Chicago: Univ. of Chicago Press.

Kurylo, E. 1996. Carter tackled tough job, put prestige on the line. *Atlanta Journal and Constitution.* Sep. 15.

Lassiter, M. D. 2006. *The silent majority: Suburban politics in the sunbelt South.* Princeton, N.J.: Princeton Univ. Press.

Lemann, N. 2000. No man's town. *New Yorker,* 42–48. Jun. 5.

Lewis, P. G., and K. Ramakrishnan. 2007. Police practices in immigrant-destination cities. *Urban Affairs Review* 42:874–900.

Lindblom, C. E. 1977. *Politics and markets.* New York: Basic Books.

Lowe, J. R. 1967. *Cities in a race with time.* New York: Random House.

Lowi, T. J. 1967. Machine politics—old and new. *Public Interest* (fall): 83–92.

Lukas, J. A. 1984. All in the family: The dilemmas of busing and the conflict of values. In *Boston, 1700–1980: The evolution of urban politics,* ed. R. P. Formisano and C. K. Burns, 241–57. Westport, Conn.: Greenwood Press.

Macedo, S., et al. 2005. *Democracy at risk.* Washington, D.C.: Brookings Institution.

March, J., and J. Olsen. 1989. *Rediscovering institutions.* New York: Free Press.

Marquand, D. 2004. *Decline of the public.* Cambridge, UK: Polity Press.

McClanahan, W. S. 2004. *Alive at 25: Reducing youth violence through monitoring and support.* Philadelphia: Public/Private Ventures, Field Report Series.

McLaughlin, M., W. R. Scott, S. Deschenes, K. Hopkins, and A. Newman. Forthcoming. Between organizing and establishment: Organizations advocating for youth. MS. Jan. 23.

McRoberts, O. M. 2003. *Streets of glory.* Chicago: Univ. of Chicago Press.

Medoff, P., and H. Sklar. 1994. *Streets of hope.* Boston: South End Press.

Milloy, C. 2007. Rhee's determination will be tested. *Washington Post,* B1, B10. Jul. 4.

Mollenkopf, J. H. 1983. *The contested city.* Princeton, NJ: Princeton University Press.

———. 1992. *A phoenix in the ashes.* Princeton, N.J.: Princeton Univ. Press.

Mollenkopf, J. H., and M. Castells, eds. 1991. *Dual city: Restructuring New York.* New York: Russell Sage Foundation.

Moore, M. H. 1988. What sort of ideas become public ideas? In *The power of public ideas,* ed. S. Kelman. Cambridge, Mass.: Harvard Univ. Press, 55–83.

Mowitz, R. J., and D. S. Wright. 1962. *Profile of a metropolis: A case book.* Detroit: Wayne State Univ. Press.

National Advisory Commission on Civil Disorders. 1968. *Report of the National Advisory Commission on Civil Disorders.* New York: Bantam Books.

Nelson, W. E. 2000. *Black Atlantic politics.* New York: State Univ. of New York Press.

Newman, H. K. 1999. *Southern hospitality: Tourism and growth in Atlanta.* Tuscaloosa: Univ. of Alabama Press.

———. 2002. *The Atlanta Housing Authority's Olympic legacy program.* Atlanta: Research Atlanta.

Newman, J., and B. McKee. 2005. Beyond the new public management? Public services and the social investment state. *Policy and Politics* 33 (4): 657–74.

Nicolaides, B. M. 2002. *My blue heaven.* Univ. of Chicago Press.

Norris, P., ed. 1999. *Critical citizens.* New York: Oxford Univ. Press.

Oakes, J., and J. Rogers. 2006. *Learning power.* Teachers College Press.

O'Connor, E. 1954. *The last hurrah.* Boston: Little, Brown.

O'Connor, T. H. 1993. *Building a new Boston.* Boston: Northeastern Univ. Press.

———. 1995. *The Boston Irish.* Boston: Northeastern Univ. Press.

Okun, A. M. 1975. *Equality and efficiency: The big tradeoff.* Washington, D.C.: Brookings Institution.

Olivera, J., and D. Rae. Forthcoming. Immigration after urbanism: The New Haven case. In *New immigrants in urban New England,* ed. H. Silver.

Orr, M., ed. 2007. *Transforming the city: Community organizing and the challenge of political change.* Lawrence: Univ. Press of Kansas.

Orren, K., and S. Skowronek. 2004. *The search for American political development.* New York: Cambridge Univ. Press.

Owens, M. L., and M. J. Rich. 2003. Is strong incorporation enough? Black empowerment and the fate of Atlanta's low-income blacks. In *Racial politics in American cities,* ed. P. Browning, D. R. Marshall, and D. H. Tabb, 201–26. New York: Longman.

Pagano, M. A., and A. O'M. Bowman. 1995. *Cityscapes and capital.* Baltimore: Johns Hopkins Univ. Press.

Payne, C. M. 2001. So much reform, so little change. In *Education policy for the 21st century,* ed. L. B. Joseph, 239–78. Champaign: Univ. of Illinois Press.

Peterman, W. 2000. *Neighborhood planning and community-based development.* Thousand Oaks, Calif.: Sage.

Peterson, P. E. 1976. *School politics Chicago style.* Chicago: Univ. of Chicago Press.

———. 1981. *City limits.* Chicago: Univ. of Chicago Press.

Pharr, S. J., and R. D. Putnam, eds. 2000. *Disaffected democracies.* Princeton, N.J.: Princeton Univ. Press.

Pierre, J. 2005. Comparative urban governance. *Urban Affairs Review* 40 (4): 446–62.

Pierre, R. E. 2007. Brokering peace. *Washington Post* (Jan. 14): C1–11.

Pierson, P. 2004. *Politics in time.* Princeton, N.J.: Princeton Univ. Press.

Pinderhughes, D. M. 1987. *Race and ethnicity in Chicago.* Urbana: Univ. of Illinois Press.

Pomerantz, G. M. 1996. *Where Peachtree meets Sweet Auburn.* New York: Penguin.

Portz, J. 2004. Boston: Agenda setting and school reform in a mayor-centric system. In *Mayors in the middle,* 96–119. Princeton, N.J.: Princeton Univ. Press.

Portz, J., L. Stein, and R. Jones. 1999. *City schools and city politics.* Lawrence: Univ. Press of Kansas.

Pruitt, B. H. 2001. *The Boston strategy: A story of unlikely alliances.* Princeton, N.J.: Robert Wood Johnson Foundation.

Putnam, R. D. 2000. *Bowling alone.* New York: Simon & Schuster.

Rae, D. W. 2003. *City: Urbanism and its end.* New Haven, Conn.: Yale Univ. Press.

———. 2006. Making life work in crowded places. *Urban Affairs Review* 41 (Jan.): 271–91.

Ramsay, M. 1996. *Community, culture, and economic development.* Albany: State Univ. of New York Press.

Rast, J. 2007. Why history (still) matters: Reconnecting to the discipline through historical institutionalism. Paper presented at the annual meeting of the American Political Science Association, Chicago.

Reed, A., Jr. 1999. *Stirrings in the jug: Black politics in the post-segregation era.* Minneapolis: Univ. of Minnesota Press.

Rich, M. J. 2003. Revitalizing urban communities: Lessons from Atlanta's empowerment zone experience. In *The status of black Atlanta, 2003,* 79–112. Atlanta: Southern Center for Studies in Public Policy, Clark Atlanta Univ.

Rich, W. C. 1996. *Black mayors and school politics.* New York: Garland.

Rokkan, S. 1966. Norway: Numerical democracy and corporate pluralism. In *Political oppositions in western democracies,* ed. R. A. Dahl, 70–115. New Haven, Conn.: Yale University Press.

Rothstein, R. 2004. *Class and schools.* Washington, D.C.: Economic Policy Institute.

Salisbury, R. H. 1964. Urban politics: The new convergence of power. *Journal of Politics* 26 (Nov.): 775–97.

Sapotichne, J., B. Jones, and M. Wolfe. 2007. Is urban politics a "black hole"? Analyzing the boundary between political science and urban politics. *Urban Affairs Review* 43:76–106.

Savitch, H. V., and P. Kantor. 2002. *Cities in the international marketplace.* Princeton, N.J.: Princeton Univ. Press.

Savitch, H. V., and J. C. Thomas. 1991. *Big city politics in transition.* Newbury Park, Calif.: Sage.

Schattschneider, E. E. 1975. *The semisovereign people.* 1960. Fort Worth: Harcourt Brace Jovanovich.

Schneider, M. 1989. *The competitive city.* Pittsburgh: Univ. of Pittsburgh Press.

Schneider, M., P. Teske, and M. Mintrom. 1995. *Public entrepreneurs.* Princeton, N.J.: Princeton Univ. Press.

Schorr, L. B. 1997. *Common purposes.* New York: Anchor Books, Doubleday.

Self, R. O. 2003. *American Babylon.* Princeton, N.J.: Princeton Univ. Press.

Sewell, W. H., Jr. 1992. A theory of structure. *American Journal of Sociology* 98 (Jul.): 1–29.

Sharp, Elaine E. 2007. Revitalizing urban research. *Urban Affairs Review* 43:55–75.

Shefter, M. 1976. The emergence of the political machine. In *Theoretical Perspectives on Urban Politics,* ed. Willis D. Hawley et al., 14–44, Englewood Ciffs, N.J.: Prentice-Hall.

Shipps, D. 2006. *School reform, corporate style.* Lawrence: Univ. Press of Kansas.

Shirley, D. 2002. *Valley interfaith and school reform.* Austin: Univ. of Texas Press.

Simon, H. A. 1969. *The sciences of the artificial.* Cambridge, Mass.: MIT PRESS.

Sirianni, C., and L. Friedland. 2001. *Civic innovation in America.* Berkeley: University of California Press.

Skocpol, T. 2003. *Diminished democracy.* Norman: Univ. of Oklahoma Press.

Small, M. L. 2004. *Villa victoria.* Chicago: Univ. of Chicago Press.

Smith, M. P., and J. R. Feagin. 1995. *The bubbling cauldron.* Minneapolis: University of Minnesota Press.

Smock, K. 2004. *Democracy in action: Community organizing and urban change.* New York: Columbia Univ. Press.

Steinmo, S., K. Thelen, and F. Longstreth, eds. 1992. *Structuring politics: Historical institutionalism in comparative analysis.* New York: Cambridge Univ. Press.

Stewart, J. 2000. *The nature of British local government.* London: Macmillan.

Stoker, G. 1995. Regime theory and urban politics. In *Theories of urban politics,* ed. D. Judge, G. Stoker, and H. Wolman, 54–71. London: Sage.

———. 1998. *Governance as theory.* UNESCO. Oxford: Blackwell.

Stoker, R. P. 1987. Baltimore: The self-evaluating city? In *The politics of urban development,* ed. C. N. Stone and H. T. Sanders, 244–66. Lawrence: University Press of Kansas.

Stone, C. N. 1976. *Economic growth and neighborhood discontent.* Chapel Hill: Univ. of North Carolina Press.

———. 1989. *Regime politics.* Lawrence: Univ. Press of Kansas.

———. 1998. Introduction: Urban education and political context. In *Changing urban education,* ed. C. N. Stone, 1–20. Lawrence: Univ. Press of Kansas.

———. 1993. Urban regimes and the capacity to govern. *Journal of Urban Affairs* 15:1–28.

————. 2003. Civic cooperation in El Paso: A case study for School Communities that Work Task Force of the Annenberg Institute for School Reform: Case studies in community partnership. http://www.schoolcommunities.org/Archive/index.html.

Stone, C., M. Orr, and D. Worgs. 2006. The flight of the bumblebee: Why reform is difficult but not impossible. *Perspectives on Politics* 4 (Sep.): 529–46.

Stone, C., and C. Pierannunzi. 2000. Atlanta's biracial colation. Paper presented at the annual meeting of the American Political Science Association, Washington, D.C.

Stone, C., and D. Worgs. 2004. Poverty and the workforce challenge. In *Workforce development politics,* ed. R. P. Giloth, 249–80. Philadelphia: Temple Univ. Press.

Sugrue, T. J. 1996. *The origins of the urban crisis.* Princeton, N.J.: Princeton Univ. Press.

Summers, M., and P. A. Klinkner. 1996. The election and governance of John Daniels as mayor of New Haven. In *Race, politics, and governance in the United States,* ed. H. L. Perry, 127–50. Gainesville: Univ. of Florida Press.

Suskind, R. 1998. *A hope in the unseen.* New York: Broadway Books.

Thelen, K. 2004. *How institutions evolve.* New York: Cambridge Univ. Press.

Thompson, J. P., III. 2006. *Double trouble.* New York: Oxford Univ. Press.

Tilly, C. 1984. *Big structures, large processes, huge comparisons.* New York: Russell Sage Foundation.

Tita, G., J. Riley, G. Ridgeway, and C. Grammich. 2003. Unruly turf: The role of interagency collaboration in reducing gun violence. *Rand Review* (fall): 1–10.

Trounstine, J. 2006. Dominant regimes and the demise of urban democracy. *Journal of Politics* 68:879–93.

Tyack, D., and L. Cuban. 1995. *Tinkering toward utopia.* Cambridge, Mass.: Harvard Univ. Press.

Usdan, M., and L. Cuban. 2003. Boston: The stars finally in alignment. In *Powerful reforms with shallow roots,* ed. L. Cuban and M. Usdan, 38–53. New York: Teachers College Press.

Varady, D. P. 2005. *Desegregating the city: Ghettos, enclaves, and inequality.* Albany: State Univ. of New York Press.

Von Hoffman, A. 2003. *House by house, block by block.* New York: Oxford Univ. Press.

Waddock, S. A. 1995. *Not by schools alone.* Westport, Conn.: Praeger.

Warren, M. R. 2001. *Dry bones rattling.* Princeton, N.J.: Princeton Univ. Press.

Wilson, W. J. 1996. *When work disappears.* New York: Knopf.

Wilson, W. J., and R. P. Taub. 2006. *There goes the neighborhood.* New York: Knopf.

Winship, C. 2002. End of a miracle? Crime, faith, and partnership in Boston in the 1990s. Kennedy School of Government, Harvard University, Rappaport Policy Notes. http://tcdata.hmdc.harvard.edu/pndata/details.php?recordID=100165.

————. 2006. Policy analysis as puzzle-solving. In *The Oxford handbook of public policy,* ed. M. Moran, M. Rein, and R. Goodin. New York: Oxford Univ. Press.

Wolfinger, R. E. 1974. *The politics of progress.* Englewood Cliffs, N.J.: Prentice-Hall.

Yee, G. 2003. From Court Street to city hall. In *A race against time,* ed. J. Cibulka and W. Boyd, 82–105. Westport, Conn.: Praeger.

13. Clarence N. Stone and the Study of Urban Politics

Jennifer Hochschild

URBAN POLITICS AND COMPARATIVE NATIONAL POLITICS

Among political scientists, the study of urban politics, whether within one nation or cross nationally, resembles the comparative study of national politics—with one crucial exception. In both the urban field and the comparative field, scholars typically come to know one or several localities very well. Their knowledge ranges across academic disciplines, encompassing language and culture, history and tradition, economic dynamics and outputs, social structures and processes, political institutions and actors, and perhaps international contexts and events. In the course of acquiring such rich knowledge, scholars frequently develop strong attachments to their location. They also often affirm the view that one needs detailed particularistic understanding of the idiosyncrasies of a given place in order to study it effectively.

Of course, some scholars of urban politics, as of comparative national politics, tend in the opposite direction. They seek out aggregated data that are standardized across locations, and they develop parsimonious theories intended to apply across particular situations. This set of scholars seeks to compare many sites along a specific, small set of dimensions rather than examining one or a few sites across an array of dimensions. They may see particular historical, cultural, geographic, or political details as extraneous complications to be set aside in the quest for explainable regularities.

The parallels continue: no matter what the approach, those who study local communities and those who study nations or regions must engage with similar intellectual and empirical concerns. Where are the boundaries of the location or locations, and should they be defined differently depending on the question at hand? What consequences flow from the fact that a given place lies within a larger political unit—Cleveland within Ohio and the United States; France within the European Union or G8? Do distinctive cultural, ethnic, religious, economic, or linguistic characteristics of the population matter for a given analytic question, or are they irrelevant? How much variation in the quality and construction of data is acceptable if one seeks to compare across locations or time periods? How can one take full account of the location or locations that one knows less well compared with the places that one knows intimately?

A final parallel is especially pertinent to this chapter. Until recently, scholars have been more inclined to do methodological battle over the right approach than to meld them or seek some alternative framing. The rise and partial fall of area studies within the field of comparative national politics is well known, and one can find traces of similar arcs within the study of urban politics. But in both fields, arguably those scholars with the most profound and valuable impact have transcended this dispute, whether by combining aggregated and particularistic analyses, or by developing broad theories flexible enough to apply in varied situations but incisive enough to frame a distinctive viewpoint.

Clarence Stone is in the latter camp, with disturbingly few peers in political science scholarship on urban politics. He is deeply knowledgeable about Atlanta, Georgia, having studied its political development for decades. He is familiar with a dozen other American cities, having studied their educational reform efforts for years. With coauthors or independently, he has developed broad theoretical frameworks—regime analysis, the "power to" approach, the systemic bias of power and inequality, the centrality of agenda setting and coordination, the urgent need for democratic decision making—that explain actions and outcomes not only in his cities but in many others as well. All of this work is undergirded by a few simple, clear principles about human nature and the conduct of social science that are easy to state and surprisingly fecund.

Before commenting on this body of work, I must point out one way in which the study of urban politics and the study of comparative national politics are emphatically not parallel: the former is largely in abeyance while the latter is thriving. The editor of the *American Political Science Review* (*APSR*) reported in 2005 that "comparative politics ... now challenges the numerical dominance of American politics submissions [to the *Review*], a turn of events that not very long ago would have been widely regarded as an extremely remote possibility" (Sigelman 2005, 138). He does not distinguish urban politics within the broader field of American politics (or within comparative politics, for that matter). But in the Introduction to this volume, Marion Orr and Valerie Johnson point out that only a tiny fraction of articles in *APSR* have ever addressed urban politics, even taking into account its heyday in the 1960s and 1970s.

Even more telling about the relative disciplinary strength of the study of urban politics and comparative national politics is membership in the American Political Science Association's organized sections. Section membership, unlike publication in journals, is completely voluntary and exhibits no competition for scarce space because every APSA member may join any number of sections for a nominal annual dues payment. In 2006, a total of 346 people belonged to the Urban Politics section; it was one of the smallest of the 34 sections. The section on Comparative Politics enjoyed 1,594 members—almost double the size of the next largest section. Membership in the Urban Politics section peaked at 467 in 1992 and has been slowly declining since. During the same period, membership in the Comparative Politics section has steadily risen from almost exactly the same starting membership in 1989. Something is working for one field and not for the other, despite considerable methodological and substantive similarities.[1]

An examination of Clarence Stone's research accomplishments shows how unfortunate this abeyance is, and it suggests some ways that scholars might be able to overcome it.[2]

OCCAM'S RAZOR AND LANYI'S BALLOON

My undergraduate classmates and I thought it a sophisticated witticism to compare Occam's razor (about which we had just learned) to Lanyi's balloon. George Lanyi was a much loved professor at Oberlin College who responded to almost any observation (in Hungarian-flavored English) that "things are much more complicated than that." He was not just an obstructionist; he could in fact demonstrate complexities and subtleties at the heart of most topics of interest to political scientists. And our labored witticism actually did point to an important issue: in seeking to explain a phenomenon or process, should one try to chip away superfluities to arrive at its essence, or should one recognize and take into account its many interactions, contingencies, and dimensions?

Clarence Stone is a devotee of Lanyi's balloon. All of the essays in this volume show in one way or another his belief that "politics . . . , business . . . , and civil society are woven together in intricate ways. . . . Urban regime analysis is therefore an effort to . . . penetrate how these various sectors are woven together. . . . The sum . . . is greater than the parts" ("Urban Politics Then and Now," this volume). He constantly points to intersections among causal forces, the need to distinguish one policy regime from another (in recent work), variations in historical trajectories, differences in governance dynamics across cities, varying interests and resources of political actors, and other ways of taming complexity without simplifying it.

Conversely, Stone is critical of scholars who adhere to Occam's razor. In his view, Paul Peterson's *City Limits* is valuable as far as it goes, but it makes simplistic distinctions that connect poorly with the messiness of actual policy making. Even more problematically, in his view, *City Limits* is premised on the claim that an economic framework is all one needs to make sense of what cities do or do not do. Stone criticizes Peterson for not attending to the political dynamics of power and choice or the social dynamics of demand and creativity. Even Robert Dahl's *Who*

Governs? (1961), with which Stone has been in "a career-long dialogue," is too sim-plistic from the vantage point of Lanyi's balloon.[3] Unlike Peterson, Dahl does attend carefully to politics—but Stone argues that like Peterson, Dahl pays too little atten-tion to systemic interactions among societal, economic, and political forces. Fur-thermore, according to Stone, Dahl defines politics too narrowly as elections, and their outcomes as visible and discrete decisions, thereby ignoring political actions ranging from agenda control to incipient protest.

A proponent of parsimony might reply that Stone is descriptively correct—Peterson builds his theory on simple distinctions among policy types and their material base, whereas Dahl focuses narrowly on electoral politics and its out-comes—but substantively mistaken. In this view, what the study of urban politics (or any politics?) needs is a few sharply delineated and straightforward theories from which one can derive testable propositions, which one should then test. After all, in this view, recognition that the urban world is complicated, interactive, and somewhat contingent is, judging by the work of too many researchers, an invita-tion to endless description and idiosyncratic interpretation of particular cases. So, a proponent of parsimony might conclude, Stone and a few other urbanists should perhaps continue to explore the complexity of city governance while most schol-ars should aim for the narrower but more rigorous goal of identifying analytic tools or models that will point to the few most relevant facts, relationships, and causes.

I do not propose to adjudicate between Occam's razor and Lanyi's balloon. This is an old debate, spread across most subfields of political science and perhaps across most social sciences. Its relevance here is twofold. First, it indicates one of Stone's distinctive and perhaps singular virtues; he is able both to insist on complexity *and* to distill from it a clear-cut, testable set of propositions. Consider urban regime analysis: Stone and his students used its broad earlier incarnation to identify diverse sorts of electoral and governance dynamics in different kinds of cities, and Stone and his coauthors have used its more narrow recent incarnation to delineate gov-ernance dynamics in distinct policy arenas within a given city or across cities.[4] Those are major achievements, comparable respectively to the broad delineation of "three worlds of welfare capitalism" (Esping-Andersen 1990) and the more fo-cused comparison among national policies of vocational training (Thelen 2004) in comparative politics.

Second, a robust discussion about the best way to explain city governance—many complex interactions or a few dominant forces—might go a long way toward reviv-ing the subfield of urban politics within political science. It would at any rate be one element of a broad strategy of (re-)connecting research on city governance with research on national governance. Let a hundred flowers bloom; scholars of urban politics should develop and encourage the use of formal models or rational choice methods to study cities, along with more traditional approaches that rely on case studies, historical trajectories, survey research, or aggregate data analyses. Stone's corpus sets the standard for one kind of methodological framework; I would urge others to adopt his breadth of vision and turn it in other directions.

HOW ARE CITIES LIKE AND NOT LIKE OTHER POLITICAL UNITS?

The broad strategy of (re-)connecting research on city governance with research on national governance must surely be substantive as well as methodological. There are plenty of links to be made. Again, Stone set the standard, drawing on Hannah Arendt's theories of power, E. E. Schattschneider's analysis of the mobilization of bias, V. O. Key's commitment to a more equal citizenry, Dahl's depiction of pluralism as a goal if not a practice, scholarship in international relations on regimes, cognitive models of framing and agenda setting, W. E. B. DuBois's recognition of the interactions between race and class, and more. Perhaps few other scholars can realistically aspire to such a broad range, but that need not prevent us from pursuing at least more particular connections.

For example, should researchers focus on the capacity of bureaucrats and other state actors to achieve their stated goals? That question could bring the classic insights of *Who Governs?* into direct contact with the thriving literature on bringing the state back in (Skocpol 1985) and bureaucratic autonomy (Carpenter 2001). Perhaps scholarship could usefully focus on path dependence of a city's development, such that its political dynamics are best explained by the timing of its origin, its early development, and choices at critical junctures. In that case, the excellent historical writing about many urban locations could be connected with theoretical work on "politics in time" and political development (Pierson 2004; Orren and Skowronek 2004). Attention to economic and public choice imperatives would start with *City Limits* but move beyond it into recent research on the role of states in a global economy or the impact of rational self-interest within institutional structures. If city councils are enough like national legislatures, then research on the pivotal voter, principal-agent relations, committee dynamics, or electoral imperatives can be brought to bear. Is racial tension in American cities analogous to ethnic conflict in nations around the world? If so, the rich literature on civil wars and intranational conflict could illuminate the history of American riots, and vice versa. Cities compete with one another, develop formal ties for mutual benefit, and trade goods, people, and information. Thus aspects of scholarly writing on international political economy, or even international security studies, could suggest intriguing analytic frameworks—including, but not limited to, regime theory. If interracial coalitions are important to city governance, as they surely are, urbanists could start

322   JENNIFER HOCHSCHILD

with Browning, Marshall, and Tabb's canonical *Racial Politics in American Cities* (1990) and then link it to the rich array of game theoretic work on coalitional strategies and failures.

Any (re-)connection between the study of politics in cities and mainstream political science writings on politics in nations will also need to attend to what is special about cities. Their geographic scale and physical location are obviously different from that of most national governments. How do size and scope matter to governance and activity? (Dahl and Tufte 1973; Katzenstein 1985; Alesina and Spolaore 2003). Cities are near the bottom of a federal system, while national legislatures and executives are near the top. How does that matter? Surely the literatures on federalism, state and regional politics, and cities have much to say to each other, both about nested relationships and about distinctive locations (Manna 2006; Baimbridge and Whyman 2004). Cities have no court system comparable in importance and visibility to the federal judicial system; how does the relative lack of a judiciary change the study of relations among branches of government? Above all, as Stone's research has shown so powerfully, cities operate through a complex web of face-to-face, neighborhood-to-neighborhood, group-to-group, business-to-business, ward-boss-to-ward-heeler relationships. People in national governments have direct connections with one another, but the nature and role of civil society is arguably dramatically different in cities than in nations (Mansbridge 1980; Berry, Portney, and Thomson 1993; Mutz 2006; Fung 2004).

Thus it makes no more sense to treat the study of urban politics as simply a miniversion of the study of national politics than it does to treat the study of urban politics as sui generis. Stone's insistence on the importance of complex interpersonal relationships in cities sometimes seems to suggest the latter, but his grounding in broad normative and analytic theories of politics, and his capacity to develop testable theories that move across locations and arenas, pulls his research back from that unhelpful path. If more scholars of both national and local politics would link propositions about cities to research on the study of nations, the field of urban politics would be stronger and more attractive to young scholars.

"POWER TO"

Stone's focus on power both in this volume and throughout his research warrants as much close attention as his research on urban regime analysis. Part of the reason is simply its existence; too much scholarship on cities (as well as other political phenomena) ignores power altogether. That observation holds both within political science and in a comparison between political science and comparable disciplines. As an indicator of the former point, consider a simple word count in JSTOR. Among

10 major peer-reviewed political science journals from 1995 to 2007,[5] the combination of words "political power" and "city" appeared 184 times, compared with "economy" and "city" 455 times, and "culture" and "city" 405 times. Nothing much should be made of these absolute numbers, but the ratios of more than two to one is at least suggestive.

As an indicator of the latter point, consider disciplines similar to political science but without the focus on power at their core. There, the study of urbanism is thriving. With the development of GIS programs and connections to an array of other disciplines, urban geography is making a comeback; it is the second largest specialty group in the Association of American Geographers (note from Elvin Wyly to author, March 14, 2007). In sociology, the section on Community and Urban Sociology has a new journal, and membership rose from "the mid-500 level" several years ago to 725 in 2006 (fall 2006 newsletter, available at http://www.commurb.org/). (The American Sociological Association is slightly smaller than the APSA.) So it is not that the study of cities is of no interest to scholars; instead, the investigation of power or politics in cities seems to be what lacks appeal.[6]

Instead of focusing on the accretion and exercise of power by human actors, urbanist political scientists typically frame their arguments in terms of structures or institutions so that theoretically disembodied forces do all the work. As Stone puts it in "Urban Politics Then and Now" (this volume), "In many urban analyses complex structures tend to be reduced to an economic imperative," whether understood as capitalist market forces or as rational self-interest. Into this partial conceptual vacuum, his robust and subtle analysis of the difference between "power over" and "power to" is a welcome insertion. Giving pride of place to power to rather than power over is an innovative move, and accords well with regime analysis. Stone notes, "Without denying that 'power over' (control) is an important facet of human relationships, let us think about 'power to' (moving from an incapacity to act toward enjoying such a capacity). . . . Interdependence becomes a central fact"— just as it is the crucial feature of regime analysis ("Urban Politics," this volume). Thinking of power as control might accord best with Occam's razor—such a definition strips the essentially contested concept down to its bare essentials—but thinking of power as effective interdependence certainly fits with Lanyi's balloon. Power thus understood is complicated, multifaceted, and hard to measure—according to proponents of regime analysis, necessarily so.

Power understood as interdependence in pursuit of capacity to achieve a goal opens a multitude of analytic possibilities, despite the difficulties in operationalizing and measuring it. It can explain total frustration of effort: the mayor can do little to improve schooling outcomes because the school board is independently elected, the school budget is separate from the city's budget, the teachers' union is concerned mainly to protect its members, the superintendent works at the pleasure of the board, advocacy groups seek an array of particular reforms, courts are overseeing expenditures for special education, the federal government is promulgating unfunded mandates, administrators are focused on developing black social capital throughout the city, and middle-class families are moving to the suburbs. And that sentence does not even mention the enormous difficulties in the best of circumstances involved in getting teenagers to concentrate on chemistry labs and vocabulary tests!

Power understood as interdependence might, however, permit a more optimistic analysis in some circumstances, explaining, for example, the breakup of old systems of domination and subordination. As Stone showed in Atlanta, sometimes the mayor needs the votes of members of previously ignored groups or neighborhoods, or downtown business leaders need the help of an insurgent mayor, or advocacy groups can use their resources to bargain for benefits to their members. "Interdependence is thus not a basis for an unceasing war of all against all. Quite the contrary, it is a foundation for seeking workable alignments. . . . There are many potential partnerships" ("Urban Politics," this volume). Stone's recent work with an array of coauthors to study educational reform politics in 11 American cities not only displays highly productive scholarly interdependence, but also documents the successes possible in the public arena—even with regard to school reform—when interacting partners pull in the same direction with a shared purpose.

I see intriguing affinities between Stone's analysis of "power to" and the concepts of some feminist theorists. Anna Yeatman, for example, describes one feminist understanding of power as "capacity . . . —an active and experimental relationship to established and not-yet-established models of self-governance. . . . A democratic state which respects . . . the rights of women . . . constitutes women as agents in their own right who are entitled to the status of a rights-bearing person" (Yeatman 1997, 153–54, emphasis deleted). That sounds very similar to Stone's analysis of how to incorporate poor neighborhoods into an urban governance regime: "The policy 'game' is . . . a more open-ended matter . . . with appreciation that long-term well-being individually and collectively involves interdependence." The new urban agenda requires "the building of associational bridges between the disconnected populations of cities and mainstream institutions" ("Urban Politics," this volume). Not-yet-established and open-ended; models of self-governance and building of associational bridges; agents in their own right and disconnected populations—the contexts of these two analyses are quite different, but the concepts and aspirations are similar.

Yeatman's description of power as capacity is echoed by other feminist theorists. The idea of

[e]mpowerment . . . center[ed] . . . on how people developed and expressed a political consciousness. . . . [It] shifted attention to communities, in addition to the more con-

ventionally studied individuals and institutions. Indeed, one could even speak of the empowerment, as opposed to the power, of an entire polity. . . . [I]ts powers were bounded by what the community thought was the purpose of the community (Flammang 1997, 33, describing the ideas of Joan Tronto; see also Hartsock 1983).

Again, one can see links between this concept and Stone and his coauthors' work on urban school reform. Their comparative study of 11 cities showed clearly that a necessary (though insufficient) condition for improving education was that salient community members, ranging from mayor to business leaders to poor parents, were jointly empowered in pursuit of a common "purpose of the community."

To my knowledge, neither Stone nor the feminist theorists have used, or are aware of, the research of the other. That lack of interaction has left the analyses on each side thinner. Flammang usefully reviews various writings on whether—or better, when—women as advocates, voters, bureaucrats, and politicians are more likely than men to focus on "power to" rather than "power over." She also addresses the more interesting question of when agencies or processes focus on empowerment rather than domination. She considers local civic organizations, welfare reform efforts, health care, and even education reform—all issues of central importance to cities—to see how new conceptions of power might affect their practices and outcomes. Stone's analysis of successful urban regimes, especially but not only in schooling, would have enhanced her discussion. Conversely, the feminists' subtle and exciting exploration of alternative ways to conceive of power, new ways to study and promote shared empowerment, and the distinctive role of women would contribute to Stone's critiques of the pluralist and power elite frameworks. It could also deepen the explanations that Stone and his coauthors provide for varying levels of success across cities in efforts to improve schooling.

It is not too late for both sides to start that discussion. What, concretely and materially, is needed to shift an urban regime from being preoccupied with domination to encouraging empowerment? What is required for mayors to learn that their chief concern should be enhancing shared capacity rather than controlling potential adversaries? Does electing women to the mayoralty or city council make a difference; do women business leaders behave differently from their male predecessors? Flammang and others have noted that community organizations are often started and maintained by women; under what circumstances can men develop the same aptitude for bridge building? The crucial move here would be to specify clearly and in a way that would lead to falsifiable propositions just what capacity building looks like, how it develops, and what it can effect. By this criterion, Stone's work is farther along than that of most feminist theorists, because he is more of a social scientist than they typically are. But overall, the study of urban politics would greatly benefit from engagement with gender politics and feminist theory (as well as vice versa).

Other arenas of political science also study "power to," although they seldom invoke the term. The study of agenda setting from a rational choice framework, and of issue framing from a psychological framework, are both close cousins to the conception of power as the capacity to accomplish a task in a complex environment. Linking Stone's focus on differentially distributed access to points of leverage for change with formal models of how actors in institutions control the options available for decision making, for example, would bring a particular type of rigor to the former and a whiff of reality to the latter. Both would benefit.

Stone's innovative analysis of power has a broader implication. A weakness of our discipline is that the central concept, power, has no consensual small set of definitions or measures, analogous to money for economists or class for sociologists. Definitions of power have ranged from Max Weber's and Robert Dahl's epigram, "A gets B to do what B would not otherwise do," to Hannah Arendt's and Richard Neustadt's claim that power is the ability to persuade, to Steven Lukes's and John Gaventa's "third face" of ideological obfuscation, to Michel Foucault's vision of power as a discipline in the capillaries. Stone adds another understanding. It is high time that more political scientists focus directly on studying power. No one should indulge the false hope of resolving the question of what it *is*, but our numerous and increasingly sophisticated measurement tools, concepts, and data sources could produce an exciting and illuminating debate, and maybe even a few points of shared insight. Urbanists could play a central role in this discussion; they have manageably sized cases, excellent comparative possibilities, well-honed concepts, a great deal of local knowledge, a passionate commitment to empowerment (in most cases), a rich array of aggregated data, and a wide set of questions that cry out for more systematic evidence and analysis.

DEMOCRACY AND INEQUALITY

Stone (like feminist theorists) is not foolish enough to jettison traditional understandings of power as control or domination. As he points out in various writings, "power over" must remain a central concept in any study of structural and interpersonal inequality. And the study of inequality in a purported democracy has been a driving motivator of his research from the earliest publications. In fact, Stone describes his career-long dialogue with *Who Governs?* not at all in methodological terms as I did above, but rather as a substantive debate with Dahl

> about the fundamental nature of political inequality in a formally democratic system.
> ... A major reason for focusing on regime rather than decision is to focus on capacities to
> shape governing arrangements, as opposed to influence on discrete decisions. Looking

at the level of governing arrangements makes the threshold issue [that is, how many political resources are needed to change the established order] salient and provides greater
opportunity to consider stratification-based bias (Note to author, January 30, 2007).

I see no reason to dispute Stone on that claim; his commitment to reducing inequality and enhancing democracy shines through in everything that he writes. To
choose only one illustration, "The challenge is to find leverage points to lessen the
impact of socioeconomic inequalities. Ultimately that is where this essay is heading.
Normatively that is what regime analysis is about" ("Urban Politics," this volume).

Two points about those sentences warrant discussion in the context of my
broader consideration of the present and future study of urban politics. First, they
show clearly how much Stone's research is rooted in moral and programmatic
rather than purely empirical or scientific commitments. In this, he resembles most
other urbanists, but arguably fewer other political scientists. For example, Peter
Dreier, John Mollenkopf, and Todd Swanstrom's book of political geography, *Place
Matters*, includes a chapter on "What Cities Can and Cannot Do to Address
Poverty," and they describe the book as "not only a synthesis of research findings
but also as a roadmap for reform" (2004, xi). J. Phillip Thompson issues a "call for
deep democracy" in the subtitle of *Double Trouble* in the hopes that his book will
"unveil . . . painful *internal* oppressions and exclusions within black politics for the
purpose of increasing the black community's power to compel similar unveiling in
broader interracial politics" (2005, ix). Even Douglas Rae, who despairs of the future
of urbanism as we have known it, concludes *City* with explicit recommendations
for "seek[ing] an urban future . . . that recaptures much of what was desirable on
the 'soft' side of urbanism" (2003, 422).

Conversely, a plurality, and perhaps a majority, of research-oriented political
scientists aspire to be "real" scientists, or at least do not see themselves to be conducting research in order to promote their normative commitments. Most scholars of comparative national politics, to return to my original point of comparison,
eschew exhortations about reform in studies of the political economy of industri-
alized nations or the nature of welfare state regimes. Similarly, most scholars of
congressional lawmaking or political party identification or principal-agent relations in bureaucracies make no effort to suggest how the House of Representatives,
the Republican Party, or the Department of Energy should do its work better. The
point holds broadly across political science. As the editor of *APSR*, Lee Sigelman,
has documented, the purpose of only 1.2% of articles in *APSR* since its inception a
century ago has been "policy prescription or criticism." Only another 2.9% of articles in *APSR* have combined "policy prescription or criticism and presentation
of empirical results." Virtually all articles in both categories were published before 1956. "If . . . contributing directly to public dialogue about the merits and

demerits of various courses of action were still numbered among the functions of the profession, one would not have known it from leafing through its leading journal" (Sigelman 2006, 467).

Like all generalizations, this one has exceptions on both sides. On the one hand, many articles and some books in the field of urban politics are carefully descriptive or explanatory, without any particular normative purpose in view. On the other hand, some scholarship on national institutions or comparative state politics *is* explicitly prescriptive. Thomas Mann and Norman Ornstein (2006) published a heartfelt plea to Congress to get back on track, and surely the many studies of the causes of ethnic conflict or civil war are written in the hope of helping to reduce their incidence. More broadly, postmodern scholarship has taught us that it is virtually impossible to escape one's own value stances in one's research, no matter how apparently esoteric or ruthlessly empirical it is. As Stone argues, "the alternatives appear not to be science versus reformism, but celebratory analysis versus critical analysis" (note to author, January 30, 2007).

Nevertheless, overt political and policy prescription is different from implicit, or unconscious, revelation of moral values. And urbanists, including Stone, do much more of the former than do most political scientists. I have no quarrel with the commitment to recommend policies or to promote particular values through one's research—I do both myself. Nevertheless, those of us who reject the ideal of a value-free, neutral social science must realize that this taste for reformism, especially because most of it comes from the liberal left, is one more way in which the study of urban politics is separated from most other empirical subfields of political science.[7] And it may have contributed to the field's relative and absolute decline in adherents. That is a price I am willing to pay, as are others, but it is a steep one.

The second point to note about Stone's claim that "the challenge is to find leverage points to lessen the impact of socioeconomic inequalities. . . . Normatively that is what regime analysis is about" is more substantive. Unlike many scholars who study race and ethnicity, he sees class dynamics as being just as important in shaping cities as, if not more important than, the black-white racial divide. Stone never loses sight of the power of race to organize structures, opportunities, and outlooks in the United States. Nevertheless, one comes away from the Atlanta books with the sense that a person's wealth arguably has more impact on his or her life chances than does race. After all, black mayors found that in order to get anything done, they needed to deal with white downtown business owners almost exactly as white mayors had done or would have done in their place. That is where the bite in "power to accomplish" really lies. And as Stone points out at the beginning of this volume's "Urban Politics Then and Now," repeated efforts to help poor neighborhoods in Atlanta have fizzled out, in part because wealthy and powerful black leaders have not given those efforts their highest commitment: "Atlanta's biracial coalition handles some matters well, but not others."

Thus, in Stone's understanding of urban regimes, elite actors almost inevitably ally with one another, and their pursuit of their own interests or their efforts to get things done for the city almost inevitably conflict with the interests of nonelites, especially the poor. Furthermore, Stone's analysis of the threshold problem in supposedly pluralist cities points to a larger structural issue with regard to class: "incumbent leadership/established arrangements enjoy substantial advantages . . . and . . . inertia is on the side of an established order. . . . Substantial resources, allies, skills etc. are needed . . . to displace that order with a new one" (note to author, January 30, 2007). And by definition, poor residents of a city lack substantial resources.

I mostly agree with Stone on this point, perhaps because I learned it from him. But the most important point is yet broader: the field of urban politics needs more newly conceived investigations of whether, when, and how urban governance is genuinely open to an array of interests and commitments, or is so tightly constrained that "democracy is a stone of Sisyphus" (to quote Stone's note once again). Dahl examined how unequal persons can effectively express political agency; Stone focuses on the structural and individual barriers to genuine change; Peterson developed the view that the relationship between classes is mutually enhancing rather than competitive, and in any case close to inevitable; Browning and coauthors sought for ways to develop coalitions across races (and therefore presumably across classes). Presumably there are other lenses through which to examine how cities and their residents contribute to the making or prevention of democracy; scholars who create them could revitalize the study of urban politics.

TOWARDS A SPATIAL THEORY OF CITIES

The boundary around a city defines the political and policy work of mayors and other urban public officials. But for many urgent concerns, that may be true more in a formal or superficial sense than in a deeper structural sense. That is, the activities of urban political actors or the trajectory of a city may be largely shaped by the horizontal relationship between a city and its adjacent communities or by the vertical relationship between a city and its state, region, national government, or supranational organization (such as the EU). This observation suggests that another way to invigorate the study of urban politics would be to develop spatial theories of politics analogous to what Paul Pierson and others have been doing for a theory of political time (Pierson 2004; Orren and Skowronek 2004; Skowronek 1993).

I do not have a fully developed argument here; that awaits more sustained attention.[8] One way to frame the enterprise would be to "direct attention to the 'politics of scale'—the processes by which scale is constructed" through state laws on taxation or incorporation, the creation of regional governance structures, devolution of decision making to neighborhoods, and so on (note from Susan Clarke to author, February 7, 2007). Alternatively, one could direct attention to the scale of politics—that is, ways in which face-to-face engagement shapes political interactions compared with ways in which links among very large numbers of voters shape distinctly different political interactions. In lieu of a developed theory, let me offer several illustrations of actual or possible analyses of the politics of space:

- Inequalities within cities are intimately, perhaps causally, connected to inequalities between cities and suburbs. As Rae argues, "resources are most available in [suburban] towns. . . . Needs are fewest in those same places. Resources are fewest on a per capita basis in New Haven [and similar cities], and needs greatest. To a very considerable extent, inequalities reinforce one another. . . . Being able to choose *where* is a more powerful instrument for deciding *what* and *how* one's family will live than anything else. . . . *[E]xit* has become even more vital than *voice*" (2003, 421, emphasis in original).
- Conversely, a suburb may be attractive socially and economically (but not politically?) to the degree that it is near a thriving city. Features ranging from the density and variety of cultural and artistic institutions and face-to-face interactions among high-end service industries such as financial firms and research hospitals, to mundane matters such as access to public transportation and airports or availability of a low-wage work force, make living in a community near a city more appealing. How suburbanites engage with the city will affect the inequalities that Rae describes.
- A "city" whose boundaries encompass a large, sparsely populated area has different resources and policy options with regard to such issues as public school desegregation, tax policy, waste treatment, water supply, and land use planning than a city whose boundaries are narrowly drawn. It will also have a different political configuration. The point is longitudinal as well as cross-sectional; how boundaries change over time will be of great importance to a spatial theory of politics.
- External interventions by encompassing political units, such as state takeovers of failing schools or judicial intervention in the creation of voting districts, might undermine local civic capacity by creating an environment in which power seems to be "out of our hands." Alternatively, activity by a larger government might help to even out disparities in political resources.
- The local business community might respond to frustration with local public bureaucracies by appealing to larger political units, such as state, national, or even supranational legislators, to mandate structural reforms in schools, health care, natural resource management, transportation, or housing policy. That intervention too could enhance or reduce inequalities, and could expand or contract resources and policy options, within cities or between cities and nearby communities.[9]

- Cities that are tightly connected with global markets, in part because of their location or topography, will have different trajectories from cities that are only loosely involved with international trade and migration (Sassen 2006).
- The topography of cities and their surrounding metropolitan areas may have important political implications; areas with a lot of rivers have more school districts than areas without, as Caroline Hoxby has pointed out.

This list is far from complete, and it is even farther from being a coherent analytic framework for studying politics in space. But I hope that it suggests some of the wide array of research endeavors that are or could be underway—and especially that it suggests how unifying these endeavors under a broader theoretical umbrella of spatial politics would enable them to add up to more than the sum of individual investigations.

CONCLUSION

Sigelman concludes his review of a century of *APSR* articles by arguing that "the period from the late 1950s through 1970 or so . . . [was] the one in which political science research was most ambitious, innovative, stimulating, and important—certainly more than it is today" (2006, 473). That was also the golden age of the study of urban politics; is that a coincidence? Sigelman deplores the growth of subfield specialization, in which "a given paper will be selected for publication because it passes muster among a narrow range of specialists rather than because it is considered to be of potentially great interest and importance to a broad range of readers" (475). My main message in this chapter is similar. Scholarship would be enhanced if students of national politics overcame their assumption that bigger is better, whether in political importance or disciplinary status. By ignoring local arenas, they miss opportunities for careful comparative research, important policy arenas, and the invitation to engage with issues of scale and scope. At the same time, scholars of urban politics need to do more to connect with other subfields of political science, to deepen the theoretical dimension of space in their research, to get more leverage from comparisons among cities within and across nations, and to develop testable, causal theories and careful measurement of concepts such as power, regime, scale, and inequality. I hope that they need not also abandon normative ideals and a commitment to reform—although they might usefully be less committed to the proposition that only the liberal left has legitimate ideas for reform. On the normative and policy dimension, they should lead rather than follow the rest of the discipline.

In all of these arenas, Clarence Stone's work has indeed led the rest of us. If this book stimulates more research of the quality of his own, it will be a success.

ACKNOWLEDGMENTS

I am grateful to generous colleagues who commented on early drafts of this chapter—Susan Clarke, Jeffrey Henig, Bryan Jones, John Mollenkopf, Marion Orr, Joshua Sapotichne, Lee Sigelman, and Clarence Stone. They preserved me from errors, pushed me to deepen my arguments, and provided valuable information and insights. They are, of course, not responsible for the claims and mistakes that remain. Thanks also to my students and colleagues who insightfully responded to my informal survey about the state of the urban politics field; their observations and complaints substantially influenced this essay.

NOTES

1. Thanks to Sean Twombly for information on APSA section membership, from the association's database.

Of course, it is possible that specialists in urban politics choose to join other sections, such as Race, Ethnicity, and Politics; Public Policy; or Comparative Politics, thus skewing the numbers and concealing their interest in the field. Market dynamics may have something to do with this: many jobs are defined as Comparative, and thus scholars so classify themselves. If so, these patterns reinforce rather than refute my claim that urban politics is a weak (and weakening?) subfield in political science. After all, one need not leave the Urban section to join another; of the 8,000 or so members of APSA who belong to at least one section, 5,200 (about two-thirds) belong to more than one section. Nevertheless, the section on Race, Ethnicity, and Politics is growing rapidly (from 248 when it was formed in 1996 to 599 in 2006), while Urban Politics is declining. And the fact that political science departments now find it useful to orient hiring and teaching around the field of comparative politics but no longer around the field of urban politics is a further indication of the relative strengths of the two arenas in disciplinary terms.

2. It is perhaps relevant that I do not consider myself an urbanist and am not usually considered one by others. However, I belong to the Urban Politics section of APSA, and my research and teaching cover many of the same topics that urbanists address, so I am a fellow traveler.

3. Stone has other crucial, and more substantive, disagreements with Dahl's *Who Governs?* (1961), which I discuss below.

4. Thanks to Archon Fung for pointing out these changes in the way that Stone has described regime analysis since its initial deployment in *Regime Politics* (1989).

5. Operationally, 2007 means the most recent year that JSTOR includes for any given journal. The journals were: *American Journal of Political Science, American Political Science Review, British Journal of Political Science, Comparative Politics, Journal of Conflict Resolution, Journal of Politics, Perspectives on Politics, Political Theory, Public Opinion Quarterly,* and *Social Science History.*

6. Another example: in the 2006 conference of the interdisciplinary Urban Affairs Association, *power* appeared in only eight unique uses in the program, which listed about 100 panels and 300 papers (http://www.udel.edu/uaa/). (One additional use referred to power stations.) In contrast, variants of *culture* appeared twice as often as *power* in the program, and *economic* appeared about four times as frequently.

7. An alternative to encouraging purportedly value-free social science in the field of urban politics would be to encourage expression of a multiplicity of values and corresponding policy recommendations. Nothing, of course, prevents people of varying ideological commitments from teaching or publishing on urban politics. Nevertheless, except for the arena of education policy

and occasionally racial politics, few political scientists generate socially or economically conservative analyses of cities' problems or opportunities. Despite important exceptions, I am fairly sure that conservatives feel less welcome at conferences or convention panels on urban issues than do scholars who identify with the left. How to change that situation remains unclear.

8. Nor is this point especially new; see, e.g., Lineberry (1975); Williams (1975); Danielson and Lewis (1996); and Hayward (2006).

9. Variants of the latter two ideas were developed by Jeffrey Henig in a note to the author and, with coauthors, in *The Color of School Reform* (1999).

REFERENCES

Alesina, A., and E. Spolaore. 2003. *The size of nations.* Cambridge, Mass.: MIT Press.

Baimbridge, M., and P. Whyman, eds. 2004. *Fiscal federalism and European economic integration.* London: Routledge.

Berry, J., K. Portney, and K. Thomson. 1993. *The rebirth of urban democracy.* Washington, D.C.: Brookings Institution.

Browning, R., D. Rogers Marshall, and D. Tabb. 1990. *Racial politics in American cities.* New York: Longman.

Carpenter, D. 2001. *The forging of bureaucratic autonomy: Reputations, networks, and policy innovation in executive agencies, 1862–1928.* Princeton, N.J.: Princeton Univ. Press.

Dahl, R. A. 1961. *Who governs?* New Haven, Conn.: Yale Univ. Press.

Dahl, R. A., and E. Tufte. 1973. *Size and democracy.* Stanford, Calif.: Stanford Univ. Press.

Danielson, M., and P. Lewis. 1996. City bound: Political science and the American metropolis. *Political Research Quarterly* 49 (1): 203–20.

Dreier, P., J. Mollenkopf, and T. Swanstrom. 2001. *Place matters: Metropolitics for the twenty-first century.* Lawrence: Univ. Press of Kansas.

Esping-Andersen, G. 1990. *The three worlds of welfare capitalism.* Princeton, N.J.: Princeton Univ. Press.

Flammang, J. 1997. *Women's political voice: How women are transforming the practice and study of politics.* Philadelphia: Temple Univ. Press.

Fung, A. 2004. *Empowered participation: Reinventing urban democracy.* Princeton, N.J.: Princeton Univ. Press.

Hartsock, N. 1983. *Money, sex, and power: Toward a feminist historical materialism.* New York: Longman.

Hayward, C. 2006. *The power of space: Identity, interest, action.* Philadelphia: American Political Science Association.

Henig, J., R. Hula, M. Orr, and D. Pedescleaux. 1999. *The color of school reform: Race, politics, and the challenge of urban education.* Princeton, N.J.: Princeton Univ. Press.

Katzenstein, P. 1985. *Small states in world markets: Industrial policy in Europe.* Ithaca, N.Y.: Cornell Univ. Press.

Lineberry, R. 1975. Suburbia and the metropolitan turf. *Annals of the American Academy of Political and Social Science* 422 (Nov.): 1–9.

Mann, T., and N. Ornstein. 2006. *The broken branch: How Congress is failing America and how to get it back on track.* New York: Oxford Univ. Press.

Manna, P. 2006. *School's in: Federalism and the national education agenda.* Washington, D.C.: Georgetown Univ. Press.

Mansbridge, J. 1980. *Beyond adversary democracy.* Chicago: Univ. of Chicago Press.

Mutz, D. 2006. *Hearing the other side: Deliberative versus participatory democracy.* New York: Cambridge Univ. Press.

Orren, K., and S. Skowronek. 2004. *The search for American political development.* New York: Cambridge Univ. Press.

Pierson, P. 2004. *Politics in time: History, institutions, and social analysis.* Princeton, N.J.: Princeton Univ. Press.

Rae, D. 2003. *City: Urbanism and its end.* New Haven, Conn.: Yale Univ. Press.

Sassen, S. 2006. *Cities in a world economy.* Thousand Oaks, Calif.: Pine Forge Press.

Sigelman, L. 2005. Report of the editor of the *American Political Science Review,* 2003–2004. *PS: Political Science and Politics* 38:137–40.

———. 2006. The coevolution of American political science and the *American Political Science Review. American Political Science Review* 100 (4): 463–78.

Skocpol, T. 1985. Bringing the state back in: Strategies of analysis in current research. In *Bringing the state back in,* ed. P. Evans, D. Rueschemeyer, and T. Skocpol, 3–41. Cambridge: Cambridge Univ. Press.

Skowronek, S. 1993. *The politics presidents make: Leadership from John Adams to George Bush.* Cambridge, Mass.: Harvard Univ. Press.

Thelen, K. 2004. *How institutions evolve: The political economy of skills in Germany, Britain, the United States, and Japan.* New York: Cambridge Univ. Press.

Thompson, J. P., III. 2005. *Double trouble: Black mayors, black communities, and the call for a deep democracy.* New York: Oxford Univ. Press.

Williams, O. 1975. The politics of urban space. *Publius* 5 (1): 15–26.

Yeatman, A. 1997. Feminism and power. In *Reconstructing political theory: Feminist perspectives,* ed. M. L. Shanley and U. Narayan, 144–57. University Park: Pennsylvania State Univ. Press.

CONTRIBUTORS

Jennifer L. Hochschild is the Henry LaBarre Jayne Professor of Government and a professor of African and African American studies. She is the coauthor of *The American Dream and the Public Schools;* and author of *Facing Up to the American Dream: Race, Class, and the Soul of the Nation; The New American Dilemma: Liberal Democracy and School Desegregation;* and *What's Fair: American Beliefs about Distributive Justice.* She is also a coauthor or coeditor of other books and articles.

Valerie C. Johnson is an associate professor of political science at DePaul University and the author of *Black Power in the Suburbs: The Myth and Reality of African American Suburban Political Incorporation,* as well as numerous scholarly articles and book chapters. Her research areas are urban education, African American politics, African American suburbanization, and juvenile incarceration. She teaches courses on urban politics, American government, race and politics, and urban education.

Marion Orr is the Fred Lippitt Professor of Public Policy and a professor of political science and urban studies at Brown University. He has published three books: *Black Social Capital: The Politics of School Reform in Baltimore, The Color of School Reform: Race, Politics, and the Challenge of Urban Education,* and *Transforming the City: Community Organizing and the Challenge of Political Change.* He is also the author and coauthor of many book chapters, journal articles, and essays on urban politics, urban school politics, and race and politics.

Clarence N. Stone is a research professor of public policy and political science at George Washington University and professor emeritus at the University of Maryland. He is the author of *Regime Politics: Governing Atlanta, 1946–1988.* His most recent book is a coauthored work, *Building Civic Capacity: The Politics of Reforming Urban Schools.* His current research interests include local agenda setting, capacity building for local democracy, and continuing attention to urban school reform.

INDEX

337

in Georgia, 186–187, 191
link to economic development, 275
paternalism, 167
pluralist view, 161–162
political incorporation, 185–186, 187, 188–191, 196–197
in Southern rural areas, 186–187
urban politics and, 7–8
See also African Americans; Atlanta, biracial governing coalition; civil rights movement; desegregation
Rae, Douglas W., 281, 327, 330
rational choice theory, 326
Reagan, Ronald, 8
redevelopment policy
attracting investment, 117, 122, 152–153
business influence, 14, 50, 272, 293
in Chicago, 143
coalitions supporting, 293
emerging agenda, 286–291
equity issues, 92
goals, 273
hospital and university expansion projects, 45–46
independent organizations, 177–179, 195, 306n40
interests in, 117–118
leadership roles, 130, 288
mayoral leadership, 272–273, 284
neighborhood focus, 286–287
opposition, 96, 233
participants in decisions, 273, 283, 288–289
persistence of poverty, 120
political economy perspective, 92–93
population displacement, 279
redistributive policies and, 275
regime theory view, 284
selective incentives, 97, 103, 104
stages, 50
study of, 14
systemic power in, 50
trade-offs, 274
unitary interest of city, 117–118, 120
See also Atlanta; New Haven
redistribution
challenges, 146, 232
coalitions supporting, 186
constraints, 182
links to development, 275
nondecision making, 273
opposition, 182, 186
policies, 273
as political strategy, 181
See also social reforms

reforms. *See* education reform; social reforms
regime analysis
alternatives, 300, 329
antecedents, 121–122
assumptions, 77, 271
comparison to pluralism, 76, 77, 84
conceptual evolution, 265
conflict management, 122
cross-city comparisons, 128–129
differences from alternatives, 271–272
electoral power, 83
factors in policy making, 77
fluid preferences, 84–85, 87–91
interdependence perspective, 282–284
leadership activities, 122–123, 124–125, 126, 131
limitations, 300
political change process, 93–94, 101–102
political economy perspective, 76–77, 92–93, 102, 122, 188, 268–269
preference formation, 85–87
relationship between business and political actors, 122
representation issues, 125
scholarship based on, 320
social reform goals, 328
state capacity, 94–95
state sufficiency, 82
structure analysis, 271
See also coalitions; preemptive power; social production model of power
Regime Politics (Stone), 14–15, 20, 265, 267, 268–269
regimes
broad agendas, 104–105
description, 13
development, 96–97, 103
durability, 271
elite alliances, 329
evolution, 269–270
influence of societal trends, 127–128
influence on policies, 13, 16–17
in international sphere, 77
limitations, 268
lower-class opportunity expansion, 98–100
maintenance, 96, 103
middle class progressive, 97–98
power in, 17
typology, 95–102
viability, 101
See also coalitions
relational power, 226, 237.
See also social production model of power
Renaissance Program (Atlanta), 268
Rendell, Edward G., 253

resistance
  to change, 146
  costs, 132
  to demands of lower-strata groups, 166
  to education reform, 211, 255, 274
  power and, 66–67
  preemptive power and, 131, 132
resources
  of business leaders, 12, 84, 167, 168, 176, 178, 188
  of governing coalitions, 95, 125, 132, 284, 293, 329
  intangible, 88
  material, 88
  mobilization, 95, 132
  preferences and, 87–88
  types, 292
  unequal distribution, 84, 85, 87–88
restructuring
  costs and benefits, 92
  effects, 96–97
  ongoing, 285
  regime theory view, 93
  See also redevelopment policy
Rhodes, Amy, 253
Ridge, Thomas, 253, 254–256, 257
Riordan, Richard, 217
Rogers, David, 49
Rokkan, S., 84, 163, 181
Rutherford, K. R., 10

Sage Foundation, 3
St. Louis, civic capacity for education reform, 209–210
Salisbury, Robert H., 7, 203, 285
San Francisco
  Children's Amendment, 293, 307–308n60
  civic capacity for education reform, 209–210
  referendum process, 98
Sapotichne, J., 5, 6
satisficing behavior, 86
Sayre, W., 3
Schattschneider, E. E., 61, 176, 301, 321
Schelling, T. C., 165
Schmoke, Kurt, 211, 219, 220
Schneider, Mark, 5
school desegregation
  in Atlanta, 19, 205
  in Boston, 215, 250, 251
  effects of struggle on civil rights leaders, 49
  in Georgia, 191
  in Pittsburgh, 214
school reform. *See* education reform
Schorr, Lisbeth, 287, 295
Schweiker, Mark, 257

sectarchy, 127–128
segregation, in Southern states, 19, 187.
  See also desegregation
Sheffield (United Kingdom), 151
Shefter, Martin, 93, 121
Sibley, John A., 191
Sigelman, L., 9–10, 327–328, 331
Simon, Herbert A., 232, 238
Sirianni, Carmen, 302
Skocpol, T., 94, 302
Skowronek, S., 300
small businesses, 289
social capital, 204, 220–221
social change
  adaptive responses of governing coalitions, 125–126
  pluralist view, 81
  See also social reforms
social control model of power, 80–81, 85.
  See also "power over"
social-investment framing, 301
social production model of power ("power to")
  description, 83–85, 226
  examples, 89
  fluid preferences and, 229–230, 234–235
  political economy perspective, 92
  preference formation, 90, 229–230
  risks, 235–236
  use of, 228, 238
  See also "power to"
social reforms
  advancing, 297–299
  feasibility, 229
  implementation issues, 230–233, 238
  issue linkages, 287
  large-scale, 232–233
  obstacles, 297–298, 300–301
  political scientists' support, 327
  promotion of social cohesion, 286, 287
  relationship to economic development, 287
  use of "power over," 227
  See also redistribution
social stratification. *See* stratification
socioeconomic groups. *See* class; stratification
Southern Regional Council, 168
spatial theory of cities, 329–331
spoils system. *See* patronage
stakeholders, 20–21, 204
state capacity, 78–80, 94–95
Stoker, G., 300
Stone, Clarence N.
  approach, 11
  career, 10–11